TAX AUTHORITY ADVICE AND THE PUBLIC

There is now almost universal acceptance that tax law is overly complex and indeterminate; and yet, there has to date been no comprehensive assessment of the role of the tax authority in the current arrangement. If the legislation and case law offer few immediate answers to the taxpayer, then the role of Her Majesty's Revenue & Customs (HMRC) in advising taxpayers becomes more apparent.

This monograph contends that the provision of advice by HMRC is desirable by virtue of the rule of law and it follows that any such advice should be correct, clear, accessible and reliable. Additionally, there should exist some means of scrutinising the advice in order to check that it satisfies these criteria.

Tax Authority Advice and the Public explores this view of HMRC's role in tax collection. It explains the deficiencies in the current system in this light, highlighting the pitfalls for taxpayers and practitioners as well as the potential remedies. Finally, the book assesses potential reforms which could be adopted in order to alleviate existing problems.

A timely and ambitious work, this book is essential reading for practitioners and academics interested in the interaction between tax administration and public law.

Tax Authority Advice and the Public

Stephen Daly

•HART•

OXFORD • LONDON • NEW YORK • NEW DELHI • SYDNEY

HART PUBLISHING
Bloomsbury Publishing Plc
Kemp House, Chawley Park, Cumnor Hill, Oxford, OX2 9PH, UK
1385 Broadway, New York, NY 10018, USA

First published in Great Britain 2020

A catalogue record for this book is available from the British Library.

Library of Congress Cataloging-in-Publication data

Names: Daly, Stephen, 1989- author.

Title: Tax authority advice and the public / Stephen Daly.

Description: Oxford ; New York : Hart, 2020. | Based on author's thesis (doctoral - University of Oxford, 2017) issued under title: HMRC and the public : the case for reform of soft law. | Includes bibliographical references and index.

Identifiers: LCCN 2020001975 (print) | LCCN 2020001976 (ebook) | ISBN 9781509930531 (hardback) | ISBN 9781509930555 (Epub)

Subjects: LCSH: Tax administration and procedure—Great Britain. | Advisory opinions—Law and legislation—Great Britain. | Soft law—Great Britain. | Great Britain. HM Revenue & Customs.

Classification: LCC KD5375 .D35 2020 (print) | LCC KD5375 (ebook) | DDC 343.4104—dc23

LC record available at https://lccn.loc.gov/2020001975

LC ebook record available at https://lccn.loc.gov/2020001976

ISBN: HB: 978-1-50993-053-1
ePDF: 978-1-50993-054-8
ePub: 978-1-50993-055-5

Typeset by Compuscript Ltd, Shannon
Printed and bound in Great Britain by CPI Group (UK) Ltd, Croydon CR0 4YY

MIX
Paper from responsible sources
FSC® C013604

To find out more about our authors and books visit www.hartpublishing.co.uk. Here you will find extracts, author information, details of forthcoming events and the option to sign up for our newsletters.

FOREWORD

For as long as there have been taxes, there have been taxpayers needing to know what is expected of them. Absent clear guidance about these expectations and the consequences of the failure to live up to them, taxpayers are at the mercy of what may appear to be arbitrary and capricious actions on the part of the tax agency. This perception, in turn, undermines respect for the rule of law and the government that is charged with upholding it.

The rule of law, and the value of human dignity that underpins it, is the basis for this book's proposals to reform the current approach of Her Majesty's Revenue and Customs (HMRC) to the provision of tax advice. Dr Stephen Daly begins with a discussion of the desirability of advice, proceeds to a taxonomy of advice currently provided by HMRC, proposes a normative framework for analysing the sufficiency of current advice in satisfying rule of law benchmarks, and undertakes such an analysis. In developing this framework – incorporating correctness, clarity, accessibility, scrutiny and reliability – the author delves deeply into caselaw, historical precedent and current developments. He discusses the current state of scrutiny of advice, and the limitations of institutions conducting that scrutiny.

But Dr Daly does not stop there. After reviewing the effectiveness of existing mechanisms available to taxpayers for holding HMRC to the advice it gives, he offers a reform agenda. He makes a compelling case for engaging the public in the development of advice, by building on existing institutions including the Working Together Group. Leaning heavily on the Australian experience of its Public Advice and Guidance Panel, the author proposes a nine-step process for developing guidance, incorporating external expert advice and proposed rule publication, with an additional step for post-publication challenges.

This, then, is an important book. Not only does it show the reader what is not working and explain why that matters, but it makes concrete and actionable recommendations for reform. The most important contribution of the book, however, is that it reminds readers that the provision of assistance is desirable and even necessary within the rule of law framework.

One of the sticky issues with guidance is, what if the guidance is wrong? How should a tax agency address this error? Dr Daly's answer to this dilemma is framed in terms of human rights, the essential human dignity of the actor. He suggests the tax agency move away from the mindset that it is *per se* unacceptable that someone, somewhere might rely on the incorrect advice to gain an advantage not afforded under the law. Rather than declining to issue advice for fear of being incorrect, the agency can mitigate that risk by adopting the nine-step process. Moreover, instead of reflexively and retroactively reneging on incorrect advice, Dr Daly proposes the tax agency embrace the concept that reliance is an important norm and instead consult with the affected parties so as to 'make an informed decision as to the comparative unfairness' of the retroactive change. This approach does not place automatic constraints on the agency's authority; rather, it ensures the agency uses its authority legitimately and in accordance with human dignity.

As an advocate for taxpayer rights, I am particularly appreciative of the attention Dr Daly pays to accessibility, including the 'practical restrictions' experienced by many seeking to hold the agency accountable in relation to its advice. Here, the author focuses our attention on the problem of post-publication challenges. The costs of challenging a position in the High Court can be an insurmountable obstacle for many taxpayers; the author persuasively makes the case that the First-tier Tribunal be able to consider taxpayers' legitimate expectations. While Dr Daly notes that the 30 million PAYE taxpayers may have limited need of advice and judicial remedies, this leaves about 7 million self-assessing taxpayers, some portion of whom are in need of or desiring advice. I suggest that without a robust advice process and an accessible tax tribunal, one cannot really say who needs advice and who doesn't.

As I noted in my 1997 and 1998 testimony before the United States Congress, because low income taxpayers cannot afford representation, the only issues that come before the courts are those raised by taxpayers with some affluence and ability to pay. Similarly, the tax agency only receives requests for guidance from those who are able to afford representation by tax professionals. This leads to an imbalance in the law; that is, the law only addresses the issues of those with the means to pay for representation.

In the United States, this inequity was addressed by the creation of a federal grant programme for low income taxpayer clinics, who have played an important role in bringing (and prevailing in) court cases, and in identifying issues for and commenting on guidance. Similarly, Dr Daly's nine-step process for identifying and issuing guidance, with its requirement of external expert consultation (which could include advocates for low and moderate income taxpayers) and proposed rule publication, and the expansion of the First-tier Tribunal's jurisdiction, will ensure that advice is not limited to the issues of the affluent alone. We may be very surprised to find what issues are lurking out there once access to justice is enhanced.

When I was drafting the proposal that ultimately became the Taxpayer Bill of Rights (TBOR), codified in the US Internal Revenue Code, I mulled over (some would say, obsessed over) the order of presentation of the rights. Ultimately, the *right to be informed* preceded all others. Without correct, clear and accessible advice that can be relied upon by the taxpayer, there is no *right to pay no more than the correct amount of tax* or to *challenge the tax agency's position and be heard*. In fact, each of the nine remaining rights in the TBOR derive from the right to be informed, including the *right to a fair and just tax system*.

This book is more than a scholarly treatise on the desirability of advice in tax administration. It is a road map for a more fair and just tax system. Dr Daly convincingly makes the case that the provision of advice conforming to his proposed normative framework respects the basic dignity of taxpayers and treats them as 'rational actors capable of choosing their own course of action'. This is an end in itself, but I suggest it also leads to improved compliance. Thus, it is in the tax agency's own self-interest to adopt the approach proposed in this book.

Nina E Olson
Washington, DC
January 2020[1]

[1] Nina E Olson is the Executive Director of the Center for Taxpayer Rights. From 2001 to 2019, she was the National Taxpayer Advocate of the US Internal Revenue Service.

ACKNOWLEDGEMENTS

The audience for an acknowledgements section is narrow. Even more so in the case of a monograph derived from a doctoral thesis. But those who do pay attention to acknowledgements will have noticed a trend. That is to put one's gratitude to family and friends for persevering through the torturous process at the end of the section. For me, that's the wrong the place for it. There are 168 hours in the week and there was rarely a week in which I spent more than a quarter of those hours working on this. The rest of the time was spent with family and friends, living and enjoying life. If I kept my sanity through this process (and some, including myself, will doubt that I ever had any), it is because I was supported unconditionally by those closest to me, in particular Ruth, my pillar.

As for the business side of things, the 40 hours or so of work per week on the thesis during my time as a doctoral student would not have been possible without the financial support provided generously by Lord Crewe's Charity, whose Lord Crewe Graduate Scholarship in the Humanities and Social Sciences was administered by Lincoln College, Oxford, and by the Faculty of Law at the University of Oxford, through the Graduate Assistance Fund. Meanwhile, the ability to travel to different parts of the UK and the world to attend conferences and research would not have been possible without the support of the Chartered Institute of Taxation through the PhD Grant Scheme (which principally funded a visiting researchship at the University of New South Wales) and the Lincoln College Graduate Research Fund.

My doctoral supervisors, Professor Judith Freedman and Professor Rebecca Williams, are owed special thanks for their patience, continuous support and expert insights which were invaluable to the development of the work, and more broadly for the development of my academic profile. Dr Glen Loutzenhiser, Edwin Simpson and Dr John Vella must also be thanked for very helpfully examining and reviewing earlier portions of the work. Segments of the book also benefitted from critique at the numerous conferences I attended between 2015 and 2018, such as the SLSA conferences in 2015 and 2016, as well as the Cambridge Tax History conference, with those conference pieces also later becoming published articles. Professor Michael Walpole from the University of New South Wales must be thanked also for arranging my visit to the University in March 2016 as well as organising several informal but important interviews with Australian tax experts. Additionally, the comments during the viva and in the report from the thesis examiners, Professor Timothy Endicott and Malcolm Gammie QC, helped enormously to clarify the scope and substance of what is now the book.

Some final thanks should go to the institutions and persons at the University of Oxford who contributed to my development generally as an academic, such as the Oxford Learning Institute, which provided excellent training courses for academic teaching, Professor Ariel Ezrachi for providing the opportunity to teach and administer academic courses and the staff at the Bodleian Law Library, who were always on hand with helpful advice for finding and searching relevant sources. The final parts of the doctoral thesis were completed when I joined King's College London as a 'postdoctoral' researcher. Fittingly, the conversion of the doctorate into a monograph was undertaken when I rejoined King's College London as a permanent academic staff member. Friends and colleagues there helped to push this work over the line, with special thanks due to Dr Natalie Pratt and Dr James Grant for reviewing some late changes to the book.

TABLE OF CONTENTS

LIST OF ABBREVIATIONS

APA	Advanced Pricing Arrangement
ATO	Australian Tax Office
C & E	Customs and Excise
CA	Court of Appeal
CAG	Comptroller and Auditor General
CGT	Capital Gains Tax
COP	Code of Practice
CRCA 2005	Commissioners for Revenue and Customs Act 2005
DC	Divisional Court
DOTAS	Disclosure of Tax Avoidance Schemes
DPP	Director of Public Prosecutions
DSS	Department of Social Security
ECHR	European Convention on Human Rights
ESC	Extra-Statutory Concession
EU	European Union
FOIA 2000	Freedom of Information Act 2000
FTT	First-tier Tribunal
GAAR	General Anti-Abuse Rule
HL	House of Lords
HM	Her Majesty
HMRC	Her Majesty's Revenue and Customs
HMSO	Her Majesty's Stationary Office
IFS	Institute for Fiscal Studies
IGT	Inspector-General of Taxation

IHT	Inheritance Tax
IR	Inland Revenue
JCPA	Joint Committee of Public Accounts
JCPAA	Joint Committee of Public Accounts and Audit
LQR	Law Quarterly Review
LSS	Litigation and Settlement Strategy
MLR	*Modern Law Review*
MP	Member of Parliament
NAO	National Audit Office
NTLG	National Tax Liaison Group
OECD	Organisation for Economic Co-operation and Development
OJLS	Oxford Journal of Legal Studies
OTS	Office of Tax Simplification
PAC	Public Accounts Committee
PACAC	Public Administration and Constitutional Affairs Committee
PFI	Private Finance Initiative
POTAS	Promoters of Tax Avoidance Schemes
PCA	Parliamentary Commissioner for Administration
PCA 1967	Parliamentary Commissioner Act 1967
PHSO	Parliamentary and Health Service Ombudsman
QBD	Queen's Bench Division
SP	Statement of Practice
TAA 1953	Taxation Administration Act 1953
TAAR	Targeted Anti-Avoidance Rule
TC	Tax Chamber
TCC	Tax & Chancery Chamber
TCEA 2007	Tribunals, Courts and Enforcement Act 2007
TCGA 1992	Taxation of Chargeable Gains Act 1992

TIOPA 2010	Taxation (International and Other Provisions) Act 2010
TSC	Treasury Select Committee
UT	Upper Tribunal
VOA	Valuation Office Agency
VAT	Value Added Tax

TABLE OF CASES

Australia

EU

European Court of Human Rights

New Zealand

Privy Council

UK

UK Tax Tribunal

TABLE OF LEGISLATION

Australia

EU

UK

Primary

Secondary

New Zealand

1

Introduction

But if taxation is the scourge of the twentieth century – the civilized evil as it were – we must learn to live with it.*

I. Introduction

There is now almost universal acceptance that tax law is overly complex and indeterminate. And yet, there has to date been no comprehensive assessment of the role of the tax authority in the current arrangement. If the legislation and case law offer few immediate answers to the taxpayer, then the role of HMRC in advising taxpayers becomes more apparent.

This book contends that the provision of advice by HMRC is desirable by virtue of the rule of law and it follows that any such advice should be correct, clear, accessible and reliable. Additionally, there should exist some means of scrutinising the advice in order to check that it satisfies these criteria. The book explains the deficiencies in the current system in light of this argument, highlighting the pitfalls for taxpayers and practitioners as well as the potential remedies. Finally, the book assesses potential reforms which could be adopted in order to alleviate existing problems. A timely and ambitious work, this book will be read by practitioners and academics interested in the interaction between tax administration and public law.

II. Background

Robert John Davies, Michael John James and Robert Gaines-Cooper claimed for tax purposes to be non-resident in the UK. Being wealthy individuals who had sought to base themselves outside the UK, the matter was of some significance. Before the Supreme Court in the 2011 case of *Gaines-Cooper*,[1] the trio sought to

* JRL Anderson in the Foreword to B Sabine, *A History of Income Tax*, 1st edn (London, George Allen & Unwin, 1966) 5.

[1] *R (Davies) v HMRC; R (Gaines-Cooper) v HMRC* [2011] UKSC 47, [2012] 1 All ER 1048 (*Gaines-Cooper* (SC)).

support their claim by relying upon guidance produced by HMRC, the UK tax authority. The argument was rejected by a majority of the Court. Beyond the merits of this particular decision, the case begs broader questions about the status of HMRC advice, its place within the legal structure, the means by which it is brought into being, and who ultimately controls it. The inquiry of this book takes its inspiration from these questions: it investigates HMRC advice, of which there are various types – from bespoke rulings to general advice in publications such as Extra-statutory Concessions, Manuals and Codes of Practice.

HMRC was formed in 2005 from a merger of the previous tax-collecting bodies, the Inland Revenue and Customs and Excise.[2] Broadly, the bodies were respectively tasked with collecting direct and indirect taxes, though HMRC also performs other functions such as the administration of tax credits[3] and the collection of student loan repayments.[4] Meanwhile, not all 'taxes'[5] are collected by HMRC; for example, council tax.[6] The merger retained the non-ministerial status of the bodies,[7] whereby ministers and the Treasury are kept at arm's length from the everyday activities of HMRC.[8] The closest that the UK has to a 'Tax Minister' is the Financial Secretary to the Treasury, to whom responsibility for oversight of HMRC has been delegated by the Chancellor of the Exchequer.[9]

HMRC's primary duty is the collection and management of taxes and credits,[10] which allows the body to do anything necessary or expedient in connection with the exercise of its functions, or incidental or conducive to their exercise.[11] This duty renders lawful the provision of advice by HMRC. As noted by Moses LJ in the Court of Appeal in *Gaines-Cooper*,[12] and affirmed by the Supreme Court,[13] it is up to HMRC to determine how best to go about performing the duty.[14] But the body has long acknowledged that the duty is best discharged by 'encouraging co-operation between the revenue and the public'.[15]

[2] For an overview, see P Tuck, D de Cogan and J Snape, 'A Tale of the Merger between the Inland Revenue and HM Customs & Excise' in P Harris and D De Cogan (eds), *Studies in the History of Tax Law: Volume 9* (Oxford, Hart Publishing, 2019).

[3] See Commissioners for Revenue and Customs Act 2005, s 5(1)(c).

[4] The Education (Student Loans) (Repayment) Regulations 2009, reg 10.

[5] The definition of a 'tax' is subject to some debate and has practical implications. See for instance M Bowler Smith and H Ostik, 'Towards a classification of the Central London congestion charge as a tax' [2011] *British Tax Review* 487.

[6] See Local Government Act 1992, s 1 and s 70, which set out who collects council tax.

[7] Explanatory Notes to the Commissioners for Revenue and Customs Act 2005, para 6.

[8] Explanatory Notes to the Commissioners for Revenue and Customs Act 2005, para 71.

[9] HMRC, '2018–19 Annual Report and Accounts' (July 2019) 72.

[10] Commissioners for Revenue and Customs Act 2005 (CRCA 2005) s 5.

[11] CRCA 2005, s 9.

[12] *R (Davies) v HMRC; R (Gaines-Cooper) v HMRC* [2010] EWCA Civ 83, [2010] STC 860 (*Gaines-Cooper* (CA)).

[13] *Gaines-Cooper* (SC) (n 1) [25] (Lord Wilson).

[14] *Gaines-Cooper* (CA) (n 12) [12].

[15] ibid.

HMRC's power to provide advice is not unconstrained. It must be construed in light of fundamental constitutional principles and rules such as Parliamentary sovereignty and those found in the Bill of Rights Act 1688/9. Article 1 provides that the suspension of laws without consent of Parliament is illegal, whilst Article 4 proscribes the levying of taxes without Parliamentary approval. Parliament decides what taxes are due, not HMRC. Further, the duty must not be performed in a way which conflicts with primary law, such as in relation to the Human Rights Act 1998 or the European Communities Act 1972. Public law standards will also be implied into the power to provide advice. For instance, the power must not be used for an improper purpose.[16] HMRC should take into account relevant considerations, and should disregard irrelevant considerations when providing advice.[17] HMRC similarly should not act in a way that is irrational.[18] But where it does something so outrageously misguided, then the body will be held to have acted unlawfully.[19]

Not only is HMRC legally empowered to provide advice, it is also desirable in principle by reason of the rule of law that the body should do so. Whilst there is no general consensus as to the precise meaning of the rule of law, it is an uncontroversial tenet that laws should act as guidance for individuals.[20] Though lacking formal legal consequences,[21] public authority advice then nevertheless does seek to guide the actions of those to whom it is addressed.[22]

It is contended in the book that a normative framework can be deduced from the rule of law, which can be tested against a system for the provision of advice. The framework consists of five benchmarks: correctness, clarity, accessibility, scrutiny and reliability. The first three relate to actual advice given by HMRC whilst the latter two relate to the structure in place for advice. These will overlap to a degree, but are sufficiently distinct so as to warrant their own individual consideration. But it will be pointed out in the book how these impact each other. When HMRC advice is placed in this framework, it is possible to investigate properly whether it satisfies these benchmarks in practice. It helps to pinpoint where deficiencies arise and allows solutions then to be proposed to remedy these issues.

[16] *Padfield v Minister of Agriculture, Fisheries and Food* [1968] AC 997 (HL).

[17] *UK Uncut Legal Action v HMRC* [2013] EWHC 1283 (Admin), [2013] SWTI 1849.

[18] *CCSU v Minister for the Civil Service* [1985] AC 374 (HL); *R v Secretary of State for the Home Department ex parte Doody* [1994] 1 AC 531 (HL), 560 (Lord Mustill).

[19] See *R v Inland Revenue Commissioners, ex parte Unilever plc* [1996] STC 681 (CA); *Al-Fayed v IRC* [2004] ScotCS 112, [2004] STC 1703 (IH); *R (Wilkinson) v IRC* [2005] UKHL 30, [2006] STC 270; and recently *HMRC v Hely-Hutchinson* [2017] EWCA Civ 1075, [2017] WLR(D) 517.

[20] See Lord Steyn, 'Democracy through law' [2002] *European Human Rights Law Review* 723, 727–28; P Craig, 'Formal and substantive conceptions of the rule of law: an analytical framework' [1997] *Public Law* 467, 487; J Raz, 'The Rule of Law and its Virtue' (1977) 93 *LQR* 195, 196; L Fuller, *The Morality of Law*, revised edn (New Haven, Yale University Press, 1969) 39, 46–90; F Hayek, *The Road to Serfdom* (Abingdon, Routledge, 1944) 54.

[21] See for instance G Weeks, *Soft Law and Public Authorities: Remedies and Reform* (Oxford, Hart Publishing, 2016) 1.

[22] See *Silver v United Kingdom* [1983] 5 EHRR 347; *R (Purdy) v Director of Public Prosecutions* [2009] UKHL 45, [2010] 1 AC 345; *R (Nicklinson) v Ministry of Justice* [2014] UKSC 38; [2014] 3 WLR 200.

The book seeks to set out the relevant law in this area in a systematic way, enriching the explanation with academic insight and providing considered reform suggestions. Whilst the book principally focuses on HMRC, it is not only to be read by those concerned with UK tax law. The book proposes a normative framework for the provision of advice which can be applied not just to HMRC, but tax authorities in other jurisdictions. Further, tax authorities are not the only public authorities which provide assistance to the public and the framework can be applied to those bodies also. Meanwhile, the book makes claims about the operation of UK public law, such as in respect of the doctrine of legitimate expectations, which should be of interest not just to UK public lawyers, but to common law public lawyers generally.

III. Justification for Study

This book is the first study which comprehensively looks at HMRC's role in providing tax advice. But there are three questions which follow: why focus on HMRC advice? To what extent does the existing literature consider the provision of advice by HMRC? And finally, why now?

As to the first question, tax commentators have noted that tax legislation has become increasingly complex and indeterminate[23] and, in consequence, there is a considerable body of literature analysing alternative structures for the promulgation of law.[24] If these reforms were adopted, or in any event if those who enact the tax laws paid greater attention to the lawmaking process, then the need for HMRC to provide advice could be substantially reduced. A critic might suggest to that end that the study of HMRC advice is misconceived and that the proper focus should be on the process that ends with Parliament enacting tax laws. Indeed, the evidence that Parliament effectively scrutinises Finance Bills is largely absent.[25] But there is little reason to believe that Parliament will become an effective scrutinising agent in the foreseeable future.[26] Former Chancellor of the Exchequer Nigel Lawson once confessed that the Treasury could use the 'arcane' language of the

[23] Treasury Committee, 'Principles of Tax Policy' (HC 2010–11, 753) paras 47–49; J Freedman, 'Interpreting tax statutes: tax avoidance and the intention of Parliament' (2007) *LQR* 53, 85 in particular fn 146.

[24] J Freedman, G Loomer and J Vella, 'Corporate tax risk and tax avoidance: new approaches' [2009] *British Tax Review* 74; R Krever, 'Plain English Drafting, Purposive Drafting, Principles-based Drafting: Does Any of it Matter?' in J Freedman (ed), *Beyond Boundaries: Developing Approaches to Tax Avoidance and Tax Risk Management* (Oxford, Oxford University Centre for Business Taxation, 2008); J Freedman, 'Improving (not perfecting) tax legislation: rules and principles revisited' [2010] *British Tax Review* 717.

[25] Institute for Fiscal Studies, 'Making Tax Law: IFS Tax Law Review Committee Discussion Paper No. 3' (March 2003) para 2.4. For an overview of the criticisms, see A Seely, 'The Budget and the annual Finance Bill' (House of Commons Briefing Paper 813, July 2019) in particular 8–11.

[26] On which, see: D Greenberg, 'Dangerous Trends in Modern Legislation' [2015] 1 *Public Law* 96.

Finance Bill, which bore 'little resemblance to the English language', to successfully evade Parliament's gaze.[27] The limitations of the Houses are also underlined by cases like the GAAR legislation, which went to a standing committee, rather than Parliament, to be analysed in detail.[28] The choice to study HMRC advice rather than the failings in the underlying law is justified accordingly by the fact that it does play and will continue to play an important role. We must see the world as it is, not as we would wish it to be.

Therefore, even if changes were to occur in the way that tax legislation is created or to the substance of the statutes, there would still be a need for HMRC to advise taxpayers (and HMRC staff) as to the operation and application of the rules. There is a limit to the level of detail that can be contained in statutes or secondary legislation or even any mandate, given the limits of language.[29] Indeed, there comes a point where even HMRC advice cannot be made even more specific. Critically, though, between that point and the legislation there is plenty that HMRC *can* do to assist. Of course, the presence of HMRC advice may have an impact on the level of detail which is contained in legislative form, but the blame for this phenomenon lies with actors external to HMRC.[30] More relevant to the actions of HMRC is the fact that there will be a relationship between the advice that it issues to a general class of taxpayers as against that which is issued to individual taxpayers. The better the former, the less need for the latter, and vice versa.

In relation to the second question concerning literature in the field, there has been little focus on the provision of advice by HMRC. Of note, however, is a 2011 book chapter from Freedman and Vella wherein the authors discussed the contours of HMRC's discretion and flagged up a number of issues, such as the difficulties encountered when seeking to rely upon HMRC advice.[31] This book should be seen as building upon the foundations set by that chapter and providing answers to the questions posed by the authors. Similarly of note are previous publications recommending that the UK introduce a system for rulings.[32] The book will also recommend introducing a system of rulings, but it will be far more comprehensive than that previously recommended, encompassing public rulings also, in addition to placing the idea of rulings more generally within the framework of HMRC advice. It is impossible to disaggregate the need for a system of individual rulings

[27] N Lawson, *The View from No 11* (London, Bantam Press, 1992) 354–55 as noted in G Loutzenhiser, *Tiley's Revenue Law*, 9th edn (Oxford, Hart Publishing, 2019) 41.

[28] N Lee, 'Editorial' (2013) 4 *Private Client Business* 143, 143.

[29] See for instance J Waldron, 'Vagueness in Law and Language: Some Philosophical Issues' (1994) 82 *California Law Review* 509.

[30] See below ch 3 in text at n 135.

[31] J Freedman and J Vella, 'HMRC's Management of the U.K. Tax System: The Boundaries of Legitimate Discretion' in C Evans, J Freedman and R Krever, *The Delicate Balance: Tax, Discretion and the Rule of Law* (Amsterdam, IBFD, 2011).

[32] A Taylor, 'Proposing a tax rulings system' (2017) 4605 *Taxation* 8; W Chan, 'Binding Rulings' (1997) 18(2) *Fiscal Studies* 189; D Sandler, *A Request for Rulings* (London, Institute of Taxation, 1994). Also, see caution urged by D de Cogan, 'A Changing Role for the Administrative Law of Taxation' (2015) 24 *Social & Legal Studies* 251, 263.

more broadly from the need for a comprehensive regime governing HMRC advice. Further, there has been work undertaken very recently on HMRC guidance by the Office of Tax Simplification.[33] This is a very useful contribution, but is narrower in scope than this study, which looks at the entire system for the provision of advice by HMRC rather than one, albeit critically important, aspect of it. Moreover, the report takes a strategic look at the general approach to providing guidance for taxpayers. But as it is a strategic look, it does not go into the level of detail about the problems in the system that this book does.[34]

Though the book will draw heavily upon the fact that HMRC advice may come as a form of soft law, the legal studies of soft law to date have differed from what is under scrutiny here. Public lawyers have generally focused upon the broader issue of administrative discretion,[35] with some notable exceptions focusing specifically upon the legal effects of soft law at a national level,[36] such as a recent book by Greg Weeks.[37] That book looks at the place of soft law in the constitution and the remedies that are available in respect of it. The book can be distinguished on several counts from the study undertaken here. First, the present study looks more specifically at one public authority – namely HMRC. Secondly, the scope of the book differs considerably, with Weeks for the majority of the book focusing on remedies (which account for one chapter in this book). Finally, the substance of the present book is as a result particularly distinct from that of Weeks' book. This book develops and applies a framework in respect of a public authority, namely HMRC, analyses problems from this perspective and proposes solutions to the problems encountered.

Although scholarship in EU law[38] and international law[39] has also focused upon soft law, it does not overlap with the subject matter in this book as such

[33] Office of Tax Simplification, 'Guidance for taxpayers: a vision for the future' (October 2018).

[34] It should be disclosed that the author of this book assisted the OTS in their study, as noted in the report: ibid 39.

[35] CK Allen, *Law and Orders*, 3rd edn (London, Stevens and Sons, 1965); KC Davis, *Discretionary Justice: A Preliminary Inquiry*, 2nd edn (Baton Rouge, Louisiana State University Press, 1971); J Jowell, *Law and Bureaucracy: Administrative Discretion and the Limits of Legal Action* (New York, Dunellen, 1975); R Baldwin and K Hawkins, 'Discretionary Justice, Davis Reconsidered' [1984] *Public Law* 570.

[36] RE Megarry 'Administrative Quasi-Legislation' (1944) 60 *LQR* 125; SA de Smith, 'Sub-delegation and circulars' (1949) 12 *MLR* 37; M Asimow, 'Nonlegislative rulemaking and regulatory reform' [1985] *Duke Law Journal* 381; R Baldwin and J Houghton, 'Circular Arguments: The Status and Legitimacy of Administrative Rules' [1986] *Public Law* 239; G Ganz, *Quasi-legislation: recent developments in secondary legislation* (London, Sweet and Maxwell, 1987); R Baldwin, *Rules and Government* (Oxford, Clarendon Press, 1995).

[37] Weeks, *Soft Law and Public Authorities* (2016).

[38] See for instance J Klabbers, 'Informal instruments before the European Court of Justice' (1994) 31 *Common Market Law Review* 997; L Senden, *Soft Law in European Community Law* (Oxford, Hart Publishing, 2004). See also Joana Mendes (ed), *EU Executive Discretion and the Limits of the Law* (Oxford, Oxford University Press, 2019).

[39] For instance J Klabbers, 'The Redundancy of Soft Law' (1996) 65 *Nordic Journal of International Law* 167; J Klabbers, 'The Undesirability of Soft Law' (1998) 67 *Nordic Journal of International Law* 381; CM Chinkin, 'The Challenge of Soft Law: Development and Change in International Law' (1989) 38 *International and Comparative Law Quarterly* 850.

instruments serve different ends. Soft international law may be used as a means of introducing a political rather than legal commitment,[40] or to create a norm which can then harden into law, either through becoming customary law or by virtue of the process of formalisation into a binding treaty.[41] Soft EU law similarly serves as a stepping stone towards development of hard law[42] and as a means of furthering integration.[43] Thus, due to different rationales for promulgation, EU law and international law scholarship on soft law is of limited applicability in a domestic setting, and in particular in the case of the use of public powers to advise. Tangentially, studies of regulation and regulatory theory have made important contributions,[44] but their focus has been on the reactions of the regulators and the regulated, rather than upon the *legal* consequences of a public authority's actions.[45] In other words, the regulation literature is more broadly concerned with the impact and effectiveness of particular rules rather than with the legal consequences flowing from them. As such, while the studies of regulation, EU soft law and international soft law have focused on the use of soft law for a particular end, this book will look at HMRC advice from a legal perspective.

The third question could be answered by simply directing the reader to the answers to the previous two questions. But specific reasons can be proffered as to why it is important *now* to consider HMRC advice. Principally, this book advances the proposition that HMRC advice is desirable by virtue of the rule of law. If we take seriously the importance of the rule of law, then any study of its manifestations should be justified on its own terms. Of course, not all taxpayers use or require HMRC advice. For instance, around 30 million people in the UK pay tax through Pay As You Earn (PAYE), as opposed to seven million who pay through self-assessment.[46] A rough estimate on the basis of these figures, even assuming that PAYE taxpayers have no other reason to engage with HMRC and that a proportion of the self-assessed have straightforward affairs,[47] will still leave

[40] O Schachter, 'Towards a theory of international obligation' in S Schwebel (ed), *The Effectiveness of International Decisions* (Leyden, Sijthoff, 1971) 13.

[41] M Shaw, *International Law*, 7th/8th edn (Cambridge, Cambridge University Press, 2014/2017) 84–88.

[42] K Wellens and G Borchardt, 'Soft law in European Community law' (1989) 14 *European Law Review* 267, 314–17.

[43] ibid 309–10.

[44] R Baldwin, C Scott and C Hood, *A Reader on Regulation* (Oxford, Oxford University Press, 1998); J Black, *Rules and Regulators* (Oxford, Oxford University Press, 1997); C Parker, C Scott, N Lacey and J Braithwaite (eds), *Regulating Law* (Oxford, Oxford University Press, 2004); J Braithwaite, T Makkai and V Braithwaite, *Regulating Aged Care: Ritualism and the New Pyramid* (Cheltenham, Edward Elgar, 2007).

[45] C Parker, C Scott, N Lacey and J Braithwaite, 'Introduction' 3–4 and J Black, 'Law and Regulation: The Case of Finance' 33–40 in C Parker, C Scott, N Lacey and J Braithwaite (eds), *Regulating Law* (Oxford, Oxford University Press, 2004).

[46] HMRC, '2018–19 Annual Report and Accounts' (2019) 26.

[47] There are multiple reasons why a PAYE taxpayer may need assistance such as in relation to the deductibility of expenses, income from other sources, or perhaps issues around other taxes such as Stamp Duty Land Tax. Even for the most straightforward of affairs, the self-assessed taxpayer will have to reach for HMRC advice on completing the return.

a large number of taxpayers that require HMRC assistance. In any event, even if a taxpayer does not directly have to engage with HMRC, the intermediary which collects the tax on HMRC's behalf may have to.

Furthermore, the book is timely as there is a momentum around dealing with HMRC advice, with those close to government, HMRC and even Parliamentarians taking up the issue. As noted already, the Office of Tax Simplification, which is a permanent independent Office of the Treasury that advises the Government on simplifying the UK tax system, was prompted to produce a report on HMRC guidance in 2018. The professional bodies – Chartered Institute of Taxation, Association of Tax Technicians and Low Incomes Tax Reform Group – have also recently decided to engage in a cross-tax project on HMRC guidance generally, while HMRC itself at the time of writing (September 2019) is conducting an internal guidance project.[48] The Treasury Select Committee too recently recommended that 'HMRC urgently reviews and improves the accessibility, quality and level of detail of guidance it makes available to vulnerable taxpayers'.[49]

IV. Book Outline

This chapter so far has sought to provide background information and to introduce the key concept around which the book is structured, namely the idea that HMRC has a legitimate and desirable role in providing advice. Additionally, it has provided an overview of the framework which will be developed and applied in order to investigate HMRC advice, as well as articulating why this area ought to be studied.

Chapter two examines the different types and categories of HMRC advice, from bespoke advice provided to individuals to more generalised advice provided to a body of taxpayers, as well as the differences between these and how they are produced. The analysis begins by looking at individual advice, which is generally issued in response to taxpayer queries. Thereafter the chapter will turn to general advice in its various categories. Meanwhile, the chapter will elaborate upon and give examples of the different 'forms' of advice.

Chapter three explores both the legality and desirability of HMRC advice. In terms of the legality of HMRC advice, there is a tension between the promulgation of HMRC advice and the legislative supremacy of Parliament. How can it be constitutionally legitimate for a public authority to effectively produce rules when that is usually the domain of the legislature? In order to answer this question, the

[48] For background, see: A Fearnside and K Willis, 'HMRC guidance: difficulties with out-of-date, inaccurate and hard to find guidance' *Tax Advisor Magazine* (1 May 2018).

[49] Treasury Select Committee, 'Disputing Tax' (HC 2017–19, 1914) 20.

chapter first revisits the fundamental tenets of 'discretion' and analyses thereafter the case law which has developed to explain HMRC's managerial discretion. In terms of the desirability of HMRC advice, the book examines both jurisprudential literature and case law relating to the European Convention on Human Rights, which expand upon the meaning of the rule of law. At its core, laws ought to act as guidance, but advice from public authorities can help to achieve this goal by elaborating upon the meaning and application of the law. To this end, HMRC advice is desirable by reason of the rule of law. From the investigation of the legality and desirability of HMRC advice is derived a normative framework, consisting of the benchmarks of correctness, clarity, accessibility, scrutiny and reliability, which is then used to test in subsequent chapters the system currently in place for HMRC advice. Compliance with this framework is not a binary matter, but rather a question of degree.

Chapter four looks at the problems which arise in respect of HMRC advice from the perspective of the normative requirements that HMRC advice be correct, clear and accessible. To this end, the chapter begins by considering instances where the advice is incorrect, such as the advice contained in ESC D33, which expressly contradicts a judgment of the High Court. It thereafter provides examples of HMRC advice that is unclear and has had the effect of producing inconsistent treatment by HMRC, such as in the case of HMRC's internal guidance on disclosures of taxpayer information. When it comes to accessibility, there are four aspects to consider, each of which can be seen operating in respect of HMRC advice. These are practical restrictions on access, lack of publication, retrospective changes and miscategorisation of advice.

Chapter five considers the different mechanisms for scrutiny that are available in respect of HMRC advice. It begins by looking at the traditional avenues for oversight that are supposed to operate to hold HMRC to account. MPs in Parliament may play only a limited role, as HMRC is a non-ministerial governmental department. To this end, external oversight is formally handed to select committees, in this case, the Treasury Select Committee and the Public Accounts Committee. The National Audit Office assists the Public Accounts Committee. However, these bodies have not historically concerned themselves with 'checking' HMRC advice. Whilst the courts could play a stronger role, they do not. The chapter further considers the role played by the Adjudicator's Office and the Parliamentary Ombudsman and taxpayers, which can in some respects be effective in scrutinising HMRC when it provides advice.

Chapter six probes the remedies which are available for taxpayers where it is argued that HMRC has departed from the advice previously provided. The chapter looks in depth at the public law remedy of legitimate expectations, but concludes that the protection offered by this doctrine is not particularly strong. The chapter thereafter very briefly looks at the private law remedies which may be available, but concludes that these will offer little comfort to taxpayers. The final part of the chapter assesses the role that is played by actors outside the tribunals and courts system, namely the Adjudicator's Office and the Parliamentary Ombudsman, and finds that these bodies can provide some protection for taxpayers.

Chapter seven sets out potential solutions to the issues encountered in respect of HMRC advice. It first explains a proposal to establish a broad, binding rulings regime. Thereafter the chapter collates the recommendations emanating from findings in earlier chapters.

Chapter eight concludes by briefly reflecting upon the study undertaken and listing the reforms recommended.

It should be highlighted at this juncture that the book makes several notable stylistic choices. The first is to refer to HMRC in the singular. More importantly, although the body only formally came into being in 2005 through the merger of the Inland Revenue and Customs and Excise, HMRC is used throughout the book to refer even to actions undertaken by either of the predecessor bodies for ease of readership. At times, it will be necessary to refer specifically to either the Inland Revenue or Customs and Excise, but for the most part, HMRC will be used. Further, the book adopts the female pronoun to refer to individual taxpayers, except where the person's identity is known, such as when referring to a case. Finally, there are many references to materials produced by HMRC and other tax organisations in the footnotes. Many of these are documents which are only available online. Rather than giving weblinks, which might expire in the future, the title of the relevant publication is used. Given that the information in these links is regularly updated, the most recent date cited on the publication is used here rather than the date it was produced.

The final matter to be noted is that the book tries to ensure that the law is correct as of September 2019.

V. Conclusion

In the latest edition of *Tiley's Revenue Law*, Loutzenhiser comments on the lack of academic study on the public law issues concerning tax:

> Although the power to tax has been at the very centre of some of our major constitutional law disputes, including the execution of a King, there has until relatively recent times been a lack of engagement with public law issues by UK tax academics.[50]

Whilst there have been several notable contributions to this area in recent years which have laid the seeds for further development,[51] it is true that the field is more

[50] Loutzenhiser, *Tiley's Revenue Law* (2019) 30.

[51] See Evans, Freedman and Krever, *The Delicate Balance* (2011); J Snape, *The Political Economy of Corporation Tax: Theory, Values and Law Reform* (Oxford, Hart Publishing, 2011); J Freedman and J Vella, 'Revenue Guidance: The Limits of Discretion and Legitimate Expectations' (2012) 128 *LQR* 192. See also SA De Smith, H Woolf and J Jowell, *Judicial Review of Administrative Action*, 5th edn (London, Sweet and Maxwell, 1995) ch 23.

sparse than should be expected given how tax collection impinges fundamentally on the relationship between citizen and state. The provision of advice by HMRC is such an area where tax administration and public law overlap, and which is in critical need of comprehensive examination. The subsequent chapters in this book will elaborate upon what it is, why it is good, what is going wrong and what can be done. As we continue to rapidly move into the era of new technology, it is important to seek answers to these questions so at least the groundwork can be laid for dealing with the inevitable significant disruption that will be caused.

2

What is HMRC Advice?

Fear and bigotry don't need explaining. They simply are, like traffic jams and taxes.*

I. Introduction

It is a great understatement to say that UK tax law today is complex. That complexity should arise is one consequence of the desire to secure equity in the tax laws,[1] in addition to pursuing other objectives.[2] If the legislation and case law offer few immediate answers to the taxpayer, then HMRC's role as administrator of the system becomes more apparent. To this end, HMRC provides vast amounts of tax advice which seek to translate for taxpayers (and tax officials) this ever more elaborate law, tax advice being a view or judgement on the consequences of tax law purposefully communicated to taxpayers as such.[3] This encapsulates a range of activities, from advising on choices afforded by legislation to the implications of transactions,[4] and comes in many different shapes and sizes, from bespoke rulings to guidance published to the world at large. Some HMRC publications may concern purely internal, administrative matters such as which person to contact in relation to particular issues. Indeed, often the interaction between HMRC and taxpayers will involve little professional judgement and may simply be signposting as to deadlines and appropriate forms. In other instances, the advice

* E Wilks, *Death Magic* (New York, Berkley Sensation, 2011).

[1] R Ewing, 'Annual report 1923–24 – 1924–25' 3 as cited in L Edmonds, *Working for all Australians 1910–2010: A brief history of the Australian Taxation Office* (Canberra, Australian Tax Office, 2010) 75.

[2] See for instance G Loutzenhiser, *Tiley's Revenue Law*, 8th edn (Oxford, Hart Publishing, 2019) 7–10; Meade Report, *The Structure and Reform of Direct Taxation* (London, George Allen & Unwin, 1978) 12; J Mirrlees, *Tax by Design: the Mirrlees Review* (Oxford, Oxford University Press, 2011) 23–33 and 35–38.

[3] This is broader than the definition adopted by the Office of Tax Simplification, which involves: 'pointing out options and then setting out which of these the taxpayer might choose and why. It may also be to identify an option that carries more risk because of some inherent uncertainty'. See Office of Tax Simplification, 'Guidance for taxpayers: a vision for the future' (October 2018) 9. However, the courts and HMRC have adopted the understanding of the meaning of 'advice' which is adopted for the purposes of this book. See for instance: *R (Aozora) v HMRC* [2017] EWHC 2881 (Admin), [2018] STC 11 [97] (Sir Kenneth Parker); HMRC, 'ADML1620' (July 2016).

[4] Chartered Institute of Taxation and Association of Taxation Technicians, 'Professional Conduct in relation to Taxation' (November 2016) 23.

will call for the exercise of professional judgement in assessing the application of complex or open-textured law to complicated facts. There is a spectrum accordingly as to the degree of judgement required to advise on the legal consequences of tax law which is encapsulated in the advice.[5] More particularly, the form of the advice may be 'substantive' as it provides the detail of a general legislative provision; 'concessionary' in the sense that the letter of the law will not necessarily be followed; 'interpretative' by reason of setting out HMRC's view of the scope and meaning of the law; 'advisory' as it is directed to taxpayers on certain tax positions; 'explanatory' in the sense of simply summarising the law or rendering it into 'plain English' even where there is no issue as to its true meaning; and 'administrative' because it sets out how HMRC proposes to administer the law, including matters relating to its general managerial discretion and cases where a specific discretion has been conferred on HMRC in some matter. Of course, these categories of forms of advice are not mutually exclusive and at times it may be impossible to distinguish between them, but they do engender different consequences, particularly in the case of concessionary advice.[6]

This chapter examines the different types and categories of HMRC advice and how they come about. The analysis begins by looking at advice provided to individual taxpayers before considering advice issued to a general body of taxpayers. The discussion of general advice lends itself also to incorporating examples of the different forms the advice may take.

II. Individual Advice

Rulings are pieces of advice issued to individual taxpayers by HMRC in response to taxpayer queries, setting out HMRC's view on the tax implications of a specified transaction or arrangement. Rulings have existed in the UK for many years, though the UK is slightly unique in that it does not operate a comprehensive system for formal rulings as arises in some other major jurisdictions. Nevertheless, informal rulings have long been provided by HMRC and its predecessor bodies. Quite separate from the system of rulings, HMRC and its predecessor bodies have also long provided assistance to individual taxpayers not just through publications or written advice, but also through helplines and other less formalised avenues.

Individual advice may also play a role in tandem with general advice. To this end, where the taxpayer is unclear about the application of general advice to her own facts, she has available to her the option, 'which may in some cases be preferable',[7] of obtaining individual advice from HMRC.

[5] This categorisation of forms of advice came directly from the thesis report prepared by the examiners of the author's doctorate, Timothy Endicott and Malcolm Gammie.

[6] This will become clear in later chapters. See for instance below ch 4 in text at n 9 and n 153; ch 5 in text at n 106; ch 6 in text at n 56; ch 7 in text at n 209 and n 274.

[7] *Aozora* (n 3) [87].

A. Informal Rulings

Though in theory an informal ruling could encapsulate any instance that advice is provided to an individual taxpayer by HMRC following a taxpayer request, whether written or not, the term 'ruling' is generally reserved for written communications between the tax authority and the taxpayer.[8] Several publications through the years from the UK revenue authorities have set out how taxpayers could receive informal rulings. For instance, Code of Practice 10[9] (which was originally published in 1995) previously set out how taxpayers could receive non-statutory rulings from HMRC. How non-statutory VAT clearances for non-business customers could be acquired was set out in VAT Notice 700/6.[10] Meanwhile a separate process was in place for business customers seeking non-statutory clearances.[11] These pieces of guidance set out the 'broad parameters and operation of the system' for informal individual rulings, and stated the 'conditions in which, and issues with respect to which, advice on the application of tax legislation' would be given.[12] However, it is clear that informal rulings predate these publications.[13]

Today, a single HMRC document entitled 'Find out about the Non-Statutory Clearance Service' provides information on when, how and on what taxpayers can get an informal ruling from HMRC.[14] A taxpayer can ask HMRC for written advice if she has fully read the relevant guidance or contacted the relevant helpline, has not been able to find the information needed and is uncertain about HMRC's interpretation of tax legislation. There is an array of instances in which HMRC will refuse to provide the advice, for example if not all relevant information has been transmitted, the taxpayer is looking for tax planning advice or the taxpayer is in effect seeking tax avoidance approval. The request for written advice is sent to the relevant team within HMRC, which processes and responds to the request. Depending on the area of law which the advice concerns, the request may go to a

[8] See for instance C Micheau, 'Tax selectivity in European law of state aid: legal assessment and alternative approaches' (2015) 40 *European Law Review* 323, 331.

[9] See HMRC, 'COP10 – HMRC Code of Practice 10 – information and advice', available at: http://webarchive.nationalarchives.gov.uk/20111005104924/http://www.hmrc.gov.uk/pdfs/cop10.htm.

[10] HMRC, 'VAT rulings: Notice 700/6' (August 2009), available at: http://webarchive.nationalarchives.gov.uk/20111005102404tf_/http://customs.hmrc.gov.uk/channelsPortalWebApp/channelsPortalWebApp.portal?_nfpb=true&_pageLabel=pageLibrary_ShowContent&id=HMCE_CL_000874&propertyType=document.

[11] HMRC, 'Clearance service for businesses – how to get certainty on significant business tax issues', available at: http://webarchive.nationalarchives.gov.uk/20111005095811/http://www.hmrc.gov.uk/cap/links-dec07.htm.

[12] J Black, 'Talking about Regulation' in M Harris and M Partington, *Administrative Justice in the 21st Century* (Oxford, Hart Publishing, 1999) 251.

[13] For instance, the case of *R v IRC, ex parte Camacq Corp* concerned an informal ruling provided by the Inland Revenue in 1989: *R v IRC, ex parte Camacq Corp* [1990] 1 WLR 191 (CA), 195. See also below in text at n 37.

[14] HMRC, 'Find out about the Non-Statutory Clearance Service' (June 2018).

specific team, as in the case of Business Investment Relief, though at other times, as in the case of VAT, the request goes to the general Non-Statutory Clearance Team.[15]

HMRC endeavours to respond to any application within 28 days. The taxpayer is free to disagree with an informal HMRC ruling, and the ruling has no impact upon statutory deadlines. Further, there is no general right of appeal against advice expressed by HMRC, but in some cases rights to appeal are set out in statute.[16] Whilst in practice such informal rulings might be perceived as binding by either HMRC or by the relevant taxpayers, the legal effect of such rulings is governed by remedies such as the doctrine of legitimate expectations and private law remedies such as promissory estoppel.[17] This is different to formal rulings which *are* legally binding.

B. Formal Rulings

As Loutzenhiser rightly points out, there 'is no general scheme whereby taxpayers can obtain advance rulings on the tax consequences of a particular transaction'.[18] Several commentators over the years have proposed the introduction of a general formalised rulings system.[19] There are, however, certain circumstances in which the legislation prescribes a clearance procedure, sometimes 'as part of broad anti-avoidance legislation'.[20] These more formal rulings are distinct from informal rulings by reason of the fact that they have statutory force *and* are automatically legally binding,[21] without the need to rely upon public or private law remedies, provided that the statutory conditions are fulfilled. HMRC has a Clearance and Counteraction Team which handles requests where advance clearance is required under particular statutory provisions, such as in relation to capital gains tax,[22] purchase of own shares by unquoted trading companies,[23] and demergers.[24] The circumstances in which a formal ruling can be requested, however, are very narrow. There are around 18 instances where legislation provides for a clearance procedure.[25] Given the breadth of the UK tax code, these form an almost negligible part of the law.

[15] See further HMRC, 'Non-Statutory Clearance Service guidance: annexes' (May 2019).

[16] For instance, some VAT-related decisions are classed as 'appealable decisions' by statute. See generally, Value Added Tax Act 1994, s 83.

[17] See below generally ch 6.

[18] Loutzenhiser, *Tiley's Revenue Law* (2019) 54.

[19] See for instance D Sandler, *A Request for Rulings* (London, Institute of Taxation, 1994). A fuller account is set out in ch 7 in text at n 51.

[20] Loutzenhiser (n 2) 55.

[21] See for instance Taxation (International and Other Provisions) Act 2010, s 220(2).

[22] See for instance, Taxation of Chargeable Gains Act 1992, ss 138(1), 139(5), 140B and 140D.

[23] Corporation Tax Act 2010, s 1044.

[24] Corporation Tax Act 2010, s 1091.

[25] According to HMRC guidance. See HMRC, 'How to apply for clearance or approval of a transaction from HMRC' (May 2019).

An example of a regime for formal rulings is that which arises in respect of Advanced Pricing Arrangements (APAs), something which in recent years has come under increased scrutiny due to concerns that these rulings may give rise to a breach of EU State aid rules.[26] An APA is a written agreement between a taxpayer and the tax authority which determines a method for resolving transfer pricing issues.[27] In the UK, the provision of APAs is governed by sections 218–230 of the Taxation (International and Other Provisions) Act 2010 (TIOPA 2010). The process for obtaining an APA is lengthy.[28] It begins with an 'expression of interest', initiated by an eligible taxpayer[29] and sent to the APA lead at HMRC, the purpose of which is to ensure that resources are not wasted on an unsuitable application and that the relevant issues are narrowed down. Following HMRC's indication that it is willing to consider the APA proposal, the taxpayer should then submit a formal APA application,[30] which HMRC aims to complete within 18–21months.[31] The agreement may be modified. There will be monitoring of the APA by HMRC and, to this end, the taxpayer should attach a compliance report[32] with the annual tax return. The APA will contain terms that allow for its revocation[33] where the business doesn't comply with the terms and conditions of the agreement, or where the identified critical assumptions cease to be valid.[34] The APA may also contain terms allowing for its modification.[35] The typical APA will last between three and five years.[36]

C. Other Channels for Individual Advice

Once upon a time, individuals would be able to simply visit the local tax office for guidance.[37] In fact, the practice of taxpayers approaching the revenue authorities goes back at least well into the nineteenth century.[38] Local tax offices no longer exist and have been replaced by regional hubs. This change was facilitated by a rapid decline in tax offices, from 600 in 2005 to 144 in 2016–17.[39] To this end, the practice of approaching the local tax inspector has now been all but abolished.

[26] For further detail, see: Micheau, 'Tax selectivity' (2015).
[27] HMRC, Statement of Practice 2/2010 (July 2019) para 1.
[28] The relevant procedure is set out in HMRC, SP 2/2010 (ibid).
[29] See TIOPA 2010, s 218(2).
[30] TIOPA 2010, s 223.
[31] HMRC, SP 2/2010 (n 27) para 36.
[32] Usually required by the agreement and as sanctioned by TIOPA 2010, s 228.
[33] On which, see TIOPA 2010, s 225.
[34] HMRC, SP 2/2010 (n 27) para 46.
[35] On which, see TIOPA 2010, s 225.
[36] HMRC, SP 2/2010 (n 27) para 25.
[37] See for instance *McGirr v Arrow One Couriers Ltd* [1983] 2 WLUK 166 [9].
[38] See for instance, C Stebbings, 'The equity of the executive: Fairness in tax law in nineteenth-century England' in P Turner (ed), *Equity and Administration* (Cambridge, Cambridge University Press, 2016) 280–81.
[39] BT, 'Smarter Working in public services: The HMRC experience so far' (September 2018) 11.

Today, however, there are still channels outside the process of rulings whereby individual taxpayers can receive advice from HMRC. Taxpayers, or tax agents working on their behalf,[40] can contact HMRC by phone on the dedicated helplines that have been established for advice in relation to issues that arise,[41] online, by post, and even via Twitter.[42] HMRC may at other times provide unsolicited advice to taxpayers, for instance in a letter following a compliance intervention.[43]

Whilst the helpline service is available to all taxpayers, more specialised help is available to the largest businesses in the UK. A Customer Compliance Manager (CCM), formerly known as a Customer Relationship Manager,[44] is assigned to the largest businesses in the UK, of which there are around 2,000.[45] The logic of assigning dedicated staff to large businesses derives from a risk-based approach to tax collection which HMRC uses as a matter of operational course.[46] Larger businesses pose a greater risk to the Exchequer and hence it follows that resources should be directed to managing the risk. The primary role of the CCM is to make sure that the business pays all the tax that is due, which involves building in-depth knowledge of the business and the sectors that it operates in. To this end, the largest businesses are able to obtain advice on technical questions directly from their CCMs.

III. General Advice

In addition to providing advice to individual taxpayers, HMRC also produces large swathes of general advice which is directed at taxpayers in a class or as a whole. HMRC,[47] the courts[48] and taxpayers[49] will often simply refer to general advice as 'guidance'. It is commonly less specific than advice provided directly to individuals, which will have an impact later when it comes to remedies that might be available to taxpayers where HMRC seeks to depart from its advice.[50] General advice, meanwhile, is to be contrasted with secondary (or subordinate

[40] HMRC, 'Dedicated helplines and contacts for tax agents' (January 2014).

[41] HMRC, 'Contact HMRC'.

[42] See for instance, HMRC, 'Tax Credits: General Queries'.

[43] HMRC, 'Admin Law Manual: ADML1800' (July 2016).

[44] HMRC, 'HCOTEG220025, Appendices: Abbreviations' (July 2016).

[45] HMRC, 'How HMRC works with large businesses' (April 2018).

[46] R Cockburn, *Small Business Tax Planning: All you need to know from start-up to retirement* (Petersfield, Harriman House Publishing, 2011) 124.

[47] For instance HMRC, 'CTM00511 Introductory: meaning of ordinary share capital: general' (May 2019).

[48] For instance *Fletcher v Thompson* [2002] EWHC 1448 (Admin) [45] (Collins J).

[49] For instance HMRC, 'Extra statutory concessions – eighth technical consultation on draft legislation' (February 2018) para 3.8.

[50] See for instance *R (Bhatt Murphy (a firm)) v The Independent Assessor* [2008] EWCA Civ 755, [2008] All ER (D) 127 [46]. See below ch 6 in text at n 37.

or delegated) legislation such as statutory instruments[51] or regulations,[52] which is generally[53] produced by HMRC pursuant to specific legislative mandate. Secondary legislation has the force of law and is binding, though it 'will be held by a court to be invalid if it has an effect, or is made for a purpose, which is *ultra vires*' in the sense of being 'outside the scope of the statutory power pursuant to which it was purportedly made'.[54] Notably, some items of general advice additionally have the force of law.[55]

For ease of reading, general HMRC advice is categorised in the book largely as it is promulgated in practice. There are to this end several distinct categories, namely Codes of Practice, Statements of Practice, Extra-Statutory Concessions, Manuals and the catch-all, 'Guidance'. Meanwhile, there exist other avenues such as through representative groups, including professional bodies, whereby HMRC provides advice to general classes of taxpayers, which is sometimes not published by HMRC. It should be noted, however, that not all information which is to be found in HMRC publications or its correspondence to groups of taxpayers should be understood as advice, as the information may be purely administrative.

A. Codes of Practice

The UK Government has defined a 'code of practice' as an authoritative statement of practice to be followed, whose prescriptions are not hard and fast rules but guidelines which may allow considerable latitude in their practical application and may be departed from in appropriate circumstances.[56] In the case of tax, Codes of Practice (COPs) are instruments which set out how HMRC will carry out its duties and are broadly authoritative statements on procedure. Only three codes are still exclusively referred to as COPs today,[57] whilst the rest have been

[51] See, for instance, Directions under Regulations 5(1) of the Income and Corporation Taxes (Electronic Communications) Regulations 2003 (SI 2003/282).

[52] See, for instance, The Investment Manager (investment transactions) Regulations 2014, which was issued in exercise of the powers conferred by Income Tax Act 2007, ss 827(2) and 825S(4) of the Corporation Tax Act 2010, s 1150.

[53] In some discrete instances, secondary legislation is not authorised per se by Parliament, but might be termed 'prerogative instruments'. For instance, double tax treaties are incorporated into UK law by way of Order in Council (see TIOPA 2010, s 2). It should be noted, however, that even then, the draft Order must be laid before and approved by the House of Commons (TIOPA 2010, s 5(2)) and also that it is an Act of Parliament that confers the power on Her Majesty. In principle, the royal prerogative can serve as the authority itself for secondary legislation (without any involvement of Parliament) as the Crown retains 'anachronistic' power to legislate by royal prerogative: (*R (Bancoult) v Secretary of State For Foreign and Commonwealth Affairs* [2008] UKHL 61, [2009] 1 AC 453 [69] (Lord Bingham)).

[54] *R (Public Law Project) v Lord Chancellor* [2016] UKSC 39, [2016] AC 1531 [23] (Lord Neuberger). For a notorious tax case where a levy was found to be ultra vires, see: *A-G v Wilts United Dairies Ltd* (1922) 38 TLR 781 (CA).

[55] See below in text at n 142.

[56] Cabinet Office, 'Guide to Making Legislation' (July 2017) para 13.12, cited in A Bradley, K Ewing and C Knight, *Constitutional & Administrative Law*, 17th edn (Harlow, Pearson Education, 2018) 612.

[57] HMRC, 'Leaflets, factsheets and booklets' (December 2016).

replaced with factsheets and leaflets[58] (though these will often still refer to the original Codes of Practice).[59] COP 9 is issued in cases where HMRC suspects tax fraud. Although generally where fraud is suspected, HMRC will seek to prosecute, COP 9 specifies that HMRC may offer the accused taxpayer instead the chance to make a full disclosure under a contractual arrangement.[60] COP 8 sets out HMRC's procedure where fraud is suspected but the contractual disclosure facility available under COP 9 is not utilised.[61] Finally, the 'Code of Practice on the Disclosure of Information' explains the law in relation to disclosure of information under the Anti-Terrorism, Crime and Security Act 2001.[62] It further describes the controls and safeguards that are in place to ensure that these disclosures conform to the law.[63] COPs are caveated that they are intended to act generally as guidance and do not generally have binding force.[64] Taking COPs as authoritative statements on procedure more generally, one might note that many other publications from HMRC would fall within this definition, such as the Litigation and Settlement Strategy (LSS),[65] which is instead categorised as 'Guidance' on HMRC's website. The LSS provides a framework through which HMRC may arrive at settlements on outstanding tax bills with taxpayers.

Given that COPs are authoritative statements on procedure, they often incorporate 'administrative' advice such as in the case of COPs 8 and 9 which set out how HMRC will exercise its discretion not to seek prosecution and instead settle the matter. What is still referred to in practice as COP 10 sets out the process for the issuance of an informal ruling by HMRC, a matter which falls squarely within its more general managerial discretion. The Code of Practice on Disclosure of Information, meanwhile, contains some 'explanatory' advice in relation to the operation of sections 19 and 20 of the Anti-Terrorism, Crime and Security Act 2001.

B. Statements of Practice

Until June 1979 the Inland Revenue Department's views on the practical interpretation of tax law were publicised in a variety of ways, including by way of answers

[58] HMRC, 'TTOG1130 – The guidance: factsheets and codes of practice: use of codes of practice' (June 2017).

[59] See for instance HMRC, 'What happens if we've paid you too much tax credits (COP 26)' (April 2019).

[60] HMRC, 'Code of Practice 9' (June 2014).

[61] HMRC, 'COP 8' (August 2014).

[62] HMRC, 'Anti-terrorism, Crime and Security Act 2001: Code of practice on the disclosure of information' (February 2002).

[63] ibid 1.

[64] See for instance HMRC, 'COP 8' (n 61) 13; Cabinet Office, 'Guide' (n 56) 106.

[65] See HMRC, 'Resolving tax disputes Commentary on the litigation and settlement strategy' (October 2017).

to Parliamentary questions and letters to professional bodies and journals.[66] The Department then consolidated the whole of this information into a list of 88 Statements of Practice (SPs)[67] and the practice thereafter has been to regularly update the list.[68] According to HMRC, SPs set out HMRC's interpretation of law and the way it will be applied in practice.[69] They explain the Department's view of the law where it is unclear; where there may be more than one interpretation or where HMRC considers it would assist taxpayers. SPs similarly may be used to make substantial statements about the way HMRC administers the tax system, how it will exercise a specific statutory discretion, or describe a practice which has no specific statutory foundation (other than section 5 of the Commissioners for Revenue and Customs Act (CRCA 2005)), but which is not, in essence, concessionary.[70]

SPs are non-binding and to this end taxpayers should be cautious about relying on them. First, SPs merely set out HMRC's view and as such may not accurately set out the law.[71] This is problematic as it is only in exceptional circumstances that HMRC will be bound to incorrect statements of the law,[72] though HMRC claims that it will not depart from its view expressed in an SP where a taxpayer has, in reliance, irrevocably changed her position.[73] Secondly, the initial caveat that they only explain HMRC's interpretation and 'do not affect a taxpayer's right to argue for a different interpretation' may serve to vitiate the possibility of binding HMRC for the reason that public law provides protection only in cases where there is an assurance which is 'devoid of relevant qualification'.[74]

SPs can embody different forms of advice, as is clear from the definition. SPs may incorporate administrative advice which sets out how HMRC will exercise a particular statutory discretion, for instance. Paragraph 74(2) of Schedule 18 of the Finance Act 1998 provides that group relief claims may be made or withdrawn outside the statutory time limits if HMRC allow it. How HMRC will exercise the discretion is further set out in Statement of Practice 5/2001.[75] SPs are equally likely to incorporate explanatory advice. For instance, SP D12 sets out a number of points of general practice which have been agreed in respect of partnerships to which section 59 of the Taxation of Chargeable Gains Act 1992 applies.[76]

[66] HM Treasury, 'Appropriation Accounts' (HC 1981-82, 76-IX) xxi.

[67] ibid.

[68] See here: HMRC, 'Statements of Practice' (January 2010).

[69] Hansard, HC Deb Vol 915, col 187 (12 July 1976). This is the definition which HMRC supplies also on its website.

[70] HMRC, 'ADML5100 – Statements of Practice: What is a Statement of Practice?' (July 2016).

[71] N Lee, *Revenue Law: Principles and Practice*, 30th edn (West Sussex, Bloomsbury Professional, 2012) 12.

[72] See below ch 6 in text at n 56.

[73] HMRC, 'ADML5100 – Statements of Practice' (n 70).

[74] See below ch 6 in text at n 137.

[75] See HMRC, 'Statement of practice 5/2001' (April 2001) paras 9–12.

[76] HMRC, 'Statement of Practice D12: Partnerships' (September 2015).

Furthermore SPs may include concessionary advice in spite of what HMRC states in its definition.[77] For instance, Statement of Practice 15 (1993) provides that HMRC is prepared to accept computations of business profits for tax purposes in figures rounded to the nearest £1,000 from single businesses or companies with an annual turnover of not less than £5 million.[78] It is not difficult to see why in practice the collapse in distinction between a statement of practice and a lawful concession arises, given that both are based upon interpretations adopted and executed by HMRC. Both will in principle then exist on the same interpretative spectrum. Thus, as was previously explicitly recognised by the Inland Revenue, there are times in which it is 'a matter of judgment whether a Statement of Practice reflected some element of concession'.[79]

C. Extra-Statutory Concessions

One of the most controversial elements of the UK tax system,[80] Extra-Statutory Concessions (ESCs) give taxpayers a reduction in tax liability to which they would not be entitled under the strict letter of the law.[81] To this end, ESCs are generally a form of concessionary advice. Such is their controversy, however, that since the landmark judgment of Lord Hoffmann in the case of *R (Wilkinson) v IRC*,[82] HMRC has embarked on a process of withdrawing or formalising ESCs into statute.[83]

According to HMRC's definition, most concessions are made to deal with what are, on the whole, minor or transitory anomalies under the legislation and to meet cases of hardship at the margins of the code where a statutory remedy would be difficult to devise or would run to a length out of proportion to the intrinsic importance of the matter.[84] There are further classes of concession not captured by HMRC's definition. Concessions may also arise where they are necessary for the practical collection and management of taxes.[85] They may also relate to instances in which it would be an abuse of power for HMRC to insist upon the strict application of the law.[86] As ESCs relate to benevolent treatment, they must

[77] A Rowland, 'Is the Revenue being Fair? Revenue Statements and Judicial Review' [1995] *British Tax Review* 115, 117.

[78] HMRC, 'Statement of Practice 15' (1993) (June 1993).

[79] HM Treasury, 'Appropriation Accounts' (n 66) xxii.

[80] On ESCs, see S Daly, 'The Life and Times of ESCs: A defence?' in D de Cogan and P Harris (eds), *Studies in the History of Tax Law: Volume 8* (Oxford, Hart Publishing, 2017).

[81] See HMRC, 'Extra-Statutory Concessions: Concessions as at 6 April 2018' (April 2018).

[82] *R (Wilkinson) v IRC* [2005] UKHL 30, [2006] STC 270.

[83] HMRC, 'Withdrawal of extra statutory concessions: Technical note and call for evidence' (January 2014) 4. The author disagrees, however, that *Wilkinson* is the catalyst for the change to HMRC practice, as expanded upon below in ch 5 in text at n 242.

[84] ibid 2.

[85] See Daly, 'Life and Times of ESCs' (2017) 178–79.

[86] ibid.

by definition arise in the taxpayer's favour.[87] Although they are intended to be of general application, this is qualified to the effect that 'special circumstances' may arise in a particular case, which will need to be taken into account in considering the application of the concession.[88] For instance, a concession will not be given in any case where an attempt is made to use it for tax avoidance.[89]

The definition of ESCs, as understood by HMRC,[90] does not distinguish between concessions which are granted in *individual cases*, variously described by other authors as remissions[91] or waivers,[92] and those that relate to *classes* of cases. Class concessions are those which are founded on fixed principles of general application affecting classes.[93] For the purposes of this book, however, references to ESCs should be taken as meaning concessions applying to classes of taxable persons rather than to individuals. Further, whilst HMRC maintains published lists of ESCs,[94] the definition of ESC itself does not distinguish between class concessions which are *published* and those which are *not* published (of which there still exists a substantial body).[95] This distinction is at times overlooked, as evidenced by Walton J's misleading assertion in *Vestey v IRC (No 2)*[96] that the list of ESCs represents a 'published code'.[97]

Crucially, concessions may only operate within a narrow legal mandate. ESCs should only be promulgated by HMRC where the tax authority believes that the concession comes within the ambit of HMRC's managerial discretion,[98] or be the result of legitimate (including purposive) interpretation.[99] This is often summed up by the phrase that 'one must be taxed by law and not untaxed by concession'.[100] The fact that ESCs by their nature come close to the line of the unlawful exercise

[87] M Gammie, '"Revenue Practice": A Suitable Case For Treatment' [1979] *British Tax Review* 304, 306; *Hansard*, HC Deb, Vol 915, col 187 (12 July 1976).

[88] HMRC, 'Extra-Statutory Concessions' (n 81).

[89] *R (Bampton) v King* [2012] EWCA Civ 1744, [2014] STC 56 [109] (Arden LJ); *R v HM Inspector of Taxes, ex parte Fulford-Dobson* [1987] BTC 158 (QBD), 166 (McNeill J).

[90] On this, see: HMRC, 'Withdrawal of extra-statutory concessions' (December 2010).

[91] J Booth, Stand and Deliver! The Inland Revenue and Non-statutory Taxation (Winchester, Waterside Press, 1998) 23.

[92] J Freedman and J Vella, 'HMRC's Management of the U.K. Tax System: The Boundaries of Legitimate Discretion' in C Evans, J Freedman, R Krever, *The Delicate Balance: Tax, Discretion and the Rule of Law* (Amsterdam, IBFD, 2011) 92.

[93] A Johnston, *Inland Revenue* (London, George Allen & Unwin Ltd, 1965) 68.

[94] See HMRC, 'Extra-Statutory Concessions' (n 81) and HMRC, 'Extra Statutory Concessions' (VAT Notice 48) (September 2017).

[95] See below ch 4 in text at n 115.

[96] *Vestey v IRC (No 2)* [1979] Ch 198 (Ch).

[97] ibid 204.

[98] *Hansard*, Vol 63, col 1171 (11 July 1984); *Wilkinson* (n 82) [21].

[99] Given that managerial discretion is founded on CRCA 2005, s 5, it could actually be argued that purposive interpretation must by its nature include giving an interpretation of the law which takes account of managerial discretion. In other words, it could simply be said that ESCs are within HMRC's powers provided that they are the result of legitimate (including purposive) interpretation rather than additionally also having to mention managerial discretion. Indeed, in Daly (n 80) that is precisely what the author did.

[100] The genesis of the quote is: *Vestey v IRC (No 2)* (n 96) 203.

of public power is a matter which will be subject to further consideration in this book, as concessions which are inconsistent with the underlying law undermine the proper and desirable function of HMRC advice[101] as well as having a significant impact upon the ability of a taxpayer to rely upon the advice.[102]

As such, it is important to distinguish between instances in which the law is rough at the penumbra and gives rise to strictly unintended consequences such as failing to give relief or encompassing cases at the fringe,[103] as against instances where the law at its core is deemed to be unfair by HMRC.[104] In the former, but not in the latter, concessions may legitimately apply (subject to coming within the acceptable limits of interpretation), although in the past ESCs have fallen into the latter category.[105] Similarly a concession may be used so as to make the effectuation of the law more workable, but may not be reformulated in such a way as to undermine the law's very intent.[106]

Some examples should help to clarify this distinction. As for the relationship between concessions and managerial discretion, HMRC is not expected to collect every last penny of tax which is due and may make concessions for the purposes of administrative convenience. An apt example arises in relation to flat rate expense allowances (FREA). These are 'expenses' arrangements which HMRC arrives at with particular industries or with particular undertakings within specific industries. Expenses incurred by employees 'wholly, exclusively and necessarily in the performance of' his or her duties of employment can be deducted from the income of that employee before it is assessed to income tax.[107] Ordinarily, an employee would have to keep all receipts for expenses incurred as a means of proving what the outgoings have amounted to. An agreement on a flat rate to be granted in respect of expenses, as in the case of an FREA, on the other hand, obviates the need to retain all of the receipts in relation to expenses and for HMRC to analyse all the receipts.[108]

Similarly, HMRC may purposively interpret the legislation in order so that it accords with the underlying legislative intent. This may arise where HMRC attempts to place the law in the context of specific sectors. For instance, the case of *R (Greenwich Property Ltd) v Commissioners of Customs and Excise ('Greenwich Property')*[109] gave rise to such a scenario in relation to the supply of zero-rated goods as regards student accommodation. Under a strict legal interpretation,

[101] See below ch 4 in text at 9.

[102] See below ch 6 in text at n 37.

[103] Johnston, *Inland Revenue* (1965) 68.

[104] *Wilkinson* (n 82) [20]; *R (Wilkinson) v Inland Revenue Commissioners* [2003] EWCA Civ 814, [2003] 1 WLR 2683 [46] (Lord Phillips); see also *Stock v Frank Jones (Tipton) Ltd* [1978] 1 WLR 231 (HL), 234 (Viscount Dilhorne).

[105] On which, see below ch 4 in text at 9.

[106] *Hansard*, Finance Bill Deb HC cols 754–55 (17 June 2008) (Philip Hammond).

[107] See Income Tax (Earnings and Pension) Act 2003, s 336.

[108] *R (Bamber) v HMRC* [2005] EWHC 3221 (Admin), [2006] STC 1035 [2]–[4] (Lindsay J).

[109] *R (Greenwich Property Ltd) v Commissioners of Customs and Excise* [2001] EWHC 230 (Admin), [2001] STC 618 (Collins J).

if universities were to rent out accommodation during summer months to non-students, they would not be entitled to claim the supply of goods was zero-rated. By 'concession',[110] the Revenue would allow a *de minimis* use of student accommodation for non-students, given that it could not be expected that the legislature would deprive relief in such circumstances. Many undergraduate and postgraduate degree programmes in the UK do not require the students to attend university during the summer months and to this end, the buildings would be left largely vacant if only registered students were entitled to live in them. The purpose of the concession, accordingly, was to 'interpret the law concerning VAT within the higher education context'.[111] An example of purposive interpretation gone awry in an ESC is that of ESC D33, which is analysed in detail in chapter four.[112] Indeed, historically there have been many concessions issued by HMRC which could not be justified either by virtue of managerial discretion or legitimate interpretation.[113]

D. Manuals

The publication of internal HMRC Manuals is one of the most interesting developments in tax law in recent years.[114] The development is sometimes put down to the Freedom of Information Act 2000,[115] but it seems the initial drive towards publication commenced in 1994, some years before the passing of the 2000 Act.[116] Prior to their publication, they were strictly confidential (although the contents were well known to inspectors who left the service for private practice).[117] HMRC's Manuals are now available online.[118] However, some information is still treated as confidential and is not published.[119] Manuals specify inter alia the procedure to be undertaken in relation to issues which arise in the collection and management of taxes. Though once considered as being directed internally only to HMRC staff, it has become clear that HMRC also maintains its Manuals for tax advisers and taxpayers, as they are an important and useful resource[120] elaborating on how HMRC seeks to apply the law in practice. This utility is evidenced in part by the number of cases where taxpayers have sought to rely upon the information

[110] The term is used comprehensively in the judgment.

[111] *Greenwich Property* (n 109) [9] (Collins J).

[112] See below ch 4 in text at n 22.

[113] See below ch 4 in text at n 9.

[114] Loutzenhiser (n 2) 53.

[115] G Morse, D Williams and S Eden, *Davies: Principles of Tax Law*, 8th edn (London, Sweet and Maxwell, 2016) 52.

[116] D Smailes, '100 years of Tolley tax' in G Aaronson et al, *Plucking the Goose: A century of taxation from the Great War to the Digital Age* (Croydon, Tolley, 2016) 50, cited in OTS, *Guidance for taxpayers* (2018) 8.

[117] ibid.

[118] HMRC, 'HMRC Manuals' (September 2018).

[119] See below ch 7 in text at n 265.

[120] A Fairpo, 'Tax Research – Online Resources' (2008) 923 *Tax Journal* 17, 17; R Cory 'The Human Rights Act 1998 and the Treasury consents regime' [2005] *British Tax Review* 412, 427.

contained in Manuals.[121] In fact, Freedman and Vella report that HMRC is beginning to put certain tax advice directly into Manuals with the expectation that taxpayers and advisers will consult them.[122]

As with other categories of advice, Manuals are qualified to the extent that they are not 'comprehensive' nor will they 'provide a definitive answer in every case'.[123] Similarly, the law as stated in the Manuals may be out of date.[124] These factors all serve to attenuate the prospect of reliance on the part of taxpayers.[125]

Not all of the information contained in Manuals can be classified as 'tax advice', such as where the Manuals refer to purely internal administrative tasks, such as who to contact in relation to particular inquiries.[126] Meanwhile that which *is* advice in the Manuals can take a variety of forms. It may be substantive – as in the case of the Alcohol Wholesales Registration Scheme Manual, which inter alia sets out the detail on the operation of Part 6A of the Alcoholic Liquor Duties Act 1979;[127] interpretative – as in the case of the Information Disclosure Guidance Manual which sets out HMRC's view on when it may disclose taxpayer information;[128] explanatory – as in the case of the 'Making and amending claims' section of the Self Assessment Claims Manual;[129] and even administrative – as with the section of the Admin Law Manual setting out how HMRC will exercise its managerial discretion to refrain from collecting tax.[130] Some of the material in Manuals also amounts to concessionary advice. For instance, on 4 August 2014, HMRC announced a change in practice in relation to the treatment of the use of unremitted foreign income or gains as collateral for a loan enjoyed in the UK.[131] It was remarked that the practice was concessionary, though the previous incarnation of the publication in a Manual made no mention of any 'concession'.[132]

E. Guidance

'Guidance' is a catch-all term for those HMRC publications which are issued to the general body of taxpayers, but are not published within the above categories.[133]

[121] For instance, *Hanover Company Services Ltd v HMRC* [2010] UKFTT 256 (TC).

[122] Freedman and Vella 'HMRC's Management of the UK Tax System' (2011) 113.

[123] HMRC, 'HMRC Manuals' (n 118).

[124] ibid.

[125] On which, see below ch 6 in text at n 56 and n 137.

[126] See for instance HMRC, 'Technical Help: How to get more help about topics in the CG Manual' (July 2019).

[127] HMRC, 'Alcohol Wholesaler Registration Scheme Manual' (July 2016).

[128] HMRC, 'Information Disclosure Guide' (March 2019).

[129] HMRC, 'SACM 3000 Making and amending claims' (April 2016).

[130] HMRC, 'ADML3400: Tests to apply' (July 2016).

[131] HMRC News, 'Remittance Basis' (August 2014).

[132] HMRC, 'Remittance Basis: Identifying Remittances: Conditions A and B: Condition B – collateral in respect of relevant debt' (October 2010). On 15 October 2015, it was announced that the concessionary treatment would not be withdrawn retrospectively, see: HMRC, 'Revenue and Customs Brief 16' (October 2015).

[133] See: HMRC, 'Leaflets, factsheets and booklets' (n 57).

This includes leaflets such as (the now defunct) Tax Bulletins,[134] Briefs,[135] Factsheets, Series and even Consultations.[136] Press releases from HMRC may also contain important information for taxpayers and, in a time prior to the internet, were a useful means of publicising new SPs and ESCs.[137] Guidance on the application of VAT laws, on the other hand, is generally found in VAT Notices[138] as with guidance on Excise in Excise Notices[139] and Tariffs in Tariff Notices.[140] Revenue and Customs briefs meanwhile announce changes in policy or set out the legal background to an issue. They generally have a short lifespan, as announced changes are incorporated into permanent guidance and the brief is then removed.[141] Many items published as Guidance could otherwise fit seamlessly within the categories of SP, COP or ESC. Somewhat confusingly, though Guidance is used as a catch-all category by HMRC for certain publications, the word 'guidance' [with a lower case 'g'] is often used by HMRC, the courts and taxpayers to refer to general advice, as noted already.

As with other items of advice, taxpayers should be cautious about relying on Guidance given that the publications are generally caveated that they are merely interpretative and by implication are not strictly binding (although some publications, such as some VAT Notices[142] and parts of the DOTAS Guidance,[143] do have the force of law).

Given the range of publications that come under the label, it is unsurprising that the instruments of published Guidance come in the full range of forms of HMRC advice. The advice in the Guidance can be substantive, such as the Guidance which details the statutory residence test;[144] concessionary – as in the case of VAT Notice 701/57 by way of which nursing agencies (or equivalent entities) may exempt the supply of nursing staff and nursing auxiliaries supplied as a principal to a third party;[145] interpretative – which arises in the instance of HMRC's interpretation of VAT liability for supplying ships, aircraft and associated services in the UK;[146] advisory – such as where settlement opportunities for taxpayers who have engaged in particular schemes are set out in Guidance;[147] explanatory – as in the case of the VAT Notice on when transactions involving land and buildings are

[134] See here http://webarchive.nationalarchives.gov.uk/20110620155444/hmrc.gov.uk/bulletins/index.htm.
[135] HMRC, 'Revenue and Customs Briefs' (July 2019).
[136] HM Government, 'Policy papers and consultations'.
[137] Gammie, 'Revenue Practice' [1979] 307.
[138] HMRC, 'VAT Notices: numerical order' (July 2018).
[139] See for instance HMRC, 'Excise Notice 39: spirits production in the UK' (July 2018).
[140] See for instance HMRC, 'Tariff Notices' (June 2019).
[141] HMRC, 'Revenue and Customs Briefs' (n 135).
[142] See for instance, HMRC, 'How to use the VAT retail Apportionment Scheme' (VAT Notice 727/4) (January 2013).
[143] HMRC, 'Guidance: Disclosure of Tax Avoidance Schemes' (April 2018) 12–13.
[144] HMRC, 'RDR3 Statutory Residence Test' (August 2016).
[145] HMRC, 'Health professionals and pharmaceutical products' (VAT Notice 701/57) (July 2018) para 6.5.
[146] HMRC, 'Ships, aircraft and associated services' (VAT Notice 744C) (January 2018) para 1.6.
[147] HMRC, 'Film production and sideways loss relief' (May 2014).

exempt from VAT;[148] or administrative – setting out the procedure that applies in the case of compliance checks.[149]

F. Other Channels for General Advice

There are other means through which HMRC can communicate general advice outside the ordinary publication scheme. For instance, HMRC engages in publicity campaigns in an effort to advise as to the legal consequences of tax law in addition sometimes to setting out how HMRC goes about finding non-compliant taxpayers.[150] Other times the advice does not come directly from HMRC as in the instance where HMRC communicates its view to representative groups who in turn pass the information on to members. In the case of *Greenwich Property*, the concession was communicated to the Committee of Vice-Chancellors and Principals of the Universities of the United Kingdom, which in turn issued a 'concordat' containing the advice from HMRC.[151] More problematically again, there are times where advice is generated within HMRC and communicated only to some outside. For instance, HMRC operates a concession known as 'liable no longer liable' by virtue of which HMRC will not require a taxpayer to register for VAT where the taxpayer's turnover is fluctuating and though it exceeds the registration threshold on one date, will fall below it on a future date.[152] It is contained in an HMRC Manual though the contents of the Manual have been redacted on the basis of 'exemptions in the Freedom of Information Act 2000'.[153] Where HMRC are alerted to the possibility that the concession applies, then it appears that it will do so, but that requires either that the taxpayer purposely (or surreptitiously)[154] communicates the salient information to HMRC or that a taxpayer is aware of the existence of the concession.

G. The Production of General Advice

Although we can clearly see the different categories of general advice and that there must be some internal process by which this is promulgated, it is not entirely clear

[148] HMRC, 'Land and property' (VAT Notice 742) (May 2012).
[149] For instance: HMRC, 'Compliance checks series – CC/FS1a' (March 2019).
[150] For instance HMRC, 'Evasion Publicity Campaign: Pre- and Post-Campaign Tracking 2012–13: Report on findings among Individuals' (2013).
[151] *Greenwich Property* (n 109) [9]. See also *R (Cameron) v HMRC* [2012] EWHC 1174 (Admin), [2012] STC 1691, [12]–[30] (Wyn Williams J) where a concession was first communicated at a meeting between trade unions and the Inland Revenue and eventually was published several years later.
[152] See: N Warren, 'Liable Not Liable: The concession not mentioned in HMRC's registration manual' *Accountingweb* (21 August 2018).
[153] See the contents of HMRC, 'VAT Manual: VATREG28000' (October 2016).
[154] As arose in the case of *Timothy Hughes and HMRC* [2018] UKFTT 407 (TC).

how these various publications come to be produced. Published sources provide some fleeting references to the relevant internal process. For instance, HMRC's Administrative Law Manual contains brief references to where ESCs and SPs originate from, namely, the Tax Admin Policy Team within Central Policy:

> If you think you may need to produce a new Statement of Practice (SP), or an amendment to an existing one, you should first contact the Tax Admin Policy Team.[155]
>
> The TAP team in Central Policy owns policy for extra-statutory concessions. You must contact them before you consider a new ESC. For assistance regarding the application of an existing ESC, you should contact the relevant technical advisor or policy owner.[156]

Other general advice seems to originate in the team which specialises in the particular area. For instance, the Capital Gains Manual is written by technical advisers in the Capital Gains Technical Group, which is part of Business, Asset and Individuals.[157]

To this end, it is unclear whether there is a systematic approach to promulgation or whether the matter is left to the discretion of the teams concerned, though the lack of public information on the matter suggests it is the latter. In this respect, it is unclear whether the different instruments are subjected to legal scrutiny within HMRC. There are examples, for instance, of mistakes in the publications which one would expect would be picked up by a lawyer (or at least an alert lawyer). For instance, in HMRC's Administrative Law Manual there is a section dedicated to the *Wilkinson* case in the context of discussing the scope of HMRC's managerial discretion.[158] However, the discussion not only neglects to mention the judgment of Lord Hoffmann and the seminal paragraphs therein, but rather only looks at Lord Phillips' (then Master of the Rolls) judgment in the Court of Appeal, neglecting entirely to mention the House of Lords judgment. The Manual notes that Lord Phillips approved of the judgment of Lord Scarman in the *Fleet Street Casuals* case. Lord Phillips did do so, but the Manual incorrectly attributes the famous Lord Diplock quote in respect of the scope of HMRC's managerial discretion to Lord Scarman. It states that:

> Lord Scarman said: '… the board are charged by statute with the care, management and collection on behalf of the Crown [of these taxes]. In the exercise of these functions, the board have managerial discretion as to the best means of obtaining for the national exchequer the highest net return that is practicable having regard to the staff available to them and the cost of collection.'

[155] HMRC, 'ADML5200: Statements of Practice: How to produce new or amended Statements of Practice' (July 2016).

[156] HMRC, 'ADML4400: Extra-statutory concessions: Who to contact before making a new extra-statutory concession' (July 2016).

[157] HMRC, 'CG99998: Technical Help: How to get more help about topics in the CG Manual' (July 2016).

[158] HMRC, 'ADML3300: Collection and Management: Case law' (July 2016).

Meanwhile HMRC will occasionally involve the public in the production of the general advice instruments. For instance, HMRC has previously endeavoured to issue 'guidance' concurrently with legislation and work with large businesses to ensure that the guidance is amended to reflect evolving commercial circumstances.[159] At times, HMRC responds to taxpayer requests for greater clarity by producing a publication setting out HMRC's view of the scope of legislative provisions.[160] Elsewhere, it has reconsidered its guidance in light of consultation with taxpayers after being better informed as to the consequences of the guidance in its previous iteration.[161] As with the question of legal scrutiny, however, there is no clear framework detailing when the public will be involved in the production of these publications and appears to be done on a purely ad hoc basis.

IV. Conclusion

The necessity of interpretation is something that stretches beyond tax law and even law itself. Laws like language require interpretation. HLA Hart explained this through the 'core and penumbra' metaphor.[162] Laws and language have a core meaning which is readily understandable. But there will also be a penumbra where the result of the application of the particular law in different situations is unclear. Where a rule states 'no vehicles in the park', it is obvious that this prohibits cars, but it is less clear if it prohibits bicycles, skateboards, or even motorised wheelchairs.

This chapter has sought to explain the different types, categories and forms of advice that HMRC produces so as to guide taxpayers as to the consequences of tax law. There are two broad types of advice – individual and general – and within these there are separate categories – most notably formal and informal in the case of individual advice; SPs, ESCs, CPs, Manuals and Guidance in the case of general advice. Cutting across these types and categories are different forms of advice – concessionary, interpretative, advisory, explanatory and administrative. What is clear is that HMRC advice can be understood as sitting on a spectrum in terms of the level of professional judgement required in the promulgation of the advice. This is principally due to interpretation, as it is the pursuit of the proper interpretation of the rules and their application which underpins all of this activity whether from the perspective of HMRC or the taxpayer.

[159] HMRC, 'Making a difference: clarity and certainty. 2006 review of links with large business' (October 2007) 9.

[160] For instance HMRC, 'Making a difference: clarity and certainty. 2006 review of links with large business' (October 2007) 9.

[161] For instance HMRC, 'Revenue and Customs Brief 16' (n 132).

[162] HLA Hart, 'Positivism and the Separation of Law and Morals' (1958) 71 *Harvard Law Review* 593, in particular 607.

Critically, the necessity of interpretation is an inevitable consequence of adopting a system where we are ruled by law and not unlimited discretion. To be ruled by law, then, is to accept that there will be some confusion as to what the rules do or do not encompass. But if this is the case, is it lawful for HMRC to assist in relation to the confusion. Even then, is it desirable that this should be the case? The next chapter will further explore these issues and pick up the theme of the rule of law, exploring it as a justification for the promulgation of HMRC advice.

3

The Role of HMRC Advice

What fate lies ahead for those unfortunate taxpayers who, while swerving to miss the potholes on a narrow road through the hills, crash into the guardrail on a wet and dark night? The likelihood is that rather than have the yellow flashing lights of 'tax assist' greet them, they are more likely to be met by dark suited gentlemen alighting from an unmarked car, with pens poised and charge sheets opened*

I. Introduction

For the VAT quarterly period ended 30 December 2007, Trinity Mirror filed their VAT return one day late. The relevant legislation in such circumstances imposed a surcharge amounting to two per cent of the VAT owed,[1] which in this case was £3.5 million. Whilst admitting liability, the taxpayers considered that the £70k penalty accordingly imposed to be disproportionate. It was upheld nevertheless in the Upper Tribunal.[2] If nothing else, the case serves as a cautionary tale about the severe legal consequences that can be brought about by the tax code: consequences taxpayers would certainly wish to be aware of!

Chapter two detailed the fact that HMRC produces advice to taxpayers which can guide them as to these consequences. But what is the legal basis for this? Even if it is legally permissible, what is the normative justification? Further, how should a system for advice operate? The purpose of this chapter, which will be split into three sections, is to provide answers to these questions. The first sets out why HMRC advice is lawful, the second elaborates upon why it is desirable in principle that HMRC should provide advice, principally because of the rule of law, and the final section sets out a normative framework for testing whether in practice HMRC advice fulfils its normative role.

* M Crowe, 'National Decisions', 'More Signposts Needed on Rocky Tax Road', National Australia Bank Limited, November 1992, 19 noted in Joint Committee of Public Accounts, 'An Assessment of Tax – A Report on an Inquiry into the Australian Taxation Office' (July 1993) 225.

[1] Value Added Tax Act 1994, s 59A(2).

[2] *HMRC v Trinity Mirror* [2015] UKUT 0421 (TCC), [2016] STC 352) [56]–[72].

II. Understanding HMRC's Role

HMRC provides advice to individual taxpayers and more generally, but the legal basis for doing so is not obvious, other than in the case of formal rulings where there is express statutory authority. How can it be constitutionally legitimate in those other instances, however, for a public authority like HMRC to effectively, through advice, produce rules for guiding the actions of taxpayers when that is traditionally understood to be the domain of the legislature? It is proposed in this section that HMRC advice generally does not conflict with the constitutional principle of Parliamentary sovereignty, but rather is a result of it. To make this clear, it is necessary to revisit the fundamental tenets of 'discretion' – distinguishing legal discretion, de facto discretion and epistemic deference – and thereafter to elaborate upon how the provision of advice comes within HMRC's managerial discretion (itself having been endowed by Parliament).

A. Discretion

i. Legal Discretion

Galligan traces the etymological roots of 'discretion' to the idea of 'good judgment'.[3] Indeed, the *Oxford Dictionary of Law* confirms this to be an accepted interpretation.[4] In modern legal usage, however, the term has come to ascribe '*autonomy* within which one's decisions are in some *degree* a matter of personal judgment and assessment'.[5] This broad definition captures the essential elements of discretion: that of *freedom to decide* (to a *degree*) within *boundaries*, such restrictions being inherent in the concept of autonomy.[6] With this, Dworkin once likened the concept of discretion to a 'hole in a doughnut',[7] the area left open by a surrounding belt of constraint. The level of discretion is inversely proportional to the intensity of constraint.[8] Critically then, legal discretion is what arises when 'someone is in general charged with making decisions subject to standards set by a particular authority'.[9] The resulting decision then will be legally respected provided that the legal standards relating to the grant of authority have not been traversed.[10]

[3] D Galligan, *Discretionary Powers*: A Legal Study of Official *Discretion* (Oxford, Clarendon Press, 1986) 8.

[4] 'discretion', J Law (ed), *Oxford Dictionary of Law*, 9th edn (Oxford, Oxford University Press, 2018).

[5] Galligan, *Discretionary Powers* (1986) 8.

[6] B Schwartz and HWR Wade, *Legal Control of Government: Administrative Law in Britain and the United States* (Oxford, Oxford University Press, 1972) 255; KC Davis, *Discretionary Justice: A Preliminary Inquiry*, 2nd edn (Baton Rouge, Louisiana State University Press, 1971) 4; K Hawkins (ed), *Uses of Discretion* (Oxford, Oxford University Press, 1992) 11; G Ganz, 'Allocation of Decision-Making Functions' [1972] *Public Law* 215, 215.

[7] R Dworkin, *Taking Rights Seriously* (London, Gerald Duckworth & Co, 1977) 31.

[8] M Kramer, *Objectivity and the Rule of Law* (Oxford, Oxford University Press, 2007) 14; J Black, *Rules and Regulators* (Oxford, Oxford University Press, 1997) 216.

[9] Dworkin, *Taking Rights Seriously* (1977) 31.

[10] This is as opposed to non-legal standards.

In the context of a governmental body which is created by Parliament, the logical first port of call with regard to legal standards will be the primary legislation which creates a power,[11] for instance, to collect and manage taxes.[12] A central task of the administrative body then is to translate this grant of power to a specific decision.[13] To this end, the body itself may have internal rules which specify the procedure for arriving at a decision, thereby incorporating a policy decision as to the ends to be achieved and the actions thusly to be pursued according to the grant of power.[14] In the case of HMRC, the Litigation and Settlement Strategy (LSS)[15] provides a clear example of such internal rules. It is an attempt to translate the parliamentary intention that HMRC should collect and manage taxes into a workable procedure. Generally, HMRC has considerable freedom in arriving at settlements with taxpayers,[16] but the LSS provides a framework through which HMRC may arrive at such settlements. For instance, wherever HMRC and a taxpayer disagree about tax due, each issue must be resolved on its own merits and not as part of any overall 'package' deal.[17] If a dispute is of an 'all or nothing' nature, HMRC will not settle out of court for less than 100% of the tax, interest and penalties due where it is believed that HMRC will likely succeed in litigation.[18] Conversely, where HMRC is unlikely to succeed in litigation, there must not be any attempt to 'split the difference'.[19] Nevertheless, these internal procedural constraints are themselves not entirely clear and thus are open to interpretation.[20]

The legal limits on discretion may be implied as well as express.[21] Discretion does not provide a carte blanche to act irrationally, but rather that *reasons* necessarily precipitate the arrival at a decision. A more apposite approach then is to acknowledge that there is autonomy to settle upon a choice for *good reasons*.[22] Accordingly, in this regard we see a convergence between discretion as it stands in modern usage and its etymological roots of *good judgment*. A further principle implied into the use of discretion is what Perry calls the 'flexibility rule',[23] though more generally it is known as the rule against fettering discretion.[24] Where a public

[11] Galligan (n 3) 208.

[12] Commissioners for Revenue and Customs Act, 2005 (CRCA 2005), s 5.

[13] G Ganz, *Quasi Legislation: recent developments in secondary legislation* (London, Sweet and Maxwell, 1987) 213; D Galligan, 'The nature and function of policies within discretionary power' [1976] *Public Law* 332, 332.

[14] Galligan (ibid) 322.

[15] HMRC, 'Resolving tax disputes: Commentary on the litigation and settlement strategy' (October 2017).

[16] See *IRC v National Federation of Self-Employed and Small Businesses Ltd* [1982] AC 617 (HL) (Fleet Street Casuals), 637 (Lord Diplock).

[17] HMRC, 'Resolving tax disputes' (2017) para 16.

[18] ibid para 18.

[19] ibid.

[20] See J Collins, 'Analysis – The tax assurance commissioner's first annual report' (2013) 1181 *Tax Journal* 22, 23; D de Cogan, '*UK Uncut Legal Action v HMRC*: legal inaction and a return to Fleet Street' [2013] 4 *British Tax Review* 552, 562 (note).

[21] See below in text at n 47.

[22] Galligan (n 3) 7.

[23] See A Perry, 'The Flexibility Rule in Administrative Law' (2017) 76 *Cambridge Law Journal* 375.

[24] See *R (Sandiford) v Secretary of State for Foreign and Commonwealth Affairs* [2014] UKSC 44, [2014] 1 WLR 2697 [54]; *R v Secretary of State for the Home Department, ex parte Venables* [1998]

body is granted discretion, it prescribes that the body may make a choice. There is nothing to this end contrary to the idea of discretion that the choice that the public body might make would be to actually restrict its choices.[25] In other words, to formulate one rule that would apply regardless of circumstances. Discretion requires us to respect the decision made by the discretion holder. However, in the case of statutory powers, it has been accepted that when Parliament grants discretion, it implies that the discretion ought to be retained and not fettered.[26] Further, Perry makes a compelling case that public bodies must not adopt an overly rigid policy and thus must retain flexibility because otherwise the public authority would fail to take into account the value of participation: it would be to refuse to a citizen the chance to make her case to the decision-maker, who has instead determined already the decision to be made.[27] Thus, where HMRC seeks to structure a statutory discretion or its managerial discretion as applied to a particular context, it must not do so in a manner which leaves no flexibility.

ii. De Facto Discretion

De facto discretion is distinct from legal discretion, but at times the two are conflated by commentators.[28] HMRC's legal discretion is the legal authority to decide between a range of choices, which is circumscribed by legal boundaries. De facto discretion, on the other hand, arises where HMRC can make determinations which have an effect, but this is not a legal effect as it is the tribunals and courts that have the legal authority to interpret legislation. For instance, where a legislative provision is broadly worded, this provides HMRC the opportunity to make a determination as to how that law should apply in practice. Taxpayers in effect will have to follow HMRC's determination, or at least if the taxpayer wishes to disagree will have to accept heightened scrutiny on her return. To this end, if a taxpayer applies to HMRC for an informal ruling but disagrees with HMRC's advice, then the taxpayer should complete the tax return in line with her own view, but draw HMRC's attention to the particular entry and explain what she has done.[29] Or where a taxpayer adopts a different view of the law from that published as the HMRC view, the taxpayer can 'protect against a discovery assessment after the

AC 407 (HL), 496 (Lord Browne-Wilkinson); *British Oxygen v Minister of Technology* [1971] AC 610 (HL), 625 (Lord Reid); *R v Port of London Authority, ex parte Kynoch Ltd* [1919] 1 KB 176 (CA), 183–84 (Bankes LJ).

[25] On this, see A McHarg, 'Administrative Discretion, Administrative Rule-making, and Judicial Review' (2017) 70 *Current Legal Problems* 267, 295.

[26] *Sandiford* (n 24) [61].

[27] Perry, 'The Flexibility Rule' (2017) 391–97. Cf McHarg, 'Administrative Discretion' (2017) 294–95.

[28] See for instance J Braithwaite, 'Making tax law more certain: A theory' (2003) 31 *Australian Business Law Review* 72, 77.

D Fernandes and K Sadiq, 'A principled framework for assessing general anti-avoidance regimes' [2016] *British Tax Review* 172, in particular 190–91.

[29] HMRC, 'Find out about the Non-Statutory Clearance Service' (June 2018).

enquiry period' by indicating that a different view had been adopted by entering this fact in the 'Additional Information' space in the return.[30]

Nevertheless it is open to taxpayers to appeal to the tribunals and thereafter courts, if challenged by HMRC, for a legal determination on the matter and the tribunals and courts have the ultimate authority to determine what the law means[31] (except in those specific instances where HMRC does in fact have the authority provided by statute to make legal determinations as in the case of formal rulings).[32] Hence the power that HMRC has to use working interpretations and apply them to facts does not amount to legal discretion to determine the rules.

iii. Epistemic Deference

Although an HMRC view of the law may not have a legal bearing, that does not mean that it has absolutely no bearing. This relates to what Paul Daly calls 'epistemic deference' – the idea that a decision-maker gives weight to a particular view expressed by some entity that is respected.[33] Thus, should HMRC express a view on a matter, then the tribunals and courts can give some weight to that view when making the legal determination. It is a factor that is taken into account in the decision-making process. The legal determination is still made by judges, and in that way HMRC's view would have no legal bearing, though it would bear some practical weight. In this way, HMRC's view could be set out in written advice given to taxpayers that ultimately influences the judge's decision.[34] For instance, the Upper Tribunal in *HMRC v Smith & Williamson*[35] and *HMRC v Glyn*[36] noted that the First-tier Tribunal in both instances had placed weight, albeit erroneously so, on the relevant HMRC guidance. HMRC's guidance on the General Anti-Abuse Rule (GAAR), as approved by the GAAR advisory panel, is unique in that it is a factor that *must* be taken into account by the tribunal or court in proceedings in connection with the GAAR.[37]

From the taxpayer's perspective, a significant risk arises where both de facto discretion and epistemic deference combine. Take, for instance, an anti-avoidance provision which is broadly drafted thereby giving de facto discretion to HMRC.

[30] See HMRC, 'Statement of Practice 1/06' (January 2006).

[31] On this, see the reference to Lord Neuberger's interjection in the case *RFC 2012 plc (in liquidation) v Advocate General for Scotland* [2017] UKSC 45, [2017] 1 WLR 2767 noted in M Gammie, 'Shooting the messenger: the proposed enabler penalty' [2017] *British Tax Review* 142, 142.

[32] See above ch 2 in text at n 18.

[33] P Daly, A Theory of Deference in Administrative Law: Basis, Application and Scope (Cambridge, Cambridge University Press, 2012) 7–9.

[34] See G Weeks, *Soft Law and Public Authorities: Remedies and Reform* (Oxford, Hart Publishing, 2016) 1–2; J Freedman and J Vella, 'HMRC's Management of the UK Tax System: The Boundaries of Legitimate Discretion' in C Evans, J Freedman and R Krever, *The Delicate Balance: Tax, Discretion and the Rule of Law* (Amsterdam, IBFD, 2011) 112–15.

[35] [2015] UKUT 666 (TCC), [2016] STC 1393 [107].

[36] [2015] UKUT 551 (TCC), [2016] STC 1020 [101].

[37] Finance Act 2013, s 211(2).

HMRC sets out its approach in advice. If the tribunal or court later applies epistemic deference to HMRC's approach, then HMRC comes close to acquiring in effect legal discretion to determine the scope and application of the law. This should concern those who believe that judicial attitudes to avoidance have shifted over time[38] and now favour HMRC.[39]

B. HMRC's Managerial Discretion

Any legal discretion that HMRC holds must be read in light of these basic building blocks. It produces freedom to make authoritative choices within the constraints of legal standards. Legislation giving HMRC duties to perform accordingly produces discretion in its hands as to how it carries out such tasks. Thus, when section 5 of the Commissioners for Revenue and Customs Act 2005 (CRCA 2005) dictates that HMRC's primary responsibility is the collection and management[40] of taxes and credits,[41] it places an overarching 'managerial discretion' in the hands of HMRC as to how it carries out these functions.[42] Section 9 of the CRCA 2005 elaborates upon this by making it clear that HMRC Commissioners may do anything which they think necessary or expedient in connection with the exercise of their functions, or incidental or conducive to the exercise of their functions.

This discretion is constrained by an array of legal rules.[43] First, it must not be used to act expressly in defiance of legislation and the case law that elaborates on the meaning of the legislation, as fundamentally it is the role of the tax authority to collect taxes prescribed as due by Parliament. Thus the discretion must not be

[38] Judges previously adopted a strict approach to statutory interpretation before moving towards purposive interpretation with *Ramsay v IRC* [1982] AC 300. See: S Daly, 'Tax Exceptionalism: A UK Perspective' (2017) 3 *Journal of Tax Administration* 95, 95–96.

[39] McCarthy and Black have speculated that the UBS case for instance might represent a departure from the previous judicial approach to avoidance cases with judges now permitted to take a much broader approach in order to strike down tax avoidance schemes. See: H Ling McCarthy and S Black, 'UBS and DB Group Services: a departure from the conventional approach?' [2016] *British Tax Review* 257.

[40] Prior to 2005, taxes were said to be under the 'care and management' of the Inland Revenue and Customs and Excise (see for instance Taxes Management Act 1970, s 1 and Value Added Tax Act 1994, Sch 11, para 1(1)). CRCA 2005, s 51(3) ensures that the references to collection and management are to be understood as meaning 'care and management'.

[41] CRCA 2005, s 5.

[42] *Fleet Street Casuals* (n 16). Discretion in the hands of Customs & Excise in this regard was identical to that of the Inland Revenue: *R v Customs and Excise Commissioners, ex p Kay & Co Ltd* [1996] STC 1500 (Keene J); *Fine Art Developments plc v Customs & Excise Commissioners* [1994] STC 668; *Customs & Excise Commissioners v Croydon Hotel & Leisure Co Ltd* [1995] STC 855.

[43] For a fuller discussion of the legal limits on discretion, see S Daly, 'Drawing the boundaries of HMRC's discretion' in R de la Feria and G Loutzenhiser (eds), *Essays in Honour of Judith Freedman* (forthcoming Oxford, Hart Publishing, 2020). The exposition of the legal limits is also given a more generous treatment by Freedman and Vella, 'HMRC's Management of the UK Tax System' (2011) 83–108.

used to usurp Parliament's role.[44] It is trite to recall that in peacetime only statute can repeal, suspend, amend or dispense with statute.[45] The discretion must be exercised too in accordance with Acts of Parliament such as the Human Rights Act 1998 and the European Communities Act 1972. Secondly, the discretion is bounded by fundamental constitutional principles such as those found in the Bill of Rights Act 1688/9. Article 1 provides that the suspension of laws without consent of Parliament is illegal, whilst Article 4 proscribes the levying of taxes without Parliamentary approval.[46] Thirdly, the discretion may not conflict with public law standards which have developed to constrain discretion.[47] As Lord Mustill explained in *R v Secretary of State for the Home Department ex parte Doody*:[48]

> Where an Act of Parliament confers an administrative power there is a presumption that it will be exercised in a manner which is fair in all the circumstances[49]

For instance, it may not be used for an improper purpose.[50] HMRC should take into account relevant considerations, and disregard irrelevant considerations when using its managerial discretion.[51] The tax authority similarly should not act in a way that is irrational.[52] Where HMRC, under the guise of collecting taxes, does something outrageously misguided, then the body will be held to have acted unlawfully.[53]

One further limit which might be considered relevant is the rule against fettering discretion, which requires that a public authority not adopt an overly rigid policy as to how it will exercise a discretion.[54] In the case of a specific statutory discretion that is granted to HMRC, such as the discretion to mitigate penalties,[55] it is easy to see how such a rule would operate. HMRC could not adopt a rigid policy whereby it would refuse to mitigate penalties unless strict criteria were met. In the case of HMRC's overarching managerial discretion, its effect is limited. For instance, it is within HMRC's managerial discretion to publish general advice

[44] *IRC v Vestey* [1980] AC 1148 (HL), 1170 (Lord Wilberforce), 1195 (Lord Edmund Davies).

[45] Lord Judge, 'Ceding Power to the Executive; the Resurrection of Henry VIII' (King's College London, April 2016) 14.

[46] On which see *Attorney-General v Wilts United Dairies Ltd* (1921) 39 TLR 781 (CA).

[47] This book purposefully seeks to avoid the debate about the origins of judicial review principles. For the purposes of this book all that matters is that these standards restrict discretion. For an overview of the debate about the origins of judicial review, see C Forsyth (ed), *Judicial Review & the Constitution* (Oxford, Hart Publishing, 2000). For an assessment of how it plays out in the context of tax, see: S Daly, 'Recent developments in tax law: vires revisited' [2016] *Public Law* 190.

[48] [1994] 1 AC 531 (HL).

[49] ibid 560.

[50] *Padfield v Minister of Agriculture, Fisheries and Food* [1968] 1 All ER 694 (HL), 706 (Lord Morris).

[51] See *UK Uncut Legal Action v HMRC* [2013] EWHC 1283 (Admin), [2013] SWTI 1849.

[52] *CCSU v Minister for Civil Service* [1985] AC 374 (HL), 410 (Lord Diplock).

[53] See *R v Inland Revenue Commissioners, ex parte Unilever plc* [1996] STC 681.

[54] See the above discussion in text at n 23.

[55] See for instance Taxes Management Act 1970, s 102; Value Added Tax Act 1994, s 70.

for taxpayers, but the rule would not affect the content of any such guidance. It would not stop HMRC from adopting an interpretation of the laws which it rigidly applied in all instances – as the interpretation of the rules does not fall within HMRC's discretion. All the rule would prevent is HMRC adopting a policy for instance of refusing to issue guidance in particular instances. This is the case also for the exercise of HMRC's discretion in the case of formal rulings – the discretion does not relate to the interpretation of the rules and hence the content of the ruling, but only arises in respect of how HMRC goes about providing the ruling.

i. Key Cases on HMRC's Managerial Discretion

Whilst it is correct to remember that this discretion is not unbounded, it must be stressed that the legitimacy of HMRC's managerial discretion in fact derives from the fact that Parliament has passed, and continues to pass, laws which HMRC must administer. Managerial discretion does not conflict with, but rather is a product of, Parliamentary sovereignty. It therefore becomes clear why the courts have endorsed the idea that HMRC has a 'wide managerial discretion' as to how it gives effect to this *primary responsibility* for the collection and management of taxes and credits.[56] HMRC's managerial discretion is endowed by Parliament and so judges should not readily interfere with decisions taken pursuant to it, as explained in three seminal judgments.

The breadth of the discretion was first explained in the *IRC v National Federation of Self-Employed and Small Businesses Ltd* ('*Fleet Street Casuals*') case,[57] wherein the House of Lords endorsed an agreement between the Inland Revenue and print workers about past and future tax liabilities. A Federation representing small businesses and self-employed individuals brought an application for judicial review of the decision to grant an 'amnesty' to a group of 'casual' newspaper workers. The amnesty purported to forego investigation into past tax liabilities of the group of casual workers in return for the completion of the two prior years' returns and future compliance.[58] For the Inland Revenue, the reason underpinning the agreement to extinguish such past liabilities, which was estimated to cost the exchequer £1 million for each year, derived from the practical inability to obtain the information about the casual workers in order to subject them to tax.[59] For instance, the workers used names such as 'Mickie Mouse of Sunset Boulevard' and 'Sir Gordon Richards of Tattenham Corner' in order to hide their true identities

[56] *Fleet Street Casuals* (n 16) 663 (Lord Roskill); 637 (Lord Diplock); 635 (Lord Wilberforce); 654 (Lord Scarman).

[57] *Fleet Street Casuals* (n 16). For a lengthy discussion of the case, see: D de Cogan, '*CIR v National Federation of Self-Employed and Small Businesses* (1981): All Grievances Converging on Tax Law' in D de Cogan and J Snape, *Landmark cases in Revenue Law* (Oxford, Hart Publishing, 2019).

[58] *Fleet Street Casuals* (n 16) 634–35.

[59] ibid 634.

from the Inland Revenue.[60] The trade unions, however, did know the details of the casual workers, but there would likely have been industrial action if the unions gave up the details of these workers.[61]

In the House of Lords hearing of the case, the starting point for the Lords on the issue of the Inland Revenue's discretion lay in the 'statutory code',[62] namely the primary statutory responsibility of the body, upon which a few points merited elaboration. The first was that there exist two separate responsibilities: that of collection and that of care and management. Secondly, it was plainly impractical to collect *every* part of tax due and it was this impracticality, which necessarily conflicted with the duty of care and management, that was accepted as giving rise to managerial discretion.[63] In other words, the effect of the literally read duty to collect *every* part of tax is diluted by the duty to care and manage,[64] thereby creating discretion.[65] Ultimately, their Lordships were satisfied that the arrangement arrived at between the Revenue and the workers, unions and employers fell within the Revenue's *wide* managerial discretion.[66] Lord Diplock went further, however, and explained that:

> [T]he board have a wide managerial discretion as to the best means of obtaining for the national exchequer from the taxes committed to their charge, the highest net return that is practicable having regard to the staff available to them and the cost of collection[67]

In the 2005 case of *R (Wilkinson) v IRC* ('*Wilkinson*'),[68] the House of Lords sought to further elaborate upon the limits of the Revenue's managerial discretion. The applicant was a widower who, had he been a widow, would have been entitled to a widow's bereavement allowance under section 262 of the Income and Corporation Taxes Act 1988. Mr Wilkinson argued inter alia that the Inland Revenue could utilise its 'managerial discretion' to extend the allowance to widowers. The House of Lords rejected the applicant's claim and held that the managerial discretion endowed upon the Revenue cannot be 'so widely construed as to concede … an allowance which Parliament could have granted but did not grant'.[69] After quoting Lord Diplock's aforementioned statement in *Fleet Street Casuals*, Lord Hoffmann

[60] *R v Inland Revenue Commissioners, Ex p National Federation of Self-Employed and Small Businesses Ltd* [1980] QB 407, 418 (CA).

[61] *Fleet Street Casuals* (n 16) 635.

[62] ibid 650 (Lord Scarman).

[63] ibid 650 (Lord Scarman); 631–32 (Lord Wilberforce); 636 (Lord Diplock); 659 (Lord Roskill).

[64] cf *New Zealand Stock Exchange v CIR* [1992] 3 NZLR 1, 3; S Griffiths, '"No discretion should be unconstrained": considering the "care and management" of taxes and the settlement of tax disputes in New Zealand and the UK' [2012] 2 *British Tax Review* 167.

[65] *Fleet Street Casuals* (n 16) 651 (Lord Scarman).

[66] ibid 663 (Lord Roskill); 637 (Lord Diplock); 635 (Lord Wilberforce); 654 (Lord Scarman). Lord Fraser declined to comment.

[67] ibid 636. This point was not expressly endorsed by the other judges in the case.

[68] [2005] UKHL 30, [2006] STC 270.

[69] ibid [21] (Lord Hoffmann).

additionally added some substance to Lord Diplock's explanation of managerial discretion:

> This discretion enables the commissioners to formulate policy in the interstices of the tax legislation, dealing pragmatically with minor or transitory anomalies, cases of hardship at the margins or cases in which a statutory rule is difficult to formulate or its enactment would take up a disproportionate amount of Parliamentary time[70]

It is noteworthy that the managerial discretion cannot be extended so as to provide a relief which Parliament did not grant even if to refuse to do so would breach the European Convention on Human Rights (ECHR).[71]

Finally, in *R (Davies) v HMRC; R (Gaines-Cooper) v HMRC* ('*Gaines-Cooper*'),[72] Robert John Davies, Michael John James and Robert Gaines-Cooper claimed for tax purposes to be non-resident. Being wealthy individuals who had sought to base themselves outside the UK, the matter was of some significance. The trio claimed that HMRC guidance, in this case a booklet known as IR20, gave rise to a legitimate expectation that non-resident status would be acquired if the residence day count were satisfied (ie less than six months in any year were spent in the UK). HMRC, on the other hand, contended that the taxpayers additionally needed to demonstrate a 'distinct break' with the UK. The majority of the court (Lord Mance dissenting) agreed with HMRC. In doing so, Lord Wilson confirmed that HMRC could use its managerial discretion to provide concessions from the strict application of the law through its advice to taxpayers:

> [T]he Revenue is entitled to apply a cost-benefit analysis to its duty of management and in particular, against the return thereby likely to be foregone, to weigh the costs which it would be likely to save as a result of a concession which cuts away an area of complexity or likely dispute.[73]

Relating this back to what we know about discretion more generally, it becomes clear why the provision of HMRC advice falls properly within HMRC's managerial discretion. HMRC must form a view on how to give effect to laws and must carry out the function of collecting and managing taxes. HMRC has adjudged that the best means of doing this is by assisting taxpayers through the provision of advice. The courts, meanwhile, have long acknowledged and supported this judgement. In *R v IRC, ex p MFK Underwriting Agents Ltd*[74] Judge J eloquently explained it as follows:

> [T]he long established practice by which the Inland Revenue gives advice and guidance to taxpayers … exists because the revenue has concluded that it is of assistance to

[70] ibid [21].

[71] See Human Rights Act 1998, s 6(2). T Prosser, *The Economic Constitution* (Oxford, Oxford University Press, 2014) 95.

[72] [2011] UKSC 47, [2012] 1 All ER 1048 (*Gaines-Cooper* (SC)).

[73] ibid [26].

[74] [1990] 1 WLR 1545.

> the administration of a complex tax system and ultimately to the benefit of the overall tax yield[75]

Sales J (as he then was) in *R (Ingenious Media and McKenna) v HMRC*[76] similarly noted that there is a rational connection between the collection of tax in an efficient, cost-effective way and communicating with the public.[77] Moses LJ put it more forcefully in the Court of Appeal in *Gaines-Cooper*[78] in a quote later endorsed by the Supreme Court:[79]

> It is trite to recall that it is for the revenue to determine the best way of facilitating collection of the tax it is under a statutory obligation to collect. But it should not be forgotten that the revenue itself has long acknowledged that the best way is by encouraging co-operation between the revenue and the public[80]

The provision of HMRC advice, then, is not a constitutional aberration. It is rooted in HMRC's managerial discretion and is a function properly executed by the body in pursuance of its responsibilities endowed by Parliament. It does not undermine the Bill of Rights Act – Parliament still has legislative supremacy and it is only with Parliamentary approval that the levying of taxes is sanctioned. HMRC's provision of advice simply seeks to give effect to Parliament's intention. Further, the advice provided by HMRC (except in the case for instance of formal rulings) does not legally determine the amount of tax due. It is the role of the tribunals and courts to determine the interpretation of legislation and how that legislation is applied to the facts. HMRC's managerial discretion then does not allow the body to provide legally determinative advice.

III. The Desirability of HMRC Advice

Explanation of the authority to provide advice does not normatively justify its proliferation. Just because HMRC can, does not mean that HMRC should. The case for HMRC advice requires a principled rationale. It is proposed here that a system for providing advice is desirable by virtue of the rule of law. This section elaborates upon why the rule of law itself is desirable, how it applies in respect of HMRC advice and how it is supported by case law concerning the ECHR. Though it is not the first time that the rule of law has been used to justify the provision of tax advice,[81] this section elaborates in greater detail about the

[75] ibid 1572 (Judge J).
[76] [2013] EWHC 3258 (Admin), [2014] STC 673.
[77] ibid [39] and [47] (Sales J).
[78] [2010] EWCA Civ 83, [2010] STC 860 (*Gaines-Cooper* (CA)).
[79] *Gaines-Cooper* (SC) (n 72) [25] (Lord Wilson).
[80] *Gaines-Cooper* (CA) (n 78) [12].
[81] See for instance B Alarie, K Datt, A Sawyer and G Weeks, 'Advance Tax Rulings in Perspective: A Theoretical and Comparative Analysis' (2014) 20 *New Zealand Journal of Taxation Law and Policy* 362, 365–69 and 386. This paper should be seen as developing upon the foundations set in that article.

merit of the rule of law, what it requires and its grounding in case law, thereby giving it greater normative force as a justification. There is an argument that can be made against using HMRC advice to advance the rule of law which is extrinsic to the advice itself and not related to the system for providing advice. This is that lawmakers will change their behaviour because of the presence of HMRC advice, producing poor, ambiguous law knowing that problems can be later fixed by HMRC. This argument will be termed the 'moral hazard' issue and though problematic does not undermine the case for HMRC advice advanced here. All of this does beg the question whether an argument can be made that there is actually an obligation on HMRC to provide advice. Though it may arise in discrete circumstances, there is no general obligation to do so.

Meanwhile other justifications, such as efficiency, are more traditionally associated with the merit of tax authorities providing advice and this section will also elaborate upon why the organising principle for this book will be the rule of law rather than these other principles. Given the attention paid to efficiency in the case law, it merits a more generous discussion than other possible justifications. This section will proceed to consider these matters in turn.

A. The Rule of Law

The rule of law has been described as the overarching principle of constitutional law.[82] Students of UK public law will be familiar with Dicey's formulation which contained three components: that government should be conducted through law, not discretion; that all should be equally subject to the law; and that the law of the constitution is not the source but the consequence of the rights of individuals as defined and enforced by the courts.[83] Of course, Dicey's conception of the rule of law has been subject to considerable criticism.[84] Indeed, although writers agree as to its importance generally, the rule of law is an elusive concept, the full contents of which are devoid of universal agreement. Notwithstanding such differences, agreement can be found in relation to one particular element of the

[82] Lord Steyn, 'Democracy through law' [2002] EHRLR 723, 727; P Craig, 'Formal and substantive conceptions of the rule of law: an analytical framework' [1997] *Public Law* 467, 487.

[83] AV Dicey, *Introduction to the law of the constitution* (Indianapolis, Liberty Classics, 1982) 120–21. Whilst the first two limbs are reasonably clear in their meaning, the third is not so and 'has caused considerable confusion': Craig, 'Formal and substantive' [1997] 473.

[84] HWR Wade and CF Forsyth, *Administrative Law*, 11th edn (Oxford, Oxford University Press, 2014) 18; F Frankfurter, Foreword to 'Discussion of Current Developments in Administrative Law' (1938) 47 *Yale Law Journal* 515, 517; J Jowell, 'The Rule of Law Today' in J Jowell and D Oliver (eds), *The Changing Constitution*, 5th edn (Oxford, Oxford University Press, 2004) 6–10. For instance, Gavin Dewry remarks that Dicey 'gave currency to a cripplingly restricted view of public law which failed to accommodate the looming reality of a twentieth century interventionist state': G Dewry, 'Public Law' (1995) 73 *Public Administration* 41, 46, noted in C Turpin and A Tomkins, *British government and the constitution: text and materials*, 7th edn (Cambridge, Cambridge University Press, 2011) 117. For a recent exploration of the imperial aspects of Dicey's account, see: D Lino, 'The Rule of Law and the Rule of Empire: A.V. Dicey in Imperial Context' (2018) 81 *MLR* 739.

concept. Most writers agree that laws ought to act as guidance.[85] Raz describes this as the 'basic idea' of the rule of law,[86] from which he subsequently deduces eight principles. The first three principles require that the law should conform to standards designed to enable it effectively to guide action.[87] These are that all laws should be prospective, open, clear, relatively stable and that the making of particular laws should be guided by open, stable, clear, and general rules.[88] In the same vein, Lord Bingham's first principle of the rule of law is that the law must be accessible and, so far as possible, intelligible, clear and predictable.[89] Lon Fuller regarded the rule of law as encompassing principles such that laws are not retroactive, but are understandable, consistent, foreseeable and stable.[90] Renowned classical liberal Friedrich Hayek meanwhile focused his conception of the rule of law on the coercive powers of the state. Nevertheless, the same principle of the law acting as guidance emerges from his definition:

> [S]tripped of all technicalities this means that government in all its actions is bound by rules fixed and announced beforehand – *rules which make it possible to foresee with fair certainty how the authority will use its coercive powers in given circumstances, and to plan one's individual affairs on the basis of this knowledge.*[91]

The general consensus clearly is that laws ought to act as guidance for individuals. A citizen should, before committing herself to any course of action, be able to know in advance the legal consequences that will follow.[92] Tasioulas labels this the 'thin' account of the rule of law.[93] The normative merit of this account is that it values human dignity.[94] It recognises individuals never as means, but as ends in themselves: rational actors capable of choosing their own course of action. The individual will weigh up the reasons to decide which action to pursue, with legal consequences providing one reason to be factored in as part of the process.[95]

In order for the rule of law to be advanced, there may be further practical requirements. Thus, the normative underpinning of the rule of law in abstract form will be furthered, and may sometimes only be fulfilled, by 'particular institutional arrangements'.[96] For instance, the content of legal rules will rarely be

[85] T Endicott, *Vagueness in Law* (Oxford, Oxford University Press, 2000) 185.
[86] J Raz, 'The Rule of Law and its Virtue' (1977) 93 *LQR* 195, 196.
[87] ibid 202.
[88] ibid 198–200.
[89] Lord Bingham, 'The Rule of Law' (2007) *Cambridge Law Journal* 67, 69. See also: Tom Bingham, 'The Rule of Law' (London, Penguin Press, 2011).
[90] L Fuller, *The Morality of Law*, revised edn (New Haven, Yale University Press, 1969) 39, 46–90.
[91] FA Hayek, *The Road to Serfdom* (Abingdon, Routledge, 1944) 54, emphasis added.
[92] *Black-Clawson International Ltd v Papierwerke Waldhof-Aschaffenberg AG* [1975] AC 591 (HL), 638 (Lord Diplock).
[93] J Tasioulas, 'The Rule of Law' in J Tasioulas (ed), *The Cambridge Companion to the Philosophy of Law* (Cambridge, Cambridge University Press, forthcoming).
[94] See for instance J Raz, *The Authority of Law* (Oxford, Oxford University Press, 1979) 221; J Finnis, *Natural Law and Natural Rights*, 2nd edn (Oxford, Oxford University Press, 2011) 272.
[95] Tasioulas, 'The Rule of Law' (forthcoming).
[96] ibid.

self-explanatory to a layperson and as such a body of persons legally trained to provide advice on the content of rules will be necessary.[97] This would thus necessitate the maintenance of a body of legal professionals in society.[98] These further practical requirements logically follow from the desirability of the rule of law, as the concept would have little utility if it could not be given effect. The rule of law without effect could be described, borrowing the famous words of Jeremy Bentham, as 'nonsense upon stilts'.[99]

Even where not *necessary* for the rule of law to be given effect, the provision of assistance will still be *desirable* given that such assistance will advance the rule of law by detailing the legal consequences of actions. Desirability is sufficient given that compliance with the rule of law is not binary but rather a matter of degree.[100] As Endicott has written, the 'rule of law is unattainable. Communities never quite achieve it'.[101] Thus it is desirable for instance for a tax authority to assist taxpayers in understanding the content of tax rules, whether by providing advice to individual taxpayers, certain classes of taxpayers or to the general body of taxpayers.

The fact that such assistance is desirable, and sometimes even necessary, from the perspective of the rule of law is recognised in the case law on the ECHR. The case law is also noteworthy for the fact that it elaborates upon the requirements of the 'thin' conception of the rule of law. The ECHR requires that intervention with certain rights and freedoms[102] be 'prescribed by law'.[103] This requires in turn that the substance of law should satisfy certain 'rule of law' benchmarks as set out in the seminal judgment of the European Court of Human Rights in the case of *The Sunday Times v United Kingdom*:[104]

> Firstly, the law must be adequately accessible: the citizen must be able to have an indication that is adequate in the circumstances of the legal rules applicable to a given case. Secondly, a norm cannot be regarded as a 'law' unless it is formulated with sufficient precision to enable the citizen to regulate his conduct: he must be able – if need be with

[97] ibid.

[98] The logical conclusion is that there should be provision of legal aid as noted by Tasioulas (n 93). Given that the professional advice of lawyers is not without cost, it would seem appropriate that there should be some provision of legal aid provided for those unable to afford the fees.

[99] Bentham famously described natural rights as 'nonsense upon stilts'. See: P Schofield, C Pease-Watkin and C Blamires (eds), *The Collected Works of Jeremy Bentham: Rights, Representation, and Reform: Nonsense upon Stilts and Other Writings on the French Revolution* (Oxford, Oxford University Press, 2002) 329–30.

[100] Tasioulas (n 93). Note though that sometimes institutions will provide assistance which is not helpful in terms of understanding the legal consequences of action, for instance where the institution provides incorrect advice. This conundrum is elaborated upon below in ch 4 in text at n 9 and ch 6 in text at n 39.

[101] Endicott, *Vagueness in Law* (2000) 185.

[102] See for instance Articles 5 and 8–11 of the ECHR.

[103] The convention actually requires that incursion upon such rights either be prescribed by law or in accordance with law. However, these phrases are synonymous. See: *The Sunday Times v UK* (1980) 2 EHRR 245, para 48.

[104] *Sunday Times* (ibid).

> appropriate advice – to foresee, to a degree that is reasonable in the circumstances, the consequences which a given action may entail. Those consequences need not be foreseeable with absolute certainty: experience shows this to be unattainable[105]

The qualities of accessibility and foreseeability accordingly must be present in order to satisfy the rule of law requirements of the ECHR. The citizen must have access to the law and the law must be formulated with sufficient clarity in order that she may foresee the consequences of not regulating her affairs in accordance with the law. The test is that of *sufficient* precision of foreseeability, as absolute certainty is recognised as unattainable.[106] Some degree of vagueness is inevitable and development of the law is a recognised feature of common law courts.[107] The sufficiency of the clarity required will vary according to the nature of the law in question and accordingly the degree of impact upon an individual.[108] For instance, a greater degree of clarity might be required in relation to state surveillance laws than that of lightly punishable obscenity laws, given the former's significant intrusion on a person's privacy[109] and the latter's need to remain flexible in order to accord to the prevailing views of society.[110]

Where public authorities provide assistance in relation to the accessibility and foreseeability of the law accordingly, they can be said to be furthering the rule of law. This can be seen for instance in the case of *Malone v UK*,[111] which concerned the law relating to the interception of communications on behalf of the police for the purposes of the prevention and detection of crime. Although the law at issue was 'somewhat obscure and open to differing interpretations',[112] the court noted the role that administrative publications could play in reducing this ambiguity:

> Detailed procedures concerning interception of communications on behalf of the police in England and Wales do exist … The public have been made aware of the applicable arrangements and principles through publication of the Birkett report and the White Paper and through statements by responsible Ministers in Parliament.[113]

In the case of *Silver v United Kingdom*,[114] the applicants were convicted prisoners who complained that the control of their mail by prison authorities constituted a breach of their rights to privacy and expression under Articles 8 and 10 of the ECHR. A question arose in the proceedings as to whether the law in this area was of sufficient quality to satisfy the rule of law requirements of Articles 8 and 10. The court found that it was not necessary that the law itself be meticulously

[105] ibid, para 49.
[106] On this, see Endicott (n 85), in particular ch 9.
[107] *R v Rimmington* [2005] UKHL 63, [2006] 1 AC 459 [35] (Lord Bingham); *SW v United Kingdom* (1995) 21 EHRR 363, para 36.
[108] *Autronic v Switzerland* (1990) 12 EHRR 485, paras 55 and 59.
[109] *Kruslin v France* (1990) 12 EHRR 547, para 33.
[110] *Muller v Switzerland* (1988) 13 EHRR 212, para 29.
[111] *Malone v UK* (1985) 7 EHRR 14. para 79.
[112] ibid.
[113] ibid.
[114] *Silver v United Kingdom* (1983) 5 EHRR 347, paras 88–89.

precise and cover every possible eventuality.[115] What was important was foreseeability. Thus the substantive law itself can be buttressed by advice provided by the relevant public authority to provide the requisite 'quality' to the law.[116] In this case, the instruments were 'Standing Orders' and 'Circular Instructions' issued by the Home Secretary to prison governors, the purpose of which was to provide guidance in relation to the control of prisoner correspondence:

> [T]he Orders and Instructions established a practice which had to be followed save in exceptional circumstances … In these conditions, the Court considers that although those directives did not themselves have the force of law, they may – to the admittedly limited extent to which those concerned were made sufficiently aware of their contents – be taken into account in assessing whether the criterion of foreseeability was satisfied in the application of the Rules.[117]

The court held accordingly that the law was sufficiently expanded upon by the Orders and Instructions so as to protect against any breach of the rule of law requirements of the ECHR.

Sometimes assistance from a public authority in relation to the accessibility and foreseeability of the law may be necessitated by the rule of law.[118] The case of *R (Purdy) v Director of Public Prosecutions*[119] ('*Purdy*') takes this concept of assistance by a public authority supplementing the underlying law to its logical conclusion.[120] Debbie Purdy suffered from primary progressive multiple sclerosis and wished to travel to Dignitas in Switzerland in order to end her life. However, she would need assistance from her husband in order to carry this out. Whilst suicide itself is not a criminal offence in the UK, it is unlawful to assist a person to commit suicide by virtue of section 2(1) of the Suicide Act 1961. The jurisdiction to institute proceedings under section 2(1) lies with the Director of Public Prosecutions (DPP), and it is well established that the DPP has discretion as to whether to take on a case.[121] Chief among the DPP's concerns when exercising this discretion is whether it is in the public interest to pursue a case.[122] It was argued accordingly that failing to promulgate a clear policy or failing to disclose the criteria that the DPP applies in cases of this kind breached the rule of law requirements of the ECHR. There was insufficient clarity as to the consequences

[115] ibid, para 88.
[116] ibid.
[117] ibid.
[118] Indeed, this was foreshadowed in the *Sunday Times* case where the court noted that in terms of foreseeability, an individual 'must be able – if need be with appropriate advice – to foresee, to a degree that is reasonable in the circumstances': *Sunday Times* (n 103) 271, §49.
[119] R (Purdy) v Director of Public Prosecutions [2009] UKHL 45, [2010] 1 AC 345.
[120] See also the gentle nudge of Lord Kerr in relation to the clarity of the law on abortion in *In the matter of an application by the Northern Ireland Human Rights Commission for Judicial Review (Northern Ireland); Reference by the Court of Appeal in Northern Ireland pursuant to Paragraph 33 of Schedule 10 to the Northern Ireland Act 1998 (Abortion)* [2018] UKSC 27, [2019] 1 All ER 173 [269].
[121] *Smedleys Ltd v Breed* [1974] AC 839 (HL), 856 (Viscount Dilhorne).
[122] *Purdy* (above n 119) [46]–[53] (Lord Hope).

flowing from the law, thereby undermining the ability of Debbie Purdy and her husband to regulate their conduct accordingly.

The Court of Appeal held that this 'failure' to promulgate a crime specific policy relating to assisted suicide did not have the effect of undermining the rule of law requirements of the ECHR.[123] The House of Lords unanimously reversed this decision. In the leading speech, Lord Hope elaborated upon the qualitative requirements of accessibility and foreseeability that the ECHR requires:

> Accessibility means that an individual must know from the wording of the relevant provision and, if need be, with the assistance of the court's interpretation of it what acts and omissions will make him criminally liable ... The requirement of foreseeability will be satisfied where the person concerned is able to foresee, if need be with appropriate legal advice, the consequences which a given action may entail.[124]

The court was of the view that DPP guidance could have the effect of supplementing these qualitative elements in order to satisfy the 'rule of law' requirement:

> The Code will normally provide sufficient guidance to Crown Prosecutors and to the public as to how decisions should or are likely to be taken whether or not, in a given case, it will be in the public interest to prosecute. This is a valuable safeguard for the vulnerable, as it enables the prosecutor to take into account the whole background of the case. In most cases its application will ensure predictability and consistency of decision-taking, and people will know where they stand.[125]

However, the Code issued by the DPP in relation to prosecutions for assisted suicide had not attained such a status.[126] The court accordingly ordered the DPP to promulgate an offence-specific policy identifying the facts and circumstances which the office-holder takes into account when deciding whether or not to consent to a prosecution under section 2(1) of the 1961 Act.[127] The DPP subsequently obliged and issued a new code.[128] Subsequently, however, the Supreme Court in *R (Nicklinson) v Ministry of Justice*[129] ('*Nicklinson*') held that this new code was still unsatisfactory in that it failed to properly reflect the prosecutorial policy of the DPP and directed the DPP to review it accordingly.[130] The DPP subsequently revised the code so as to align the policy with the publication.[131]

The provision of assistance by a tax authority in the form of advice in principle, then, advances the rule of law, rendering the individual better informed of

[123] ibid [79].
[124] ibid [41].
[125] ibid [54].
[126] ibid [55].
[127] ibid [1] (Lord Phillips); [56] (Lord Hope); [64], [67], [69] (Baroness Hale); [86] (Lord Brown); [101] (Lord Neuberger).
[128] The Director of Public Prosecutions, 'Policy for Prosecutors in Respect of Cases of Encouraging or Assisting Suicide' (February 2010).
[129] *R (Nicklinson) v Ministry of Justice* [2014] UKSC 38, [2014] 3 WLR 200.
[130] ibid [144], [146] (Lord Neuberger); [195] (Lord Mance); [206] (Lord Wilson); [254] (Lord Sumption); [323] (Lady Hale).
[131] DPP, 'Policy for Prosecutors' (2010) was revised in October 2014.

the legal consequences that will flow from her actions. This is more than simply stating that advice provides certainty.[132] The rule of law requires accessibility in addition to foreseeability or certainty of outcome. Further, certainty is vague in terms of its underlying merit, whereas the rule of law is 'good' as it values human dignity. The fact that advice may be addressed to non-humans, such as companies or other legal entities, does not defeat the claim that the rule of law justifies the provision of advice. Such entities are simply 'legal fictions' and are controlled and operated ultimately by humans. To this end, the humans behind the fiction will still need to know the legal consequences of their actions, in order to decide upon the appropriate course of action. It is irrelevant also that advice may be given to a tax agent working on behalf of a taxpayer, as the taxpayer will ultimately take a decision on the basis of the advice from the agent. It is critical to recall that it is the decision to engage in a particular action which is central to the issue of the rule of law.

It should finally be noted that this argument could also be partially put in the language of 'structuring' discretion. It has long been orthodox thought that the provision of advice acts as a means of 'structuring' administrative discretion.[133] Through this process, the public body sets out policies as to how discretionary power will be exercised. Such is the orthodoxy of the merit of this proposition that it has come to be recognised as a significant tenet of the constitutional framework.[134] Structuring HMRC's statutory and managerial discretion through advice (in so far as the advice is accessible to the public) accordingly advances the rule of law as it informs individuals about how the rules will be applied to them and hence the legal consequences of their actions.

B. Moral Hazard

The term 'moral hazard' is adopted to refer to the risk that the provision of advice will have an adverse effect on the behaviour of lawmakers. The effect is principally due to the fact that the system for the provision of advice by HMRC is not, nor can it be, separated from the broader context of the social, political and legislative system within which HMRC operates.[135] The concern is that legislation might

[132] Certainty is regularly used as the justification for the provision of advanced rulings. See, for instance, M Diller, P Kortebusch, G Schneider and C Sureth-Sloane, 'Boon or Bane? Advance Tax Rulings as a Measure to Mitigate Tax Uncertainty and Foster Investment' (2017) 26 *European Accounting Review* 441; Y Givati, 'Resolving Legal Uncertainty: The Fulfilled Promise of Advance Tax Rulings' (2009) 29 *Virginia Tax Review* 137, 147; W Chan, 'Binding Rulings' (1997) 18 *Fiscal Studies* 189, 192–95.

[133] Proposed most notably in Davis, *Discretionary Justice* (1971).

[134] *Secretary of State for the Home Department v Pankina* [2010] EWCA Civ 719, [2010] 3 WLR 1526 [15] (Sedley LJ). See also *R (Alconbury Developments Ltd) v Secretary of State for the Environment, Transport and the Regions* [2001] UKHL 23, [2003] 2 AC 295 [143] (Lord Slynn).

[135] JA Jones, 'Tax law: rules or principles?' [1996] 6 *British Tax Review* 580, 593; S James and I Wallschutzky, 'The Design of an Appropriate System of Tax Rulings' (1995) 5 *Revenue Law Journal* 175, 188.

be drafted more broadly and in more generalised terms, knowing that the scope can be narrowed down or the legislation explained thereafter in HMRC advice.[136] Another consequence might be the decision not to use secondary legislation at all. In this way, complexity can move from legislation to tax authority advice.[137] This would be detrimental from the perspective of the rule of law, as laws themselves would become less foreseeable. It would no doubt be undesirable for myriad other reasons too, such as in relation to democracy, the separation of powers and the legitimacy of law.

This has arisen particularly in the anti-avoidance context in recent years. For instance, section 16A of the Capital Gains Tax Act 1992 is a targeted anti-avoidance rule (TAAR) which is drafted in very broad terms.[138] Section 16A(1) provides as follows:

> For the purposes of this Act, "allowable loss" does not include a loss accruing to a person if – (a) it accrues to the person directly or indirectly in consequence of, or otherwise in connection with, any arrangements, and (b) the main purpose, or one of the main purposes, of the arrangements is to secure a tax advantage.

During the consultation process, professional bodies criticised the breadth of the provision for catching 'objectionable' and 'unobjectionable' transactions alike as Freedman and Vella note.[139] The Government and HMRC sought to assure those concerned that the provision only caught objectionable transactions and that guidance to that effect did not seek to cut down on the scope of the provision, but simply reflected their understanding.[140] This interpretation of the provision was rejected by the bodies with the guidance thus appearing concessionary and inconsistent with the underlying law.[141]

Another example cited by Freedman and Vella is that of the TAAR introduced by section 75A of the Finance Act 2003 in relation to Stamp Duty Land Tax.[142] Again, the provision is drafted incredibly broadly, with HMRC guidance seeking to cut down its scope.[143] The Upper Tribunal in the case of *Project Blue v HMRC*[144] was far from convinced that this was satisfactory. Morgan J noted that HMRC's guidance provided that the body would not seek to apply the

[136] On this issue in the related context of general guidance issued by tax authorities, see Freedman and Vella (n 34) 117; T Bowler, 'Countering tax avoidance in the UK: which way forward?' (Institute for Fiscal Studies, 2009) 18–19.

[137] This was mentioned in the parallel context of guidance: Bowler (ibid) 162.

[138] Freedman and Vella (n 34) 117.

[139] ibid.

[140] ibid, where the following are cited: Chartered Institute of Taxation, 'Draft TAAR – Chartered Institute of Taxation Comments' (9 February 2007); Chartered Institute of Taxation, 'Targeted Anti-Avoidance Rule (TAAR) for Capital Losses Comments of the Chartered Institute of Taxation' (1 June 2007); and The Tax Faculty of the Institute of Chartered Accountants in England and Wales, 'Avoidance through the creation and use of capital losses' (8 February 2007) *Taxrep* 07/07.

[141] Freedman and Vella (n 34) 117.

[142] ibid.

[143] See P Cannon, 'New SDLT general anti-avoidance rule' (2007) 874 *Tax Journal* 6.

[144] *Project Blue v HMRC* [2014] UKUT 564 (TCC), [2015] STC 745.

provision to transactions it considered to have already been taxed appropriately, but that this was not the way that the provision operated as a matter of law.[145] The provision applies in a mandatory way whenever the facts of the case come within the words of the section.[146]

Whilst the moral hazard issue is problematic from the perspective of the rule of law, it does not in fact undermine the argument advanced here that HMRC advice is desirable. It is certainly a risk, but the risk arises because of the actions of stakeholders extrinsic to the advice.[147] HMRC's responsibility is as a tax authority. It is the responsibility of lawmakers to write the laws and decide upon which form they ought to take. To the extent that the lawmakers fail in their duty, that is their responsibility and not the fault of HMRC for providing advice. What certainly can be recommended is that insofar as HMRC's views may be taken into account during the lawmaking process, the body should refrain from suggesting that broad legislation can be cut down by advice and should instead urge legislators to articulate intent clearly through legislation.

C. Is there an Obligation to Provide Advice?

Given the desirability of the provision of advice by reason of the rule of law, can it be argued that there is a general positive obligation to provide advice? The short answer is no. One would expect such an obligation to be set out in statute, as arises in specific instances such as with formal rulings.

There may, however, be times in which an obligation to provide advice can be implied. For instance, given the judgments of *Purdy* and *Nicklinson*, HMRC may be obliged to provide advice where a provision of the ECHR is engaged and failure to do so would undermine the rule of law requirements of the ECHR. This argument was tried, though failed, in *Privacy International v HMRC*,[148] but it is unclear from the judgment whether the claimant specifically invoked the ECHR to make the argument.[149] The case concerned the power of HMRC to disclose information about its export control functions to the NGO Privacy International. Given that this involved taxpayer information, HMRC refused the NGO's request on the basis of its duty of confidentiality. HMRC's guidance on the duty is ambiguous on permissible derogations.[150] To this end, counsel for Privacy International invited the High Court to direct HMRC to provide sufficiently clear guidance on

[145] ibid [50].
[146] ibid. See also *Project Blue Ltd v HMRC* [2018] UKSC 30, [2018] STC 1355 [43] (Lord Hodge).
[147] There are other stakeholders that are intrinsic to that advice on the other hand as they have a role in relation to scrutinising advice or holding HMRC to advice, such as the Adjudicator's Office, Parliamentary and Health Service Ombudsman, tribunals and courts and taxpayers who are consulted.
[148] *Privacy International v HMRC* [2014] EWHC 1475 (Admin), [2015] STC 948.
[149] ibid [180]–[185].
[150] See below ch 4 in text at n 64.

when disclosure of taxpayer information may be made. This would force HMRC to address itself in a deliberate manner on the issue of disclosure and then to make public its position.[151] Although citing the obvious appeal of such a suggestion, the Court rejected the invitation for two reasons. First, the Court noted that there had only been two cases which had grappled with the issue.[152] Accordingly, this was not an especially solid platform upon which to intervene.[153] Secondly, for the pragmatic reason that HMRC would have to consult the CPS and their views on the issues arising are not before the Court.[154]

Neither are particularly strong reasons for rebuttal, it might be noted, given that the primary focus of any such rebuttal ought to have been on the clarity of the advice and the impact of its ambiguity. On the first reason, the judge dedicated some 106 paragraphs to articulating the factors that may be relevant to a decision to disclose taxpayer information,[155] thereby providing the very platform he said was lacking. As for the second reason, the invitation to direct HMRC did not require the body at that moment to provide detailed guidance, but rather merely invited it to consider its position and put it more firmly in detail available to the public at a later date. Accordingly, the fact that HMRC would have to consult the CPS could have been readily accommodated in the direction.

EU law provides another situation where an obligation may arise in specific instances to provide advice. The EU principle of legal certainty, which mirrors the foreseeability and accessibility requirements of the rule of law, can impose on HMRC an obligation to facilitate the effectuation of rights granted by EU law. This obligation can be discharged through the provision of advice. The Merger Directive, which seeks to neutralise the fiscal obstacles to cross-border mergers, for instance provides taxpayers broadly with rights to non-taxation on certain transactions.[156] One condition of this, however, is that there is no tax avoidance motive behind the transaction.[157] In *Euro Park Service v Ministre des finances et des comptes publics*,[158] a company governed by French law was wound up by its sole shareholder and sought tax deferral in accordance with Article 4(1) of the Merger Directive. The deferral, however, was denied on the basis that ministerial approval (required by national law) was not sought, and secondly would not have been given, since the transaction was not justified by commercial reasons but rather was carried out to avoid or evade tax. However, the French legislation did

[151] *Privacy International* (n 148) [180].
[152] ibid [185].
[153] ibid.
[154] ibid.
[155] ibid [74]–[179]; see also [61].
[156] Council Directive 2009/133/EC of 19 October 2009 on the common system of taxation applicable to mergers, divisions, partial divisions, transfers of assets and exchanges of shares concerning companies of different Member States and to the transfer of the registered office of an SE or SCE between Member States [2009] OJ L 310/34.
[157] Article 15(1).
[158] Case C-14/16 *Euro Park Service v Ministre des finances et des comptes publics* (ECJ, 8 March 2017).

not specify the detailed rules for the ministerial approval. Therefore the French legislation itself did not comply with the principle of legal certainty[159] and in order to comply with EU law it would have been necessary for the administrative practice and guidance to remedy this by providing such certainty. The Court of Justice, however, found that the tax administration's practice was not sufficiently precise, clear and foreseeable to enable taxpayers to ascertain their rights.[160] Put another way, once the legislation was found to be inadequate, the obligation fell to the tax administration to provide assistance to taxpayers to help them realise their rights, but the tax administration failed in respect of this obligation. This duty could have been given effect through the provision of individual and general advice, thereby highlighting the point that there can be circumstances in which EU law could require HMRC to provide advice.

Finally, some tax provisions, such as those which allow HMRC to charge or reduce penalties, are geared towards compliance rather than revenue raising. An example is the statutory penalty regime, which, as put by Geraint Jones QC, 'is not intended by Parliament to be a revenue raising device. The obvious intention of Parliament [is] … to encourage compliance'.[161] Given that Parliament's intent is to produce compliance in such a case, then it could be argued that HMRC is under a positive obligation to further that Parliamentary intent by providing unsolicited advice to taxpayers. A pertinent example arises from a series of First-Tier Tribunal decisions wherein Geraint Jones QC held it unfair that HMRC failed to notify late-paying taxpayers that penalties were accruing, notwithstanding the fact that the provisions imposed no such express duty on HMRC.[162] Although this line of argument was overturned by the Upper Tier on the basis of 'jurisdiction',[163] Geraint Jones QC nevertheless took it as an 'admission' of probable unfairness on the part of the Revenue that it chose to reform its approach and subsequently provide notifications to potentially late paying taxpayers.[164]

D. Other Normative Justifications

Other normative justifications for the provision of advice by HMRC may be propounded. For instance, efficiency is often lauded as a reason for tax authorities to assist taxpayers.[165] The argument goes as follows: efficiency in collection is

[159] ibid para 41. See also Advocate General Wathelet's Opinion at para 53.

[160] *Euro Park Service* (n 158), para 44.

[161] *Hilltop Syndicate Shoot v The Commrs for HMRC* [2012] UKFTT 26 (TC) [25]. See also: *Hok Limited v The Commrs for HMRC* [2011] UKFTT 433 (TC) [10]; *Sunset Travel Limited v The Commrs for HMRC* [2012] UKFTT (471) (TC) [16].

[162] *Hok* (ibid) [10]; *Sunset Travel Limited* (ibid) [16].

[163] *Hok v R & C Commrs* [2012] UKUT 363 (TCC) [55].

[164] *Royal Institute of Navigation v R & C Commrs* [2012] UKFTT (472) (TC) [26].

[165] See for instance the justification for the introduction of rulings in New Zealand, as noted by Alarie, Datt, Sawyer and Weeks, 'Advance Tax Rulings' (2014) 367. Efficiency may also be invoked as a benefit of the rule of law – see Jowell, 'The Rule of Law Today' (2004) 19–20.

desirable[166] as it reduces the cost of tax collection and hence allows the tax authority to use its resources in a manner which will best result in it achieving its primary objective, which in the case of HMRC is to collect revenues due and bear down on tax avoidance and evasion.[167]

Efficiency in respect of advice can be seen in two respects. First, assistance in the form of advice reduces the prospect of taxpayers misapplying or misinterpreting the law and thereby producing incorrect tax outcomes. The result may be a loss of revenue, from taxes due, for the public purse and will be that the tax authority will have to expend resources in correcting the incorrect tax outcome. Secondly, engaging with taxpayers through the provision of advice also leads to efficiency in the sense that it highlights for HMRC the activities or proposed activities of taxpayers, information which the tax authority would otherwise have to discover of its own volition and incur cost in doing so.[168] This occurs where individual taxpayers (including their agents) or representative bodies approach HMRC for advice and in the process provide pertinent background information about the relevant activities.[169] It also occurs where HMRC consults with taxpayers and representative bodies when promulgating general advice.[170] Advice in this sense is just one of many initiatives in which tax authorities engage in order to acquire information about the activities of taxpayers, some of whom pose a particular risk to the Exchequer. For instance, HMRC engages in co-operative compliance with the UK's largest businesses.[171] The idea is that this gives the taxpayer an incentive to voluntarily provide information to a greater extent and as early as possible to HMRC, allowing the authority to better focus resources on those with a greater tax compliance 'risk' profile. In exchange, the tax office keeps the taxpayer informed in a timely manner about HMRC thinking on the taxpayer's tax affairs.[172] Similarly, many jurisdictions, including all EU Member States,[173] operate a scheme for the advanced disclosure of tax avoidance schemes. This enables tax authorities to engage in effective risk-based investigations and allows the Government to get to grips quickly with potential legislative loopholes so that these could be eradicated

[166] See for instance A Smith, *The Wealth of Nations* (London, W Strahan and T Cadell, 1776), Book V, Ch II, Pt II; J Mirrlees, *Tax by Design: the Mirrlees Review* (Oxford, Oxford University Press, 2011) 22 and 42; Kay and King term tax collection costs as 'pure social loss': J Kay and M King, *The British Tax System*, 5th edn (Oxford, Oxford University Press, 1990) 15.

[167] HMRC, 'HM Revenue and Customs single departmental plan' (June 2019).

[168] See N Sugarman, 'Federal Tax Rulings Procedure' (1954) 10 *Tax Law Review* 1, 5; D Oliver 'Advance Rulings' [1996] 6 *British Tax Review* 578, 579.

[169] As arises in the case of applications for Advance Pricing Agreements (APAs), see HMRC, 'Statement of Practice 2/2010' (November 2016) para 34.

[170] On which, see below ch 5.

[171] On which, see D de Widt and L Oats, 'Risk Assessment in a Co-operative Compliance Context: A Dutch-UK Comparison' [2017] *British Tax Review* 230.

[172] HMRC, TCRM1000 (March 2017).

[173] On which, see Council Directive (EU) 2018/822 of 25 May 2018 amending Directive 2011/16/EU as regards mandatory automatic exchange of information in the field of taxation in relation to reportable cross-border arrangements [2018] OJ L 139/1, Recitals 4 and 13.

at the next available opportunity.[174] For these reasons, the courts in the UK, as noted already, have long supported the decision on the part of HMRC (and its predecessor bodies) to actively assistant taxpayers.[175]

The idea that schemes for providing advice produce efficiency, however, does not go undisputed. For instance, there is an argument that uncertainty is actually beneficial for the public purse in the sense that it may lead taxpayers to 'over-comply'[176] with the law.[177] This argument, however, is misconceived. Efficiency is to be judged by the cost incurred as against the taxes collected. Monies not due as tax but received should not be factored into considering the efficiency of a collection initiative. Whilst the extra money may be a bonus for the Treasury, it says nothing about how efficient a tax authority is in carrying out the task of tax collection. Efficiency is about the cost of collecting taxes due, not the cost of collecting monies not due.

A better reason for not relying upon efficiency as a normative justification,[178] however, is that it is vulnerable to empirical challenge. Of course, some empirical studies suggest that the provision of advice leads to greater tax compliance. For instance studies have shown a correlation between the quality of advice provided to taxpayers and levels of compliance.[179] Indeed, HMRC itself believes people are more likely to pay the right tax when they find HMRC easy to deal with and if they understand what is expected of them, and that customer service and tax compliance should therefore be taken together in considering how it delivers services.[180] However, there is a risk that the better the service that HMRC provides becomes, the more reliant taxpayers in turn become without any corresponding increase in compliance.[181] To this end taxpayers could switch from using private agents to assist in tax compliance thus shifting costs from individual taxpayers to HMRC. Furthermore, the efficiency justification may have the effect of removing equity from the provision of assistance to taxpayers if it can be demonstrated that it is more efficient to provide advice to those that pay more taxes in absolute terms. Indeed, the fact that HMRC invests in a 'resource-intensive, relationship-managed service for the largest customers'[182] appears to bear this out.

[174] See for instance: HMRC, 'Disclosure of Tax Avoidance Schemes (DOTAS) Consultation Document' (9 December 2009) 4.

[175] See above in text at n 74.

[176] Alarie, Datt, Sawyer and Weeks (n 81) 367.

[177] See for instance S Scotchmer and J Slemrod, 'Randomness in Tax Enforcement' (1989) 38 *Journal of Public Economics* 17. Cf L Osofsky, 'The Case Against Strategic Tax Law Uncertainty' (2011) 64 *Tax Law Review* 489.

[178] This is as opposed to a legal justification for the exercise of discretion. As is evident from the Moses LJ comment in *Gaines-Cooper* quoted above, it is not the proper role of a judge to second-guess how HMRC should go about the task of collecting tax. In that instance, they have a wide managerial discretion.

[179] National Audit Office and Tax Administration Research Centre, 'The effect of HMRC Taxpayer Assistance on compliance: An experimental investigation' (December 2017); National Audit Office, 'The quality of service for personal taxpayers' (HC 2016–17, 17) 10 and paras 3.3–3.6.

[180] HC Committee of Public Accounts, 'HM Revenue & Customs performance in 2014–15: Sixth Report of Session 2015–16' (HC 2015–16, 393) 6.

[181] NAO and TARC, 'The quality of service' (n 179) para 3.8.

[182] HMRC, 'Large Business strategy' (September 2014).

Relying upon the rule of law as a justification, however, avoids the empirical problem because what the rule of law requires is simply that people are provided with the relevant information so that they can understand the legal consequences of their actions. It does *not* in turn require that taxpayers actually better comply with their obligations. In relation to equity across taxpayers, a component of the thin conception of the rule of law is that laws should be accessible to those affected by them, and thus should make no distinction between differently placed taxpayers.[183]

That is to answer why the rule of law is to be preferred to efficiency as a justification, but there are other principles that could also justify the provision of advice, such as trust, tax morale and even democracy. For instance, it is imperative that we should be able to trust our public officials.[184] The argument accordingly would be that the provision of advice is conducive to increasing trust.[185] Tax morale, which can be broadly understood as the intrinsic motivation to pay tax,[186] could assist as a justification in so far as it could be argued that tax authority advice raises morale.[187] As regards justifying HMRC advice on the basis of democracy, Thomas and Elliott have written that 'Genuine democracy calls for the widest possible public involvement'.[188] Democracy is about much more than the occasional vote.[189] It entails engagement with citizens and turns on citizens participating in the political process.[190] Accordingly, the argument would go as follows: the public ought to be involved in the formulation of policies that directly impact it,[191] whether in respect of individual advice or general advice to taxpayers.

The question which follows is why focus solely upon the rule of law? Two reasons are offered in response. First, as explained in this chapter, the courts have developed further and further the idea that laws, and guidance in respect of those

[183] See section IV on accessibility.

[184] For an overview of trust and taxation generally, see: S Goslinga, L Van Der Hel-Van Dijk, P Mascini and A van Steenbergen (eds), *Tax and Trust* (The Hague, Eleven International Publishing, 2018).

[185] Using trust as a justification for the provision of advice would provide further normative weight to the suggestion that taxpayers should have some form of right to bind tax authorities to their advice. See for instance: C Forsyth, 'Wednesbury Protection of Substantive Legitimate Expectations' [1997] *Public Law* 375, 375; C Forsyth, 'The Provenance and Protection of Legitimate Expectations' (1988) 47 *Cambridge Law Journal* 238, 239.

[186] B Torgler, 'Tax morale, rule governed behaviour and trust' (2003) 14 *Constitutional Political Economy* 119, 125.

[187] It is notable that there is a rich body of literature on the relationship between tax morale and compliance. A good starting point is B Torgler, *Tax Compliance and Tax Morale: A Theoretical and Empirical Analysis* (Cheltenham, Edward Elgar Publishing, 2007). Interestingly, the need to take into account tax morale (written as 'taxpayer perceptions of th[e] integrity' of the tax system) when managing the tax system is set out in primary legislation in New Zealand. See Tax Administration Act 1994, s 6(2)(a).

[188] R Thomas and M Elliott, *Public Law*, 3rd edn (Oxford, Oxford University Press, 2017) 173.

[189] R Kirkham, 'The Constitutional Role of the Ombudsman' (2006) 10 *The International Ombudsman Yearbook* 120, 128.

[190] D Galligan, *Due Process and Fair Procedures* (Oxford, Oxford University Press, 1994) 128.

[191] P Craig, *Administrative Law*, 8th edn (London, Sweet and Maxwell, 2016) 450; P Daly, 'Administrative Law: A Values-Based Approach' in J Bell, M Elliott, J Varuhas and P Murray (eds), *Public Law Adjudication in Common Law Systems: Process and Substance* (Oxford, Hart Publishing, 2015) 29.

laws, ought to comply with the rule of law and, to this end, the concept has traction in terms of legal argumentation. Secondly, and more importantly, the rule of law is generally agreed to be a matter of fundamental constitutional importance and it should follow that an exploration of its impact upon the provision of advice to the public is merited on its own terms.

IV. A Normative Framework for HMRC Advice

Given the underlying principle of the rule of law, the next logical question is how this can be given practical effect in a system for providing advice. It is contended here that a normative framework can be deduced, which can be tested against a system for the provision of advice. The framework consists of five benchmarks, which build on the ideas of foreseeability and accessibility. The first three relate to actual advice given by HMRC whilst the latter two relate to the structure in place for advice. These will overlap to a degree but are sufficiently distinct so as to warrant their own individual consideration.

The first is that advice should illuminate the correct tax outcome (*correctness*). HMRC advice should allow a taxpayer to better understand the legal consequences of her actions. But where the advice is misconceived, then the taxpayer is not properly informed as to the legal consequences. The second is that advice should be clear, and hence foreseeable, though some tolerance must be accepted in terms of ambiguity (*clarity*). The third is that advice ought to be accessible to all (*accessibility*), within which there are four aspects to consider. The first is that the taxpayer should have advice available to her. Clearly, this objective is undermined where a regime for giving advice is open to some and not to others, or where advice given to one taxpayer is relevant, but not made available, to another taxpayer. Given the underlying value of human dignity, it would be bizarre if the rule of law were to openly sanction disparate treatment of human beings. But whilst it might be *desirable* to universalise access to advice, it must be accepted that total equality of treatment is not feasible due to resource constraints and there will have to be trade-offs. Focus should accordingly be on whether the compromises are justified. Thus, decisions, which should be interrogated, must be made both in relation to the scope of what advice will be provided and the category of persons to whom advice will be provided. Advice, on the other hand, which exists but is simply not supplied to all for whom it might be relevant, is more clearly problematic from an accessibility point of view and is the second aspect that needs to be considered. The third aspect is the ability to know how the advice applies at any given time. Retrospective changes to advice hinder this, as accessibility requires stability over time,[192] and finally, mingling of different categories of advice misleads taxpayers and those charged with oversight.

[192] Tasioulas (n 93). See also C Sunstein, *Legal Reasoning and Political Conflict*, 2nd edn (Oxford, Oxford University Press, 2018) 104. Lon Fuller once remarked that 'every departure from the principles

The fourth benchmark is that of *scrutiny*. From the perspective of the thin account of the rule of law, scrutiny of advice is important as it ensures that the advice is correct, clear and accessible, thereby enhancing these qualities. The thin account of the rule of law does not require any particular form of scrutiny – whether from inside the organisation or outside. What matters is what works, as scrutiny is judged as effective insofar as it is instrumental in bringing about correctness, clarity and accessibility of advice. The fifth is that advice should be reliable (*reliability*). Taxpayers to the greatest extent possible ought to be entitled to rely upon advice which affects them. Reliability is intimately related to the idea of foreseeability. In order for the advice to be of utility to a taxpayer, to advance her understanding of the legal consequences of her action, she must be able to rely upon it. Otherwise, its weightlessness undermines its power to provide guidance. To this end, there must be appropriate mechanisms in place to ensure that the tax authority does not renege on its advice.

Though these five benchmarks form the normative framework, it is important to recognise that these are ideals of a desirable system for the provision of advice. Compliance with them accordingly is not a binary matter, but rather a question of degree.[193] Further, there are other considerations that may be viewed as important and thus at times override the values of the rule of law underpinning the framework.[194] To this end, it is permissible to take the view that comprising the normative benchmarks is at times legitimate. It follows that it is permissible for policymakers too to take into account other considerations. For instance, there might well be other reasons, such as accountability and democracy, why scrutiny from parties outside HMRC would be desirable. Scrutiny may help ensure greater participation by those affected by the advice.[195] It guards to a degree against exploitation by certain interest groups or the production of biased advice.[196] Further, given that the tax authority will be exercising a public power, there is a legitimate claim that it should be subject to external scrutiny.[197]

Finally, the benchmarks have an interdependent relationship. The degree to which advice is clear and correct will have a direct bearing on its reliability, whilst the level of scrutiny afforded to the advice will impact its correctness and clarity.

of law's inner morality is an affront to man's dignity'. See L Fuller, *The Morality of Law* (New Haven, Yale University Press, 1964) 162.

[193] As noted already, Tasioulas (n 93) makes an equivalent remark in respect of the rule of law.

[194] Such as the need to combat tax avoidance. For instance, HMRC will refuse to provide an informal ruling where it relates to an avoidance scheme. HMRC, 'Find out about the Non-Statutory Clearance Service' (June 2018). For a different take on the values that might be relevant, see R Prebble and J Prebble, 'Does the Use of General Anti-Avoidance Rules to Combat Tax Avoidance Breach Principles of the Rule of Law?' (2010) 55 *St Louis University Law Journal* 21.

[195] Craig, *Administrative Law* (2016) 468.

[196] This is noted in relation to the parallel context of general guidance: D Schoenbrod, *Power without Responsibility – How congress abuses the people through delegation* (New Haven, Yale University Press, 1993) 21; R Stewart, 'The Reformation of American Administrative Law' (1975) 88 *Harvard Law review* 1667, 1684–85.

[197] Treasury Committee, 'Principles of Tax Policy' (HC 2010–11, 753) para 43.

To this end, chapters five and six are structured so as to correspond to the problems illuminated in chapter four.

V. Conclusion

This chapter has sought to elaborate upon the role of HMRC advice, assessing both its lawfulness and desirability. The provision of HMRC advice is a proper exercise of its managerial discretion which has been sanctioned by Parliament, though the discretion is subject to myriad legal constraints. Assistance from HMRC is a desirable feature in a tax system, meanwhile, as it promotes the rule of law. HMRC advice provides guidance to taxpayers as to the legal consequences of their actions, thereby valuing human dignity.

Through the process of justifying the provision of HMRC advice, a normative framework against which the system for the provision of advice can be judged was developed. It is formed of five benchmarks, namely correctness, clarity, accessibility, scrutiny and reliability. Compliance with this framework is not a binary matter, but rather a question of degree. In subsequent chapters this framework will be used to test the provision of tax advice by HMRC and to structure the consideration of potential future reforms.

4

Problems with Advice

No doubt this kind of near-law will be with us for some years to come; in its benign form, that is to be hoped for, in its malignant form feared*

I. Introduction

Over the years, many have cited the problems relating to HMRC advice. Most notable is the criticism of David Williams in an influential *British Tax Review* article in 1979.[1] Williams cited various members of the bench who openly criticised the practice of extra-statutory concessions (ESCs) in their judgments, such as Wills J in *Swayne v IRC*,[2] Scott LJ in *Absalom v Talbot*,[3] Ungoed Thomas J in *IRC v Clifforia Investments Ltd*,[4] and Walton J in the series of *Vestey* cases[5] (views which were subsequently endorsed by the House of Lords).[6] There is merit in these criticisms. HMRC advice should be consistent with the underlying law (correctness), sufficiently clear as to guide taxpayers as to their rights and obligations under the law (clarity) and accessible to those affected by it (accessibility).[7] The purpose of this chapter is to demonstrate how HMRC advice in practice may fail to satisfy these requirements.[8] This chapter will use examples of these problems

* RE Megarry, 'Administrative Quasi-Legislation' (1944) 60 *LQR* 125, 128.

[1] D Williams, 'Extra-Statutory Concessions' [1979] *British Tax Review* 137. See: *Vestey v IRC* [1980] AC 1148 (HL), 1194 (Lord Edmund-Davies). Lord Edmund-Davies' speech in turn has been cited by McNeill J in *R v HM Inspector of Taxes, ex parte Fulford-Dobson* [1987] BTC 158 (QBD), 165–66; *Adrian John Wilkinson v The Commissioners of Inland Revenue* [2002] EWHC 182 (Admin), [2002] STC 347 [27] (Moses J); *R (Wilkinson) v Inland Revenue Commissioners* [2003] EWCA Civ 814, [2003] 1 WLR 2683, 2696.

[2] [1899] 1 QB 335 (QBD), 344.

[3] [1943] 1 All ER 589 (CA), 598.

[4] [1963] 1 WLR 396 (Ch), 402.

[5] *Vestey v IRC (No 1)* [1979] Ch. 177 (Ch), 197 and *Vestey v IRC (No 2)* [1979] Ch 198 (Ch), 202, 203–204.

[6] *Vestey v IRC* (above n 1) 1170–73 (Lord Wilberforce) and 1194 (Lord Edmund-Davies).

[7] The professional bodies – CIOT, ATT and LITRG – have engaged in a cross-tax project on HMRC guidance generally, while HMRC are at the time of writing conducting an internal guidance project. For background, see: A Fearnside and K Willis, 'HMRC guidance: difficulties with out-of-date, inaccurate and hard to find guidance' *Tax Advisor Magazine* (1 May 2018).

[8] This chapter is derived in part from S Daly, 'Oversight of HMRC Soft-Law: Lessons from the Ombudsman' (2016) 38 *Journal of Social Welfare and Family Law* 343, available at www.tandfonline.com/doi/full/10.1080/09649069.2016.1228147 <copyright Taylor and Francis>.

where deliberate choices have been made either by HMRC or by legislators in order to support the argument that more needs to be done if the thin account of the rule of law is to be taken seriously.

II. Correctness

For HMRC advice to advance the rule of law, taxpayers should be advised as to the legal consequences of their actions. But advice which is incorrect clearly conflicts with this rationale and can be seen arising in three respects. The first is where concessions are provided which are inconsistent with the underlying law. Concessions are singled out for special treatment given that these, by definition, are in tension with the underlying substantive law and there is greater scope accordingly for concessions to go beyond what is permissible. Secondly, where the advice has misconceived the law and thirdly where the law has been correctly interpreted but incorrectly applied.

A. Concessions which are Inconsistent with the Underlying Law

Many writers have highlighted that strong lobbying and interest groups may exploit the process of promulgating advice,[9] and successfully obtain concessions from the law. The prospect of such exploitation is unsettling for several reasons. There is the potential removal of horizontal equity between taxpayers within the same class. It exposes 'a Revenue official to temptation'[10] to make de facto changes to the law to fit their personal morality. The most troubling issue in this vein is that it may allow HMRC decisions to undermine the authority of Parliament where there is an inconsistency with the underlying law, consequently undermining the rule of law. Although some flexibility must be given to HMRC as to the effectuation of its role in managing and collecting taxes, Lord Hoffmann surmised that this only 'enables the commissioners to formulate policy *in the interstices of the tax legislation*' (emphasis added)[11] and does not allow the commissioners to concede 'an allowance which Parliament could have granted but did not grant'.[12] The point of this constriction is that it prevents HMRC from playing fast and loose with tax

[9] D Schoenbrod, *Power without Responsibility – How congress abuses the people through delegation* (New Haven, Yale University Press, 1993) 21; K Brooks, 'A Reasonable Balance: Revenue Authority Discretions and the Rule of Law in Canada' in C Evans, J Freedman and R Krever (eds), *The Delicate Balance: Tax, Discretion and the Rule of Law* (Amsterdam, IBFD, 2011) 71.

[10] *Absalom v Talbot* (n 3) 598 (Scott LJ).

[11] *R (Wilkinson) v IRC* [2005] UKHL 30, [2006] STC 270 (*Wilkinson*) [21].

[12] ibid.

legislation. This would, as one judge hyperbolically noted, effectively 'reverse the result of the Civil War'.[13]

There are many examples from the history of HMRC and its predecessor bodies of pressure groups extracting benevolent treatment from HMRC which may conflict with the underlying law. The classic example of such favouritism is a concession which operated from at least World War II[14] until 2003[15] in relation to miners' free coal. Miners were entitled to coal for personal use by virtue of their employment. This is a taxable benefit in kind as it is something that is capable of being converted into money or something of direct monetary value to the employee.[16] During World War II, however, miners were given cash payments in lieu. By virtue of a concession, the rationale of which the Office of Tax Simplification was unable to ascertain,[17] this cash in lieu payment was not chargeable to tax.[18] The practice continued to operate for either free coal or the payment in lieu until the concession was put into legislation in 2003.[19] Around the middle of the concession's lifetime, at which point it was estimated to be costing circa £30 million per annum,[20] Walton J in *Vestey (no 2)* expressed his bewilderment at the practice:

> [U]pon what basis have the commissioners taken it upon themselves to provide that income tax is not to be charged upon a miner's free coal and allowances in lieu thereof ... If this kind of concession can be made, where does it stop; and why are some groups favoured as against others?[21]

It need not necessarily be the case that taxpayers have explicitly sought to extract concessions. Sometimes HMRC can of its own initiative provide relief from the underlying law in a manner going beyond the scope of what is permissible. ESC D33 is a particularly apt example. Despite several attempts in recent years to update or legislate the concession,[22] at the time of writing (September 2019) it is still operative.[23] This is a class concession relating to capital gains tax (CGT). By way of background, CGT is levied[24] on any gain[25] accruing to a chargeable

[13] *M v Home Office* [1994] 1 AC 377, 395 (Lord Templeman).

[14] Inland Revenue, 'A List of Extra Statutory Wartime Concessions given in the Administration of Inland Revenue Duties' (October 1944) Cmd 6559.

[15] It was enacted in Income Tax (Earnings and Pensions) Act 2003, s 306.

[16] HMRC, 'EIM00530 – Employment income: benefits in kind taxable as earnings: meaning of money's worth' (April 2018).

[17] Office of Tax Simplification, 'Review of tax reliefs Final report' (March 2011) 57.

[18] Inland Revenue, 'A List of Extra-Statutory Wartime Concessions' (1944) 248.

[19] Income Tax (Earnings and Pensions) Act 2003, s 306.

[20] HM Treasury, 'Appropriation Accounts 1980/81' (HC 1981–82, 76-IX) xxi.

[21] *Vestey (No 2)* (n 5) 203.

[22] For instance, HMRC in July 2014 released a consultation paper in which it sought responses on a proposal to legislate ESC D33. See: HMRC, 'Legislating Extra Statutory Concession D33' (July 2014) 10.

[23] See ESC D33 in HMRC, 'Extra-Statutory Concessions: Concessions as at 6 April 2018' (April 2018); HMRC, 'Capital Gains Manual: CG13020' (July 2019).

[24] By virtue of Taxation of Chargeable Gains Act 1992 (TCGA 1992), s 1.

[25] TCGA 1992, s 15.

person[26] from the chargeable disposal[27] of a chargeable asset.[28] A chargeable asset in turn is defined in very broad terms as *any form of property*, whether situated in the UK or not, including:

(a) options, debts and incorporeal property generally, and
(b) any currency other than sterling, and
(c) any form of property created by the person disposing of it, or otherwise coming to be owned without being acquired.[29]

In *O'Brien v Benson's Hosiery (Holdings) Ltd* ('*O'Brien*'),[30] a director under a seven-year service contract with the taxpayer, Benson's Hosiery, was released from his obligations in return for payment to the taxpayer of £50,000. The House of Lords held that the £50,000 was subject to CGT on the basis that the contractual right of the taxpayer to the director's services was an asset which could be and had been turned to account. The case of *Zim Properties v Proctor* ('*Zim Properties*'),[31] which is the catalyst for ESC D33, follows from this case.[32] *Zim Properties* concerned a settlement arrived at between a firm of solicitors and Zim, the taxpayer. Owing to alleged negligence on the part of the solicitors, the sale of three properties fell through. The solicitors settled the matter for £69,000, which the Inland Revenue in turn assessed to tax. In line with *O'Brien*, the court held that a right to bring an action is an 'asset' for the purposes of CGT,[33] provided such action is not vexatious or frivolous.[34] Further, Warner J held that the capital sum was not derived from any underlying asset, in this case the three properties, but rather from the right of action itself.[35]

For taxpayers generally, this case would have had a wide-ranging effect. The 'gain' which is subject to CGT is calculated by deducting the acquisition cost,[36] exemptions[37] and reliefs[38] from the proceeds of the disposal of the asset. As such, rights of action would be assessable to tax in their own right and the acquisition cost, exemptions and reliefs relating to a separate, but obviously related, asset would not be deductible. An anomalous position thus arises whereby the £69,000 could not be reduced by costs, reliefs or exemptions of a separate asset as it arose

[26] TCGA 1992, s 2.
[27] TCGA 1992, ss 21–27.
[28] TCGA 1992, s 21(1).
[29] ibid.
[30] [1980] AC 562 (Ch).
[31] [1985] STC 90 (Ch). On which, see D Salter, '*Zim Properties Ltd v Proctor* (1985): Compromise of Action, Compensation and CGT' in D de Cogan and J Snape, *Landmark cases in Revenue Law* (Oxford, Hart Publishing, 2019).
[32] *Zim Properties* (n 31) in particular, 104–08.
[33] See TCGA 1992, s 37(1).
[34] *Zim Properties* (n 31) 106.
[35] ibid 108–09.
[36] TCGA 1992, s 38.
[37] For instance TCGA 1992, s 3.
[38] For instance TCGA 1992, ss 169H–169V and 222–26).

from a claim of negligence, but if the firm of solicitors had simply smashed up a property, causing £69,000 in damage, then that sum would be![39]

ESC D33 was introduced in 1988[40] to combat this anomaly by extending the range to which an underlying asset would be engaged. In other words, despite the strict legal position, the Revenue would treat a cause of action relating to an underlying asset as being derived itself from that underlying asset. The relevant acquisition cost (or portion thereof) could thus be deducted, and it would be eligible for statutory reliefs and exemptions in connection with the asset. The chargeable gain would be significantly reduced as a result, or the computation may even result in a 'loss'. This treatment is explained in paragraphs 8–10 of ESC D33:

> **8. Relief by concession**
>
> Where a gain arises on the disposal of a right of action, the case may alternatively, by concession, be treated in accordance with the following paragraphs of this statement.
>
> **9. Underlying assets**
>
> Where the right of action arises by reason of the total or partial loss or destruction of or damage to a form of property which is an asset for capital gains tax purposes, or because the claimant suffered some loss or disadvantage in connection with such a form of property, any gain or loss on the disposal of the right of action may by concession be computed as if the compensation derived from that asset, and not from the right of action. As a result a proportion of the cost of the asset, determined in accordance with normal part-disposal rules, and indexation allowance, may be deducted in computing the gain. For example if compensation is paid by an estate agent because his negligence led to the sale of a building falling through, an appropriate part of the cost of the building may be deducted in computing any gain on the disposal of the right of action.
>
> The gain may be computed by reference to the original cost of the underlying asset, with time-apportionment if appropriate if the asset was acquired before 6 April 1965, or by reference to its market value on 6 April 1965. For disposals on or after 6 April 1988, the gain may be computed in appropriate cases by reference to the value of the asset on 31 March 1982.
>
> **10. Other reliefs and exemptions**
>
> If the relief was or would have been available on the disposal of the relevant underlying asset, it will be available on the disposal of the right of action. For example, if compensation is derived from a cause of action in respect of damage to a building suffered by reason of professional negligence, and the compensation is applied in restoring the building, deferment relief under Section 23, TCGA 1992 will be available as if the compensation derives from the building itself and not from the right of action.
>
> Other reliefs which may become available in this way include private residence relief, retirement relief and roll-over relief. HMRC Board will be prepared to consider extending time limits in cases where because of a delay in obtaining a capital sum in

[39] On part disposals, see: TCGA 1992, s 42.

[40] HMRC, 'Legislating Extra Statutory Concession D33' (n 22) 10.

> compensation, the normal time limit allowed for a relief has elapsed. If the right of action relates to an asset which is specifically exempt from capital gains tax, such as a motor car, any gain on the disposal of the right of action may be treated as exempt.

HMRC has claimed that this extension to the range of that which will qualify as an underlying asset is supported by the case of *Pennine Raceway Ltd v Kirklees Metropolitan Council (No 2)*[41] wherein Pennine Raceway held a licence to conduct drag racing on a disused airfield. When Kirklees Metropolitan Council rejected planning permission, the value of the licence dropped. The Council paid compensation to Pennine and the Court of Appeal held that this compensation reflected the loss in value of the licence.[42] But there is a clear distinction between these two instances. There is no doubt that the licence in *Pennine Raceway* represented an underlying asset and the direct consequence of not obtaining planning permission would have been to reduce the value of the licence. To take an example, if I ask you to sell my house and you set fire to it instead, you have caused directly the reduction in value for which I ought to be compensated. However, if you simply fail to sell my house (having promised to do so), my claim against you in negligence will be to compensate me for the harm caused by poor service,[43] not for any reduction in the value of the house (which may be caused by the market). The crucial distinction is between compensation for harm caused by a poor service as against compensation for an action which directly causes loss in value. The example accordingly is of false equivalence and cannot serve as the basis for extending the range of what will qualify as an underlying asset.[44]

To reiterate Lord Hoffmann's appraisal, a concession may only be granted within the interstices of legislation but cannot relieve tax which Parliament has prescribed as due. Could the concession here then be characterised as mere purposive interpretation and as such legitimate? The answer to this question must equally be 'no', as the success of that argument hinges on some ambiguity in relation to the meaning of the legislative text or need to construe the legislation in a way to make the collection of tax workable. But the High Court in *Zim Properties* clearly set out that the capital sum may derive from the right of action itself and so, this argument must make way for the ultimate conclusion that the concession goes beyond what is legally permissible by reason of its ambition to overrule a judicial decision.[45]

[41] [1989] STC 122 (CA).

[42] HMRC (n 22) 12.

[43] More specifically, the claim will be for the economic loss caused by the breach of your duty of care towards me. See, for starters, *Hedley Byrne & Co Ltd v Heller & Partners Ltd* [1964] AC 465, [1963] 2 All ER 575 (HL).

[44] HMRC even appears to accept this, as can be gleaned from its response to submissions on the consultation about legislating ESC D33: HMRC, 'Legislating Extra Statutory Concession D33: Summary of Responses' (November 2015) 5.

[45] David Southern QC equally holds that the concession in effect overrules *Zim Properties*: D Southern, 'Changes to the taxation of compensation (ESC D33)' (Chancery Bar Association/Revenue Bar Association, March 2015) 6, available at www.chba.org.uk/for-members/library/all-london-seminars/2015-seminars/changes-to-the-taxation-of-compensation-esc-d33.

Perhaps even more controversially, where a right of action arises that does not involve an underlying form of property, the ESC holds that any gain accruing on the disposal of the right of action would be exempt from CGT. This treatment was explained in para 11 of ESC D33:

> **11. No Underlying Asset**
>
> A right of action may be acquired by a claimant in connection with some matter which does not involve a form of property which is an asset for capital gains tax purposes. This may be the case where professional advisers are said to have given misleading advice in a tax or other financial matter, or to have failed to claim a tax relief within proper time. Actions may be brought in relation to private or domestic matters. Where the action does not concern loss of or damage to or loss in connection with a form of property which is an asset for capital gains tax purposes, the approach in paragraph 9 above of treating the compensation as deriving from the asset itself is not appropriate. In these circumstances any gain accruing on the disposal of the right of action will be exempt from capital gains tax.

As with paragraphs 8–10, the argument for purposive interpretation again is moot given that this paragraph *directly* contradictions the decisions in *Zim Properties* and in *O'Brien*. HMRC has argued, however, that the concession was justified initially on grounds of administrative convenience.[46] That might be persuasive in the case of a negligible amount of compensation. When the concession was introduced in 1988, however, there was no limit to the amount that would be exempted by the Inland Revenue from CGT. In January 2014, further, HMRC set a limit of £500,000 below which there would be no question of CGT. It is difficult to foresee any circumstance in which the administrative cost and inconvenience of collecting gains on amounts of up to £500,000 would outweigh the benefit.

Of course, if HMRC were to amend its practice by withdrawing ESC D33, the awards granted might well take account of the tax that must be paid on receipt, thereby being increased in order to include a tax charge. But whilst taxpayers might be no worse or better off in that scenario, the Exchequer is certainly worse off in the current scenario than legally it ought to be. The ultimate problem for HMRC in relation to ESC D33 is that a right of action is recognised as an asset for the purposes of CGT – that such is the case, however, is Parliament's will. The constitution dictates that HMRC obey the law not as a matter of grace but as a matter of necessity.[47]

B. Legal Misconception

At other times, HMRC advice may be incorrect not by reason of the interposition of a concessionary element, but by reason of the true legal position being

[46] HMRC (n 22) 13.

[47] See *M v Home Office* (n 13) 395 (Lord Templeman). See also *R (Evans) v Attorney General* [2015] UKSC 21, [2015] 2 WLR 813 [52] (Lord Neuberger) cited in Salter (n 31) 326.

misconceived. HMRC's approach to the doctrine of legitimate expectations is an example of this. The doctrine of legitimate expectations provides a remedy to a citizen against a public authority where that institution has evoked an expectation that the public authority shall follow a particular course of action but seeks to resile from doing so. The Administrative Law Manual sets out HMRC's approach as to when it will give effect to a legitimate expectation that a taxpayer will be treated in accordance with incorrect advice:

> **Incorrect Advice to Customers: When incorrect advice can be binding**
>
> HMRC is only bound by incorrect advice in circumstances where all of the following tests are met:
>
> - The customer made it plain he or she was seeking fully considered advice and indicated what it would be used for
> - The customer provided all information relevant to the query
> - The advice given by HMRC was clear, unambiguous and without qualification
> - The customer acted in reliance on the advice (i.e. he or she did or refrained from doing something as a direct consequence of the advice)
> - *The customer would suffer detriment if the correct statutory position were applied; (e.g. he would be financially worse off than if the correct advice had been given in the first place)*
> - To apply the correct statutory position would be so unfair as to constitute an abuse of power (see ADML1400).
>
> A customer can only suffer detriment if he or she is subject to real harm or loss. It is not sufficient to merely suffer disappointment or upset.[48]

HMRC place particular reliance upon the need for the taxpayer to demonstrate detrimental reliance: that the customer would suffer detriment if her expectation of treatment were not upheld. To characterise detrimental reliance as an *essential* element to a legitimate expectations claim is incorrect, however. As set out by Scheimann LJ in *R (Bibi) v Newham LBC*:

> To disregard the legitimate expectation because no concrete detriment can be shown would be to place the weakest in society at a particular disadvantage. It would mean that those who have a choice and the means to exercise it in reliance on some official practice or promise would gain a legal toehold inaccessible to those who, lacking any means of escape, are compelled simply to place their trust in what has been represented to them.[49]

Whilst not being a per se requirement, the presence of detrimental reliance is generally an indication that a legitimate expectation should be upheld. It would be the exception, rather than the rule, that detrimental reliance will not be present for the court to give effect to the expectation.[50] So the true legal position

[48] HMRC, 'Admin Law Manual: ADML1300' (July 2016) (emphasis added).

[49] [2001] EWCA Civ 607 [55], [2002] 1 WLR 237.

[50] *R v Department of Education and Employment, ex parte Begbie* [1999] EWCA Civ 2100 [48] (Peter Gibson LJ).

accordingly, as concisely summarised by Whipple J in *R (Hely-Hutchinson) v HMRC* ('*Hely-Hutchinson*')[51] is that the circumstances in which HMRC may have to give effect to a legitimate expectation 'can travel beyond cases of detrimental reliance (although the fact that a taxpayer has relied to his or her detriment on the Commissioners' promise is in many cases the source of the complaint of unfairness)'.[52] Additionally concerning about the guidance in question is that Whipple J pointed out this misconception in relation to the necessity of detrimental reliance in *Hely-Hutchinson* in October 2015[53] but the Administrative Law Manual remains uncorrected at the time of writing (September 2019).[54]

C. Misapplication

Finally, there are instances which arise in which the law itself has not been improperly understood by HMRC but rather has been applied incorrectly to the facts, for instance because an overly narrow interpretation is adopted in order to apply general advice to particular facts. An example which nicely demonstrates this phenomenon can be seen in the 'Annual Report for 1994'[55] of the Parliamentary Commissioner for Administration ('Ombudsman').[56] This case concerned the application of what at the time was Statement of Practice A31. By way of SP A31, the Inland Revenue could compensate taxpayers for expenses caused by serious or persistent mistakes on the part of the Inland Revenue. This policy can now be found in HMRC guidance and has been broadened to the effect that taxpayers may be compensated for mistakes or unreasonable delay on the part of HMRC which causes the taxpayer to incur costs.[57] It has an interesting history, owing its genesis to investigation and pressure placed upon the Inland Revenue by both the Ombudsman and the Select Committee on the Parliamentary Commissioner for Administration in the 1970s. Sir Norman Price, then Chairman of the Board of the Inland Revenue, wrote to the Select Committee in 1975 to reveal that the concerted pressure had forced him to reconsider the Board's previous policy, which was a blanket refusal to cover the expenses of taxpayers. The review led him to the conclusion that the rigidity of the policy created severe unfairness in those instances where the taxpayer's costs arose directly out of a serious error on the part

[51] [2015] EWHC 3261 (Admin), [2016] STC 962.

[52] ibid [43].

[53] ibid [76].

[54] Although the decision was overturned on appeal, the Court did not reject Whipple J's decision that comparative unfairness in addition to detriment is a relevant consideration. See *HMRC v Hely-Hutchinson* [2017] EWCA Civ 1075, [2017] WLR(D) 517 (*Hely-Hutchinson* (CA)) [92].

[55] Parliamentary commissioner for administration, 'Annual Report for 1994' (HC 1994/95, 307) [56].

[56] The role of the Parliamentary Commissioner for Administration has since been subsumed within the body of the Parliamentary and Health Service Ombudsman.

[57] HMRC, 'Complain about HMRC'.

of the Board itself. The Chairman acknowledged that this could occur in various different circumstances, ranging from cases where no responsible official, acting in good faith with proper care, could reasonably have made such an error to cases where the original action was based upon a pardonable error, but which manifests itself into something much more serious if it persists. As a result, the Chairman decided that as a matter of principle, the Board should consider compensation in cases of this kind and accordingly a new practice emerged.[58]

The provision of compensation to cover loss caused by mistakes or unreasonable delays is undoubtedly lawful, though not because a claim would lie against HMRC in negligence.[59] The provision of compensation to this end would come within the scope of HMRC's managerial discretion, justified most likely on the basis of the principle of good administration.[60] Further, the Ombudsman can advise HMRC to provide compensation owing to injustice caused by maladministration[61] and the courts on judicial review can require HMRC to do so.[62] To this end, it would be strange if HMRC could only be compelled to provide compensation, but could not do so of its own volition in order to avoid being so forced. However, though the law had been understood correctly in the Revenue's general advice, its application as documented in the 1994 case study was incorrect as argued by the Ombudsman and belatedly accepted by the Chairman of the Inland Revenue. The complainants were a firm of accountants who highlighted an error on the part of the Inland Revenue in assessing tax due, but were advised by the District Inspector and the Revenue's Executive Office for the region that the resulting accountants' fees of £146.88 would not be repaid. The Chairman of the Board sought to excuse the errors on the part of the Revenue as 'pardonable' but following the advice of the Ombudsman that the department's reading of A31 was 'unjustifiably restrictive' agreed to pay the accountants' costs and to review the internal guidance issued to officers.

III. Clarity

From a rule of law perspective the justification for HMRC advice is that it supplements the underlying law by providing further guidance as to its minutiae, thus

[58] Select Committee on the Parliamentary Commissioner for Administration, 'First report from the Select Committee on the Parliamentary Commissioner for Administration together with the proceedings of the committee and minutes of evidence, session 1974–75' (HC 1974–75, 454) 106–07.

[59] On this, see *Neil Martin Ltd v HMRC* [2007] EWCA Civ 1041, [2008] Bus LR 663.

[60] See for instance ibid [19] where the Court of Appeal, in recalling the High Court's decision, highlights HMRC's understanding that the provision of compensation is discretionary.

[61] See for instance Parliamentary Commissioner for Administration, 'Second report of the Parliamentary Commissioner for Administration' (HC 1973–74, 106) 7.

[62] Senior Courts Act 1981, s 51 and CPR 44.2. If a judicial review case is transferred to the Upper Tribunal, costs can also be awarded against the losing party, see: The Tribunal Procedure (Upper Tribunal) Rules 2008, r 10(3)(a). The Upper Tribunal is a superior court of record, meaning it has the same jurisdiction as the High Court: Tribunals, Courts and Enforcement Act 2007, s 3(5).

rendering the citizen better informed of the legal consequences that will flow from her actions. That contention is, however, thwarted where the citizen is denuded of the ability to follow HMRC advice. Put another way, this deprives the advice of the very integrity it requires to render it complementary to the underlying law. This may arise in several scenarios. The first is where the taxpayer is deprived of an avenue of redress against HMRC where it seeks to resile from its position and to this end, chapter six explores 'reliability' in relation to tax law. Another manifestation of this is where the advice is unclear, which itself has an impact on reliability. Whilst there is a spectrum in respect of clarity, HMRC's approach should be to ensure that the advice is clear for the taxpayer to whom the advice is directed. Thus different levels of detail and nuance will be required in order to direct an ordinary taxpayer in advising on her affairs as against a taxpayer with complex affairs in need of sophisticated assistance.[63] The task of HMRC should be to assess what is the level of clarity necessary for a reasonable taxpayer in the circumstances to be better equipped to understand the legal consequences of her actions.

Whilst there is a range of examples from which to choose in order to demonstrate the level of vagueness in HMRC advice which is unacceptable, the paradigm is where the advice is so vague as to be open to conflicting interpretations. This is what has arisen in the case of HMRC's advice on the scope of its duty of confidentiality. By way of background, the function of collecting taxes, bestowed upon HMRC by virtue of section 5 of the Commissioners for Revenue and Customs Act 2005 (CRCA 2005), would be a difficult task if it were not for an array of wide-ranging powers which allow HMRC to extract and hold significant amounts of information about taxpayers.[64] Owing to this position of responsibility in relation to individuals' private information, HMRC is bound by a duty of confidentiality, 'a well established principle of the law of confidentiality'.[65] Enshrined in section 18 of CRCA 2005, it provides that 'officials may not disclose information which is held by the Revenue and Customs in connection with a function of the Revenue and Customs'. The duty is not without limit, however, and exceptions for instance may be made 'for the purposes of a function of the Revenue and Customs'.[66] HMRC elaborates on the limited circumstances in which disclosure of taxpayer information may be made 'for the purpose of a[n] [HMRC] function' to persons outside HMRC in its Internal Manual 'Information Disclosure Guide'.[67] Information may

[63] The Office of Tax Simplification in its report on guidance made a distinction between the different users of HMRC guidance: see: Office of Tax Simplification, 'Guidance for taxpayers: a vision for the future' (October 2018) 4–5.

[64] See for instance Finance Act 2008, Sch 36.

[65] *R (Ingenious Media and McKenna) v HMRC* [2016] UKSC 54 [17], [2016] 1 WLR 4164 (*Ingenious Media* (SC)).

[66] CRCA 2005, s 18(2)(a)(i). More exceptions are found at s 18(b)–(h).

[67] HMRC, 'Information Disclosure Guide' (March 2019).

be disclosed for the purpose of an HMRC function, such as the collection of tax for instance, where the following requirements are satisfied:

- Failing to do so would result in HMRC being significantly less effective or efficient in carrying out its functions;[68]
- Any detrimental impacts on individuals or legal entities that may result from the disclosure are proportionate to the expected benefits;[69] and
- There are no viable alternatives that could achieve the same outcome without the same (or a similar) level of disclosure.[70]

An example of such a situation, as provided in the Information Disclosure Guide, would be where a tax enquiry could be concluded more quickly by revealing information obtained from a third party. In this instance, it might be judged that disclosure of the information ahead of being required to reveal it by an order in court proceedings would render it likely for the taxpayer to recognise and agree to her true tax liability. This early disclosure would therefore be more resource efficient for both HMRC and the customer.[71] The previous incarnation of the Manual, in particular section IDG40430,[72] set out HMRC's position in essentially the same terms. It was stated therein that disclosure of information was lawful where:

- Only the minimum level of information about the customer would be disclosed to allow the function to be carried out,[73] and
- The making of the disclosure is necessary for the exercise of HMRC's functions.[74]

IDG40430 defined 'necessary' as pivoting upon whether making disclosure would enable an official to carry out the functions of the department.[75]

As should have become apparent, this Manual is quite bare and, other than the specific example cited, does not make entirely clear under what circumstances HMRC may disclose confidential information. Whilst it is true that some tolerance in respect of the clarity of advice must be afforded, the ambiguity in relation to this Manual is insufficient for the reason that it gives rise to contradictory positions within HMRC. This state of affairs has become clear in light of the conflicting approaches adopted by HMRC as revealed by the cases of *R (Ingenious Media and McKenna) v HMRC* ('*Ingenious Media*')[76] and *Privacy International v HMRC* ('*Privacy International*').[77]

[68] HMRC, 'IDG40415' (March 2019).
[69] ibid.
[70] ibid.
[71] ibid.
[72] This is the iteration which was used by the taxpayers in the *Ingenious* case, referred to later in this Section. See *R (Ingenious Media and McKenna) v HMRC* [2015] EWCA Civ 173, [2015] STC 1357 (*Ingenious Media* (CA)), [35].
[73] ibid.
[74] ibid.
[75] ibid.
[76] [2013] EWHC 3258 (Admin), [2014] STC 673 (*Ingenious Media* (HC)); *Ingenious Media* (CA) (n 72) *Ingenious Media* (SC) (n 65).
[77] [2014] EWHC 1475 (Admin), [2015] STC 948.

Privacy International concerned the power of HMRC to disclose information about its export control functions to the NGO Privacy International. The NGO alleged that a UK company, Gamma International, had supplied malware to repressive regimes in countries such as Bahrain and Ethiopia. It was claimed that Gamma International supplied the equipment illegally to those states in breach of export regulations. Accordingly, Privacy International inquired of HMRC – the enforcer of export regulations – whether such equipment had been supplied. HMRC responded that it had no power to provide information about its investigations by virtue of section 18 of the CRCA 2005 and that the provision imposed strict controls on the disclosure of information:[78]

> [T]he starting point of this legislation is that without specific legal authority officials of HMRC may not disclose any information held by HMRC in connection with its functions … and it is a criminal offence to reveal any information from which persons … might be identified. Consequently HMRC cannot comment on individual cases, and in particular we will be unable to keep you or other third parties informed of the progress of any investigations.[79]

The tenor of the letter indicated that HMRC's view was that there were no exceptions that could apply to authorise HMRC to disclose information.[80] This blanket refusal, the judge pointed out, was misconceived and served as one of the reasons the judge remitted the decision to HMRC to be considered again.[81]

Ingenious Media concerned an 'off the record' disclosure by David Hartnett, then Permanent Secretary for Tax at HMRC, to journalists from *The Times*. The conversation concerned tax avoidance schemes which were taking advantage of the 'Film Partnership' legislative provisions. Over the course of the meeting, Hartnett referred specifically to the appellants, Ingenious Media and Patrick McKenna, as marketers of such avoidance schemes;[82] expanded that the appellants had contributed to depriving the public purse of circa £5 billion;[83] explained that McKenna had personally used such schemes[84] and pronounced such schemes as 'scams for scumbags'.[85] Some of these comments were later quoted in articles published by the journalists on 21 June 2012.[86]

HMRC's justification for the disclosure, with which both the High Court and Court of Appeal agreed,[87] and which was encouraged by the Public Accounts

[78] ibid [17].
[79] ibid.
[80] ibid [18].
[81] ibid [63]–[73].
[82] *Ingenious Media* (CA) (n 72) [9].
[83] ibid [10].
[84] ibid [11].
[85] ibid.
[86] A Mostrous, F Schlesinger and R Watson, 'Screen play: how movie millions are moved offshore' *The Times* (21 June 2012); F Schlesinger, 'World of glitz and glamour that's on the Revenue's radar', *The Times* (21 June 2012).
[87] *Ingenious Media* (HC) (n 76) [38]–[51]; *Ingenious Media* (CA) (n 72) [26]–[30], [37]–[47].

Committee,[88] was that the disclosure was necessary for the purpose of tax collection.[89] In both the High Court and Court of Appeal, it was held that the disclosures by HMRC were in accordance with HMRC's Manual.[90] It is notable accordingly that in *Ingenious Media*, HMRC contested that it had a relatively wide power to disclose information, whilst in *Privacy International*, the body sought to refuse a request to disclose information on the basis that it had no power to do so. Such a conflict was not lost on Green J:

> The irony of the *Ingenious Holdings* [sic] case as applied in the present case is that in that case the HMRC was arguing for a broad power to disclose information based upon a relatively loose nexus between the information disclosed and the functions of the HMRC and in circumstances where they could be indiscrete and in fact disparaging about both a company (Ingenious Holdings) and an individual who promoted tax avoidance schemes. In the present case however HMRC has moved to the absolute other end of the spectrum and in the Decision letter and in subsequent correspondence denied that it has any power at all to disclose information and has adopted a narrow approach towards disclosure which ostensibly contradicts its own arguments in *Ingenious Media*.[91]

Even more disconcerting is the fact that HMRC's standpoint on disclosure in *Ingenious Media* contradicted the previous position advocated by Hartnett before the Public Accounts Committee in 2011. Hartnett's response to questioning around the scope of the duty of confidentiality was that disclosure of taxpayer information might in fact *hinder* the efficient collection of tax, thereby somewhat undermining the argument adopted in *Ingenious Media*.[92] Meanwhile, one month after the High Court decision in *Ingenious Media* was handed down, HMRC's policy on disclosure of taxpayer information in the case of work deaths changed.[93] By reason of its duty of confidentiality, HMRC would no longer provide work history information to a requesting coroner. These apparent conflicting interpretations of the law relating to breaches of confidentiality seem to be guided by expediency and not principle,[94] as HMRC shifts the goal posts according to the exigencies of the particular predicament. The inconsistent approach is the outward manifestation of the vague, ambiguous directions: the inexorable outcome of insufficiently clear advice. In sum, the problem with this piece of advice is that it can produce conflicting

[88] Public Accounts Committee, 'HM Revenue & Customs 2010–11 Accounts: tax disputes' (HC 2010–12, 1531) 9, paras 6 and 7.

[89] The Supreme Court unanimously disagreed, however, with the lower courts' reasoning, see *Ingenious Media* (SC) (n 65). That does not take away from the argument here which concerns HMRC's justifications for disclosures of information.

[90] See *Ingenious Media* (HC) (n 76) [44] and [60]–[61]; *Ingenious Media* (CA) (n 72) [30] and [37]–[47]. The Supreme Court's judgment however made no mention of the Manual.

[91] *Privacy International* (n 77) [60].

[92] PAC, 'HM Revenue & Customs 2010–11 Accounts: tax disputes' (n 88) Ev 67; see A Goodall, 'Taxpayer Confidentiality: Hartnett sets out HMRC view for MPs' (2011) 1098 *Tax Journal* 2.

[93] *R (HMRC) v HM Coroner for the City of Liverpool* [2014] EWHC 1586 (Admin), [2015] QB 481 [7].

[94] G Sanitt, 'Ingenious Media and HMRC's duty of confidentiality' (2015) 1256 *Tax Journal* 8, 9.

approaches to an area of law which is particularly sensitive for taxpayers. Further, despite the issue being litigated several times in recent years, HMRC has decided not to publish advice which would provide greater clarity.

IV. Accessibility

Minor errors on the part of taxpayers can have significant consequences. It is of utmost importance accordingly that those who are affected by tax law or HMRC interpretations and policies in pursuance of that law should have the ability to know the extent of their liability or their rights. Those persons who are affected by HMRC advice ought to be able to access it. There are four aspects to accessibility that will be analysed here. First, issues around accessibility are most notable where there are practical restrictions on access to HMRC advice. The second aspect to consider is where HMRC operates internal policies that affect classes of taxpayer but these policies are unpublished. Thirdly, taxpayers ought to know how the HMRC advice applies at any given time. Retrospective changes to advice hinder this capability. Finally, a taxpayer should have the ability to know which parts of HMRC advice the taxpayer can rely upon. Where pieces of HMRC advice contain concessionary elements, the taxpayer will be unwittingly placed in a precarious position.

A. Practical Restrictions

In theory HMRC advice can be accessed by all, though there are practical aspects that ought not to be ignored. For instance, whilst HMRC operates helplines and thus anybody with the use of a phone can contact HMRC for advice, this presupposes that a taxpayer even realises that she may need HMRC assistance or clarification. If the taxpayer does not have computer access then she will not have read HMRC's general advice which would direct her to some obligation or entitlement (which might lead her in turn to contacting HMRC directly for an informal ruling).[95]

Even beyond such practical restrictions, the substantive (as opposed to theoretical) entitlement to HMRC advice will necessarily be impacted by resource constraints or policy decisions, and this is where the tension with the thin account of the rule of law is particularly present. Whilst it might be desirable to universalise access to HMRC advice with each individual taxpayer entitled to timely, bespoke advice, it is plainly not feasible and there will have to be trade-offs. Thus, decisions

[95] On 'digital exclusion', see Office of National Statistics, 'Exploring the UK's digital divide' (March 2019).

must be made in relation to both what advice is produced by HMRC and to whom it is provided. But these decisions must be justified. The more advice that HMRC wishes to provide, then the more general it would have to be. Where less advice is produced, but of a more bespoke nature, then the persons to whom the advice will be directed will be a narrower category.

These decisions can be seen for instance in respect of advice to individual taxpayers. In terms of the scope of the advice that HMRC will provide, the body will not provide a ruling where the advice relates to avoidance, whether the request is for a formal ruling and its interaction with the General Anti-Abuse Rule,[96] or an informal ruling and avoidance generally.[97] Meanwhile only a narrow category of taxpayers, in a very limited set of circumstances, will be entitled to formal rulings, with all the benefits that come with such rulings including expertise on technical issues and also the fact that they are binding.[98] At the same time, the general population of taxpayers will have to content themselves with informal rulings – granted, however, that the policy decision about whether to legislate for binding rulings lies with Parliament and not HMRC. Further, we can see that the largest taxpayers even when obtaining individual advice, though not in the form of a formal ruling, will generally have better access to HMRC. A Customer Compliance Manager is assigned to the largest businesses in the UK, of which there are around 2,000.[99] The overall outcome of this approach is undoubtedly to favour larger taxpayers in respect of the resources that are dedicated to ensuring that their tax affairs are in order.[100] This is to be contrasted with other jurisdictions who no doubt will also have biases in terms of resource allocation, but at the same time operate a comprehensive formal ruling system, such as Australia.[101]

Finally, it should be recognised that resource constraints will have an impact on the timeliness of HMRC advice. Where a taxpayer seeks individual advice or where HMRC recognises the need for general advice, it should be provided promptly. Informal rulings will generally take less than 28 days, though this will be longer in the case of VAT rulings or complicated rulings.[102] A formal ruling may take longer, depending on the type of ruling requested. For instance, an Advanced Pricing Arrangement typically takes 18–21 months to complete.[103] On the other hand, a clearance relating to the transaction in land anti-avoidance provisions must be given within 30 days of notification.[104] General advice is provided on a

[96] HMRC, 'How to apply for clearance or approval of a transaction from HMRC' (May 2019).

[97] HMRC, 'Find out about the Non-Statutory Clearance Service' (June 2018).

[98] See above ch 2 in text at n 18.

[99] HMRC, 'How HMRC works with large businesses' (April 2018). See above ch 2 in text at n 45.

[100] To this end, the Treasury Select Committee recently recommended that HMRC reviews and improves the accessibility, quality and level of detail of guidance it gives to vulnerable taxpayers, owing to concerns raised by the Low Income Tax Reform Group and Chartered Institute of Taxation. See Treasury Select Committee, *Disputing Tax* (HC 2017–19, 1914) 19–20.

[101] See for instance Taxation Administration Act 1953, Sch 1, subs 359-5(2) and 359-10(1).

[102] HMRC, 'Find out about the Non-Statutory Clearance Service' (n 97).

[103] HMRC, 'Statement of Practice 2/2010' (November 2016) para 36.

[104] See for instance Income Tax Act 2007, s 770(4).

more ad hoc basis, though lobbying from representatives may result in general advice being provided at the time, or at least close to the time, that legislation is introduced.[105] In terms of HMRC's helplines, the department has set targets of answering customers' calls within five minutes, leaving no more than 15 per cent of callers waiting for more than 10 minutes to speak to an adviser.[106]

Given that these issues are in tension with the rule of law, justifications ought to be assessed. Dealing with timing first, the targets that HMRC has set for itself seem sensible and broadly in line with those adopted in other jurisdictions.[107] Meanwhile the consequence that larger taxpayers may have better access to HMRC, whilst unfortunate from an equality perspective, naturally follows from HMRC's primary objective as large taxpayers pose a greater risk to the Exchequer. This is to 'collect revenues due and bear down on avoidance and evasion',[108] which is agreed between HMRC and the Treasury.

Some of these decisions are not dictated per se by resources. Take the decision to restrict access to rulings due to tax avoidance for instance. The restriction falls in line with HMRC's primary objective. Whilst this might not easily square with the thin account of the rule of law, it is unlikely to see the Treasury or HMRC shift away from this position. It is possible for the normative framework advanced here to accommodate other values and policy decisions. Compliance with the framework is not binary, but is a matter of degree.[109] In any event one could try to justify the restriction insofar as the rule of law merely requires guidance rather than detailed specifics. Thus, rules may be left purposefully vague so that individuals would be discouraged from pushing their boundaries.[110] On the other hand it is difficult to generate any coherent justification as to why Parliament has decided that formal rulings are available only in 18 scenarios.[111]

B. Publication

It could be argued that it should not be necessary that HMRC advice be published as HMRC is required generally to tax a person in accordance with a particular

[105] See for instance HMRC, 'Company distributions: Consultation Document' (December 2015) and HMRC, 'Company distributions: Summary of Responses' (March 2016) 10, 14, 16 and 17. See further ch 5 in text at n 290.

[106] HMRC, '2018–19 Annual Report and Accounts' (July 2019) 38; HMRC, 'HM Revenue and Customs single departmental plan' (June 2019).

[107] See for instance C Waerzeggers and C Hillier, 'Introducing an Advance Tax Ruling (ATR) regime' (2016) 2 Tax Law IMF Technical Note 6 (albeit in the context of binding rulings).

[108] HMRC, 'Single departmental plan' (n 106).

[109] Tasioulas says this also in relation to the rule of law: J Tasioulas, 'The Rule of Law' in J Tasioulas (ed), *The Cambridge Companion to the Philosophy of Law* (Cambridge, Cambridge University Press, forthcoming).

[110] J Waldron, 'Vagueness in Law and Language: Some Philosophical Issues' (1994) 82 *California Law Review* 509, 536.

[111] According to HMRC guidance. See HMRC, 'How to apply for clearance or approval of a transaction from HMRC' (May 2019).

practice even if the taxpayer is unaware of the practice.[112] However, this theoretical basis in reality only holds where a taxpayer approaches HMRC, which in turn then applies the treatment, and in any event assumes that HMRC operates error-free.[113] These practical issues and the rule of law would dictate that advice should so far as possible be publicised to those who may fall within its scope. Some jurisdictions as a result, though not the UK, publish formal rulings. Given that this will engage the issue of taxpayer privacy, provision can be made for the redaction of identifying information as in Australia.[114]

As regards general HMRC advice and, in particular, concessions, the history of the Inland Revenue merits criticism. Practitioners have written about many instances where HMRC offered class concessions which are not published. Michael Nolan in 1981 wrote about the profit of a company being taxed as if it were the income of the shareholders unless it could be proved that the profits were needed for the purpose of reorganisation of the company.[115] This practice which was well known by the Bar prior to 1966, was revealed in a letter from the Revenue in 1966 to a professional accountancy body, but was not explicitly published in a press release until 1973.[116] Similarly, the Inland Revenue went through a process of reviewing all ESCs in the mid-1980s and published dozens of previously unpublished extra-statutory class concessions.[117] For this reason, the number of active Inland Revenue listed ESCs grew from 122 in 1980[118] to 169 by 1987.[119] Similarly, the review of concessions in the aftermath of *Wilkinson*[120] has served to bring to light a number of concessions which were previously unpublished.[121] A consultation paper on draft legislation was produced in November 2008,[122] which sought to place a number of concessions on a statutory footing. Three of

[112] *R (Gallaher Group Ltd) v Competition and Markets Authority* [2018] UKSC 25, [2018] 2 WLR 1583 [29] (Lord Carnwath); *R (Bancoult) v Secretary of State for Foreign and Commonwealth Affairs (No 2)* [2008] UKHL 61, [2009] 1 AC 453 [182] (Lord Mance).

[113] On this, see E Troup, 'Unacceptable Discretion: Countering Tax Avoidance and Preserving the Rights of the Individual' (1992) 13 *Fiscal Studies* 128, 134–35. On this, see also *LH Bishop Electrical Co. Ltd v HMRC* [2013] UKFTT 522 (TC), [2013] STI 3433 where Judge Mosedale held that non-publication could be *Wednesbury* unreasonable.

[114] ATO, 'Publishing of private rulings' (7 May 2018).

[115] M Nolan, 'The Unsatisfactory State of Current Tax Law' [1981] 3 *Statute Law Review* 148, 151.

[116] See also J Booth, *Stand and Deliver! The Inland Revenue and Non-statutory Taxation* (Winchester, Waterside Press, 1998) 180.

[117] Inland Revenue, 'Tax Bulletin Issue 32' ('A Hundred Years of Inland Revenue Extra Statutory Concessions').

[118] Board of Inland Revenue, 'Extra-statutory concessions in operation at 8 August 1980' (IR1 (1980)).

[119] See: Board of Inland Revenue, 'Inland Revenue extra-statutory concessions as at June 1985' (IR1 (1985)) and Board of Inland Revenue, 'Extra-Statutory Concessions Supplement' (IR1 (Supp) (1987)).

[120] *Wilkinson* (n 11).

[121] See, for instance, HMRC, 'Withdrawal of extra statutory concessions – Technical Note' (December 2009) 13, for an unpublished concession which allowed VAT to be charged on school inspections supplied under contract to Ofsted.

[122] HMRC, 'Extra-statutory Concessions – Technical Consultation on draft Legislation' (November 2008) 35–36.

these concessions, however, were previously unpublished.[123] For instance, the paper enlisted a concession allowing modest expenses for travel and subsistence by self-employed persons.[124] Although this departed from the strict position otherwise outlined in HMRC's Manual,[125] it can be traced back to a written answer in the House of Commons in 1976. Robert Sheldon, then Financial Secretary to the Treasury, wrote that a self-employed person 'may be allowed a deduction for modest expenditure on meals consumed in the course of a travelling occupation or an occasional business journey outside the normal pattern'.[126] As such, although the concession has existed since 1976, it had nevertheless not been formally published. The other two unpublished concessions listed in this document related to an extra-statutory exemption from duty of spirits-based flavourings[127] and a concession relieving goods supplied for consumption during EU rail journeys from VAT, which dated back to the opening of the Channel tunnel in 1994.[128] In a document from April 2009, HMRC further sought comments on its proposal to remove two other unpublished concessions.[129] One related to grants provided by the Highlands and Islands Enterprise.[130] Some of these grants were strictly taxable as revenue receipts, but by concession from HMRC were treated as capital receipts. The other related to the longstanding unpublished concession entitled 'Equitable Liability'.[131] This concession concerned the acceptance of time-barred returns in instances where there was never a legal right to adjust the liability. This concession can be traced back at least to 1897 wherein the Revenue acknowledged that it remitted tax debts on grounds of equity.[132] Nevertheless, the concession was not published until 1995.[133]

Even today, post-*Wilkinson*, there is evidence of unpublished concessions issued to classes of taxpayers.[134] Indeed, John Avery Jones recently noted that 'It is sad to have to relate that unpublished concessions still exist'.[135] An example is the 'liable no longer liable' concession. Taxpayers are under an obligation to register

[123] ibid 5–6. Although there are five unlisted concessions in this document, two of these were previously to be found in HMRC manuals.

[124] ibid 31.

[125] HMRC, 'BIM37900 – Wholly and exclusively: expenditure having an intrinsic duality of purpose: contents' (May 2019).

[126] Hansard (HC Deb) Vol 922, cols 66–67W (6 December 1976).

[127] HMRC, 'Extra-statutory Concessions – Technical Consultation on draft Legislation' (n 122) 30.

[128] ibid 42.

[129] HMRC, 'Withdrawal of Extra-statutory Concessions – Technical Note' (April 2009).

[130] ibid 14.

[131] ibid 15.

[132] Public Accounts Committee, 'Second report from the committee of public accounts' (HC 1897–98, 261-VIII).

[133] Inland Revenue, 'Tax Bulletin: Issue 18' (August 1995).

[134] See for instance M James, *Taxation of Small Businesses 2016–2017*, 9th edn (London, Spiramus Press, 2016) 42.

[135] JA Jones, 'The equity of the executive: A commentary' in P Turner (ed), *Equity and Administration* (Cambridge, Cambridge University Press, 2016) 294 referring to *LH Bishop* (n 113) [510].

for VAT where they make taxable supplies in excess of the registration threshold.[136] The effect of the concession is that HMRC will not require a taxpayer to register for VAT where the taxpayer's turnover is fluctuating and though exceeds the registration threshold on one date, will fall below it on a future date.[137] It is contained in an HMRC Manual though the contents of the manual have been redacted on the basis of 'exemptions in the Freedom of Information Act 2000'.[138]

Finally, it is notable that in the UK, advice to individual taxpayers is not published. Whilst it would be impossible to publish all advice provided to individuals through informal rulings or other means, it would be possible to publish in redacted form the advice that is provided by way of formal ruling.[139] The redaction would have the effect of protecting taxpayer confidentiality, as required by section 18 of CRCA 2005.

C. Retrospective Changes

HMRC's general approach to advice is that it will not make retrospective changes. This is obviated, however, where it materialises that the relevant advice is in fact incorrect in law. Accordingly, where there is a change in HMRC advice and additional tax can be recovered from a taxpayer the starting point is that any tax due should be collected unless there is an overwhelming reason to not do so.[140] This approach undermines the ability of taxpayers to know what relevant HMRC advice applies at any given time, undermining the rule of law which requires stability over time.[141]

There are a series of examples which evidence this approach in practice. For instance, HMRC released guidance in 2005 which concerned inheritance tax (IHT). Finance Act 2004 introduced provisions which sought to limit the efficacy of IHT avoidance schemes. Prior to 2005, a variety of approaches were adopted to circumvent the IHT charge.[142] Sometimes, this would involve the asset owner (the 'settlor') setting up two trusts; selling the assets, financed by a loan from the settlor, to one trust (in which she had an interest); and placing the loan thereafter in the second trust (in which she had no interest or derived no benefit whatsoever).[143]

[136] Value Added Tax Act 1994, s 3; Sch 1, para 1; Sch 2, para 1; Sch 3, para 1; Sch 3A, para 1.

[137] See: N Warren, 'Liable Not Liable: The concession not mentioned in HMRC's registration manual' *Accountingweb* (21 August 2018).

[138] See the contents of HMRC, 'VAT Manual: VATREG28000' (October 2016).

[139] This occurs in Australia, for instance, ATO, 'Publishing of private rulings' (May 2018).

[140] Institute of Chartered Accountants in England and Wales, 'Legitimate Expectation and Reliance on HMRC Guidance' (Technical Release 06/13), 14. See also: HMRC, 'ADML1200 Incorrect Advice to Customers: Collection and management' (July 2016) and HMRC, 'ADML1605 What this means in practice: Incorrect Advice to Customers' (July 2016).

[141] Tasioulas, 'Rule of Law' (forthcoming).

[142] E Chamberlain and C Whitehouse, 'HMRC debacle? The efficacy of home loan schemes is in question' (2011) 167 *Taxation* 15, 16.

[143] ibid 15–16.

The scheme would have the effect of, on the death of the settlor, reducing the IHT charge on the assets in the first trust to nil as the loan would cancel out the value of the assets (assuming the assets did not appreciate in value).[144] As for the transfer of the debt to the second trust, lifetime transfers of assets are charged to IHT if the transferor dies within seven years of the transfer.[145] Accordingly, if the settlor survives seven years, then the transfer of the debt to the second trust also escapes tax.

Finance Act 2004 had the effect of seriously curtailing the efficacy of these schemes. By reason of paragraphs 11(6) and (7) of Schedule 15, the loan would be an 'excluded liability' and so would not be taken into account when calculating the IHT charge. Crucially for present purposes, HMRC's guidance in 2005 provided that it would challenge those schemes in which the loan was repayable on demand, but would accept those schemes where the debt was repayable only after the death of the asset owner who settled the trusts.[146] In 2010, however, HMRC amended the guidance to state that it would no longer accept as valid those schemes[147] and issued guidance in 2011 setting out in full the new approach.[148] Cases closed prior to the change in guidance would remain closed, but those where there was an open enquiry would be subject to the new interpretation.[149] This had the effect of retrospectively changing the tax treatment afforded to those who are unlucky enough still to have enquiries open.[150]

This approach to retrospective changes in HMRC advice was equally applied in relation to 'specialty debts' (a debt recorded in a deed) whereby HMRC changed the view it had adopted in its Manual. Previously, HMRC treated the debts as being situated in the jurisdiction 'where the instrument happens to be' (where the debt was created 'under seal') but from January 2013 would treat the debt as being situated in the jurisdiction where the debtor resides.[151]

It might be argued that the rule of law concern in the case of retrospective changes is misguided, as HMRC is simply seeking to correct past mistakes. Is it really a rule of law issue then if a taxpayer receives correct advice as to the true legal consequences of her actions if that advice replaces incorrect advice? Surely,

[144] ibid 16. Inheritance Tax Act 1984, s 49(1) provides that interest in possession trusts are subject to IHT on the value of the assets. As per *St Barbe Green v Inland Revenue Commissioners* [2005] EWHC 14 (Ch), [2005] STC 288, liabilities against the assets are deductible in deducing the relevant value.

[145] Inheritance Tax Act 1984, s 3A.

[146] E Chamberlain, 'Home loans: an update on common Inheritance Tax mitigation schemes' (April 2013) *Step Journal* 26, 27–28.

[147] T Harris, M McLaughlin, I Wunschmann-Lyall and C Erwood, *Core Tax Annual: Inheritance Tax 2011/12* (West Sussex, Bloomsbury Professional, 2011) 427.

[148] Chamberlain, 'Home loans' (2013) 28.

[149] M McLaughlin, I Wünschmann-Lyall and C Erwood, *Core Tax Annuals: Inheritance Tax 2015/16* (West Sussex, Bloomsbury Professional, 2015).

[150] See also *Hely-Hutchinson* (CA) (n 54).

[151] HMRC, 'IHTM27079 'Foreign property: specialty debts: bonds and debentures under seal' (May 2019).

the rule of law is undermined where laws are not applied correctly? This book argues[152] that incorrect advice does not undermine the rule of law in an aggregate sense, as taxpayers on the whole are better advised where HMRC produces advice, even if some is incorrect. Even in an individual case, the underlying value of the rule of law, namely human dignity, is respected where taxpayers are advised as to the de facto consequences of their actions. These arguments in any event are predicated on the assumption that HMRC's change in advice results in the new advice being legally correct, but whether this is the case is not a simple issue beyond the instance where a court has determined the new advice to be correct.

D. Mingling

Some publications are labelled as Guidance when they are more aligned with Codes of Practice, Statements of Practice, ESCs and so on. The sense overall from the available sources is that HMRC does not have a coherent streamlined system for the production of HMRC advice.[153] Where there is no framework for decisions as to whether HMRC advice should be produced, how this should occur and in what category of publication the advice should be placed, there will be inevitably be miscategorisation of HMRC advice.

Miscategorisation of different types of advice can have real practical consequences. First, it leads to incoherency in that the underlying text does not accord with the definition proposed at the beginning of the publication. If one of the purposes of HMRC advice is to inform taxpayers as to their rights and obligations under the law, then this objective will be undermined by this confusing presentation. Secondly, and more worryingly, it can be a trap for the unwary taxpayer who had assumed, for instance in the case of Guidance, that the publication contained merely a description of the law rather than some concessionary element. An issue of protection arises for the taxpayer where a concession is present as it may indicate that the advice is in fact incorrect and this may serve as a legal justification for HMRC going back on its advice.[154] A prudent taxpayer would be wary of relying upon concessions accordingly but might unwittingly fall into the trap of doing so and thereafter have her protection rescinded. Finally, miscategorisation undermines supervision of HMRC advice, as it directs attention away from issues where oversight is particularly warranted. This is notable again in respect of concessions as these instruments require more intense scrutiny to ensure that they do not overreach their proper boundaries. ESCs as a result of such issues are, at least in theory,

[152] See further below ch 6 in text at n 53.
[153] See above ch 2 in text at n 155.
[154] *Hely-Hutchinson* (CA) (n 54). See further below ch 6 in text at n 56.

supposed to be scrutinised by the National Audit Office & the Public Accounts Committee.[155]

There is much evidence of this issue of miscategorisation unfortunately having arisen in practice. In the wake of *Wilkinson*, HMRC acknowledged the existence of a number of ESCs which were incorrectly categorised in Manuals. For instance, if a taxpayer incurs capital expenditure on replacing plant or machinery, the taxpayer can claim by concession a revenue deduction for the replacement expenditure (a 'renewals allowance') for the purposes of income tax or corporation tax.[156] This concessionary treatment was previously not acknowledged and the treatment was to be found in a Revenue Manual, rather than in the list of published ESCs.[157] Similarly, disabled individuals without disabled persons' badges could previously calculate the private use benefit of their automatic company car based on the price and emissions of the equivalent manual car. This was acknowledged by HMRC as a concession post-*Wilkinson*[158] but had previously been found in a Revenue Manual.[159] On 4 August 2014, HMRC announced a change in practice in relation to the treatment of the use of unremitted foreign income or gains as collateral for a loan enjoyed in the UK.[160] It was remarked that the practice was concessionary, whilst the previous incarnation of the publication in a Revenue Manual however made no mention of any 'concession'.[161]

Concessions have also been found in HMRC Guidance, rather than in the published list of ESCs. For instance, it was previously prescribed[162] that HMRC would not issue penalties for late filing of certain returns provided they were received by 19 July following the end of the tax year (ie 5 April).[163] A similar concession operated in HMRC Guidance to the effect that a motor vehicle would be treated as a zero-rated supply if it were supplied to a disabled wheelchair user

[155] Treasury Minute dated 31 December 1897 on the Reports relating to Civil and Miscellaneous Accounts, 1895–96 in Public Accounts Committee, 'Second report from the committee of public accounts' (HC 1897–98, 261) 147–49. See below, however, ch 5 in text at n 106.

[156] HMRC, 'Withdrawal of Extra-statutory Concessions – Technical note and call for evidence' (December 2011).

[157] See: HMRC, 'BIM46935: Renewals allowances for capital expenditure on plant and machinery' (May 2019).

[158] HMRC, 'Withdrawal of Extra-statutory Concessions – Technical note and call for evidence' (above n 156).

[159] HMRC, 'EIM24900 PAYE: Company cars for disabled drivers without blue badges'.

[160] HMRC News, 'Remittance Basis' (August 2014).

[161] HMRC, 'Remittance Basis: Identifying Remittances: Conditions A and B: Condition B – collateral in respect of relevant debt' (October 2010). On 15 October 2015, it was announced that the concessionary treatment would not be withdrawn retrospectively; see HMRC, 'Revenue and Customs Brief 16' (October 2015).

[162] HMRC, 'CWG5 Class 1A National Insurance contributions on benefits in kind – A guide for employers', para 25.

[163] HMRC, 'Withdrawal of extra statutory concessions – Technical note and call for evidence' (above n 156).

and shortly after adapted for their specifications.[164] Ordinarily, this treatment was reserved for supplies of vehicles *already* adapted for use by a disabled person.[165] A previous concession found in VAT Guidance allowed dining rooms and kitchens to be zero-rated as residential accommodation for students and school pupils if they were used 'predominantly' by the students.[166] Strictly, zero-rating would only apply where the buildings were used 'solely' for a relevant residential purpose.[167] Finally, an ESC once operated to allow hotels, inns, boarding houses and similar establishments to apply the 'reduced value rule' where a long-term resident had vacated the accommodation with no continuing right to the accommodation during their absence.[168] The provision of sleeping accommodation in a hotel, inn, boarding house or similar establishment is standard rated for VAT purposes.[169] However where accommodation is provided to an individual for a period of over 28 days, VAT need only be charged on that part of the payment that is not for accommodation. This is the 'reduced value rule'.[170] Strictly, the rule would cease to apply if there were *any* break in the residence, such as even a weekend away.[171] By concession published in HMRC Public Notice 709/3, the rule would continue to apply if a long-term resident left for an occasional holiday; or if a student left during vacation and returned to the same accommodation the following term.[172]

V. Conclusion

There is certainly some merit in the arguments of those such as David Williams who have criticised the way in which HMRC has used its advice. HMRC have been found on occasion to favour particular classes of persons and to produce advice inconsistent with the underlying law. To go beyond the boundaries of the power to issue advice is a matter of constitutional impropriety regardless of whether concessions to particular classes of taxpayers might be defensible for non-legal reasons. Purposeful departure from the wording of statutes aside, legal misconceptions and misapplication too fail to enlighten taxpayers as to the true legal consequences of their actions. Unduly ambiguous pieces of advice meanwhile serve to undermine the rule of law justification for the very existence of HMRC advice.

[164] HMRC, 'Withdrawal of extra statutory concessions – Technical note' (December 2010) 11.
[165] VAT Act 1994, Sch 8, Group 12, Items 2(f), 2A and Note 5L.
[166] HMRC, 'Withdrawal of extra statutory concessions – Technical note and call for evidence' (January 2014) 9–10.
[167] VAT Act 1994, Sch 8, Group 5, Items 1 and 2.
[168] HMRC, 'Technical note and call for evidence' (2014) 11.
[169] VAT Act 1994, Sch 9, Group 1, Item 1, para (d).
[170] VAT Act 1994, Sch 6, para 9.
[171] HMRC, 'Technical note and call for evidence' (n 166) 11.
[172] See now, HMRC, 'VAT Notice 709/3: hotels and holiday accommodation' (February 2019).

It is clear too from the foregoing investigation that several issues in respect of the accessibility of HMRC advice will arise. Admittedly, as a starting point, resource limitations will dictate that access will need to be compromised. Not all taxpayers can be entitled to the same bespoke, expert and timely advice, though provision can be made to minimise inequalities of assistance. In any event, advice should where possible be publicised to those it concerns, retrospective changes should be guarded against and mingling of advice containing concessionary elements should be avoided.

The problems of correctness, clarity and accessibility also have the effect of undermining the reliability of HMRC advice.[173] However, the most immediate and pressing question which should follow from a reading of this chapter must be: how are these problems permitted to propagate? To answer that question, we should turn to consider the mechanisms for scrutiny which operate in respect of HMRC advice.

[173] To which we will turn in ch 6.

5

Scrutiny

> HMRC has considerable power at its disposal, but with that power comes a responsibility to act proportionately, appropriately and fairly, and with regard for the law and its own internal procedures.*

I. Introduction

HMRC occupies a curious space in the state. As a non-ministerial body,[1] the traditional elements of individual ministerial responsibility are eschewed.[2] Ministers and the Treasury are at arm's length from the everyday activities of HMRC.[3] But there is nevertheless a nexus such as to make them at least politically responsible for indiscretions of the body.[4] The Treasury Select Committee has highlighted the resulting paradox:

> It is regrettable that the HMRC's relationship with HM Treasury can give rise to a situation where a Minister can recognise publicly that a problem exists in a department which is within his remit, but tell Parliament that he is powerless to take action to bring about improvement.[5]

The level of Ministerial and Treasury involvement is limited to providing directions of a general nature which shall be complied with by HMRC.[6] For instance,

* Parliamentary and Health Service Ombudsman, 'Annual Report 2008–09' (HC 2008–09, 786) 12 (Ann Abraham). Cf D Oliver, 'Ombudsmen in search of a role' (1978) 41 *MLR* 446, 452.

[1] Explanatory Notes to the Commissioners for Revenue and Customs Act 2005, para 6.

[2] On individual responsibility, see: C Turpin and A Tomkins, *British government and the constitution: text and materials,* 7th edn (Cambridge, Cambridge University Press, 2011) 573–91. On issues of accountability, see: M Flinders, *Delegated Governance and the British State* (Oxford, Oxford University Press, 2008) ch. 6; J Rutter, *The Strange Case of Non-Ministerial Departments* (Institute for Government, October 2013) 7–11.

[3] See Explanatory Notes to the Commissioners for Revenue and Customs Act 2005, para 71.

[4] For instance, George Osborne came in for a lot of criticism in relation to HMRC's settlement with Google of its past tax affairs in the first half of 2016. See G Parker and V Houlder 'Backlash builds against Google tax deal' *The Financial Times* (25 January 2016); J Freedman, 'UK institutions for tax governance: reviewing tax settlements' [2016] *British Tax Review* 7, 8.

[5] Treasury Select Committee, *Closing the Tax Gap: HMRC's Record at Ensuring Tax Compliance* (HC 2010–12, 1371) para 90.

[6] Commissioners for Revenue and Customs Act 2005, s 11.

HMRC and the Treasury together have a 'policy partnership' arrangement whereby the Treasury leads on strategic tax policy and policy development. HMRC leads on policy maintenance and implementation.[7] HMRC's Single Departmental Plan is an example of this policy partnership arrangement in practice. This is a joint venture between the Financial Secretary to the Treasury (a junior ministerial post) and HMRC's Permanent Secretaries and sets out HMRC's objectives as well as how it is intended they shall be achieved.[8] Formal control of the everyday actions of HMRC accordingly does not arise at a ministerial level, but rather is exercised by senior civil servants. In HMRC, the Chief Executive and Permanent Secretary is responsible to Parliament for the department's expenditure and performance.[9] This means that the buck should stop with civil servants in terms of inadequacies in HMRC advice. What can be gleaned from chapter two, however, is that internal scrutiny of advice, if it occurs at all, is done on an *ad hoc* basis and there is no general oversight framework.[10]

An assessment of the scrutiny exercised by external bodies and parties is accordingly necessary.[11] Whilst the previous chapter concerned problems with HMRC advice as it is produced, this and the subsequent chapter are concerned with the system of advice (though obviously there will be a symbiotic relationship between the system and the resulting advice). Parliament can exercise control through select committees, the formal vehicles through which scrutiny of HMRC is to take place. An independent body meanwhile performs external audits and the tribunals and courts undertake indirect regulation. Other channels of scrutiny have been created and have developed over the years, as in the case of the Adjudicator's Office ('Adjudicator') and Parliamentary and Health Service Ombudsman ('Ombudsman'). It is not necessary for scrutiny to take place only in Westminster or The Strand, however. Taxpayers and organisations representing taxpayers, including professional bodies, can play an important role in the scrutinising process too. This chapter will, however, demonstrate that there are serious shortcomings in terms of how these bodies scrutinise HMRC advice. Whilst some aspects are positive – for instance the contribution of the Adjudicator, the Ombudsman and taxpayers – the conclusion which must be arrived at is that there is inadequate examination of the correctness, clarity and accessibility of HMRC advice.[12]

[7] HMRC, 'IDG52200: Information disclosure Gateways with other government departments: HM Treasury (HMT)' (March 2019).

[8] HMRC, 'HM Revenue and Customs single departmental plan' (June 2019).

[9] See HMRC, 'Code of governance for resolving tax disputes' (October 2017) 13.

[10] See above ch 2 in text at n 155.

[11] There has been much criticism over the years of the degree of scrutiny to which HMRC is subjected. See, for instance, House of Lords Select Committee on Economic Affairs, 'Tackling Corporate Tax Avoidance in a Global Economy: is a New Approach Needed?' (HL 2013–14, 48) para 124; Judith Freedman evidence para 122; Margaret Hodge para 119.

[12] This chapter is derived in part from S Daly, 'Oversight of HMRC Soft-Law: Lessons from the Ombudsman' (2016) 38 *Journal of Social Welfare and Family Law* 343, available at: www.tandfonline.com/doi/full/10.1080/09649069.2016.1228147.

This chapter will proceed by first assessing the part played by Parliament, through its select committees along with the Comptroller and Auditor General and National Audit Office. Secondly, the roles of the Adjudicator and Ombudsman will be considered. The limited contributions of the tribunals and courts will then be assessed before finally turning to the involvement of taxpayers and representative groups.

II. Parliamentary Scrutiny

A. Treasury Select Committee

The Treasury Select Committee (TSC) is appointed by the House of Commons to examine the expenditure, administration and policy of HM Treasury, HMRC and associated public bodies.[13] It was established in 1979 as The Treasury and Civil Service Select Committee[14] and, along with other departmental committees, owes its genesis to the Procedure Committee, which was founded under James Callaghan's Labour administration in 1976[15] and recommended the introduction of committees in 1978.[16] The object was to rationalise the system for parliamentary scrutiny of government departments.[17]

In order to perform its primary function of examining expenditure, administration and policy, the committee has the power to 'send for persons, papers and records'.[18] Its power to summon witnesses, not merely from public institutions but also from industry and academia,[19] is unqualified 'except to the extent that it conflicts with the privileges of the Crown and of the Members of the House of Lords, or with the rights of Members of the House of Commons'.[20] Although the TSC itself cannot enforce its order, a refusal to comply can be reported to the House, which might thereafter treat the refusal as contempt.[21] In practice, however, the formal power is rarely used and the committees prefer to proceed

[13] For statutory authority, see Standing Order No 152.

[14] The title was changed to 'TSC' during the 1992–97 Parliament. See: Treasury Select Committee, *Second special report* (HC 1995–96, 24) ii.

[15] P Laugharne 'The Treasury and Civil Service Select Committee during the Thatcher Administration' (2007) 26 *Parliamentary History* 225.

[16] Select committee on procedure, 'First Report' (HC 1977–78, 588-I).

[17] ibid xlviii.

[18] Standing Order No 152(4)(a).

[19] Standing Order No 152(4)(a); J McFall, 'The Treasury Select Committee: its reach and its role in the financial crisis' (2009) 29 *Economic Affairs* 53, 53.

[20] W McKay, M Hutton and A Sandall (eds), *Erskine May's Treatise on the Law, Privileges, Proceedings and Usage of Parliament*, 23rd edn (Oxford, Butterworths, 2004) 647, noted in O Mba, 'Transparency and accountability of tax administration in the UK: the nature and scope of taxpayer confidentiality' [2012] *British Tax Review* 187, 193.

[21] Turpin and Tomkins, *British government* (2011) 620.

by invitation rather than by command.[22] How exactly this power interacts with other legal provisions is also not entirely clear. Though the rules are provided in a Standing Order, thereby suggesting that primary legislation ought to take precedence where there is a clash, the power of contempt is vested in Parliament rather than in courts, thereby complicating the issue. During the 'Settlements' scandal, wherein questions were raised over settlements that HMRC arrived at with several multinationals,[23] senior members of HMRC refused to answer questions from another select committee, the Public Accounts Committee (PAC), which has the same power to send for 'persons, papers and records'.[24] The refusal was based on an assertion that employees of HMRC were proscribed from relinquishing taxpayer information on the basis of the duty of confidentiality enshrined in section 18 of the Commissioners for Revenue and Customs Act 2005.[25] This notoriously led to Anthony Inglese, former General Counsel and Solicitor at HMRC, being forced to swear an oath as the Committee was 'not able to get answers' from the lawyer.[26] After taking the oath he nevertheless continued to hold firm, refusing to disclose taxpayer information.[27] The PAC did not seek to sanction Inglese and this unfortunate episode is probably as close as we will ever come to a clash between rules of law and powers of Parliament in a tax context.

From this cursory overview of the TSC's remit, it would appear that the body is concerned more broadly with aspects of administration, policies undertaken and value for money, than the scrutiny of HMRC advice. Analysis of the TSC's[28] relationship with HMRC, through examination of the reports undertaken by the body relating to HMRC since the inception of the TSC, reveals this to be precisely the case.

During the short 2015–17 Parliamentary session, the TSC reported on the appointment of various figures in HMRC,[29] and HMRC proposals in respect of 'Making Tax Digital'.[30] In respect of the latter, the Committee did at several times recommend that HMRC should produce 'clear guidance' so as to smooth the transition to digitalisation,[31] but left it to HMRC to tease out what in substance such advice should look like. This is similar to the recommendation of the TSC

[22] ibid.

[23] See: National Audit Office, 'Settling large tax disputes' (June 2012).

[24] Standing Order No 148.

[25] Public Accounts Committee, 'HM Revenue & Customs 2010–11 Accounts: tax disputes' (HC 2010–12, 1531) 9–12; Ev 3, Q25, Q33 (David Hartnett); Ev 113, Q84 (Lesley Strathie).

[26] ibid Ev 44, Q533. Inglese retired shortly after and may take some minor comfort from the fact that his position was later upheld by the Supreme Court in *R (Ingenious Media and McKenna) v HMRC* [2016] UKSC 54, [2016] 1 WLR 4164.

[27] See for instance PAC, 'Tax disputes' (n 25) Q582.

[28] It should be noted that this analysis also includes TSC's sub-committee.

[29] See Treasury Select Committee, 'Appointment of Jon Thompson as Chief Executive of HMRC' (HC 2016–17, 232) and Treasury Select Committee, 'Appointment of Edward Troup as Executive Chair of HMRC' (HC 2016–17, 498).

[30] Treasury Select Committee, 'Making Tax Digital' (HC 2016–17, 927).

[31] ibid 23, 30, 40–41.

in the 2017–19 session wherein the body investigated the conduct of tax enquiries.[32] The TSC recommended that HMRC reviews and improves the accessibility, quality and level of detail of guidance it gives to vulnerable taxpayers, owing to concerns raised by the Low Incomes Tax Reform Group and Chartered Institute of Taxation.[33]

This recent, surface-level focus by the TSC upon the need for particular pieces of HMRC advice and for the advice to be of a particular quality stands out as it contrasts with the concerns the body more routinely focuses upon. During the 2010–15 session, the TSC examined the (approximately) six million under- and overpayments of tax revealed in September 2010,[34] the tax gap[35] (including through questioning of David Hartnett, then Permanent Secretary for Tax at HMRC over the Goldman Sachs revelations)[36] and the operation of the PAYE system.[37] Additionally, Lin Homer (former Chief Executive of HMRC) produced a letter for the TSC with information concerning the publication of HMRC's Business Plan 2014–16,[38] whilst the TSC also held an inquiry into revelations that a significant number of UK residents had secret Swiss bank accounts possibly being used to evade UK taxes.[39]

Over the course of the 2005–2010 session, the TSC investigated the closure and movement of offices, relationship with Mapeley,[40] staff morale,[41] child trust funds,[42] administration issues (such as data security[43] and tax credits[44]), expenditure,[45] and the merger of the Inland Revenue and Customs and Excise departments.[46]

For the 2001–2005 session, the TSC probed the Spring Departmental Reports (which investigates policies, strategies, expenditure and organisational matters),[47]

[32] Treasury Select Committee, 'Disputing Tax' (HC 2017–19, 1914). This is the only report during that session which related to HMRC at the time of writing, September 2019.

[33] ibid 19–20.

[34] Treasury Select Committee, '16th Report: Administration and effectiveness of HM Revenue and Customs' (HC 2010–12, 731).

[35] Treasury Select Committee, '29th Report – Closing the Tax Gap: HMRC's record at ensuring tax compliance' (HC 2010–12, 1371).

[36] ibid 20.

[37] Treasury Select Committee, 'HMRC's operation of the PAYE system' (HC 2010–12, 479-I).

[38] L Homer, 'Letter to Andrew Tyrie, Chair of the Treasury Select Committee' (3 July 2014).

[39] Treasury Select Committee, 'HM Revenue and Customs and HSBC' (HC 2014–15, 1071).

[40] Mapeley STEPS is a private sector consortium to which the ownership and management of the estates of the Inland Revenue and Customs and Excise were transferred.

[41] Treasury Select Committee, 'Minutes of Evidence for 25 June 2008' (HC 2007–08, 852-I).

[42] Treasury Select Committee, 'Child Trust Funds follow up' (HC 2007–08, 537-I); Treasury Select Committee, 'Minutes of Evidence for 30 November 2005' (HC 2005–06, 738-I).

[43] Treasury Select Committee, 'Minutes of Evidence for 29 October 2008' (HC 2007–08, 1097-III).

[44] Treasury Select Committee, 'Minutes of Evidence for 14 March 2007' (HC 2006–07, 382-I); Treasury Select Committee, '6th Report: The administration of tax credits' (HC 2010–12, 811).

[45] Treasury Select Committee, 'Minutes of Evidence for 22 November 2006' (HC 2006–07, 51-I); Treasury Select Committee, 'Minutes of Evidence for 26 and 12 October 2005' (HC 2005–06, 524-I, II).

[46] Treasury Select Committee, 'Minutes of Evidence for 24 January 2007' (HC 2006–07, 192-I).

[47] Treasury Select Committee, 'Minutes of Evidence for 30 June 2004' (HC 2003–04, 908-I); Treasury Select Committee, 'Minutes of Evidence for 21 July 2004' (HC 2003–04, 835-I); Treasury Select Committee, 'Minutes of Evidence for Wednesday 4 June 2003' (HC 2002–03, 746-I). In addition to further organisational matters analysed by the body: Treasury Select Committee, 'Minutes of Evidence for Wednesday 26 June 2002' (HC 2001–02, 1011).

fraud relating to excise duty[48] and alcohol duty,[49] the merger of the Inland Revenue and Customs and Excise,[50] the transfer of the management of their estates to Mapeley STEPS,[51] the working family tax credit,[52] and the administrative costs of tax compliance.[53] The TSC further reported on the performance of the self-assessment system,[54] on restricting the use of offshore tax structures, the implementation of tax credits, and the suspension of National Insurance Contributions Deficiency Notices (which essentially state that one owes National Insurance).[55]

Between 1997 and 2001, the TSC reported on matters relating to Customs and Excise such as the body's success in achieving compliance;[56] tackling the shadow economy;[57] the impact of non-compliance on compliant businesses;[58] the potential for closer working with the Inland Revenue;[59] and the collection of excise duties.[60] Customs and Excise also gave evidence on updates in connection with recommendations from previous reports.[61] Meanwhile, the TSC conducted a significant report into the Inland Revenue's approach to compliance.[62] From 1992 to 1997, the Inland Revenue and Customs and Excise were mentioned in a series of ancillary reports.[63] Furthermore, during the 1994/95 session, following significant losses in

[48] Treasury Select Committee, 'Minutes of Evidence for 17 November 2004' (HC 2003–04, 1281-I).

[49] Treasury Select Committee, 'Minutes of Evidence for Wednesday 14 November 2001' (HC 2001–02, 371-I).

[50] Treasury Select Committee, 'Ninth Report: The Merger of Customs & Excise and the Inland Revenue' (HC 2003–04, 556).

[51] Treasury Select Committee, 'Fourth Report: The Handling of the Joint Inland Revenue/Customs and Excise Steps PFI Project' (HC 2002–03, 184).

[52] Treasury Select Committee, 'Minutes of Evidence for Wednesday 19th June 2002' (HC 2001–02, 975).

[53] Treasury Select Committee, '7th Report: The Administrative Costs of Tax Compliance' (HC 2003–04, 269).

[54] Treasury Select Committee, 'Inland Revenue: Self Assessment Systems' (HC 2001–02, 681); see also: Treasury Select Committee, 'Minutes of Evidence for Wednesday 6th March 2002' (HC 2001–02, 681-I).

[55] Treasury Select Committee, 'Tenth Report: Inland Revenue Matters' (HC 2002–03, 834).

[56] Treasury Select Committee, 'Second Report' (HC 1999–00, 53).

[57] ibid.

[58] ibid.

[59] ibid.

[60] Treasury Select Committee, 'Sixth Report' (HC 2000–01, 237).

[61] Treasury Select Committee, 'Minutes of Evidence for Wednesday 1 November 2000' (HC 1999–00, 953).

[62] Treasury Select Committee, 'Sixth Report' (HC 1998–99, 199).

[63] Treasury Select Committee, 'Third Report: the 1996 Budget' (HC 1996–97, 129); Treasury Select Committee, 'Third report: the 1995 budget' (HC 1995–96, 79); Treasury Select Committee, 'First report: the cross border market in excise products' (HC 1995–96, 24); Treasury and Civil Service Committee, 'Fourth report: Simplified estimates and resource accounting together with the proceedings of the committee, minutes of evidence and appendices' (HC 1994–95, 212); Treasury and Civil Service Committee, 'The city research project: Minutes of evidence' (HC 1994–95, 533); Treasury and Civil Service Committee, 'Financial Services Regulation: Minutes of evidence' (HC 1994–95, 187-I); Treasury and Civil Service Committee Sub-Committee, 'The role of the Civil Service '(HC 1993–94, 27-I); Treasury and Civil Service Committee Sub-Committee, 'The role of the Civil Service' (HC 1993–94, 27-VIII); Treasury and Civil Service Committee sub-committee, 'The role of the Civil Service: minutes of evidence' (HC 1992–93, 390-VIII); Treasury and Civil Service Committee, 'Sixth report: The role

revenue as a result of an exponential increase in personal imports of beer, wine and tobacco following the opening of the European Single Market in 1993, the TSC undertook an extensive report into cross-border shopping.[64]

During the 1987–1992 sitting of Parliament, both bodies were mentioned in ancillary reports,[65] provided information for reports on general matters not pertaining specifically to the work of either body[66] and submitted evidence for the (then) recently introduced system of departmental reports.[67] The TSC commissioned a report compiling the effect of manpower losses at both departments[68] and elsewhere made a number of recommendations on the use of economic statistics.[69]

From 1983 to 1987, as with the previous sitting, both bodies were referred to in ancillary reports,[70] provided evidence for reports on general matters[71] and supplied

of the Civil Service' (Interim report) (HC 1992–93, 390); Treasury and Civil Service Committee Sub-Committee, 'The role of the Civil Service: minutes of evidence' (HC 1992–93, 390-VII).

[64] Treasury and Civil Service Committee, 'First report: Cross border shopping' (HC 1994–95, 35).

[65] Treasury and Civil Service Committee, 'Eighth report: Progress in the next steps initiative' (HC 1989–90, 481); Treasury and Civil Service Committee, 'Sixth report: The presentation of information on public expenditure' (HC 1988–89, 217); Treasury and Civil Service Committee, 'Fifth report: Developments in the Next Steps Programme' (HC 1988–89, 348); Treasury and Civil Service Committee Sub-Committee, 'The civil service management reform: the next steps' (HC 1987–88, 494-I); Treasury and Civil Service Committee, 'Seventh report: Public expenditure and estimates' (HC 1987–88, 506); Treasury and Civil Service Committee, 'Second report: The government's public expenditure plans 1988–89 to 1990–91' (HC 1987–88, 292). The Inland Revenue was additionally mentioned in a report on the 1988 budget, see: Treasury and Civil Service Committee, 'Fourth report: The 1988 budget' (HC 1987–88, 400).

[66] Treasury and Civil Service Committee, 'First report: The 1990 autumn statement' (HC 1990–91, 41); Treasury and Civil Service Committee, 'Sixth report: Public expenditure' (HC 1989–90, 466); Treasury and Civil Service Committee, 'Second report: The work of the valuation office' (HC 1989–90, 223); Treasury and Civil Service Committee, 'Third report: International debt strategy' (HC 1989–90, 138); Treasury and Civil Service Committee, 'Third report the European Commission's proposals on the approximation of indirect taxation' (HC 1987–88, 248).

[67] Treasury and Civil Service Committee, 'Fifth report: The new system of departmental reports' (HC 1990–91, 290).

[68] Treasury and Civil Service Committee, 'Manpower losses in the revenue departments' (1988–89, 155-I).

[69] Treasury and Civil Service Committee, 'Official economic statistics' (HC 1989–90, 671); Treasury and Civil Service Committee, 'Official economic statistics' (HC 1988–89, 181-I); Treasury and Civil Service Committee, 'Official economic statistics' (HC 1988–89, 181-II).

[70] Treasury and Civil Service Committee, 'Fifth report' (HC 1986–87, 84); Treasury and Civil Service Committee, 'Third report' (HC 1986–87, 153); Treasury and Civil Service Committee, 'International credit and capital markets' (1985–86 HC 464-I); Treasury and Civil Service Committee, 'Sixth report: The government's expenditure plans 1985–86 to 1987–88' (HC 1984–85, 213); Treasury and Civil Service Committee, 'Sixth Report: Estimates 1984–85' (HC 1983–84, 516); Treasury and Civil Service Committee, 'Fourth report: The 1984 budget' (HC 1983–84, 341); Treasury and Civil Service Committee, 'Second report: The structure and form of financial documents presented to Parliament' (HC 1984–85, 110).

[71] Treasury and Civil Service Select Committee, 'Civil service recruitment, training & career management & public service manpower' (HC 1986–87, 358-I); Treasury and Civil Service Committee, 'The financial and economic consequences of UK membership of the European communities' (HC 1984–85, 57-II); Treasury and Civil Service Committee Sub-Committee, 'Acceptance of outside appointments by Crown servants' (HC 1983–84, 302); Treasury and Civil Service Committee Sub-Committee, 'The financial and economic consequences of UK membership of the European communities' (HC 1984–85, 57-I).

information on expenditure.[72] The TSC specifically reported on the monitoring of corporate tax receipts;[73] VAT;[74] tax office delays at the Inland Revenue;[75] and organisational issues (such as systems for tackling the illicit drug trade and deferment guarantees on warehoused goods) at Customs and Excise.[76]

Finally, during the 1979–1983 session, both bodies were cited in tangential reports,[77] provided evidence for general reports[78] and submitted information for a report on the structure of income taxation.[79]

It is not doubted that the TSC provides a 'vital link in the British democratic system'[80] by examining the expenditure, administration and policy of HMRC. Nevertheless, the TSC is most at home when crunching figures, asking hard-hitting questions of HMRC's internal inefficiencies and assessing its policies for tackling emerging issues. The analysis of the reports undertaken here confirms

[72] Treasury and Civil Service Committee, 'Supply estimates 1987–88' (HC 1986–87, 332-I); Treasury and Civil Service Committee, 'Supply estimates 1987–88' (HC 1986–87, 332-I); Treasury and Civil Service Committee, 'Supply estimates' (HC 1985–86, 38-i); Treasury and Civil Service Committee, 'Memoranda on long-term trends in resources and public expenditure' (HC 1984–85, 141); Treasury and Civil Service Committee, 'Supply estimates 1985–86' (HC 1984–85, 369-I).

[73] Treasury and Civil Service Committee, 'Sixth report' (HC 1986–87, 293).

[74] Treasury and Civil Service Committee, 'Fourth report' (HC 1986–87, 45).

[75] Treasury and Civil Service Committee, 'Inland revenue: tax office delays' (HC 1985–86, 165-I).

[76] Treasury and Civil Service Committee, 'Sixth Report: Estimates 1984–85' (HC 1983–84, 487-I); Treasury and Civil Service Committee, 'Sixth Report: Estimates 1984–85' (HC 1983–84, 516).

[77] Treasury and Civil Service Committee, 'Memorandum on efficiency and effectiveness in the civil service' (HC 1982–83, 118); Treasury and Civil Service Committee, 'First special report' (HC 1982–83, 46); Treasury and Civil Service Committee, 'Fourth report: International monetary arrangements: international lending by banks' (HC 1982–83, 21); Treasury and Civil Service Committee, 'Civil service pay' (HC 1982–83, 19-I); Treasury and Civil Service Committee Sub-Committee, 'Efficiency and effectiveness in the Civil Service' (HC 1980–81, 360-III); Treasury and Civil Service Committee, 'Seventh report: Civil service manpower reductions' (HC 1980–81, 423); Treasury and Civil Service Committee, 'Fifth report: The 1981 budget and the government's expenditure plans 1981–82 to 1983–84' (HC 1980–81, 232); Treasury and Civil Service Committee Sub-Committee, 'Efficiency and effectiveness in the Civil Service' (HC 1980–81, 360-II); Treasury and Civil Service Committee, 'Fourth report' (HC 1979–80, 712).

[78] Treasury and Civil Service Committee, 'Third report: Efficiency and Effectiveness of the Civil Service' (HC 1981–82, 236); Treasury and Civil Service Committee, 'Budgetary reform in the UK' (HC 1981–82, 137); Treasury and Civil Service Committee, 'The 1981 budget and the government's expenditure plans 1981–82 to 1983–84' (HC 1980–81, 232-I); Treasury and Civil Service Committee, 'First report: The future of the Civil Service Department' (HC 1980–81, 54); Treasury and Civil Service Committee, 'Fifth report: The 1981 budget' (n 77); Treasury and Civil Service Committee Sub-Committee, 'Tax changes in the March 1980 Budget' (HC 1979–80, 554-I, II and III); Treasury and Civil Service Committee, 'Second report: The budget and the government's expenditure plans 1980–81 to 1983–84' (HC 1979–80, 584); Treasury and Civil Service Committee, 'Efficiency of the Civil Service' (HC 1979–80, 333-II, IV, V and VII); Treasury and Civil Service Committee, 'Fourth report: Civil Service manpower reductions' (HC 1979–80, 712).

[79] Treasury and Civil Service Committee Sub-Committee, 'The structure of personal income taxation and income support' (HC 1981–82, 331); Treasury and Civil Service Committee, 'Third special report: The Structure of Personal Income Taxation and Income Support' (HC 1982–83, 386); Treasury and Civil Service Committee Sub-Committee, 'The structure of personal income taxation and income support' (HC 1982–83, 20-I); Treasury and Civil Service Committee Sub-Committee, 'The structure of personal income taxation and income support' (HC 1982–83, 20-II).

[80] McFall, 'The Treasury Select Committee' (2009) 54.

that it focuses broadly on aspects of administration, policies undertaken and value for money, and not, importantly, the scrutiny of HMRC advice.

B. Comptroller and Auditor General, National Audit Office and PAC

The Comptroller and Auditor General (CAG), National Audit Office (NAO), and PAC operate an interrelated supervisory role over HMRC.[81] The CAG carries out examinations into the economy, efficiency and effectiveness with which governmental departments use their resources in discharging their functions.[82] The officeholder accordingly has considerable discretion to decide what areas of tax administration to examine,[83] although the primary function has, since the office's inception in 1866,[84] been to examine accounts on behalf of the House of Commons.[85] The CAG is head of the NAO,[86] which has approximately 800 staff,[87] and an officer of the House of Commons.[88] Being an auditor, the NAO's primary function is executed by way of auditing the financial statements of government departments and evaluating value for money within public spending.[89] The NAO also carries out investigations into areas of concern,[90] such as the report into the settling of large tax disputes by HMRC, otherwise known as the 'Settlements' scandal.[91] Additionally, the body acts on an international level,[92] for instance carrying out external audits for other international organisations.[93] The NAO also supports the services of Parliament[94] by presenting its reports to the PAC[95] which, like the TSC, is a select committee of the House of Commons. Most reports of the NAO and CAG are used as the basis of PAC hearings.[96]

[81] This section develops an argument made in S Daly, 'The Life and Times of ESCs: A defence?' in P Harris and D de Cogan (eds), *Studies in the History of Tax Law: Volume 8* (Oxford, Hart Publishing, 2017) 192–93. This section more generally is derived in part from that contribution.

[82] National Audit Act 1983, s 6(1).

[83] National Audit Act 1983, s 1(3); National Audit Office, 'Increasing the effectiveness of tax collection: a stocktake of progress since 2010' (February 2015) (HC 2014–15, 1029-I).

[84] Exchequer and Audit Departments Act 1866 created the post.

[85] J McEldowney, 'Public Expenditure and the Control of Public Finance' in J Jowell and D Oliver, *The Changing Constitution*, 7th edn (Oxford, Oxford University Press, 2011) 357.

[86] National Audit Act 1983, s 3(1)(a).

[87] National Audit Office, 'About us'.

[88] National Audit Act 1983, s 1(2).

[89] NAO (n 87).

[90] ibid.

[91] NAO, 'Settling large tax disputes' (n 23).

[92] NAO (n 87).

[93] T Daintith and A Page, *The Executive in the Constitution: Structure, Autonomy, and Internal Control* (Oxford, Oxford University Press, 1999) 194.

[94] NAO (n 87).

[95] Daintith and Page, *The Executive in the Constitution* (1999) 197.

[96] NAO (n 87); NAO, 'Increasing the effectiveness of tax collection' (n 83) 5; McEldowney, 'Public Expenditure' (2011) 356.

The PAC was established in 1861 by a resolution of the House of Commons.[97] It is appointed to examine 'the accounts showing the appropriation of the sums granted to Parliament to meet the public expenditure, and of such other accounts laid before Parliament as the Committee may think fit'.[98] Together with the NAO and CAG accordingly, the committee is provided with the authority to scrutinise HMRC and hold it to account for its administration of the tax system.[99] The bodies' main method of affecting change is through recommendations to government,[100] but at times they choose to heighten awareness of the underlying issues by courting publicity.[101] For this reason, although the constitutional importance is not in dispute here,[102] the bodies may stir up ill feelings.[103]

By way of powers, the PAC has the same power to send for 'persons, papers and records'[104] as the TSC. The CAG, meanwhile, has right of access to all such documents as may be reasonably required for executing its functions.[105]

Unlike the TSC, the three entities have a distinct mandate apropos HMRC advice, specifically ESCs, traceable back to a Treasury Minute from 1897.[106] The Bank of England held part of the estate of Alexander III of Russia and a concession attempted to exempt this segment from death duty.[107] The Treasury, perturbed by such gratuitous relaxations of the law by the Inland Revenue, put in place a process for overseeing individual and class concessions. Individual concessions above £50 would be furnished yearly to the CAG, together with the reasons for the dispensations.[108] The CAG would thereafter use her 'discretion with care and tact' and report to the PAC any particular concession that it was considered ought to be highlighted.[109] It was stressed that class concessions, meanwhile, should be put on a statutory footing at the earliest opportunity.[110] Although the PAC was clearly concerned with the use of concessions, it is notable that their cessation was not suggested.

Accordingly, and distinct from the case of the TSC, it is not necessary to comprehensively analyse the bodies' relationship with HMRC in order to

[97] *Hansard*, HC Deb Vol 166, cols 329–30 (31 March 1862). See now: Standing Order No 148.
[98] Standing Order No 148(1).
[99] NAO (n 83) 5.
[100] NAO (n 83) 5.
[101] Daintith and Page (n 93) 198.
[102] McEldowney (n 85) 356. See generally G Drewry (ed), *The New Select Committees*, 2nd edn (Oxford, Oxford University Press, 1989).
[103] See: Public Leaders Network, 'Public accounts committee "theatrical exercise in public humiliation"' *The Guardian* (9 March 2012).
[104] Standing Order No 148.
[105] National Audits Act 1983, s 8.
[106] Public Accounts Committee, 'Second report from the committee of public accounts' (HC 1897–98, 261-VIII) 147–48.
[107] D Tallon, I Young, P Elliott and D Dave, *Inland Revenue Practices and Concessions: 1984/85 Bound Volume* (London, Oyez Longman, 1984) 11.
[108] PAC (n 106) 148.
[109] ibid.
[110] ibid.

understand the capacity of the trio of the PAC, CAG and NAO and their level of supervision over HMRC advice. This can be extrapolated by analysing the level of scrutiny afforded by the triumvirate to HMRC class concessions. Since 1897, PACs and CAGs have regularly asserted that class concessions ought to be regularised by statute at the earliest practicable opportunity. In this regard, however, the bodies' have demonstrated their own limited focus. The bodies have concerned themselves historically with simply questioning why concessions have not been put on a statutory footing. They have not been concerned with issues of clarity, correctness or accessibility. For instance, the CAG in the report for the year ending 31 March 1953 noted the following:

> As the remissions still without statutory cover had become rather numerous I asked for information as to the principal concessions which continued in force, and the intentions of the Department with regard to seeking such cover.[111]

In the report for the year ended 31 March 1968, the CAG similarly directed the Inland Revenue towards regularising concessions, rather than analysing the substance:

> The Committee of Public Accounts of Session 1966–67 endorsed the view expressed in Treasury Minute of 31 December 1897 that statutory cover should be sought for remissions applicable to classes at the earliest opportunity.[112]

Likewise, in the report for the year ended 31 March 1981, the CAG reiterated the focus of the bodies on placing concessions in legislation, and not on expending time reviewing the interstices of ESCs:

> Over the years successive Committees of Public Accounts have endorsed the view, first expressed by the Treasury in 1897, that wherever possible extra-statutory class concessions should be placed on a statutory footing at the earliest opportunity.[113]

In 1991, the PAC intimated again its unease with published ESCs, but did not apply any scrutiny to the corpus of the existing class concessions:

> We learnt that three concessions which were suitable for legislation were over 50 years old and that one concession which had been classified as temporary was also 50 years old[114]

Finally, the practice of the CAG, NAO and PAC submitting ESCs to scrutiny appears to have completely lapsed, with no mention of the issue by either body since 1998.[115]

[111] Comptroller and Auditor General, 'Appropriation accounts of the sums granted by Parliament for revenue departments for the year ended 31st March 1953' (HC 1953–54, 12-XXIV) x.

[112] Comptroller and Auditor General, 'Appropriation accounts of the sums granted by Parliament for civil services, classes I–V, for the year ended 31st March 1968' (HC 1968–69, 53-LI) x.

[113] Comptroller and Auditor General, 'Appropriation accounts on the sums granted by Parliament for classes XIII–XIV for the year ended 31st March 1981' (HC 1981–82, 76-IX) xi.

[114] Public Accounts Committee, 'Second report: Inland Revenue Department' (HC 1990–91, 71) x.

[115] Comptroller and Auditor General, 'General report' (HC 1997–98, 251-XIX) 31.

What these examples serve to demonstrate is that although these entities have been given a specific mandate to scrutinise ESCs, and although the bodies have nominally noted this in the reports (at least up until 1998), they have failed to interrogate the relevant ESCs for consistency with the law or clarity or indeed to have raised issues in respect of accessibility. It was the Chancellor of the Exchequer who conducted a review in the mid-1980s into the publication of ESCs, and specified thereafter that administrative practices would be subject to a regular biannual review to identify any which should properly be classified as ESCs.[116] In this regard, the issue of publication does not appear to have been considered by the CAG, NAO and PAC to be a matter for scrutiny, much less issues surrounding practical limitations or accessibility, retrospectivity and mingling.

III. The Adjudicator and Ombudsman[117]

The Ombudsman has 'carved for itself a distinctive niche'[118] in the public law framework.[119] The original purpose of the office was to act as an aid to Parliamentary scrutiny of the Executive,[120] the other supervisory mechanisms such as questioning by MPs in the House of Commons and indirect oversight by the courts having been deemed no longer suited to the task.[121] But the role of the office is broader than originally conceived and it acts 'as a source of dispute resolution, as a guardian of good public administration, and as a systematic check upon departmental effectiveness'.[122] The work of the Ombudsman is now complemented in the case of HMRC by the Adjudicator, to which complaints must be issued prior to proceeding to the Ombudsman.[123] Established in 1993, the body was initially to investigate complaints in relation to the Inland Revenue.[124] The Adjudicator is now responsible

[116] *Hansard*, HC Deb Vol 79, cols 188–89 (16 May 1985).

[117] This part borrows heavily from S Daly, 'Oversight of HMRC soft law: lessons from the Ombudsman' (2016) 38 *Journal of Social Welfare and Family Law* 343.

[118] A Abraham, Preface to R Kirkham, 'Parliamentary Ombudsman: Withstanding the Test of Time' (HC 2006–07, 421) 1.

[119] For more, see: R Gregory and G Giddings, 'Practice and Prospects of the ombudsmen in the United Kingdom' (Lampeter, Edwin Mellon Press, 1995).

[120] Abraham, Preface to Kirkham, *Parliamentary Ombudsman* (2006–07) 1.

[121] P Leyland and G Anthony, *Textbook on Administrative Law*, 8th edn (Oxford, Oxford University Press, 2016) 132.

[122] Abraham (n 118) 2. See also D Oliver, 'Ombudsmen in search of a role' (1978) 41 *MLR* 446, 452; Parliamentary Commissioner for Administration, 'Report for 1983' (HC 1983–84, 322) 1.

[123] HMRC, 'Complain about HMRC. See to that end The Adjudicator's Office, HMRC and VOA, Service Level Agreement for the provision of complaints adjudication services for HM Revenue & Customs and Valuation Office Agency by the Adjudicator's Office' (July 2018) para 5.12 and Appendix C.

[124] Inland Revenue Press Release, 17 February 1993, reprinted in [1993] 13 *Business Law Review* 98 as noted in PE Morris 'The Revenue Adjudicator – the first two years' [1996] *Public Law* 309, 309 fn 5.

for complaints in relation to HMRC and the Valuation Office Agency (VOA),[125] and has a similar remit to that of the Ombudsman.[126] Unlike the Ombudsman, the Adjudicator does not have a statutory footing, but is instead predicated upon a contractual relationship with HMRC.[127] The Adjudicator is neither an employee of HMRC nor a civil servant, and is thus not subject to any direction from HMRC in respect of any individual complaint or type of complaint.[128]

An analysis of the reports from the Adjudicator and Ombudsman reveals that these bodies can be useful in scrutinising the correctness, clarity and accessibility of HMRC advice.

A. The Adjudicator

The Adjudicator's role is to consider whether HMRC and the VOA have applied their standards, guidance and codes of practice fairly and consistently.[129] Critically, the Adjudicator can look at complaints about mistakes, unreasonable delays, poor or misleading advice, processes, whether a policy has been followed, inappropriate staff behaviour and the use of discretion.[130] To this end, the remit of the Adjudicator clearly encompasses overseeing HMRC advice. There are a range of matters, on the other hand, that the Adjudicator may not consider, such as matters of government or departmental policy, or complaints where there is a specific right of determination by any court, tribunal, or other body that could consider the complaint.[131] The breadth of the Adjudicator's jurisdiction runs in parallel to that of the Ombudsman, but the Adjudicator is a prior step in the complaints machinery.[132] Complainants should approach first the Adjudicator before approaching the Ombudsman (through their MP) if still dissatisfied. Given its placing in the machinery for complaints, the Adjudicator has been called a 'middle tier' between the internal complaints process and the Ombudsman.[133]

In terms of powers the Adjudicator has full access to HMRC's records and can interview relevant staff.[134] Where the Adjudicator thinks that either HMRC or the VOA have fallen short, the body will recommend what they need to do to put

[125] Up until 2016 the Adjudicator's Office also investigated complaints into the Insolvency Service. See: Adjudicator's Office, 'Annual Report 2017' (September 2017) 28.

[126] Adjudicator, HMRC and VOA, 'Service Level Agreement' (2018) paras 5.1–5.23.

[127] ibid para 5.3; C Harlow and R Rawlings, *Law and Administration*, 3rd edn (Cambridge, Cambridge University Press, 2009) 458.

[128] D Oliver, 'The Revenue Adjudicator: a new breed of Ombudsperson?' [1993] *Public Law* 407, 407–08.

[129] See Adjudicator, HMRC and VOA (n 123) para 5.1.

[130] See ibid para 5.10.

[131] See ibid para 5.12.

[132] ibid para 5.12 and Appendix C.

[133] Harlow and Rawlings, *Law and Administration* (2009) 458.

[134] Adjudicator, HMRC and VOA (n 123) para 5.13; Oliver, 'The Revenue Adjudicator' [1993] 408.

matters right.[135] This may include making suggestions for broader service improvements where this is considered to be of benefit to the wider public. Additionally, these powers may be used to recommend *ex gratia* payments, recompense and other payments to complainants such as covering expenses incurred in pursuing complaints and compensation for loss of time in pursuing complaints.[136] But critically, the body can only issue recommendations that are in accordance with HMRC's powers and guidance.[137]

The influence of the Adjudicator slightly departs from that of the Ombudsman. Undoubtedly, the opinion of the Adjudicator holds significant sway with HMRC. For instance, in the years 2018/19,[138] 2016/17,[139] 2015/16,[140] 2014/15,[141] 2013/14,[142] 2012/13,[143] 2011/12,[144] 2010/11,[145] 2009/10[146] and 2008/09,[147] all the Adjudicator's recommendations were accepted by HMRC.[148] This reflects the general agreement between the Adjudicator and HMRC that the recommendations, although not binding, will be accepted and followed in all but exceptional circumstances.[149] Furthermore, the ability of the Adjudicator to publicise non-compliance with a recommendation represents a potent weapon in the armoury of the Office.[150] However, the power of the Ombudsman's findings is bolstered by the fact of its link with Parliament, as the Ombudsman is an officer of the House of Commons. The status of the Adjudicator as independent of the House of Commons means the Office cannot benefit from this political power.[151] However, the case of *R (Bradley) v Secretary of State for Work and Pensions* ('*Bradley*')[152] adds a legal edge to recommendations from the Ombudsman, and by analogy the Adjudicator. Therein it was

[135] Adjudicator, HMRC and VOA (n 123) para 5.5.

[136] Oliver, 'The Revenue Adjudicator' (n 128) 408.

[137] See Adjudicator, HMRC and VOA (an 123) paras 5.1, 5.2 and 5.20.

[138] Adjudicator's Office, 'Annual Report 2019' (June 2019) 22 and 32. In the 2018 report, HMRC accepted all the recommendations, though it is not clear if the VOA did: Adjudicator's Office, 'Annual Report 2018' (July 2018) 16 and 28.

[139] Adjudicator's Office, 'Annual Report 2017' (n 125) 35.

[140] Adjudicator's Office, 'Annual Report 2016' (September 2016) 12 and 24.

[141] Adjudicator's Office, 'Annual Report 2015' (September 2015) 12 and 22.

[142] Adjudicator's Office, 'Annual Report 2014 Learning is paramount!' (July 2014) 12 and 22.

[143] Adjudicator's Office, 'Annual Report 2013 The Adjudicator calls for greater organisational learning' (June 2013) 12, 17 and 22.

[144] Adjudicator's Office, 'Annual Report 2012 A year of challenges' (July 2012) 12, 18 and 22.

[145] Adjudicator's Office, 'Annual Report 2011 A year of record breaking performance' (July 2011) 12, 18 and 22.

[146] Adjudicator's Office, 'Annual Report 2010 continuous improvement driving performance learning lessons' (September 2010) 12, 17 and 20.

[147] Adjudicator's Office, 'Annual Report 2009' (September 2009) 15.

[148] It is worth noting that most complaints to the Adjudicator's Office relate to tax credits. See for instance, Adjudicator's Office, 'Annual Report 2016' (n 140) 12.

[149] Oliver (n 128) 408. See Adjudicator, HMRC and VOA (n 123) para 5.19–5.20.

[150] Morris, 'The Revenue Adjudicator' [1996] 313.

[151] ibid.

[152] [2008] EWCA Civ 36, [2009] QB 114.

found that a government department could only reject an Ombudsman's finding of maladministration 'on cogent reasons'[153] and that any decision to reject a finding may itself be judicially reviewed and quashed if judged to be irrational.[154] Should an entity, such as HMRC, decide not to act as the Adjudicator or Ombudsman recommends, the implication is that the injured party may challenge a decision not to follow the recommendation on the basis that to refuse to do so would be irrational. Similarly, should the entity decide not to act on the basis that the conclusion of the Adjudicator or Ombudsman as to the relevant facts is inaccurate, the affected party is able to go to court to check whether the authority has good reason to reject the findings of fact.

Given its remit, powers, and influence it should be unsurprising that the Adjudicator can prove effective in scrutinising instances where HMRC advice was inconsistent with the law, insufficiently clear, and inaccessible, leading to change in respect of these problems. A case study in the 2014 Annual Report evidences the ability of the Adjudicator to force HMRC to change published advice where the instrument incorporates a position which is inconsistent with the law. HMRC advice provided that the cost of court fees could be deducted from claims for tax refunds. This was incorrect as a matter of law and following the investigation and recommendation from the Adjudicator the advice was amended to reflect the correct legal position.[155] Meanwhile the 2018 Annual Report details how the Adjudicator can work with HMRC to deal with misapplications of its advice. Therein the Adjudicator explained that it had continuously highlighted that HMRC was not correctly following its own advice, namely ESC A19.[156] This concession provides that in certain circumstances arrears of tax will not be pursued where delays have been caused by HMRC errors.[157] The body accordingly worked with HMRC to ensure its correct application, helping the Process Design team to redesign the internal guidance in order to make the intent and application clearer and more consistent for their customers.

A case study in the 2007 Annual Report meanwhile highlights the ability of the Adjudicator to tackle issues in respect of both lack of clarity and non-publication. HMRC operated a Flat Rate VAT scheme. However, the advice on the matter was contradictory and unclear, leading the Adjudicator to recommend that the advice should be amended, which HMRC accepted,. Furthermore, the Adjudicator expressed concern about the fact that entities could be retrospectively added to the Flat Rate VAT scheme, but that this was not widely published. Rather, the clear advice on retrospection was available to businesses applying electronically, but not to other applicants. To this end, it was recommended that HMRC consider

[153] ibid [51], [72] (Sir John Chadwick).
[154] ibid [95] (Sir John Chadwick).
[155] Adjudicator's Office, 'Annual Report 2014' (n 142) 17.
[156] Adjudicator's Office, 'Annual Report 2018' (July 2018) 14.
[157] See HMRC, 'Extra-Statutory Concessions: Concessions as at 6 April 2018' (April 2018).

whether the advice could be expanded to a wider audience.[158] It is now to be found in an HMRC Manual online.[159]

Overall it is clear that the Adjudicator makes a positive contribution to the scrutiny of HMRC advice, but there are some limitations. For instance, where there is incorrect advice which is favourable to a taxpayer, there is no incentive for the taxpayer to raise a complaint and hence for the Adjudicator to be involved to ensure that HMRC applies the law correctly. In any event even where published concessions arise, the Adjudicator's approach is to ensure that the concessions are applied consistently and fairly, rather than to question their lawfulness. In terms of accessibility, the limitations of the Adjudicator become clearer. The Adjudicator cannot question governmental or departmental policy, thereby exempting the policy decisions which restrict access to HMRC advice from scrutiny. The Adjudicator will have little reason to care about mingling. Meanwhile, when it comes to retrospectivity the Adjudicator can be of little assistance. The Adjudicator, to recall, can seek to ensure that HMRC follows its policies.[160] However, when it comes to retrospective changes, it is clear HMRC policy that the body will generally go back on incorrect advice and collect tax due.[161] To this end, the Adjudicator will only be able to assist in respect of retrospective changes if this would be in line with HMRC's own policy,[162] which is very strict (though a separate policy can be invoked to ensure that a taxpayer is compensated for the costs incurred as a result of misleading advice).[163] This is borne out, for instance, by a case study from the Adjudicator's 2007 Annual Report.[164] Therein a taxpayer had been assured by HMRC that it should not charge VAT on some of its supplies and to that end repaid to the taxpayer sums incorrectly collected. Later, however, HMRC changed its position and required the taxpayer to repay the VAT that it ought to have collected. The taxpayer argued that this was unfair, but the Adjudicator did not uphold the taxpayer's complaint about the retrospective change in advice.[165]

B. Ombudsman

The Ombudsman's remit, drafted in very broad terms, is to investigate complaints of 'maladministration' by government departments and some other

[158] Adjudicator's Office, 'Annual Report 2007' (September 2007) 38–39.

[159] See HMRC, 'VAT Flat Rate Scheme: FRS3000' (July 2016).

[160] See Adjudicator, HMRC and VOA (n 123) para 5.10.

[161] This is subject to detailed consideration in ch 6.

[162] Though the Adjudicator will enforce the official HMRC policy where the requirements are met. See for instance Adjudicator's Office, 'Annual Report 2009' (n 147) 30–31; Adjudicator's Office, 'Annual Report 2006' (2006) 34–45.

[163] See Adjudicator's Office, 'Annual Report 2012' (n 144) 17.

[164] Adjudicator's Office, 'Annual Report 2017' (n 125) 22.

[165] The Report officially notes that the taxpayer's complaint was partially upheld, but this was only insofar as HMRC had not adequately explained the position to the taxpayer.

public bodies[166] (including HMRC)[167] causing 'injustice' to a member of the public.[168] The complaint must be raised within one year of the grievance arising.[169] Both 'maladministration' and 'injustice' are not defined. Richard Crossman, the Minister of Housing and Local Government who played a significant role in passing the bill through Parliament,[170] nonetheless opined that it would be a 'wonderful exercise' to try to define the former by reference to a catalogue of the qualities which would make up maladministration: 'bias, neglect, inattention, delay, incompetence, ineptitude, perversity, turpitude, arbitrariness and so on'.[171] Injustice, on the other hand, is said to encompass 'not merely injury redressable in a Court of Law',[172] but also, in Crossman's words, 'the sense of outrage aroused by unfair or incompetent administration, even where the complainant has suffered no actual loss'.[173] The threshold of 'injustice' is surpassed by virtue of the citizen being 'affected by the maladministration in some way'.[174] The implication from these attempts at definitions is that a broad approach is to be taken to the question of what constitutes maladministration causing injustice.[175] Although maladministration is not intended to encompass questioning the 'merits of a decision',[176] the condition, in practice, has not been strictly followed.[177]

In a similar vein, although the Ombudsman is not permitted by reason of section 5 of the governing Act to investigate complaints where the aggrieved person has a right of appeal, reference or review to or before a tribunal[178] or through proceedings in a court of law,[179] the officer may do so where it is not reasonable to expect the aggrieved person to have sought such redress.[180] The effect of this

[166] Parliamentary Commissioner Act 1967 (PCA 1967), s 5(1)(a).
[167] PCA 1967, s 4, Sch 2 (as amended).
[168] PCA 1967, s 5(1)(a).
[169] PCA 1967, s 6 (3).
[170] Leyland and Anthony, *Administrative Law* (2016) 137.
[171] *Hansard*, HC Deb Vol 734, col 51 (18 October 1966).
[172] SA De Smith, H Woolf and J Jowell, *Judicial Review of Administrative Action*, 5th edn (London, Sweet and Maxwell, 1995) para 1–102.
[173] *Hansard* (n 171). See also: *R v Parliamentary Commissioner for Administration, ex parte Balchin* [1998] 1 PLR 1 (Admin), 11 (Sedley J).
[174] T Endicott, *Administrative Law*, 4th edn (Oxford, Oxford University Press, 2015) 495.
[175] HWR Wade and C Forsyth, *Administrative Law*, 11th edn (Oxford, Oxford University Press, 2014) 74; Harlow and Rawlings (n 127) 533; M Seneviratne, *Ombudsmen: Public Services and Administrative Justice* (Oxford, Butterworths, 2002) 45–46.
[176] PCA 1967, s 12(3); *R v Local Commissioner for Administration, ex p Bradford Metropolitan City Council* [1979] QB 287 (CA), 311H (Lord Denning MR); *R v Local Commissioner for Administration, ex p Eastleigh Borough Council* [1988] QB 855 (CA), 863 (Lord Donaldson MR).
[177] Endicott, *Administrative Law* (2015) 490–92; Harlow and Rawlings (n 127) 533; Kirkham, *Parliamentary Ombudsman* (n 118) 7–8. For instances of the Ombudsman questioning the merits of decisions, see: Parliamentary and Health Service Ombudsman, 'Tax Credits: Getting it wrong?' (HC 2006–07, 1010) 9–10; Parliamentary Ombudsman, 'Annual report 1999–00' (HC 1999–00, 593) 31; Parliamentary commissioner for administration, 'Annual report for 1990' (HC 1990–91, 299) 16.
[178] PCA 1967, s 5 (2)(a).
[179] PCA 1967, s 5 (2)(b).
[180] PCA 1967, s 5 (2).

drafting is to attempt to separate issues of law from administration, placing the latter but not the former within the ambit of the Ombudsman's powers.[181] It is, however, merely a 'modest attempt to avoid overlapping remedies',[182] and there have been many cases investigated in practice where legal remedies would have been available.[183] There is one condition, though, which does undoubtedly restrict the remit of the Ombudsman. In order for a complaint to be investigated, it must come through the relevant MP for the aggrieved constituent,[184] before being referred to the Ombudsman (with the complainant's consent).[185]

The utility of the office is ensured by its wide powers of investigation.[186] The officer has almost unfettered access to papers and persons, a 'striking advantage' of the Ombudsman over MPs' questioning.[187] The officer may effectively compel any Minister, officer, member, or person related to the purportedly offending department to furnish information or produce documents.[188] As the investigation takes place in private, any secrecy or confidentiality condition of that person's employment is obviated,[189] except in relation to Cabinet proceedings.[190] The Ombudsman has the same powers as a court to summon and examine witnesses.[191] The recommendations of the Ombudsman, which can range from the issuance of an apology[192] to financial compensation,[193] seek to restore the complainant to the position she would have been in had the maladministration not occurred.[194] Recommendations may also be directed towards broader, systemic change, as arose in relation to the introduction of compensation for expenses incurred by reason of official error on the part of HMRC.[195]

The potency of the Ombudsman's investigations derives from its founding constituents. The Ombudsman is an officer of the House of Commons and

[181] Leyland and Anthony (n 121) 140; Kirkham (n 118) 5.

[182] Harlow and Rawlings (n 127) 539.

[183] Wade and Forsyth, *Administrative Law* (2014) 76–77.

[184] PCA 1967, s 5(1)(a). A related condition implicit in s 5 is that the complainant must be a UK resident, or the complaint must relate to rights and obligations accruing in the UK (PCA 1967, s 6(1)).

[185] PCA 1967, s 5(1)(b).

[186] Kirkham (n 118) 6.

[187] KC Wheare, *Maladministration and its Remedies* (London, Stevens and Sons, 1973) 144.

[188] PCA 1967, s 8(1).

[189] PCA 1967, s 8(3).

[190] PCA 1967, s 8(4).

[191] PCA 1967, s 8(2). See however PCA 1967, s 11(3).

[192] Parliamentary Commissioner for Administration, 'Third report of the parliamentary commissioner for administration' (HC 1973–74, 281) 12; Parliamentary Commissioner for Administration, 'Annual report for 1988' (HC 1988–89, 301) 16; Parliamentary and Health Service Ombudsman, 'Annual Report 2010–11' (HC 2010–11, 1404) 17.

[193] Parliamentary Commissioner for Administration, 'Second report of the Parliamentary Commissioner for Administration' (HC 1973–74, 106) 7.

[194] Parliamentary and Health Service Ombudsman, 'Equitable Life: a decade of regulatory failure' (HC 2007–08, 815-I) 377.

[195] See for instance Parliamentary Commissioner for Administration, 'Annual report for 1995' (HC 1995–96, 296) para 54.

is appointed by the Crown on the advice of the Prime Minister. The body is accountable to Parliament through the medium of the Public Administration and Constitutional Affairs Committee (PACAC).[196] Reports on the investigations undertaken are laid before the PACAC,[197] whilst individual findings and recommendations are dispatched to the referring MP.[198] The names of the complainants are anonymised.[199] Although the Ombudsman holds no formal powers to compel compliance with any of the office's recommendations, the involvement of the PACAC[200] and referring MP[201] is generally sufficient to ensure compliance on the part of the offending public body. As Roskill LJ noted in *Congreve v Home Office*,[202] 'no criticism of a government department could be more devastating'.[203] Further, as noted already, the case of *Bradley* should ensure that HMRC act very carefully when deciding whether the reject any recommendations from the Ombudsman.

As with the Adjudicator, research into the Ombudsman's reports demonstrates that the Ombudsman has been effective to an extent in remedying failings of HMRC advice in relation to correctness, clarity and accessibility. In terms of combatting inconsistency between the law and the corresponding advice, a pertinent example is that of a case concerning the collection of betting duty from an on-course bookmaker.[204] As it stood at the time, possession of a valid betting duty card was necessary before a bookmaker could stand at a race meeting. Before these cards could be issued, the bookmaker had to pay a deposit calculated by reference to estimated duty liability. The complainant in this case, who had held a bookmaker's permit for about 14 years, received a demand for payment of £35. It was said that he owed betting duty amounting to over £200 for the previous year and the amount of £35 was required as a deposit if he wished to obtain further betting duty cards while the matter was being investigated. During the course of the investigation, the Ombudsman found that Customs Notice No 455 (which provided that cards would not be issued until all duty due was paid) was inconsistent with the Department's legal advice about the circumstances in which officials were empowered to refuse to issue a card. Subsequent to this issue being highlighted, the Department corrected Customs Notice No 455 so as to properly reflect the underlying legal position. This was that Customs officers were not empowered to

[196] Parliamentary and Health Service Ombudsman, 'Annual Report 2011–12' (HC 2011–12, 251) 5.
[197] PCA 1967, s 10(4).
[198] PCA 1967, s 10(1).
[199] For instance, see: Parliamentary and Health Service Ombudsman, 'Selected summaries of investigations by the Parliamentary and Health Service Ombudsman Volume 1, report 1' (February and March 2014) (HC 2014–15, 566).
[200] Harlow and Rawlings (n 127) 534.
[201] Wade and Forsyth (n 175) 69.
[202] [1976] QB 629 (CA).
[203] ibid, 654–55. See also: *Seifert and Lynch v Pensions Ombudsman* [1997] 1 All ER 214, 222 noted in Harlow and Rawlings (n 127) 482–83.
[204] Parliamentary Commissioner for Administration, 'Annual report for 1976' (HC 1976–77, 116) 8.

refuse the issue of a betting duty card to a bookmaker on the ground of being in arrears with duty payment, but merely to require additional security as a condition of the issue of a card.[205]

Meanwhile, the recommendations in the damning 'Tax Credits: Getting it wrong?' report,[206] dealing with the systemic problems encountered following the introduction of tax credits, highlight the Ombudsman's ability to force changes to the way HMRC applies its advice so as to ensure it is correctly applied. The Ombudsman recommended that HMRC develop feedback mechanisms to enable staff to learn from complaints about the unreasonable application of COP 26.[207] This is the Code of Practice which sets out the procedure for remedying overpayment of tax credits.[208] The report also recommended that HMRC should ensure that proper consideration is given to the impact of recovery decisions on the individuals and families concerned. Both recommendations were accepted.[209] In terms of the latter, HMRC responded by ensuring in future that any time a question of 'hardship' were to arise, it would be put to the Debt Management and Banking Unit in HMRC, who are specialists in determining the question of hardship.[210]

In combatting the lack of clarity of some pieces of advice, the Ombudsman has also intervened at times to good effect, as arose in relation to ESC A5 (now obsolete).[211] The concession specified that it was Inland Revenue practice not to assess removal expenses borne by an employer where an employee '*has* to change residence' (emphasis added) as a result of a transfer to another post within an organisation. This was said only to apply if the employee was forced to travel at least 25 miles or over an hour by public transport. In the case itself, the employee's new office was 20 miles from his residence, but his employer, for commercial reasons, thought it essential for him to live within five miles of the new branch. The Ombudsman did not find that there was maladministration in the case in failing to apply the terms of the concession to the employee in question, but did query the wording of the concession as it failed to make clear the degree of necessity required by the phrase '*has* to change residence'. Accordingly, the Chairman of the Board of Inland Revenue accepted that the concession was seriously ambiguous and that it needed to be reviewed and improved.

In another case concerning internal advice issued to department officials, the Ombudsman found that actions of Customs officials had been contrary to legal advice, but also that the advice to the officials in the case had been fragmented

[205] Parliamentary Commissioner for Administration, 'Fifth report of the parliamentary commissioner for administration [cases investigated 1st February to 30th April, 1976]' (HC 1975–76, 496) 812.

[206] PHSO, *Tax Credits: Getting it wrong?* (n 177).

[207] ibid 12, 38.

[208] See: HMRC, 'What happens if we've paid you too much tax credits (COP 26)' (April 2019).

[209] Parliamentary and Health Service Ombudsman, 'Annual Report 2007–08' (HC 2007–08, 1404) 20.

[210] PHSO (n 177) 13, 38.

[211] Parliamentary Commissioner for Administration, 'Annual report for 1987' (1987–88 HC 363) 13.

and imprecise.[212] The affected citizen, a holidaymaker, was returning to the UK with furniture, but had improperly completed a declaration form. The question for Customs officials was whether this was 'reckless' or 'careless', but during the interview, the holidaymaker had not been advised that 'recklessness' was being considered. The woman had been given a Rule II caution by the Customs officials, but not a Rule III caution,[213] before she was offered the option of court proceedings or payment of a sum to compound proceedings. The proper legal course of action in instances where there have been allegations of recklessness was in fact to refer to the department's solicitor, but the officials were not clearly informed of this. The department accordingly agreed to make administrative changes in the procedures to shore up these inadequacies in the internal advice. That case also serves to demonstrate the two-way nature of HMRC advice; even where it is primarily directed at officials, it can nevertheless impact taxpayers.

By having such unencumbered access to internal documents and people, the Ombudsman is well placed to understand internal HMRC advice and to provoke publication where the advice enshrines policies, procedures or interpretations which impact taxpayers. By way of example, the Ombudsman's investigations for the year 1991 revealed a previously unpublished extra-statutory practice.[214] The Inland Revenue was allowing repayments of tax to be made outside the statutory six-year time limit laid down by section 43 of the Taxes Management Act 1970, where the claim is delayed by reason of mistakes made by the Inland Revenue or by another government department. Following the Ombudsman's inquiry into a complaint from a taxpayer who belatedly discovered that he had not received the benefit of old age allowance to which he had had an entitlement since the mid-1970s (for which the Inland Revenue made an *ex gratia* payment of £1,930.17), the Inland Revenue agreed to look into the possibility of publishing the existence of the practice and undertook to ensure that it was promulgated in the Revenue's internal instructions to tax offices. The concession was subsequently published that year as ESC B41.[215] In another case where a citizen accused Customs officials of having damaged his property when his luggage was being searched at a port of entry, the result of the Ombudsman's investigation was the revision of internal advice and its publication as a Code of Practice.[216] The particular officials were wearing outer coats, thereby concealing their name badges, contravening Customs and Excise advice ('Traveller's Charter'). Meanwhile, internal advice on dealing

[212] Parliamentary Commissioner for Administration, 'Annual report for 1982' (HC 1982–83, 257) 16–17.

[213] Rule II of the Judges' Rules provided that a caution was to be issued as soon as an officer had evidence which would afford reasonable grounds for suspecting that a person has committed an offence. Rule III provided that where a person is charged with or informed that she may be prosecuted for an offence, she shall be cautioned. See: A Keane and P McKeown, *The Modern Law of Evidence*, 10th edn (Oxford, Oxford University Press, 2014) 383.

[214] Parliamentary Commissioner for Administration, 'Annual report for 1991' (HC 1991–92, 347) 15.

[215] See: Inland Revenue, 'IR1 (Supp)' (1991).

[216] PCA, 'Annual report for 1995' (n 195) para 67.

with complaints was also not followed. Subsequent to this investigation, Customs and Excise modified its internal policy and thereafter published it as 'Complaints and putting things right: our code of practice' in January 1996.[217]

Unlike the Adjudicator, however, the Ombudsman is not constrained by what HMRC says in its codes of practice or other published advice, and can look beyond these in order to consider whether injustice has been caused.[218] This means that its remit in preventing HMRC from retrospectively changing its advice is broader. To this end, in a case concerning overpaid tax credits, HMRC was prevented from collecting monies due because it had previously issued incorrect advice.[219] HMRC sent the taxpayer a notice demanding repayment of £1,673.57, but when she queried the assessment, she was assured that there was no overpayment. This assurance was incorrect, but the Ombudsman held HMRC to it because of its delaying and mishandling of the case. Critically, however, the Ombudsman made no mention of the financial detriment condition which would have to be satisfied in order for the Adjudicator to assist a taxpayer in such an instance.

As with the Adjudicator, the contribution that the Ombudsman has made to scrutinising HMRC advice to ensure its correctness, clarity and accessibility should not be overstated. The limitations of the Adjudicator, in terms of having an incentive to ameliorate incorrect favourable advice, questioning policy decisions or caring about mingling, apply also the Ombudsman. Whilst the Ombudsman is not barred per se from questioning policy decisions that affect accessibility, it is difficult to see how these would be the cause of injustice by maladministration on the part of HMRC. This is particularly so given that the taxpayer concerned would be complaining about the non-existence of rights, rather than positive actions leading directly to harm.

IV. The Tribunals and Courts

Whilst traversing the delicate separation of powers, the tribunals and courts can play an important constitutional role in 'checking' administrative discretion,[220] mindful to protect individuals' liberty from any unjustified encroachments by the executive.[221] Given that it is promulgated under HMRC's managerial discretion, there is no reason in principle why the tribunals or courts should not also

[217] Now found in: HMRC, 'Complain about HMRC'.

[218] This was noted in Parliamentary and Health Service Ombudsman, 'Annual Report 2001–02' (HC 2001–02, 897) 35.

[219] PHSO, 'Annual Report 2007–08' (n 209) 20.

[220] KC Davis 'Judicial Control of Administrative Action' (1966) 66 *Columbia Law Review* 635; KC Davis, *Discretionary Justice: A Preliminary Inquiry*, 2nd edn (Baton Rouge, Louisiana State University Press, 1971).

[221] *R v Secretary of State for the Home Department, ex parte Simms* [1999] 3 WLR 328, [2000] 2 AC 115 (HL), 131–32.

undertake a residual supervisory function in respect of HMRC advice.[222] However, scrutiny by these bodies by way of judicial review[223] is weak in practice for two primary reasons. First, the opportunity for intervention in order to advise HMRC to correct its advice, to make it clearer and render it more accessible, is severely limited. Of course, there are frequent challenges by taxpayers in relation to HMRC advice. But these disputes revolve around whether HMRC advice has been applied correctly,[224] not that changes should be made because HMRC advice is incorrect, unclear or inaccessible. Meanwhile, those that are directly affected by HMRC advice are unlikely to bring challenges where it operates in their interest.[225]

Third parties, on the other hand, will face the issue of *locus standi*.[226] Section 31(3) of the Senior Courts Act 1981 provides that 'the court shall not grant leave to make such an application unless it considers that the applicant has a *sufficient interest* in the matter to which the application relates' (emphasis added). However, this hurdle is not insurmountable. To this end, there is a trend in tax cases for allowing 'public-spirited'[227] taxpayers to bring challenges, even where there is no direct interest in a case.[228] In *IRC v National Federation of Self-Employed and Small Businesses Ltd* ('*Fleet Street Casuals*'),[229] where a group representing 50,000 taxpayers challenged the lawfulness of an agreement between the Inland Revenue and workers on Fleet Street, the House of Lords ultimately found that the group did not have sufficient interest to challenge the decision.[230] The case lays

[222] Indeed, there is precedent for the courts doing so, as seen already in the cases of *R (Purdy) v Director of Public Prosecutions* [2009] UKHL 45, [2010] 1 AC 345 and *R (Nicklinson) v Ministry of Justice* [2014] UKSC 38, [2014] 3 WLR 200. See also *Gillick v West Norfolk and Wisbeck Area Health Authority* [1985] UKHL 7, [1986] AC 112.

[223] Senior Courts Act 1981, s 31A allows the High Court to transfer judicial review proceedings to the Upper Tribunal. Later in this book it shall be recommended that the jurisdiction of the First-tier Tribunal be expanded. See below ch 7 in text at n 295.

[224] See generally below ch 6.

[225] A serious problem as highlighted in the scholarship on ESCs over the years: D Williams, 'Extra-Statutory Concessions' [1979] *British Tax Review* 137; M Gammie, 'Extra-Statutory Concessions' [1980] *British Tax Review* 308.

[226] See for instance *R (On the application of David Edwards) v The Environment Agency, Secretary of State & Rugby Ltd* [2004] EWHC 736 (Admin), [2004] 3 All ER 21.

[227] Wade and Forsyth (n 175) 590–92.

[228] *UK Uncut Legal Action Ltd v HM Revenue and Customs* [2013] EWHC 1283 (Admin), [2013] SWTI 1849 (*UK Uncut Legal Action*), [11].

[229] [1982] AC 617 (HL).

[230] The reasoning of the Lords differed on the matter, however. Lord Wilberforce held that generally no taxpayer has sufficient interest in asking the court to investigate the tax affairs of another taxpayer (633D), and though there may be a case of sufficient gravity where a taxpayer may (633E), this was not such a case (635F–636A). Lord Fraser found that there was no sufficient interest on the basis that no individual taxpayer has sufficient interest to challenge the assessment of another and that this was not a case of exceptionally grave or widespread illegality on the part of the public authority (646G–647B). Lord Scarman held that the group representing the taxpayers did not have sufficient interest because they had failed to show reasonable grounds for believing that the failure to collect tax from the Fleet Street casuals was an abuse of the revenue's managerial discretion (655A). Lord Roskill found that there was no sufficient interest once one considered the relevant statutory duty of the Inland Revenue, to collect tax in light of taxpayer confidentiality, and the particular complaint along with the relief sought, which required interfering with the affairs of individual taxpayers where there was no evidence

down the general rule that one taxpayer will not generally have sufficient interest to challenge HMRC's dealings with another, though it is notable that several of the Lords nevertheless did scrutinise the relevant Revenue decision.[231]

A taxpayer may be able to overcome this hurdle where an argument can be made that a taxpayer is interested not as a general taxpayer but as a competitor, as occurred in the case of *R v Attorney General, ex parte ICI*.[232] The facts are slightly unique in that the application of the relevant tax provisions to the applicant's competitors would have a bearing on the applicant's place in the market.[233] Moreover, a third party that is not a competitor may be granted standing provided that there are sufficiently strong grounds for showing that HMRC has acted unlawfully.[234] In *UK Uncut v HMRC*,[235] an action from an advocacy group contesting, inter alia, that HMRC had failed to comply with its own internal guidance when settling an outstanding tax bill with Goldman Sachs was allowed to proceed to full hearing.[236] The reasoning behind the grant of permission to bring judicial review proceedings was not particularly fleshed out. Simon J simply held that:

> The claimants have legitimate arguments that the courts have recently adopted a more relaxed approach to the rules about standing compared to the position in [the *Fleet Street Casuals* case in] 1982, and that they fall into a category which has standing to bring judicial review proceedings in the present case.[237]

At the full hearing, Nicol J explained that the reason why other taxpayers may have 'sufficient interest' to challenge the decision by the Revenue to waive tax in certain situations is 'because an over-generous approach to one taxpayer may correspondingly increase the burden on all other taxpayers'.[238]

Secondly, assuming judicial opportunity to intervene, it is suggested that the influence of judges on HMRC's handling of its advice is limited, or at least more limited than might be expected. For instance, despite the fact that Whipple J pointed out in October 2015[239] that HMRC's advice on legitimate expectations in its Administrative Law Manual was wrong, it remains uncorrected at the time

of grossly improper pressure or motive (662E–663B). Lord Diplock on the other hand would have preferred to decide the case not on the specific ground of no sufficient interest, but upon the more general ground that it had not been shown that 'the board did anything that was ultra vires or unlawful' (637D–E).

[231] ibid 637C–D (Lord Diplock); 654B (Lord Scarman) for instance.

[232] [1987] 1 CMLR 72.

[233] ibid, in particular [108].

[234] *R v Secretary of State for Foreign and Commonwealth Affairs, ex parte World Development Movement Ltd* [1995] 1 WLR 386 (DC).

[235] n 228.

[236] On which, see D de Cogan, '*UK Uncut Legal Action v HMRC*: legal inaction and a return to Fleet Street' [2013] *British Tax Review* 552, 555 fn 26.

[237] n 228 [9].

[238] ibid [41].

[239] *R (Hely-Hutchinson) v HMRC* [2015] EWHC 3261 (Admin), [2016] STC 962 [76].

of writing (September 2019).[240] Meanwhile, the fallout from *R (Wilkinson) v IRC* ('*Wilkinson*')[241] is generally held out as an example of the courts' impact as regards HMRC advice. It has largely become received wisdom that HMRC's recent restriction on the use of ESCs is a direct result of Lord Hoffmann's criticism of their use in *Wilkinson*.[242] However, further analysis of the period proceeding the decision, closer scrutiny of the judgment and comparison with the events following the *Vestey* series of cases serve to undermine this argument and highlight the relative weakness of the court's influence. In *Wilkinson*, the applicant was a widower who, had he been a widow, would have been entitled to a widow's bereavement allowance under section 262 of the Income and Corporation Taxes Act 1988. Mr Wilkinson argued, inter alia, that HMRC could utilise its 'managerial discretion' to extend the allowance to widowers. The House of Lords rejected the applicant's claim and held that the managerial discretion endowed upon HMRC cannot be so widely construed as to concede such an allowance which Parliament could have granted but did not grant.[243]

Subsequent to this judgment, HMRC engaged in a process of reviewing all existing ESCs. Where possible, concessions which overreached the discretion were put on a statutory footing.[244] Elsewhere, HMRC found concessions which in reality were not concessionary and were withdrawn.[245] Some concessions were found to be dormant as few taxpayers, and in some cases no taxpayers, had sought their application for many years.[246] For instance, HMRC could not trace a single occasion when concessionary treatment of Roman Catholic religious communities, which dated back to at least 1921, had been invoked. Further, however, HMRC has not added a single concession to the list of published ESCs which relate to taxes previously under the management of the Inland Revenue.[247] Whilst the review itself, along with the regularisation or removal of unlawful concessions, is certainly merited, it is advanced for several reasons that *Wilkinson* is not the impetus for these actions.

First, the initial reaction post-*Wilkinson* can more aptly be characterised as one of inertia than one of urgency, on the part of the Treasury, HMRC and NAO.

[240] The Court of Appeal did not reject this aspect of Whipple J's decision. See: *HMRC v Hely-Hutchinson* [2017] EWCA Civ 1075, [2017] WLR(D) 517 [92].

[241] [2005] UKHL 30; [2006] STC 270.

[242] Institute of Chartered Accountants in England and Wales, 'Legitimate Expectation and Reliance on HMRC Guidance' (Technical Release 06/13) 16; J Freedman and J Vella, 'Revenue Guidance: The Limits of Discretion and Legitimate Expectations' (2012) 128 *LQR* 192, 194.

[243] *Wilkinson* (n 241) [20] (Lord Hoffmann).

[244] See for instance, The Enactment of Extra-Statutory Concessions Order 2014 (SI 2014/211).

[245] For instance, 'F18 Treatment of income tax in Canada on capital gains deemed to arise on a person's death'. See: HMRC, 'Withdrawal of extra statutory concessions – Technical note and call for evidence' (January 2014) 18.

[246] HMRC, 'Withdrawal of extra statutory concessions – Technical Note' (December 2009) 12.

[247] Compare the list of ESCs as at 31 August 2005 ((HMRC, 'Extra-Statutory Concessions' (31 August 2005) to that as at 6 April 2018 (HMRC, 'Concessions as at 6 April 2018' (n 157) 2).

The Finance Acts of 2006[248] and 2007[249] gave a statutory footing to only one ESC relating to direct tax each respectively. The Income Tax Bill 2006–07 (which subsequently became the Income Tax Act 2007) sought to incorporate a modest four class concessions, only two of which were listed expressly in the HMRC publications as concessions.[250] However, neither ESC was incorporated into the final Act. The NAO in its annual accounts from 2005–06[251] and 2006–07[252] noted the continuing use of concessions,[253] but made no comment on their legality post-*Wilkinson*. Similarly, the relevant Treasury ministers were unconcerned about the continued use of concessions after *Wilkinson*. On 2 May 2006, opposition MPs expressed concern about the legal standing of concessions post-*Wilkinson*. Julia Goldsworthy (at the time Liberal Democrat MP for Falmouth and Camborne) proposed an amendment to legislation which sought to abolish the corporation tax starting rate and non-corporate distribution rate. The amendment was tabled amid concerns that many small clubs and societies would once again have to pay corporation tax on very small amounts of income as a result of the abolition of the nil-rate corporation tax band.[254] Julia Goldsworthy was unconvinced that this problem could be remedied by concession alone, given the judgment in *Wilkinson*.[255] Mark Hoban (then Conservative MP for Fareham) similarly relayed the concern of professional bodies who, although having been assured by HMRC that the issue would be tackled with a concession, were anxious that such a concession would lack legal standing.[256] John Healey (then Financial Secretary to the Treasury) swiftly rebutted their concerns, without substantive recourse to the decision in *Wilkinson*:

> For many years, the Inland Revenue and, latterly, HMRC have not sought corporation tax returns from clubs and unincorporated associations with very small tax liabilities. That practice was established before the introduction of the starting rate of corporation tax, and it will not be affected by the changes in clause 26 [of the incoming legislation]. Any club or society that is unclear about its tax position should ask its local HMRC office for advice … Sensible practices are already in force within HMRC to ensure that the corporation tax regime is applied reasonably in respect of clubs and unincorporated associations.[257]

[248] Finance Act 2006, s 64.

[249] Finance Act 2007, s 62.

[250] 'Explanatory Notes to the Income Tax HC Bill' (2006–07) para 14.

[251] National Audit Office, 'HM Revenue & Customs 2005–06 Accounts: The Comptroller and Auditor General's Standard Report' (July 2006).

[252] National Audit Office, 'HM Revenue & Customs 2006–07 Accounts: The Comptroller and Auditor General's Standard Report' (July 2007).

[253] See National Audit Office, 'HMRC 2005–06 Accounts' (n 251) para 3.46 and National Audit Office, 'HMRC 2006–07 Accounts' (n 252) para 3.19.

[254] *Hansard*, HC Deb Vol 445, col 924 (2 May 2006).

[255] ibid, col 925.

[256] ibid, col 924.

[257] ibid.

With such an assurance accordingly that HMRC would continue to operate its 'sensible' concessionary practice, Julia Goldsworthy withdrew her amendment.[258] On 26 June 2007, Theresa Villiers (Conservative MP for Chipping Barnet) expressed concern about the implications of *Wilkinson* as regards widely drafted Targeted Anti-Avoidance Rules, which were to be combatted by concessions.[259] The Chief Secretary to the Treasury (Mr Stephen Timms), in a manner similar to John Healey, rebutted this concern in swift fashion:

> The hon. Member for Chipping Barnet referred to a famous comment … that "[a] taxpayer should be taxed by law not untaxed by concession". I see the sense in that comment, but in circumstances such as those I described an innocent taxpayer might have to pay tax in situations that we did not expect when we drafted the legislation. I suspect that a reference to the words of Mr. Justice Walton, or indeed Lord Upjohn, would probably not satisfy someone who found themselves in that position.[260]

In other words, it was the Treasury's view that such a concession to the professional bodies would be within the powers of HMRC, without actually substantiating why, or how, such would be consistent with *Wilkinson*.

Secondly, it does not appear from the case that HMRC *had* misconceived the scope of its managerial discretion before *Wilkinson*. The speech of Lord Hoffmann did little more than reiterate the definition which is given to ESCs at the beginning of HMRC's relevant publication. This definition, *unchanged* from its first appearance in 1987,[261] is as follows:

> An Extra-Statutory Concession is a relaxation which gives taxpayers a reduction in tax liability to which they would not be entitled under the strict letter of the law. Most concessions are made to deal with what are, on the whole, minor or transitory anomalies under the legislation and to meet cases of hardship at the margins of the code where a statutory remedy would be difficult to devise or would run to a length out of proportion to the intrinsic importance of the matter.[262]

Lord Hoffmann, in almost perfect symmetry, defined the discretion to issue ESCs as follows:

> This discretion enables the commissioners to formulate policy in the interstices of the tax legislation, dealing pragmatically with minor or transitory anomalies, cases of hardship at the margins or cases in which a statutory rule is difficult to formulate or its enactment would take up a disproportionate amount of Parliamentary time.[263]

What Lord Hoffmann added in his speech was that HMRC's discretion to grant ESCs may not be construed 'so widely as to enable the commissioners to

[258] ibid col 925.
[259] *Hansard*, HC Deb Vol 462, col 248 (26 June 2007).
[260] ibid cols 250–51.
[261] Inland Revenue, Press Release, 25 September 1987, [1987] *Simon's Tax Intelligence* 724, para 5.
[262] HMRC, 'Concessions as at 6 April 2018' (n 157) 2.
[263] *Wilkinson* (n 241) [21].

concede … an allowance which Parliament could have granted but did not grant'.[264] It appears from the history of the case, however, that this was precisely HMRC's thinking on the issue at the time. At no stage in the litigation did the Inland Revenue appear to misconceive the boundaries of its discretion. Rather, it was the applicant widower who sought to have concessionary treatment extended. The Inland Revenue, on the other hand, had argued throughout the case, at the High Court,[265] Court of Appeal[266] and House of Lords[267] respectively that its managerial discretion could not be extended so as to grant an ESC to the widower as it would contradict Parliament's intention.

Thirdly, that *Wilkinson* could alone be the catalyst is unconvincing when contrasted with the non-reaction of the Commissioners to the judicial denunciations of ESCs in the series of *Vestey* cases some 25 years earlier. The Inland Revenue had argued in the *Vestey* cases that it was entitled to arrive at a working solution to incredibly complex and problematic legislation such that in any given case the Revenue would divvy up the tax payable on income arising in trusts, as it considered prudent.[268] The courts in turn concerned themselves more broadly with concessions. In somewhat caged language in *Vestey v IRC (No 1)*, Walton J questioned their legal basis:

> I am quite unable to understand upon what principle of law the Crown … feels itself entitled to mitigate [the monstrous results of the legislation] by such concessions as it chooses to make. One should be taxed by law, and not be untaxed by concession.[269]

Walton J was less equivocal in *Vestey v IRC (No 2)*:

> In the first place, I, in company with many other judges before me, am totally unable to understand upon what basis the Inland Revenue Commissioners are entitled to make extra-statutory concessions … This is not a simple matter of tax law. What is happening is that, in effect, despite the words of *Maitland, The Constitutional History of Eng*land (1909), p. 305, commenting on the Bill of Rights, 'This is the last of the dispensing power,' the Crown is now claiming just such a power.[270]

The House of Lords in *Vestey v IRC*[271] echoed the sentiments of Walton J. Lord Wilberforce held that the Inland Revenue's 'frightening'[272] and 'remarkable'[273] claim to a discretionary power in the case did not involve a process 'of construction,

[264] ibid.
[265] *Adrian John Wilkinson v The Commissioners of Inland Revenue* [2002] EWHC 182 (Admin), [2002] STC 347 [28] (Moses J).
[266] *R (Wilkinson) v Inland Revenue Commissioners* [2003] EWCA Civ 814, [2003] 1 WLR 2683, 2687.
[267] *Wilkinson* (n 241) [8].
[268] *Vestey v IRC (No 1)* [1979] Ch 177 (Ch), 194–95; *Vestey v IRC (No 2)* [1979] Ch 198 (Ch); *Vestey v IRC* [1980] AC 1148 (HL), 1169.
[269] *Vestey (No 1)* (n 268) 197.
[270] *Vestey (No 2)* (n 268) 203.
[271] *Vestey v IRC* (n 268).
[272] ibid 1172.
[273] ibid 1171.

even one of strained construction, but is one of rewriting the enactment'.[274] This would give rise to a course of interpretation 'which Parliament might certainly have taken, but which it has manifestly avoided'.[275] The courts, 'acting on constitutional principles, not only should not, but cannot, validate'[276] the Revenue's proposition as it would give rise to 'taxation by self-asserted administrative discretion and not by law'.[277] Lord Edmund-Davies similarly stated, 'it is surely high time to consider the basis of this claim by the executive to make such extra-statutory concessions'.[278]

Despite the clear denunciations by the justices in the *Vestey* cases of the use of HMRC's managerial discretion to effect concessions, the practice was not discontinued. In fact, the number of active Inland Revenue listed ESCs grew from 122 in 1980[279] to 169 by 1987,[280] reaching a peak of 179 by 1993.[281] Accordingly, the *Vestey* cases and the House of Lords *Wilkinson* judgment diverge at two distinct points. First in respect of the level of criticism afforded to the Inland Revenue in the former as against the brief two-paragraph explanation by Lord Hoffmann in the latter. Secondly, in that the Revenue was arguing for a wide discretionary power in the former (which it lost), but expressly contended against such jurisdiction in the latter (which it won), some 25 years subsequently. On the basis of this contrast and the fact that the tax authority's understanding of discretion clearly matured in the interim two decades, one would have logically expected the revenue bodies to have reviewed the existing concessions post-*Vestey* and not for HMRC to review concessions post-*Wilkinson*. The idea that *Wilkinson* could spur the review process alone, given the striking contrast with the continued use of ESCs following severe criticism in the *Vestey* cases, does not stand up to scrutiny.

V. Taxpayers and Representative Groups

Consultation generally serves an important democratic function as it gives parties a chance to have a say in those policies and rules which affect them.[282] This has been acknowledged by HMRC and the Government generally in respect of the contribution taxpayers and representative groups, including professional bodies,

[274] ibid 1170.
[275] ibid.
[276] ibid 1172.
[277] ibid 1173.
[278] ibid 1194.
[279] Board of Inland Revenue, 'Extra-statutory concessions in operation at 8 August 1980' (IR1 (1980)).
[280] See: Board of Inland Revenue, 'Inland Revenue extra-statutory concessions as at June 1985' (IR1 (1985)) and Board of Inland Revenue, 'Extra-Statutory Concessions Supplement' (IR1 (Supp) (1987)).
[281] Board of Inland Revenue, 'Extra-statutory concessions in operation at 31 December 1993' (IR1 (1994)).
[282] See for instance D Galligan, *Due Process and Fair Procedures* (Oxford, Oxford University Press, 1994) 128.

can make to the process of tax-policy formation.[283] As set out in 'Tax Consultation Framework', the Government and HMRC endeavour to engage interested parties on changes to tax policy and legislation at each key stage of developing and implementing the policy.[284] This includes:

- making clear at what stage the engagement is taking place so that its scope is clear;
- carrying out at least one formal, written, public consultation in areas of significant reform;
- setting out, as the policy develops, its strategy for stakeholder engagement including planned formal consultation periods, informal discussions, working groups and workshops;
- consulting, where possible, on the policy design, draft legislation and implementation of anti-avoidance and other revenue protection measures, provided this does not present additional risk to the Exchequer;
- minimising the occasions on which it consults only on a confidential basis. Where confidential consultation has been necessary the Government will be as transparent as possible about its outcome and consult openly if pursuing the policy change further;
- providing feedback which sets out the Government's response to the views received and makes clear what changes, if any, have been made to the planned approach as a result of those views.[285]

By consulting on tax policy, this gives interested parties the opportunity to scrutinise the process including calling for general or individual advice to be made available, thereby impacting accessibility, and where advice is provided to assist in relation to its correctness and clarity. In the context of the rule of law then, individual taxpayers and organisations which represent taxpayers can play an important role in relation to HMRC advice.

The commitment to open consultation on tax policy is supported by the practical evidence, though it should be cautioned that open consultation alone does not guarantee effective consultation.[286] Between 1 March 2013 and 26 September 2019, there were 259 publications on which there was consultation.[287] Between 14 February 2013 and 22 February 2010, HMRC put out and finalised consultation

[283] HM Treasury and HMRC, 'Tax Consultation Framework' (March 2011) 2; 'Tax policy making: a new approach' (June 2010) 3; HMRC, 'Making a difference: clarity and certainty. 2006 review of links with large business' (October 2007) 9.

[284] See: HM Treasury and HMRC, 'Tax Consultation Framework' (n 283) 4–5.

[285] ibid 3.

[286] See, for instance, House of Lords Select Committee on Economic Affairs, 'The Finance Bill 2008: Volume 1 Report' (HL 2007–08, 117-I) paras 12–39, noted in T Prosser, *The Economic Constitution* (Oxford, Oxford University Press, 2014) 98.

[287] This information was taken from the gov.uk website on 26 September 2019.

on 106 publications.[288] Between 11 February 2010 and March 2005, the number of publications produced for consultation was 136.[289]

The foregoing, however, has been concerned with the engagement of taxpayers in policy-making generally. What about the specific case of the promulgation of HMRC advice? In this regard, HMRC has previously endeavoured to issue published advice concurrently with legislation and work with large businesses to ensure that the advice is amended to reflect evolving commercial circumstances.[290] In other instances, consultation on tax policy matters can serve as the catalyst for the production of HMRC advice. For instance, in November 2010, the coalition Government announced plans to introduce a 'Patent Box', a preferential regime for profits arising from patents.[291] Further to this, HM Treasury and HMRC put out a consultative document in June 2011 seeking responses to government proposals. Responses indicated that detailed advice would additionally be required[292] and HMRC accordingly followed suit. A similar timeline arose in the case of the Summer Budget 2015 wherein it was announced that there would be reforms to the way dividend income is taxed. A consultation document was produced in December 2015,[293] and owing to concerns raised in the responses to the document, HMRC agreed to introduce advice to clarify the scope of the new provisions and to give practical examples as to how the new regime will operate.[294] Most pertinently, consultation has led to HMRC amending its advice after considering the views of taxpayers. On 4 August 2014, HMRC announced a change in practice set out in its advice in relation to the treatment of unremitted foreign income or gains used as collateral for a loan enjoyed in the UK.[295] A transitional period to 5 April 2016 was to take place in order to allow taxpayers to make necessary arrangements in their affairs so that they would align with the change in advice. Representative bodies voiced their concerns at the new arrangements, highlighting that many taxpayers had entered into arrangements prior to August 2014 in reliance on HMRC's advice, which would be very difficult to unwind. In light of the responses from the taxpaying community, HMRC agreed to amend its published advice so that its change would only take effect prospectively, thereby catching only those arrangements entered into *after* August 2014.[296]

[288] This information was taken from webarchive.nationalarchives.gov.uk on 22 July 2019 which displayed a snapshot of the HMRC website at 2 October 2013.

[289] This information was taken from webarchive.nationalarchives.gov.uk on 22 July 2019 which displayed a snapshot of the HMRC website at 2 October 2013.

[290] HMRC, 'Making a difference: clarity and certainty. 2006 review of links with large business' (October 2007) 9.

[291] See HMRC, 'Corporation Tax: the Patent Box' (January 2007).

[292] HM Treasury and HMRC, 'The Patent Box: December 2011 response to consultation' (December 2011) 12, 18 and 23.

[293] HMRC, 'Company distributions: Consultation Document' (December 2015).

[294] HMRC, 'Company distributions: Summary of Responses' (March 2016) 10, 14, 16 and 17.

[295] HMRC News, 'Remittance Basis' (August 2014).

[296] HMRC, 'Revenue and Customs Brief 16 (2015): remittance basis treatment of foreign income and gains used for loan collateral' (October 2015).

The provision of some channel to allow individual taxpayers to provide input on HMRC advice seems a prudent course of action. Some pieces of HMRC advice provide a formal means of doing so, such as in the case of the Business Income Manual, where there is a feedback link which directs an interested party to email a particular person to provide suggestions or comments about the advice.[297] But the presence of a channel allows taxpayers to provide unprompted assistance to HMRC. For instance, a 2016 paper produced by the Tax Law Review Committee of the IFS[298] details an example where initial HMRC advice was that stamp duty was payable on a court order which approved a scheme of arrangement, a formal means of restructuring a company in the UK.[299] The correct understanding is that stamp duty is payable on the instrument transferring the shares,[300] and it is normal practice that the terms of a scheme of arrangement require an instrument separate to the court order to actually transfer the shares (the court order itself merely approving the transferral). A taxpayer contacted HMRC in order so that this guidance could be revised and after months of discussion and consultation HMRC agreed to change the guidance.[301]

In sum, HMRC clearly demonstrates a commitment to consultation with taxpayers on policy matters, and importantly, it takes account of the views of taxpayers on the necessity for published HMRC advice at times to supplement the underlying law and in turn a willingness to amend the advice following critique by the community. A criticism which can be leveled is the ad hoc nature of the current regime in relation specifically to the promulgation and amendment of HMRC advice. Thus, whilst the Tax Consultation Framework determines HMRC's engagement with taxpayers on policy matters, there is silence on when HMRC will decide to promulgate or amend advice or policy following engagement with taxpayers and representative groups.

VI. Conclusion

Non-ministerial public bodies are generally utilised in OECD countries for the purpose of tax collection.[302] This is desirable insofar as it prevents politicians from getting their hands in the till or interfering in individual tax decisions. Such merit must however be weighed against the disadvantage of accountability having to be ensured through channels alternate to ministerial responsibility. As a result,

[297] HMRC, 'Business Income Manual: BIM Feedback' (May 2019).

[298] Disclosure: the author has been a member of the Committee since 2019.

[299] See Institute for Fiscal Studies, 'The Case for the Abolition of Stamp Duty' (November 2016) 12.

[300] See Finance Act 1999, Sch 13, para 1.

[301] See HMRC, 'Stamp Duty and Stamp Duty Reserve Tax: transfer schemes of arrangement' (November 2015).

[302] OECD, 'Tax Administration in OECD and Selected Non-OECD Countries: Comparative Information Series (2010)' (March 2011) 15.

formal oversight of HMRC is left to a number of bodies, namely select committees along with the NAO and CAG, and assessment of their role in scrutinising HMRC advice reveals why myriad issues of correctness, clarity and accessibility arise. The TSC tends to focus broadly on aspects of administration, policy and prudence, but not the scrutiny of the substance of HMRC advice. The focus of the NAO, CAG and PAC respectively has been on holding governmental departments to account over spending. Finally the tribunals and courts are hampered, it is suggested, by the twin handicaps of limited scope for intervention and lack of impact to date.

The current framework for scrutiny is not entirely without merit. The Adjudicator can provide valuable scrutiny. At the same time, owing to increasing exploration of the 'flexibility' contained within the governing 1967 statute, the Ombudsman has become a 'valuable tool in the ongoing process of calling the government to account'.[303] Within the office's sprawling ambit have inevitably come HMRC's advisory activities which the Ombudsman has demonstrated an ability to scrutinise. However, the contributions that the Adjudicator and Ombudsman have made and can make should not be exaggerated. Engagement with taxpayers and representative groups, albeit in an ad hoc fashion, has been demonstrated to be both something that HMRC is willing to engage in and that has demonstrable benefits. Finally, whilst the NAO and CAG currently perform a limited role, it does not follow that they lack the institutional competence to provide scrutiny of advice.[304]

Where the problems of correctness, clarity and accessibility go unresolved, an inevitable consequence of the lack of robust scrutiny, the taxpayer will not benefit from the HMRC advice as is required by the rule of law rationale advanced in this book. Moreover, these problems will have an impact also on the reliability of HMRC advice, as will be explained in the following chapter.

[303] Kirkham (n 118) 20.
[304] See below ch 7 in text at n 277.

6

Remedies

> But public servants are human, and it is human to err. They are not immune from the weaknesses which afflict the rest of mankind. They may, by words or conduct, arouse expectations which are later dashed*

I. Introduction

In order for the rule of law to be advanced, taxpayers to the greatest extent possible ought to be entitled to rely upon advice which affects them. Without reliability, the advice is essentially weightless and will fail to assist a taxpayer in understanding the legal consequences of her action(s). To this end, there ought to be appropriate mechanisms in place to ensure that the tax authority does not renege on its advice. Of course, formal rulings are binding on HMRC, as are instruments of general advice which have the force of law, such as some VAT notices.[1] But even outside of this context, it is the published position of HMRC that its advice can be binding, and so on paper that ought to be the end of the discussion. But HMRC qualifies this general position in several respects.[2] First, it must be demonstrated that the taxpayer's position falls within the scope of the advice. Secondly, there are particularities in respect of individual advice in that the taxpayer must have directed HMRC to all material facts and made HMRC aware of the purpose of the request for advice. Thirdly, there must not be a conflict with HMRC's duty to collect tax. This duty, as HMRC interprets it, means that HMRC must depart from its advice where there is for instance a change in the law or a change in the understanding of the law. It also means that the advice will not be binding where it is incorrect, though this is qualified to the extent that a taxpayer will be protected where she can show financial detriment would occur if the correct advice were applied.[3]

* Lord Bingham, Foreword to R Moules, *Actions against Public Officials: Legitimate Expectations, Misstatements and Misconduct* (London, Sweet and Maxwell, 2009).

[1] See, for instance, HMRC, 'How to use the VAT retail Apportionment Scheme' (VAT Notice 727/4) (January 2013). On formal rulings, see above ch 2 in text at n 18.

[2] See together HMRC, 'When you can rely on information or advice provided by HM Revenue and Customs' (March 2009) and HMRC, 'Admin Law Manual: ADML1300' (July 2016).

[3] There is confusion on this point in the publicly available HMRC guidance cited ibid. In the 'Admin Law Manual' it is also mentioned that it must be demonstrated that HMRC's conduct amounts to an abuse of power, but then (circularly) provides that an abuse of power would arise where a taxpayer can demonstrate financial detriment.

Even before assessing how HMRC follows this position in practice, these qualifications alone suggest that taxpayers need to be aware of the potential remedies available to them where HMRC seeks to renege on its advice.[4]

Where HMRC produces advice upon which the taxpayer seeks to rely, public law provides protection in the form of the doctrine of 'legitimate expectations'. Private law may in theory be of assistance to taxpayers, though this merits only brief consideration given that legitimate expectations is a much more developed taxpayer protection. There may be a temptation of those who are legally trained to fetishise legal protection, but any study of taxpayer remedies would be incomplete without consideration of the protections afforded outside the tribunals and courts system. In particular, the Adjudicator's Office ('Adjudicator') and Parliamentary and Health Service Ombudsman ('Ombudsman') can provide relief for taxpayers, though the jurisdiction and enforcement capability of these bodies suggest that their impact is necessarily limited. The overarching thesis in this chapter is that there are serious shortcomings in relation to the remedies available in terms of providing reliability for taxpayers.

The chapter will proceed by examining first how public law can assist taxpayers, assessing principally the common law doctrine of legitimate expectations though supplementing this discussion with consideration of its interaction with the European Convention on Human Rights ('ECHR') and EU law. The chapter will then briefly consider private law remedies. Finally, the chapter will consider the protections afforded outside the tribunals and courts system.

II. Public Law

The doctrine of legitimate expectations provides relief where a public authority goes back on an earlier indication that it would follow a certain course. If successfully invoked, it can provide a substantive remedy for a taxpayer. In other words, a substantive benefit in the form of the non-payment of money to HMRC.[5] Although the doctrine is one which has been in constant flux for several decades,[6] the broad tenets of a successful claim for a substantive remedy under this doctrine in tax

[4] This book is only concerned with holding HMRC to its advice. It does not consider the consequences for taxpayers in terms of distress and worry caused by HMRC for which taxpayers may be entitled to compensation. HMRC does provide payment for such distress: HMRC, 'Complaints and Remedy Guidance: CRG3200' (November 2018).

[5] This is to be contrasted with procedural remedies, such as a right to be consulted, which can also be granted in the case of legitimate expectations: *R (Bhatt Murphy (a firm)) v The Independent Assessor* [2008] EWCA Civ 755, [2008] All ER (D) 127 [47]–[49].

[6] *R v Inland Revenue Commissioners, ex parte Unilever plc* [1996] STC 681695 (Simon Brown LJ); *R (Nadarajah and Abdi) v Secretary of State for the Home Department* [2005] EWCA Civ 1363 [69] (Laws LJ). It is probably more settled now as a result of the Supreme Court decision in *R (Gallaher Group Ltd) v Competition and Markets Authority* [2018] UKSC 25, [2018] 2 WLR 1583. On which, see: S Daly and J Tomlinson, 'Administrative Inconsistency in the Courts' (2018) 23 *Judicial Review* 190.

cases are relatively set. The first is that there must exist a 'legitimate expectation'[7] and the second is that frustrating this expectation would be unlawful,[8] though these two limbs are not mutually exclusive.

On the first limb, the initial pronouncement of the law in this area came in the case of *R v Inland Revenue Commissioners, ex parte MFK Underwriting* ('*MFK Underwriting*').[9] Therein Bingham LJ (as he then was)[10] set out two conditions necessary for an expectation to be legitimate in tax, from which there has been little subsequent divergence.[11] The first is that the taxpayer placed all her cards face upwards on the table.[12] This condition is applicable only where an individual taxpayer has sought out a ruling from HMRC.[13] In such an instance, she must give full details of the specific transaction on which she seeks the ruling and she must indicate the purpose of the ruling sought, in other words, that she seeks to rely upon it.[14] The second condition is that the taxpayer received a promise, representation or assurance, or there was an established practice,[15] which was clear, unambiguous and devoid of relevant qualification.[16] Although a 'literal reading' of Bingham LJ's judgment might suggest this condition would not apply to communications directed at taxpayers generally,[17] it has later come to be accepted that it does.[18] In the case, he remarked that a statement formally published by HMRC to the world 'might safely be regarded as binding, *subject to its terms*, in any case falling clearly within them' (emphasis added).[19] Logically, however, a case would fall clearly within the scope of a publication *only* if the terms were clear and unambiguous.[20] Similarly, 'its terms' would need to be unqualified as a condition precedent to creating an expectation upon which there could be any reliance.[21]

The second limb of the doctrine is that frustrating the expectation must be unlawful and the onus shifts to the public authority to demonstrate that it

[7] See *R (Davies) v HMRC; R (Gaines-Cooper) v HMRC* [2011] UKSC 47, [2012] 1 All ER 1048 [25]–[29] (Lord Wilson).

[8] *United Policyholders v AG of Trinidad and Tobago* [2016] UKPC 17, [2016] 1 WLR 3383 [38] cited approvingly in *R (Hely-Hutchinson) v HMRC* [2017] EWCA Civ 1075, [2017] STC 2048 (*Hely-Hutchinson* (CA)) [36].

[9] [1990] 1 WLR 1545 (CA). This dicta was affirmed in *R (Bancoult) v Secretary of State for Foreign and Commonwealth Affairs (No 2)* [2008] UKHL 61, [2009] 1 AC 453 [60] (Lord Hoffmann).

[10] Throughout this chapter he will be referred to as Bingham LJ given that at issue throughout is his judgment in *MFK Underwriting*.

[11] The most recent tax case on legitimate expectations to reach the Supreme Court was that of *Gaines-Cooper* (n 7) wherein the court based its analysis on Bingham LJ's formula ([28]).

[12] *MFK Underwriting* (n 9) 1569.

[13] ibid.

[14] ibid.

[15] This aspect is added here due to the later judgment of *Unilever* (n 6).

[16] *MFK Underwriting* (n 9) 1569.

[17] ibid.

[18] *Bancoult* (n 9) [60]; *Gaines-Cooper* (n 7) [29] (Lord Wilson).

[19] *MFK Underwriting* (n 9) 1569.

[20] See *R (Tunbridge Wells BC) v Sevenoaks Magistrates' Court* [2001] EWHC 897 (Admin), [41] (Sullivan J).

[21] See: *Bancoult* (n 9) [60] (Lord Hoffmann); *Gaines-Cooper* (n 7) [29] (Lord Wilson).

is acting lawfully.[22] As this limb of the doctrine developed this was sometimes understood as an action on the part of a public authority which is so unfair as to amount to an 'abuse of power',[23] or 'conspicuously unfair'.[24] But claims for legitimate expectations should no longer be couched in such language. Following the decision in *R (Gallaher Group Ltd) v Competition and Markets Authority* ('*Gallaher*'),[25] it is clear that the doctrine of legitimate expectations is not a *sui generis* ground of review, but rather that an unlawful action in respect of a legitimate expectation must be grounded in the accepted grounds for judicial review.[26] Generally, this will require HMRC to demonstrate that refusing to give effect to the legitimate expectation is not *unreasonable*.[27] In the context of legitimate expectation tax cases, this essentially invites a balancing exercise between, on the one hand, detriment to the private interest of the individual in frustrating an expectation as against the detriment to the public interest, on the other hand, in giving effect to it.[28] Mere unfairness as such, which could be characterised as 'a bit rich' but nevertheless understandable, will not suffice.[29] It is necessary that the decision by HMRC to renege on its earlier communication is so *unreasonable* that it should not be permitted to stand.[30] An example of such unreasonableness would be HMRC reneging on an earlier agreement with immediate effect.[31] Giving the taxpayer a reasonable transitional period in which to rearrange her affairs, on the other hand, would not.[32]

Interestingly it is not necessary that the commitment on which the claim for legitimate expectation is grounded is actually communicated to the affected party. The orthodox case where the doctrine will assist a taxpayer is where she has received information from HMRC on which she then acts. However, the doctrine

[22] *Paponette & Ors v Attorney General of Trinidad and Tobago (Trinidad and Tobago)* [2010] UKPC 32, [2012] 1 AC 1 [37] (Dyson SCJ). On which, see: *R (on the application of) v General Medical Council* [2013] EWCA Civ 327, [2013] 1 WLR 2801 [58] and *In the matter of an application by Geraldine Finucane for Judicial Review* (Northern Ireland) [2019] UKSC 7 [64] (Lord Kerr).

[23] *R v North and East Devon Health Authority (ex p Coughlan)* [2001] QB 213 (CA), [2000] 3 All ER 850 [57] (Lord Woolf); *In Re Preston* [1985] 1 AC 835, 864H, [1985] STC 282 (HL) (Lord Templeman).

[24] *Unilever* (n 6) 695 (Simon Brown LJ).

[25] *Gallaher* (n 6).

[26] Which has a certain circularity as there is no common consensus on the categorisation of the grounds for review; see M Elliott and R Thomas, *Public Law*, 3rd edn (Oxford, Oxford University Press, 2017) 497. See *CCSU v Minister for the Civil Service* [1985] AC 374 for the famous tripartite categorisation.

[27] See *Gallaher* (n 6), in particular [41]. In the High Court in *R (Hely-Hutchinson) v HMRC* [2015] EWHC 3261 (Admin), [2016] STC 962 (*Hely-Hutchinson* (HC)), the taxpayer succeeded essentially on the ground that there were relevant considerations which were not taken into account. That case was overturned in the Court of Appeal (*Hely-Hutchinson* (CA) (n 8)) and in any event preceded the Supreme Court judgment in *Gallaher*.

[28] See: *Coughlan* (n 23) [57] (Lord Woolf).

[29] *Unilever* (n 6) 697 (Simon Brown LJ).

[30] ibid; *R v Inland Revenue Commissioners, ex parte Unilever plc* [1994] STC 841, 849 (Macpherson J).

[31] For instance, *Unilever* (n 6).

[32] *R (Cameron) v HMRC* [2012] EWHC 1174 (Admin), [2012] STC 1691 (Wyn Williams J) [70]–[71]. See also: *R (Bamber) v HMRC* [2005] EWHC 3221 (Admin), [2006] STC 1035 [59] (Lindsay J).

also imposes a requirement on public bodies to act consistently across persons, unless there is a good reason not to.[33] Of course, when it comes to the balancing act between private and public interests in terms of assessing the *reasonableness* of reneging on the earlier commitment, the person will have a stronger claim where she acted in reliance on the advice. The claim will be stronger again where she has relied on the advice to her detriment.[34] It is for this reason that above it was noted that HMRC's position does not properly reflect the correct legal position on when advice can be binding. To recall, HMRC's position is that it must collect tax where the advice is incorrect unless it can be demonstrated that there is financial detriment. But the correct legal position is less strict – yes, financial detriment *can* demonstrate unreasonableness on the part of HMRC and it will be in exceptional circumstances where its absence is not fatal for substantive legitimate expectations claims, but it is not the *only* way to demonstrate unlawful conduct.[35]

The two limbs to the doctrine are not mutually exclusive, but are interrelated. For instance, the clarity of a representation will have a bearing upon whether resiling from it would be unreasonable.[36] By this standard, bespoke advice to an individual taxpayer is likely to be much more targeted than general advice, thus by its nature making it more likely to be unreasonable to resile from it.[37] On the other hand, if a taxpayer were to have concealed material information in the request for a ruling, HMRC would not be acting improperly in refusing to give effect to it.[38]

A. Inaptness of the Doctrine of Legitimate Expectations

Having set out the initial framework within which legitimate expectation claims are assessed, it is now possible to move on to the overarching argument of this section, namely that the doctrine of legitimate expectations provides insufficient protection for taxpayers seeking to rely upon HMRC advice. There are five key

[33] *Gallaher* (n 6) [29] (Lord Carnwath); *Bancoult* (n 9) [182] (Lord Mance). The fact that the doctrine protects various interests is well explained in R Williams, 'The Multiple Doctrines of Legitimate Expectations' (2016) 132 *LQR* 639.

[34] See *R (Bibi) v Newham London Borough Council* [2001] EWCA Civ 607, [2002] 1 WLR 237 (Schiemann LJ) [29]; *R v Department of Education and Employment, ex parte Begbie* [1999] EWCA Civ 2100 [48] (Gibson LJ); *Bancoult* (n 9) [60] (Lord Hoffmann). For a tax case where this arises, see *R (Aozora) v HMRC* [2017] EWHC 2881 (Admin), [2018] STC 11 [98] (Sir Kenneth Parker). The courts' focus on detriment overlooks the possibility of developing the doctrine on the basis of what David Owens calls 'authority interest'. The basic idea is that once a promise has been given, the control over that promise shifts to the promisee and so the promisee should control whether the promise is not given effect. The virtue of this position is that 'human beings often want such authority for its own sake (not just to facilitate prediction or coordination)'. See: D Owens, 'A Simple Theory of Promising' (2006) 115 *Philosophical Review* 51.

[35] This was noted by Whipple J in *Hely-Hutchinson* (HC) (n 27) [64] and accepted by the Court of Appeal: *Hely-Hutchinson* (CA) (n 8) [92].

[36] See: *Tunbridge Wells BC* (n 20) [41] (Sullivan J).

[37] *Bhatt Murphy* (n 5) [46].

[38] See *R v IRC, ex p Matrix Securities Ltd* [1994] 1 WLR 334.

problems for taxpayers, which broadly map on to issues of correctness, clarity and accessibility under assessment in earlier chapters. The first two relate to satisfying the second limb, binding HMRC even in the case of incorrect advice ('Correctness') and relatedly, negating HMRC's desire to maintain control ('Control'). The second two relate to satisfying the first limb of a successful claim, namely demonstrating sufficient clarity on the part of HMRC ('Clarity') and not being caught by a qualification ('Qualifications'). Finally, there is the issue of access to justice ('Access').

i. Correctness

Though the doctrine of legitimate expectations generally performs an important function in holding public authorities to their representations or practices, a cynic might note that it is at its most useful in tax where, but for a representation of HMRC, monies would otherwise have been due.[39] But that begs a critical question concerning HMRC's duties – how can it be within HMRC's powers to uphold an expectation that it will not collect tax which it has a duty to collect? The answer is that it is within HMRC's powers to uphold an expectation even if this means collecting less tax than is due.[40] But in order to explain the answer in this particular context it is necessary to start by noting that a public authority must act lawfully, including by acting within its powers (*intra vires*).[41] HMRC would accordingly be acting ultra vires if it sought to sell financial products,[42] or to levy taxes.[43] Given that the duty is to collect tax, this requires at a minimum that HMRC not act directly contrary by explicitly agreeing not to investigate or challenge a taxpayer's future affairs in return for a fixed sum of money, as occurred in *Al-Fayed v Advocate General for Scotland (CIR)*.[44] But it has already been established that it is within HMRC's powers to provide assistance to taxpayers in the form of advice,[45] and this is so even if the advice is incorrect in the sense of misunderstanding a taxing provision (procedural or substantive)[46] or its application to the facts.

[39] *R (on the application of Lower Mill Estate Ltd and Conservation Builders) v Revenue and Customs Commissioners* [2008] EWHC 2409 (Admin), [2008] BTC 5743 [22] (Blake J). It is left open here whether there is such a thing as *the* right answer in tax as to how much tax is due by talking only of a mistake leading to *an* answer which is incorrect.

[40] See ch 3 section II B i.

[41] The doctrine of ultra vires is one of the cornerstones of the UK's constitutional framework and in broad terms forms the basis for judicial intervention. See *Boddington v British Transport Police* [1998] UKHL 13; [1999] 2 AC 143, 171 (Lord Steyn); *R v Hull University Visitor, ex parte Page* [1993] AC 682 (HL), 701 (Lord Browne-Wilkinson). For prerogative powers and non-statutory bodies, see for instance, *R v Panel on Take-overs and Mergers, ex parte Datafin* [1987] QB 815 (CA).

[42] See on this point, the case of *Hazell v Hammersmith and Fulham LBC* [1992] 2 AC 1 (HL).

[43] *Attorney-General v Wilts United Dairies Ltd* (1921) 39 TLR 781 (CA).

[44] [2004] ScotCS 112, [2004] STC 1703 (IH).

[45] See ch 3 in text at n 74.

[46] By this I mean to include both those provisions which impose or relieve taxes, and those provisions which impose obligations on either HMRC or the taxpayer as to the procedure to be followed in order to comply with the substantive provisions.

Were it otherwise, there would be undesirable consequences that it must be assumed were not intended by Parliament.[47] For instance, it would result in injustice for taxpayers who sincerely placed reliance upon HMRC's advice.[48] It would also be impractical, for HMRC would be held to be acting beyond its powers every time it makes a mistake, which itself would produce the perverse incentive to delay or avoid decisions indefinitely for fear of making mistakes. Or indeed, conversely, the incentive might be to be cavalier, knowing that any mistakes can later be corrected.[49] To this end, Bingham LJ in *MFK Underwriting* rightly rejected as too narrow the notion that any mistake on the part of the tax authority resulting in less tax collected would be in conflict with the statutory duty.[50] Indeed, despite what counsel may have argued in the case, Leonard Beighton, the Director-General of the Inland Revenue, recognised that the Revenue could be bound by assurances 'however unsound the rulings might have been'.[51] Moreover, HMRC's practice is to let past mistakes lie, thereby accepting that mistakes are within its powers. For instance, by way of ESC A19 taxpayers can ask HMRC not to seek taxes due if it has made a mistake because it did not act on information provided.[52]

One could seek to invoke the Bill of Rights Act 1688/9, Article 1 of which provides that the suspension of laws without consent of Parliament is illegal, whilst Article 4 proscribes the levying of taxes without Parliamentary approval. Thus HMRC mistakes which either result in more or less tax than is due could be constitutionally problematic, though in response it should be countered that, for the reasons already listed, Parliament's will is not undermined as it can be taken to have intended that mistakes are within the powers it granted HMRC.

Further, it does not undermine the rule of law rationale for providing advice if the advice is itself occasionally wrong. In a parallel context, Lord Reed noted in *AXA General Insurance Ltd v Lord Advocate*[53] that 'the protection of the rule of law does not require that every allegation of unlawful conduct by a public authority

[47] In an earlier article, I was more hesitant to suggest this – but even if this proposition is incorrect, an alternate argument on the basis of common law constitutionalism can produce the same result. See S Daly, 'Recent developments in tax: *vires* revisited' [2016] 2 *Public Law* 190. The argument would go as follows: incorrect advice may be unlawful. But it is also unlawful for HMRC to act contrary to the principle of good administration. Thus, the role of the court in such an instance would be to balance the two unlawful actions against each other. This latter argument ought to be credited to Rebecca Williams with whom the author had invaluable discussions when writing the aforementioned article. See also: P Craig, 'Representations by Public Bodies' (1977) 93 *LQR* 398, 413–17.

[48] P Craig, *Administrative Law*, 8th edn (London, Sweet and Maxwell, 2016) 700. Though Craig was speaking in the context of ultra vires expectations, the argument still applies as in the situation discussed here the issue is whether there ought to be an expanded category of actions which should count as ultra vires.

[49] See *Rowland v Environment Agency* [2003] EWCA Civ 1885, [2005] Ch 1 [103] (May LJ); *Stretch v West Dorset DC* (1999) 77 P & CR 342, [1998] 3 EGLR 62 (CA) 66–67 (Peter Gibson LJ).

[50] See *MFK Underwriting* (n 9) 1567C and 1568F. See also *Gaines-Cooper* (n 7) [26] (Lord Wilson).

[51] L Beighton, 'The Finance Bill process: scope for reform?' [1995] *British Tax Review* 33, 41.

[52] See in HMRC, 'Extra-Statutory Concessions: Concessions as at 6 April 2018' (April 2018). See also ESC B41 in that list and HMRC, 'What happens if we've paid you too much tax credits (COP 26)' (April 2019).

[53] [2011] UKSC 46, [2012] AC 868.

must be examined by a court'.[54] What is important, it is submitted, is that on the whole taxpayers are better advised as to the legal consequences of their actions because HMRC provides advice. Moreover, the designation of advice as incorrect in such a context is far from straightforward – does it take the Supreme Court determining it to be incorrect or would it suffice simply if there was a legal opinion to that effect? Further, whilst incorrect advice does not help individuals understand the *true* legal consequences of their actions, it does help individuals understand the de facto consequences of their actions. In terms of planning their lives then, human dignity, the value which underpins the thin account of the rule of law, is offended by removing this foreseeability about the consequences of actions. But it should go without saying that HMRC of course should still strive to ensure that the advice is correct.[55]

However, whilst the presence of a mistake does not render the advice unlawful, it will nevertheless prove problematic for taxpayers as it affords HMRC a strong argument (though not a 'trump card')[56] that it has a 'good reason' to frustrate the expectation – namely that Parliament has prescribed that more tax is due – hence shielding HMRC from an accusation of irrationality.[57] To this end, it is often remarked by the courts that a taxpayer's prima facie legitimate expectation is to be taxed in accordance with the law.[58] There is a strong public interest in the imposition of taxation in accordance with the law.[59] It is for this reason that HMRC will be held to be acting lawfully where it retrospectively changes its advice where a mistake has been made.

For instance, in the case of *Hely-Hutchinson v HMRC*[60] the Court of Appeal held that the fact that the guidance which the taxpayer sought to rely on contained an error inter alia justified HMRC's decision not to honour its previous advice. In 2003, the Inland Revenue issued guidance in respect of the calculation of capital gains tax on sales of share options.[61] In 2009, HMRC acknowledged that the guidance contained an error of law and produced revised guidance.[62] As regards closed cases where the 2003 guidance was relied upon, HMRC has applied the terms of

[54] ibid [170].

[55] See ch 4 in text at n 8.

[56] *Hely-Hutchinson* (HC) (n 27) [43] (Whipple J).

[57] On mistakes see for instance *Gallaher* (n 6) [62] (Lord Briggs); *R (O'Brien) v Independent Assessor* [2007] 2 AC 312 (HL) [30] (Lord Bingham); *Customs and Excise Comrs v National Westminster Bank plc* [2003] EWHC 1822 (Ch), [2003] STC 1072 [66] (Jacob J).

[58] *MFK Underwriting* (n 9) 1569; *R (Greenwich Property Ltd) v Commissioners of Customs and Excise* [2001] EWHC 230 (Admin); *Lower Mill Estate* (n 39) [13] (Collins J); *Gaines-Cooper* (n 7) [28] (Lord Wilson).

[59] *Samarkand Film Partnership No. 3 & Ors v Revenue And Customs* [2017] EWCA Civ 77, [2017] STC 926 (*Samarkand* (CA)) [115].

[60] *Hely-Hutchinson* (CA) (n 8). Part of this discussion is extracted from a longer case note that the author has written: S Daly, 'Legitimate expectations and HMRC advice' (2018) 77 *Cambridge Law Journal* 265. For another example where a mistake was critical, see: *R (Veolia and Viridor) v HMRC* [2016] EWHC 1880 (Admin), [2016] STI 2201.

[61] Inland Revenue, 'Technical Note' (January 2003).

[62] HMRC, 'HMRC Brief 30/09: Shares acquired before 10 April 2003 by exercising employee share options – allowable deductions' (July 2019).

the 2003 guidance. Where the case was open in 2009, as in the case of the taxpayer Ralph Hely-Hutchinson, HMRC applied the less favourable 2009 guidance. The Court of Appeal found that HMRC's decision to do so was lawful, critically noting that HMRC had 'good reason' to depart from it.[63] This was because it contained a mistake, but the Court did little to elaborate upon the circumstances in which a mistake can be said to have arisen. What about the case where it is highly unclear whether HMRC has previously made a mistake? What counts as a mistake – does internal legal advice pointing out a possible mistake suffice? What if a tribunal or other judge finds against an HMRC interpretation?[64] Perhaps the lack of reasoning is explained by the fact that HMRC's error was particularly obvious and hence it went without having to be said that in such an obvious case HMRC could reverse its position. But that explanation is difficult to square with the Court's statement earlier in the judgment that it was 'not concerned with the correctness of HMRC's view'.[65]

In any event, it is clear that in many cases HMRC will be found to have acted lawfully by frustrating a legitimate expectation if the underlying advice contained a mistake. Taxpayers can be more confident in cases where they can demonstrate detrimental reliance, as courts are generally comfortable with holding it to be unlawful in such circumstances to frustrate the expectation.[66] The taxpayer needs to be able to show something akin to positive causation[67] – for example, where a taxpayer builds student accommodation thinking it will be entitled to relief,[68] or sells a family home and moves abroad[69] or, in the case of a seafarer, sets off from anchorage before midnight.[70] The detriment of simply having to pay the tax that is due will not suffice alone – recalling that a taxpayer's prima facie expectation is to be taxed in accordance with the law[71] – nor will the detriment caused by events external to the reliance on the advice.[72]

[63] *Hely-Hutchinson* (CA) (n 8) [62]–[65].

[64] Indeed, HMRC has previously ignored First-tier Tribunal decisions which it dislikes. The *HSBC Holdings plc and The Bank of New York Mellon Corporation v HMRC* [2012] UKFTT 163 (TC) decision, which was not followed in HMRC, 'Revenue and Customs Brief 14/12' (May 2012), as noted in T Bowler, 'HMRC's Discretion: The Application of the *Ultra Vires* Rule and the Legitimate Expectation Doctrine' (Institute for Fiscal Studies, December 2014) para 3.1.

[65] *Hely-Hutchinson* (CA) (n 8) [3].

[66] *Bibi* (n 34) [29] (Schiemann LJ); *Begbie* (n 34) [48] (Peter Gibson LJ); *Bancoult* (n 9) [60] (Lord Hoffmann).

[67] In *Aozora* (n 34) [98], Sir Kenneth Parker found against the taxpayer's claim for legitimate expectation, noting that in order to demonstrate that it was unlawful for HMRC to resile on the expectation, the taxpayer would have to be able to show that 'but for the advice that unilateral tax credit was available, it would not have made the business decision that it did, but would have made a business decision that was more favourable from a tax point of view'.

[68] *Greenwich Property* (n 58).

[69] *Cameron* (n 32).

[70] Adopting the facts of *Gaines-Cooper* (n 7).

[71] See text at n 58. Though this would be different in the case where a taxpayer would account for the tax but for the legitimate expectation and pass on the cost to an end consumer as in *R (Biffa Waste Services Ltd) v Revenue and Customs* [2016] EWHC 1444 (Admin), [2017] Env LR 10.

[72] *Hely-Hutchinson* (CA) (n 8) [92].

Further, taxpayers may also succeed if they can show comparative unfairness because a similarly placed taxpayer has received different treatment, though we have yet to see a successful tax case to date where this argument by a taxpayer has succeeded.[73] The problem lies in finding a comparator in a 'materially identical'[74] position, rather than simply finding another taxpayer who has been treated differently. In *Hely-Hutchinson*, the taxpayer argued that the relevant comparator was people who submitted their tax returns in reliance on the 2003 guidance, but the Court of Appeal held that the relevant comparator group was those taxpayers whose returns were still open when the 2009 guidance was introduced.[75] And the taxpayer was treated the same as those in the latter category, though not those in the former category.

Perhaps in the future, the Court may also accept the rule of law rationale advanced in this book, or at least the human dignity aspect underpinning the principle, as an important factor in determining whether it would be unlawful to resile from incorrect advice. But as it currently stands, beyond exceptional circumstances where detrimental reliance or comparative unfairness or something akin to either can be demonstrated, the orthodox position that one cannot rely upon incorrect advice holds. The taxpayer accordingly is severely hindered by an inability to rely upon advice which contains incorrect information. The taxpayer is also hindered, at a broader level, by the uncertainty as to whether HMRC should discover a mistake at a later date and rescind the previous treatment.

ii. Control

A bolder proposition is that the doctrine of legitimate expectations is hampered by HMRC's desire to maintain control over use of its advice, so as to counteract unforeseen advantages being gained by taxpayers. The desire to maintain control most likely stems from discomfort with the idea that HMRC is to blame for reduced revenues for the exchequer. Several arguments are advanced in support of this contention, drawing upon the prevalence of 'qualifications' and HMRC's approach to changes of interpretation. In the first instance, the assertion is borne out by the very insertion of 'qualifications' such as health warnings and provisos. In *R (Davies) v HMRC; R (Gaines-Cooper) v HMRC* (*Gaines-Cooper*),[76] HMRC argued successfully that the insertion of the 'health warning' encouraging contact

[73] Whipple J upheld the taxpayer's complaint in the High Court in *Hely-Hutchinson* on the basis that HMRC should also take into account the comparative unfairness of treating taxpayers with open cases differently from persons whose cases are closed (*Hely-Hutchinson* (HC) (n 27) [71]). Although the decision was overturned by the Court of Appeal, the Court did not reject Whipple J's decision that comparative is a relevant consideration – *Hely-Hutchinson* (CA) (n 8) [52]–[65]. For another failed tax case invoking comparative unfairness, see *City Shoes v HMRC* [2018] EWCA Civ 315, [2018] STC 762.

[74] See *Hely-Hutchinson* (CA) (n 8) [53] and [62].

[75] See *Hely-Hutchinson* (CA) (n 8) [64].

[76] *Gaines-Cooper* (n 7).

with HMRC in any case of difficulty in applying the relevant guidance, prevented HMRC from being bound *ab initio*.[77] Given that this judgment was handed down in 2011, the continued use of health warnings indicates that the purpose is to reserve to HMRC control over the use of its published advice. By extension, the inclusion of provisos precluding reliance in a case of 'tax avoidance' similarly seeks to endow broad discretion upon HMRC. HMRC uses the word 'avoidance' to mean bending the rules of the tax system to gain a tax advantage that Parliament never intended,[78] but this is not a definition from the case law, and nor is it a statutory definition of tax avoidance.[79] By using its own broader definition, HMRC can take a wide approach as to what it might define as 'avoidance', giving the body the opportunity to counteract use of its advice by the taxpayer which it dislikes. The explicit insertion is crucial, as noted by Collins J in *R (Greenwich Property Ltd) v Commissioners of Customs and Excise ('Greenwich Property')*[80] as such a proviso must be expressed and cannot merely be implied into communicated material.[81]

Secondly, the approach to changes in legal advice reinforces the contention that HMRC seeks to reserve discretion to counteract benefits perceived to be undue, given that it is not forced to do so. HMRC's position in such an instance is that it is generally bound to follow the new legal interpretation.[82] Carnwath J (as he then was) in *R v Customs and Excise Commissioners, ex parte F & I Services Ltd*[83] noted that a 'bona fide change of legal opinion within the commissioners *might* be expected' (emphasis added) to preclude the previous advice from being binding prospectively.[84] But HMRC may also seek to apply the new legal interpretation retrospectively, as occurred in the case of *Hely-Hutchinson*, where the new interpretation applied to all who had previously sought to rely on the 2003 guidance and whose cases were still open in 2009. In neither case, particularly in the latter, is it an *obligation* for HMRC to do so. Of course, it is under a duty to collect taxes and there is a strong public interest in collecting taxes which are due. But a change of legal opinion does not prove that taxes are due, no more than an unfavourable

[77] ibid [32] (Lord Wilson); [64] (Lord Hope); [66] (Lord Walker).

[78] HMRC, 'Tax avoidance: an introduction' (September 2016).

[79] On case law, see: M Devereux, J Freedman and J Vella, 'Tax Avoidance' (Oxford University Centre for Business Taxation, December 2012) 3–7. Some judges have attempted to do so. See for instance: *IRC v Willoughby* [1997] 4 All ER 65 (HL), [1997] STC 995, 1003h–1004a (Lord Nolan). On statutes, see: A Seely, 'Tax avoidance and tax evasion' (House of Commons Briefing Paper 7948, May 2019) 3. The General Anti-Abuse Rule legislation for instance does not define avoidance, but simply 'abusive' practices (see Finance Act 2013, s 207). The Disclosure of Tax Avoidance Schemes regime on the other hand uses hallmarks to define avoidance (see for instance Tax Avoidance Schemes (Prescribed Descriptions of Arrangements) Regulations 2006 (SI 2006/1543), reg 6).

[80] *Greenwich Property* (n 58).

[81] ibid [24]–[25].

[82] Institute of Chartered Accountants in England and Wales, 'Legitimate Expectation and Reliance on HMRC Guidance' (Technical Release 06/13) 14; *Southern Cross Employment Agency Ltd v HMRC* [2014] UKFTT 088 (TC), [21].

[83] *R v Customs and Excise Commissioners, ex parte F & I Services Ltd* [2000] STC 364 (QBD).

[84] ibid 377; affirmed by Robert Walker LJ in the Court of Appeal: *F & I Services Ltd v Customs and Excise Commissioners* [2001] EWCA Civ 762, [2001] STC 939 [66].

non-final tribunal or court decision proves that taxes are not due, and vice versa. HMRC has the power to make mistakes and when it realises a potential mistake, its *obligation* is to consider its options.[85] It may be lawful to renege on prior commitments as in *Hely-Hutchinson*, but it may be lawful also to take other approaches.[86]

iii. Clarity

A legitimate expectation can only arise on the basis of HMRC advice which is of sufficient clarity. The manner in which this condition has been interpreted[87] opens it up to two alternate criticisms, however: that fulfilling the condition is exceedingly difficult; and/or that the requirements for its satisfaction are so malleable as to deprive HMRC advice of its normative, rule of law utility.[88] Both points can be best illustrated by examining the successful legitimate expectation cases, thereafter contrasting them with unsuccessful cases wherein conditions were implied into the advice. This detailed analysis of the case law also will serve the practical purpose of assisting taxpayers who are engaged in disputes with HMRC as to whether they can rely on HMRC advice.[89]

In *R v Inland Revenue Commissioners, ex parte Unilever plc*,[90] the question was whether HMRC could resile from its previous conduct, wherein over the course of 20 years it had accepted tax relief claims from taxpayers outside the statutorily prescribed period.[91] The Court of Appeal held that HMRC acted unlawfully by resiling from this trend, enforcing the time bar and denying the taxpayers claims for relief. The conduct on the part of HMRC had given rise to an unequivocal expectation that relief claims would be accepted beyond the statutory time period.[92] The case of *R (Cameron) v HMRC* ('*Cameron*')[93] concerned two seafarers who successfully contended that they were entitled to the seafarer's

[85] The Court of Appeal in *R v Hertfordshire CC Ex p Cheung* [1986] 3 WLUK 310 found that there was an implied discretion to reconsider cases which were decided on a mistaken view of the law. On which see: C Lewis, 'Judicial review: time limits and retrospectivity' [1987] *Public Law* 21.

[86] As with ESC A19, ESC B41 and COP26 noted at n 52.

[87] J Maugham, 'What can you legitimately expect?' (2013) 1114 *Tax Journal* 13, 13; K Smith and R Doran 'GSTS Pathology LLP: When do legitimate expectations end?' (2013) 1177 *Tax Journal* 16, 16. Many cases falter at this hurdle. For instance, *R (Corkteck) v HMRC* [2009] EWHC 785 (Admin), [2009] STC 1681; *MFK Underwriting* (n 9).

[88] The generality of the criteria for establishing a legitimate expectation has also been highlighted by the courts, see: *Nadarajah* (n 6) [67] (Laws LJ). See also Williams, 'Multiple Doctrines' (2016).

[89] There is another case not included here in which the taxpayer was successful in invoking the doctrine, namely, *R (on the application of GSTS Pathology LLP and others) v Revenue and Customs Commissioners* [2013] EWHC 1801 (Admin), [2013] STC 2017, which has been relied on in later cases. It is not mentioned here because at issue was an injunction, rather than substantive relief long term from the monies otherwise payable.

[90] *Unilever* (n 6).

[91] Income and Corporation Taxes Act 1988, s 393(11)(2).

[92] See also *R (ABCIFER) v Secretary of State for Defence* [2003] EWCA Civ 473, [2003] QB 1397, [72]; cf P Sales and K Steyn, 'Legitimate expectations in English public law: an analysis' [2004] *Public Law* 564, 575.

[93] *Cameron* (n 32).

deduction from their earnings because they had relied upon guidance. The 'eligible period' for seafarer's deduction was calculated by reference to days of absence from the UK,[94] which in turn pivoted upon whether a person was absent the UK at midnight.[95] However, determining whether a seafarer was in or outside the UK, defined by a 12-mile radius, at midnight would be incredibly difficult and onerous to prove. To this end, a concession was issued in guidance published to seafarers whereby if the boat upon which the seafarer was present left its berth or anchorage prior to midnight, the seafarer would be taken to have left the UK.[96] HMRC contended that this concession would only apply where the ship was destined for another country.[97] The taxpayers' understanding was that this concession would apply regardless of whether the ship was ultimately destined for another country, but would be satisfied simply if it left the UK.[98] The guidance upon which they sought to rely read as follows:

> A day of absence from the UK is any day when you are outside the UK at the end of that day (midnight). We normally treat a vessel as having left the UK at the moment it leaves berth or anchorage, on a voyage which will take it outside UK territorial waters. Arrival times are treated in a similar way.[99]

Wyn Williams J found that this wording unequivocally provided that, once outside at midnight, the seafarer would be treated as being absent the UK.[100] It is difficult, from a reading of the text, to arrive at any other conclusion, and HMRC did not press this point. HMRC's case, in reality, pivoted upon whether this 'concession' was superseded by a subsequent, narrower concession.[101] In *Greenwich Property*,[102] the University of Greenwich had decided to create a new student residence. Half had been completed with the University's own funds, with the other half funded through a Private Finance Initiative (PFI). The PFI agreement prescribed that the accommodation would be let privately during the summer months. The applicant sought to rely upon a published concession[103] from HMRC to the effect that the building would be zero-rated,[104] notwithstanding the fact that students would not be the sole inhabitants of the residential accommodation. This published concession read as follows:

> Higher education institutions are in a peculiar position as they know that some use is likely to be made of student accommodation for non-qualifying purposes during vacations but such use is difficult to quantify. In the circumstances, because in any event tax

[94] Income Tax (Earnings and Pensions) Act 2003, s 378.
[95] Income Tax (Earnings and Pensions) Act 2003, s 378(4).
[96] *Cameron* (n 32) [22].
[97] ibid [34].
[98] ibid [42], [53].
[99] ibid [22].
[100] ibid [78].
[101] ibid [23]–[33], [63], [73]–[74], [82].
[102] *Greenwich Property* (n 58).
[103] Although not in the list of published ESCs.
[104] Value Added Tax Act 1994, Sch 8.

> will be collected in respect of this non-qualifying vacation use and provided that the new building is clearly intended primarily for use as student accommodation for ten years from the date of its completion, then we are content for higher education institutions to disregard the 10% de minimis rule and to issue a certificate for the construction or acquisition of such a building as 'relevant residential' building under Group 8 of the zero-rated schedule.

The thrust of the concession was that HMRC would treat the building as zero-rated if the University could demonstrate its primary use for ten years would be student accommodation.[105] HMRC contended that to fall properly within the terms of the concession, it was necessary for the University itself to rent out the property during the summer months and not the PFI provider.[106] Collins J rejected this on the basis that there could be no logical distinction between such an activity being undertaken by the University itself or a third party, and that both instances fell squarely within the terms of the concession.[107] Therein, however, Collins J highlighted the significant height of the threshold facing an applicant in a legitimate expectation claim. The taxable person must demonstrate that she has acted strictly in accordance with what the concession permits and has complied with all the conditions necessary to obtain the relief.[108] There can be *no* ambiguity:

> *Any doubt* should be resolved in favour of the tax being payable according to the statutory provision since, if there is doubt, or the language of the concession is ambiguous, the taxpayer should inquire of the Commissioners whether what he intends to do falls within the concession.[109]

Collins J allowed the concession to be relied upon given that there was no doubt as to the applicability of its terms in this case. There was no mention in the concession as to whether it was necessary or not for the University itself to rent out the accommodation in the summer months. As with *Cameron*, HMRC did not push the point. Rather, HMRC's overarching claim was that the concession was being utilised as a tool for tax avoidance.[110] This too was the case with *R (Biffa Waste) v Revenue and Customs*[111] where the main issue of the proceedings was not the clarity of the ruling which was given to the taxpayer, but whether that ruling applied only to the specific facts on which it was given or whether it could be applied to analogous situations (which the Administrative Court accepted it could).[112]

[105] *Greenwich Property* (n 58) [9].
[106] ibid [21].
[107] ibid [23].
[108] ibid.
[109] ibid [23]. Emphasis added.
[110] ibid [21]–[25]. Although generally provisos in HMRC publications ensure that they cannot be utilised for tax avoidance purposes, the Concordat to the CVCP contained no such qualification; see ibid [25].
[111] *Biffa Waste* (n 71).
[112] ibid [85]–[129].

R v Customs and Excise Commissioners, ex parte Kay,[113] meanwhile concerned the recovery of overpaid VAT by opticians. HMRC had made representations in a Business Brief[114] to the relevant taxpayers which stated that they were entitled to repayment of overpaid VAT:

> Any claims for repayment with statutory interest which date back to 1 September 1988 should now be submitted by opticians to their local VAT office, together with details of the apportionment used, where that is still to be agreed with the local office.

It was subsequently identified in the brief that any such claims should be made before 12 March 2001.[115] The Court held that this amounted to a clear representation upon which the taxpayers were entitled to rely.[116] As with *Cameron* and *Greenwich Property*, HMRC's contention that it was not bound by an expectation did not revolve around the terms of the publication, but on this occasion was based upon an understanding that legislation would later be introduced retrospectively to counter the repayment duties and as such ought not to be bound by the publication.[117]

In these cases, the advice contained assurances that the judges accepted as clear and to an extent it could be argued that HMRC too accepted this, given that it often had to explore fallback arguments separate from the issue of clarity. These cases are very much the exception to the rule: most cases will not overcome the 'no ambiguity' bar. This can be demonstrated by looking at cases wherein HMRC and the courts interpreted conditions or provisions *into* the relevant advice that were not apparent on first reading. In *Gaines-Cooper*,[118] the need for a 'distinct break' was read into HMRC's published material. The taxpayers claimed that HMRC guidance gave rise to a legitimate expectation that non-resident status would be acquired if the residence day count were satisfied (ie less than six months in any year were spent in the UK).[119] HMRC, on the other hand, contended that the taxpayers additionally needed to demonstrate a 'distinct break' with the UK.[120] The majority of the Supreme Court (Lord Mance dissenting) agreed with HMRC, notwithstanding that the guidance itself made no explicit reference to the concept.[121] Lord Wilson gave the leading speech and is seen in this following paragraph to interpolate such a meaning into the words of the guidance:

> [The] paragraphs [in the Guidance] must be read compendiously. *They shared one important feature: they all referred to 'visits' on the part of the individual to the UK*. If he

[113] [1996] STC 1500 (QBD) (Keene J).
[114] Customs and Excise, 'Business Brief 8/95' (May 1995).
[115] ibid; *Kay* (n 113) 1524.
[116] *Kay* (n 113) 1527.
[117] ibid 1515.
[118] *Gaines-Cooper* (n 7).
[119] ibid [30].
[120] ibid [79].
[121] ibid [30].

> usually resides in the UK, he will go abroad as a visitor but, if he has left the UK and has adopted a usual residence abroad, he will come to the UK as a visitor: *we are not visitors in the country of our usual residence*. The reference to visits to the UK therefore underlined the need for a change in the individual's usual residence and *therefore, by ready inference, for a distinct break* in the pattern of his life in the UK.[122]

Freedman and Vella described the majority's approach to the construction of HMRC's guidance in this case as 'questionable',[123] as regards its departure from the plain language of the text. The forced reasoning of Lord Wilson in the extracted piece supports this conclusion. It requires a linguistic double leap: first, to imply that the reference to visits brings to mind the idea that one cannot be a visitor in the country of one's usual residence and secondly, to imply that this, '*by ready inference*', requires a 'distinct break' from the UK.

Similar 'reading in' was initially successful in the case of *Ingenious Media*, which arose out of an episode where David Hartnett (then Permanent Secretary for tax at HMRC) disclosed the details of the investigation of particular taxpayers to journalists from *The Times*.[124] The taxpayers claimed that the exposure breached a legitimate expectation created by an HMRC Manual.[125] The relevant publication indicated that HMRC could disclose customer information for the purpose of an HMRC function, with examples provided such as:

- passing HMRC debt details to the Official Receiver in bankruptcy work;
- providing the police with details of a forthcoming visit so they can assess the health and safety risk (see IDG40460);
- making inquiries about a HMRC customer with a third party (see IDG30400);
- carrying out distraint in a public place.[126]

Being a non-exhaustive list, the Manual thereafter stressed that disclosure of information would be proper if this enabled HMRC to carry out its functions more effectively.[127] An *ejusdem generis* reading of the above examples, however, is highly unlikely to direct the reader to permit the disclosure of case-specific details to the media as occurred in that case. An example of a disclosure of the same order might be sharing taxpayer information with the media in order that journalistic investigations would not undermine a police raid,[128] which is a far cry from imparting

[122] ibid [42] (emphasis added).

[123] J Freedman and J Vella, 'Revenue Guidance: The Limits of Discretion and Legitimate Expectations' (2012) 128 *LQR* 192, 192.

[124] *R (Ingenious Media and McKenna) v HMRC* [2013] EWHC 3258 (Admin), [2014] STC 673 (*Ingenious Media* (HC)); *R (Ingenious Media and McKenna) v HMRC* [2015] EWCA Civ 173, [2015] STC 1357 (*Ingenious Media* (CA)); *R (Ingenious Media and McKenna) v HMRC* [2016] UKSC 54 [17], [2016] 1 WLR 4164 (*Ingenious Media* (SC)). This case is discussed in ch 4 in text at n 81.

[125] *Ingenious Media* (HC) (n 124) [28].

[126] ibid [25]; *Ingenious Media* (CA) (n 124) [35].

[127] *Ingenious Media* (HC) (n 124) [25]; *Ingenious Media* (CA) (n 124) [35].

[128] *Ingenious Media* (SC) (n 124) [35].

it generally to journalists because it may result in more efficient tax collection. The High Court and Court of Appeal nevertheless upheld HMRC's action as being in line with the Manual on the basis that it would bolster both relations between the media and HMRC and, in turn, the efficient collection of tax.[129] With a harmonious relationship would come a quid pro quo: the media would hand over evidence of tax avoidance to HMRC and the engagement would additionally ameliorate public confidence in the administration of the tax system.[130] That such disclosure is viewed as being of the same order as that of use for distraint and debt collection demonstrates the breadth of interpretation which the courts can potentially apply to HMRC advice. Of course, the Supreme Court ultimately held that HMRC's disclosure was unlawful,[131] but made no comment on HMRC's Manual, or whether the taxpayers could expect on the basis of information in the Manual that HMRC would not disclose information (though it can probably be inferred that the Supreme Court disagreed with the lower courts on the issue).

In *R (ELS Group) v HMRC*[132] an issue before the Court of Appeal was whether HMRC guidance could apply retrospectively. The relevant guidance, Business Brief BB4/10, contained a concession which limited the quantum of VAT a business had to charge when seconding its own staff. The court was required to construe the guidance in order to determine whether its terms were capable of being applied retrospectively (ie whether the taxpayer was entitled to rely at a later time upon the guidance, having failed at the relevant time to elect for the treatment under the guidance). HMRC contended that 'concessions should be given a relatively narrow construction in recognition of the fact that they involve a derogation from statute'.[133] This was accepted by Patten LJ, to whom it seemed 'that the most influential contextual element in the process of construction must be the statutory default position'.[134] As the guidance itself did not in clear words state that it could be applied retrospectively, the taxpayer could not be said to be entitled to the concessionary treatment. The fact that the concession operated:

> [I]n effect as a decision by HMRC not to collect tax that becomes statutorily due … militates strongly in my view against giving the concessions any greater scope than a fair and normal reading of the language of the concession dictates.[135]

Moreover, to extend the concession retrospectively to fit the current case would 'create an obvious inconsistency' with the relevant legislation 'and is a powerful reason why the concession should be assumed and interpreted not to have that effect'.[136] In brief then, the Court placed significant reliance upon the proper legal

[129] *Ingenious Media* (HC) (n 124) [44] and [60]–[61]; *Ingenious Media* (CA) (n 124) [30] and [37]–[47].
[130] *Ingenious Media* (HC) (n 124) [44].
[131] *Ingenious Media* (SC) (n 124).
[132] [2016] EWCA Civ 663, [2016] STC 2417.
[133] ibid [23].
[134] ibid [24].
[135] ibid [35].
[136] ibid [36].

position in order to determine the meaning and scope of the HMRC advice, even if this correct legal position was not actually mentioned in the advice itself.

On the one hand, it might be said that the successful cases demonstrate just how clear the advice must have been in order for the taxpayer to prevail in a legitimate expectation claim. But on the other hand, the cited unsuccessful cases might demonstrate an altogether different proposition – namely, that what is important is not the content of the advice itself, but the interpretation and interpretative methodology of the deciding judge. The argument that the advice should be understood in light of implied material is always open to HMRC.[137]

iv. Qualifications

In order to ground a legitimate expectation, the HMRC advice must be 'devoid of relevant qualification'. The sheer ubiquity of qualifications in general advice, rather than in individual advice, undermines this potential. For instance, many publications contain 'health warnings' in the form of: 'This Publication gives you information about X, and how HMRC interprets the legislation in the context of applying X to an individual's circumstances'.[138]

There is a clear trend of courts being inclined to find that such health warnings undermine the prospect of a legitimate expectation from arising. In the case of *Hanover Company Services Ltd v HMRC*,[139] the First-tier Tribunal (FTT) noted obiter that such a health warning *precluded* the creation of a legitimate expectation, though that puts the point too strongly.[140] Collins J in *Thompson v Fletcher*[141] more accurately summarised the problem as being that a 'health warning' can serve to vitiate the possibility of an expectation arising, as it makes it 'absolutely clear that readers should not be [*sic*] assume that the guidance is comprehensive'.[142] The issue of health warnings also came to bear in *Gaines-Cooper*. The majority of the Supreme Court held that the claim to a legitimate expectation could not be made out, partly because of the presence of a health warning.[143] The guidance upon which the applicants sought to rely was prefaced as follows:

> The notes in this booklet reflect the law and practice at October 1999. They are not binding in law and do not affect rights of appeal about your own tax. You should bear in mind that the booklet offers general guidance on how the rules apply, but whether

[137] Though this was not successful in *R (Vacation Rentals) v HMRC* [2018] UKUT 383 (TCC), where the Upper Tribunal opined that HMRC sought to advance an interpretation of the relevant guidance which was 'inappropriately technical and rigorous' ([76]).

[138] See for instance HMRC, 'RDR3 Statutory Residence Test' (August 2016).

[139] [2010] UKFTT 256 (TC).

[140] ibid [49].

[141] [2002] EWHC 1448 (Admin), [2002] STC 1149.

[142] ibid [47]. See also the cases prior and subsequent to *Hanover*. See: *Cameron* (n 32); *B&J Shopfitting Services v HMRC* [2010] UKFTT 78 (TC); *Kay* (n 113).

[143] *Gaines-Cooper* (n 7) [32] (Lord Wilson); [64] (Lord Hope); [66] (Lord Walker).

the guidance is appropriate in a particular case will depend on all the facts of that case. *If you have any difficulty in applying the rules in your own case, you should consult an Inland Revenue Tax Office.*[144]

Provisos to HMRC materials can provide much the same effect. These are found, for instance, attached to HMRC's published list of ESCs which provides that concessions will not be given in any case where an attempt is made to use them for tax avoidance.[145] This proviso resulted in an ESC not applying to a taxpayer in the case of *R v Inspector of Taxes, ex parte Fulford-Dobson*[146] as the court held that the taxpayer was attempting to use the concession for avoidance purposes.[147] In dismissing the taxpayer's contention that a legitimate expectation arose on the basis of representations in an HMRC Manual, the Upper Tribunal in *Samarkand*[148] placed significant weight on a caveat precluding reliance where 'there is, or may be, avoidance of tax'.[149] It followed that the taxpayers had to take the Manual in its entirety and could not 'take out the plums they liked and ignore the duff they did not'.[150] The Court of Appeal noted that the guidance was 'permeated with qualifications relating to tax avoidance'[151] and agreed with the Upper Tribunal's reasoning on the point.[152]

v. Access

Access to the tribunals and courts is also an obstacle to the protection of taxpayers from HMRC reneging on written representations. Access is circumscribed by the requirement that a claim based on legitimate expectations be brought in the High Court rather than the FTT,[153] costs and the scope for judicial review applications.

For a time, there was considerable uncertainty as to the scope of the tribunal's power to hear issues of public law.[154] In *Oxfam v HMRC*,[155] Sales J (as he then was) embarked on an analysis of analogous case law relating to the jurisdiction

[144] ibid [32] (Lord Wilson) (emphasis added).

[145] HMRC, 'Concessions as at 6 April 2018' (n 52) 2.

[146] [1987] BTC 158 (QBD).

[147] ibid 166–69. See also: *R (Bampton) v King* [2012] EWCA Civ 1744, [2014] STC 56 [109] (Arden LJ).

[148] *Samarkand Film Partnership No 3, Proteus Film Partnership and three partners v HMRC* [2015] UKUT 211 (TCC), [2015] STC 2135.

[149] ibid [154].

[150] ibid [172].

[151] *Samarkand* (CA) (n 59) [126].

[152] ibid [114], [124] and [130].

[153] It should be noted that where it is 'just and convenient' to so do, the Administrative Court may transfer the case to the Upper Tribunal, as occurred for instance in *R (Capital Accommodation (London)) v HMRC* [2012] UKUT 276 (TCC), [2013] STC 303, but was refused in *R (Hankinson) v HMRC* [2009] EWHC 1774 (Admin), [2009] STC 2158.

[154] Differently constituted tribunals arrived at differing conclusions upon this matter. See: *HOK Limited v The Commissioners for Her Majesty's Revenue and Customs* [2011] UKFTT 433 (TC). Cf *Revenue and Customs Commissioners v Hok Limited* [2012] UKUT 363 (TCC), [2013] STC 225.

[155] [2009] EWHC 3078 (Ch), [2010] STC 686.

of similar tribunals and also the relevant statutory wording, before concluding that the FTT had jurisdiction to hear public law matters. However, this judgment has been later refined as only relating to the determination of input tax for the purposes of section 83(c) of the Value Added Tax Act 1994.[156] The result now is that a taxpayer will have to commence judicial review proceedings in the High Court, as well as pursue the substantive case in the tax tribunal.[157] This resulting duplication has been criticised by John Avery Jones:[158]

> I do not see this as a matter of principle. The High Court certainly has power to review all exercises of discretions by Customs for those who can afford to go there; why should not the Tribunal if they are qualified to decide the more difficult substantive part of the appeal?[159]

It is certainly questionable why an expert tribunal cannot determine all the issues surrounding a case which comes before it.[160] One could counter that it is necessary to ensure that public law issues are dealt with at a higher level due to the fact that the FTT is not constituted wholly by judges.[161] However, there is a certain air of 'fig leaf'[162] logic to the argument, considering that in the case of some taxing provisions, the tribunal does in effect decide upon public law issues. For instance, the tribunal will take account of excess of jurisdiction, unlawfulness or impropriety on the part of HMRC when evaluating the reasonableness of a taxpayer's excuse for avoiding a penalty.[163] Indeed, as the author has pointed out the tribunal considers issues in respect of all the grounds of judicial review thereby underlining its competence to hear public law claims.[164]

The practical ramifications of having to commence judicial review in the High Court were highlighted in *William Bourne v HMRC*.[165] For the ordinary taxpayer, without the benefit of representation, the requirement to commence dual proceedings is 'tantamount, in practice, to denying that appellant the ability to pursue that claim'.[166] The unrepresented taxpayer is unlikely to go to the expense of funding two sets of proceedings,[167] and may be unaware of the relevant procedure,

[156] *Rotberg v HMRC* [2014] UKFTT 657 (TC).

[157] Even in the case of Value Added Tax Act 1994, s 83(c) Sales J in *Oxfam* recommended that taxpayers should still take this duplicative route, see: *Oxfam* (n 155) [80].

[158] JA Jones, 'The reform of the tax tribunals: a story of uncompleted business' [2006] *British Tax Review* 282, 291–93.

[159] ibid 291.

[160] See ch 7 in text at n 295.

[161] As per The Qualifications for Appointment of Members to the First-tier Tribunal and Upper Tribunal Order 2008, s 2(2) and (4), members of the First-tier Tribunal may be non-judges who are accountants or who have substantial experience in tax matters.

[162] This phrase is borrowed from J Laws, 'Law and democracy' [1995] *Public Law* 72, 79.

[163] Jones, 'The reform' [2006] 291, fn 54.

[164] S Daly, 'Public Law in the Tax Tribunals and the Case for Reform' [2018] 1 *British Tax Review* 94.

[165] [2010] UKFTT 294 (TC).

[166] ibid [24].

[167] E Troup, 'Unacceptable Discretion: Countering Tax Avoidance and Preserving the Rights of the Individual' (1992) 13 *Fiscal Studies* 128, 134.

namely that the taxpayer must institute judicial review proceedings within 90 days of HMRC's decision,[168] and should simultaneously stay these proceedings behind the substantive appeal.[169]

In practical terms, cost is perhaps the greatest obstacle to a taxpayer seeking to advance a legitimate expectation claim. Proceedings must be commenced in the High Court (Administrative Court).[170] The cost of commencing judicial review proceedings (now £154), of requesting a reconsideration a judicial review application at a hearing (£385)[171] and of pursuing the claim if permission is granted (now £770)[172] is prohibitive generally and will almost completely deter persons with disputes worth under £1,000. The Court has discretion also to award costs against an unsuccessful judicial review applicant.[173] Where the Court decides to make an order, the general rule is that the unsuccessful party will be ordered to pay the costs of the successful party.[174] Litigants may apply to the Court to have their judicial review case heard by the Upper Tribunal,[175] but the Court must be satisfied that transferring the case would be 'just and convenient'.[176] In any event, costs can also be awarded against the losing party[177] and the same costs-shifting rule which operates in the High Court probably also applies given that the Upper Tribunal in such an instance is exercising concurrent jurisdiction.[178] The extent to which some Court fees can be avoided meanwhile depends upon when, in the litigation, the case is transferred to the Upper Tribunal. On the other hand, there is currently no fee for taking a case to the First-tier Tax Tribunal and each side generally bears its own costs.[179]

Finally, section 84 of the Criminal Justice and Courts Act 2015 has the effect of introducing another barrier to access for claimants. This provides that the High Court must refuse to grant relief on an application for judicial review if it appears to the Court to be *highly likely* that the outcome for the applicant would not have been substantially different if the conduct complained of had not occurred

[168] CPR 54.5.

[169] Ministry of Justice, 'Pre-Action Protocol for Judicial Review' para 5.

[170] Senior Courts Act 1981, s 31.

[171] Generally a necessity given that most Judicial Review applications are refused on paper, see: Ministry of Justice, 'Judicial Review: Proposals for further reform' (September 2013) 8.

[172] See HM Courts and Tribunals Service, 'EX50A: 24 July 2018' (July 2018) 4.

[173] Senior Courts Act 1981, s 51 and CPR 44.2.

[174] Judiciary for England and Wales, 'The Administrative Court Judicial Review Guide 2018' (July 2018) para 23.1.2.

[175] Tribunals, Courts and Enforcement Act 2007 (TCEA 2007), ss 15–21.

[176] Senior Courts Act 1981 s 31A(3); TCEA 2007 s 19(1).

[177] See TCEA 2007, s 29; The Tribunal Procedure (Upper Tribunal) Rules 2008 (SI 2008/2698 (L 15)), r 10(3)(a).

[178] Senior President of Tribunals, 'Costs in Tribunals: Report by the Senior President of Tribunals' (December 2011) para 138.

[179] For a helpful overview, see: A Keats, 'When to claim costs at a tax tribunal', *AccountingWeb* (8 February 2019). See The Tribunal Procedure (First-tier Tribunal) (Tax Chamber) Rules 2009 (SI 2009/273 (L 1)), r 10 for when costs can be awarded.

(although the Court retains a discretion to grant relief for reasons of exceptional public interest).[180] The same applies to the permission stage, although this only arises where the defendant brings the motion, or where the Court decides this of its own motion, that the outcome would have been substantially the same.[181] It is the words 'highly likely' which are at issue. Previously judges had a discretion to refuse relief where the same outcome would have been 'inevitable', a much higher standard.[182] The amendment was significantly criticised, most notably by Lord Pannick, whose *Times* article on the issue[183] became a focal point for the debate as the bill passed through the houses.[184]

It could be argued that although this amendment is undesirable from the perspective of reducing the scope for holding public authorities to account in respect of unlawful actions,[185] the private rights of claimants are unaffected. In other words, if the claimant can demonstrate a right to a remedy which is more than nominal, the case will still proceed and, to this end, the amendment should not hinder access to the courts for taxpayers seeking to hold HMRC to its advice (given that taxpayers claims' should generally be for non-nominal remedies). This, however, is to overlook the obfuscating nature of the amendment. Judicial review targets generally the propriety of the decision-making process, and only exceptionally, for instance where unreasonableness is demonstrated, the decision itself. By reducing the standard to 'highly likely' from 'inevitable', the judge is forced to consider in outline the merits of the decision and to place herself in the shoes of the decision-maker, hypothesising whether it was highly likely that she too would arrive at the same decision.[186] By introducing this possibility, it increases the scope for the judge to decide that the claimant's action should be dismissed. The consequence of the change is to make it more difficult for a claimant to bring an action and to seek relief.

B. Using the ECHR and EU Law

In order to be comprehensive, it should be mentioned that as a matter of public law, there are additional options that can be pursued by taxpayers in order to seek

[180] Criminal Justice and Courts Act 2015, s 84(1). See Senior Courts Act 1981, s 31(2A) and (2B).

[181] Criminal Justice and Courts Act 2015, s 84(2). See Senior Courts Act 1981, s 31(3D). Here the court may disregard the requirement for reasons of exceptional public interest. See Senior Courts Act 1981, s 31(3E).

[182] In respect of taking into account irrelevant considerations for instance, see *R (FDA) v Secretary of State for Work and Pensions* [2012] EWCA Civ 332, [2013] 1 WLR 444 [67] (Elias LJ).

[183] D Pannick, 'Why judicial review needs protection from our politicians' *The Times* (20 February 2014).

[184] See, for instance, *Hansard*, HC Deb Vol 582, col 697 (17 June 2014) (Andy Slaughter); *Hansard*, HL Deb Vol 754, col 1557 (30 June 2014) (Baroness Campbell).

[185] And, in this sense, the amendment ignores the 'plurality of purposes' served by judicial review: S Nason, *Reconstructing Judicial Review* (Oxford, Hart Publishing, 2016) 15.

[186] *Hansard*, Criminal Justice and Courts Bill Deb col 106 (13 March 2014) (Angela Patrick); *R (Cooper) v Ashford Borough Council* [2016] EWHC 1525 (Admin), [2016] PTSR 1455 [86] (John Howell QC).

to enforce legitimate expectation claims against HMRC. Most notably, taxpayers can seek to invoke the ECHR and EU law. However, it should be made clear that an argument which fails on the common law legitimate expectation claim will most likely derive little benefit from these routes.[187]

Article 1 of the First Protocol to the ECHR protects the 'peaceful enjoyment of possessions', within which a claim for a substantive legitimate expectation can be made. However, Article 1 Protocol 1(2) is deferential towards signatory states in respect of tax. It provides that deprivation of possessions may be justified 'in the public interest', as provided by law. In particular, states are entitled 'to control the use of property in accordance with the general interest or to secure the payment of taxes or other contributions or penalties'. There are, accordingly, significant hurdles for a taxpayer seeking to invoke the ECHR in order to advance a legitimate expectation claim in respect of HMRC advice – the first is demonstrating that she comes within the scope of the provision by holding a 'possession'; the second is finding the infringement not to be justified; and the third is that, even if justified, she must demonstrate that any such justification is not proportionate.

A legitimate expectation claim must be incidental to a property right in order for it to garner the protection of the First Protocol.[188] Thus, if a property right is present,[189] for instance such as a right to recover input tax,[190] a claim to a legitimate expectation can be considered.[191] But the problem lies in demonstrating that a sufficiently strong claim in law is present so as to amount to a 'possession'.[192] Demonstrating such a strong claim only brings us back to the question of whether a legitimate expectation is made out as a matter of national law, thereby essentially adding nothing to the common law protection. However, assuming that one can be made out, the ECHR will generally not assist beyond what the common law legitimate expectation doctrine can provide. This is because HMRC will be justified in reneging on a legitimate expectation if it does so in order to secure the payment of tax and will have little difficulty in an ordinary case demonstrating the action to be proportionate given that national authorities are afforded 'a wide margin

[187] This aligns with what might be at least the anecdotal observation that litigants are better advised to ground arguments generally in established administrative and constitutional law principles. In this context, Dinah Rose has said that '[Blackstone's commentaries get] much more purchase with a common law judge in many occasions than the human rights act'. See 'Magna Carta: Myth and Meaning' discussion from 19.28, available at: www.intelligencesquared.com/events/magna-carta-myth-and-meaning. For instance, see *R (Unison) v Lord Chancellor* [2017] UKSC 51, [2018] 1 CMLR 35, where the constitutional principle of access to justice arrived at the same result as EU law ([66]–[85] and [89] in particular (Lord Reed)).

[188] *Prince Hans-Adam II of Liechtenstein v Germany* (42527/98) [2001] ECHR 463, para 83.

[189] See *R (on the application of Carvill) v IRC* [2003] STC 1539 (QBD) [49].

[190] On which, see *Bulves AD v Bulgaria* (3991/03) [2009] STC 1193; *Aleena Electronics Ltd v HMRC* [2011] UKFTT 608 (TC) [38]–[44].

[191] It may even be contested in the First-tier Tribunal rather than the High Court, as was tried in *Aleena Electronics Ltd v HMRC* [2011] UKFTT 608 (TC).

[192] For a helpful recent overview of what amounts to a possession in the context of tax, see: *R (on the Application of Rowe and Others) v HMRC; R (on the Application of Vital Nut Co Ltd and Others) v HMRC* [2017] EWCA Civ 2105, [2017] WLR(D) 830 [158]–[185] (McCombe LJ).

of appreciation',[193] particularly in tax cases.[194] Cases that have succeeded on the proportionality ground have involved an interference 'so burdensome, arbitrary, unfair or excessive, relative to any community or public interest, as to preclude its being regarded as reasonably founded'.[195] Take, for instance, the case of *R.Sz v Hungary*.[196] There the taxpayer was among a group of persons singled out for additional taxation, some time after the original receipt of the monies, leading to almost total deprivation of the money received.

The principle of legitimate expectation in EU law,[197] meanwhile, can assist taxpayers where the claim concerns EU law, for instance because the relevant HMRC advice relates to VAT or the Directive on Administrative Cooperation.[198] The EU doctrine of legitimate expectations protects an individual in a situation in which a relevant public body gives precise, unconditional and consistent information, in whatever form, thereby leading that individual to entertain well-founded expectations.[199] This definition does not appear to provide anything of substance to differentiate it from the common law doctrine.[200]

However, beyond that provided by common law, the EU doctrine may be of assistance to taxpayers as it potentially provides greater reliability for expectations predicated on incorrect advice, though this depends on the particular error. In *Elmeka NE v Ypourgos Oikonomikon*,[201] the taxpayer received an assurance from the Greek tax authority that its supply of services was exempt from VAT, though this was incorrect. The Court of Justice noted that the doctrine of legitimate expectations formed part of the EU legal order.[202] The taxpayer's expectation would be binding on the Greek Government, subject to the national court determining whether the taxpayer could reasonably have believed that the public authority which provided the incorrect advice was competent to rule on the application of the exemption to its activities.[203] The question of competence here was particular to the facts as the Greek Government argued that the organ of the tax authority which provided the advice was not the correct department to which requests for advice were to be directed.

[193] See for instance, *AXA* (n 53) [126] (Lord Reed).

[194] *Rowe and Vital Nut* (n 192) [197] (McCombe LJ).

[195] See also *Allan v HMRC* [2015] UKUT 16 (TCC) [52] (Barling J).

[196] [2013] ECHR 628, [2013] ECHR 41838/11.

[197] Cases C-181/04 to C-183/04 *Elmeka NE v Ipourgos Ikoomikon* [2006] ECR I-8167, para 31.

[198] Council Directive 2011/16/EU of 15 February 2011 on administrative cooperation in the field of taxation and repealing Directive 77/799/EEC [2011] OJ L 64/1.

[199] Joined cases C-630/11 P to C-633/11 P *HGA and Others v Commission* (ECJ, 13 June 2013) para 132. See also Case C-289/91 *Mavridis v Parliament* [1983] ECR 1731, para 21.

[200] See for instance *Infinis Energy Holdings Ltd v HM Treasury* [2016] EWCA Civ 1030, [2017] STC 414. For an in-depth discussion of the EU law on legitimate expectations, see: P Craig, *EU Administrative Law*, 3rd edn (Oxford, Oxford University Press, 2018) ch 18. See also T Tridimas, 'Indeterminacy and legal uncertainty in EU law' in J Mendes (ed), *EU Executive Discretion and the Limits of the Law* (Oxford, Oxford University Press, 2019).

[201] Cases C-181/04 to C-183/04 *Elmeka NE v Ypourgos Oikonomikon* [2006] ECR I-8167.

[202] ibid para 31.

[203] ibid paras 35–36.

The judgment of the Court should be read alongside the Advocate General's opinion in the case, which elaborates upon the narrow circumstances which led to this outcome.[204] She noted that the same result would not be arrived at where the underlying error related to community law which is unambiguous.[205] Nor where the community law in question, which has been misconceived in the advice, is that of 'general interest' in the sense that Member States have no natural vested interest in the correct application of the Community rules concerned.[206] State aid, for instance, is an example where the rules only work if all Member States act scrupulously in implementing them, whereas there is a perceived economic incentive conversely for Member States not to apply them in individual instances. The integrity of the Schengen area provides another example of a general interest situation where deviations have an impact across Member States rather than being internal to a single state.[207] This case, however, concerned VAT, and more particularly, it concerned a trader who believed its supplies to be exempt. Had these not been exempt, the trader would simply have passed on the charge to the consumer (subject to price elasticity). In sum then, beyond the protection provided by the common law doctrine of legitimate expectations to taxpayers seeking to hold HMRC to its advice, the ECHR can only provide assistance in extreme circumstances. Meanwhile, EU law will be helpful only in situations where HMRC advises in relation to EU law in which it is competent,[208] the relevant law is not unambiguous and honouring the incorrect advice does not have an impact on the scope or effectiveness of EU law.[209]

Finally, it should be noted that the ECHR and EU law may assist in respect of retrospective changes in advice where this is done because of a change in the law. As noted in respect of the ECHR,[210] the rule of law requires that laws be foreseeable and accessible, with respect to which retrospective changes in law necessarily conflict.[211] EU law similarly guards against retrospective changes as these conflict with the principle of legal certainty.[212] A detailed discussion of these options, however, is outside the scope of this book as, in both instances, the taxpayer will in reality have to attack the change in law rather than HMRC's change of position in light of the law.

[204] Cases C-181/04 to C-183/04 *Elmeka NE v Ypourgos Oikonomikon* [2006] ECR I-8167, Opinion of AG Stix-Hackl.

[205] ibid para 45. See also cases Cases C-31/91 to C-44/91 *Alois Lageder SpA v Amminiistrazione delle Finanze dello Stato* [1993] ECR I-01761, para 35.

[206] ibid.

[207] See on this Case C-606/10 *Association nationale d'assistance aux fronteires pour l'etrangers (ANAFE) v Ministre de l'Interieur, de L'Outre-mer, des Collectivites territoriales et de l'Immigration* (ECJ, 14 June 2012).

[208] Namely, procedural and substantive tax laws as opposed to laws which it is not tasked with administering, such as the state aid rules.

[209] Case 210/87 *Remo Padovani and the successors of Otello Mantovani v Amministrazione delle finanze dello stato* [1988] ECR 6177 para 22.

[210] See ch 3 in text at n 102.

[211] *Axa* (n 53) [119] (Lord Reed).

[212] Case 98/78 *Firma A Racke v Hauptzollamt Mainz* [1979] ECR 69, para 20.

III. Private Law

For the sake of completeness, it should be noted there are remedies in private law which in theory could assist a taxpayer in holding HMRC to its advice, but these are underdeveloped for this purpose. The most notable is estoppel.[213] This provides broadly that a party, including for our purposes a public authority, can be estopped from resiling from an earlier commitment to another party because it would be unjust or inequitable to do so.[214] However, this is much narrower and less developed than the legitimate expectations doctrine. Indeed, as Bradley, Ewing and Knight have noted, it is 'not likely to be of any utility in the near future'.[215] The oft-cited statement from Lord Hoffmann in *R v East Sussex County Council, ex parte Reprotech (Pebsham) Ltd*[216] in particular drives such pessimism. Although the private law concept of estoppel was helpful in the development of the doctrine of legitimate expectations, its reserves for that purpose have been exhausted:

> It seems to me that in this area, public law has already absorbed whatever is useful from the moral values which underlie the private law concept of estoppel and the time has come for it to stand upon its own two feet.[217]

There are several key limitations to the use of estoppel for present purposes which demonstrate that its scope is far narrower than the doctrine of legitimate expectations. First, the claimant must show generally show detriment,[218] whereas as noted already this is not the case with legitimate expectations. This is because public law forces the relevant public authority to take into account a broader range of factors, such as the interests of the general public, when exercising its powers.[219] Second, estoppel cannot be allowed where it would require a public body to act outside its powers,[220] and even more problematically cannot be used to estop a public authority from exercising a statutory discretion or performing a public duty.[221] This will prove fatal for a taxpayer where HMRC argues that more tax is due than

[213] Others would include negligent misstatement, but only very specific circumstances would assist for this cause of action, as the taxpayer would need to demonstrate a 'special relationship'. On this, see *Hedley Byrne & Co Ltd v Heller & Partners Ltd* [1964] AC 465 (HL), [1963] 2 All ER 575. See more generally, G Weeks, *Soft Law and Public Authorities: Remedies and Reform* (Oxford, Hart Publishing, 2016) chs 9 and 10.

[214] *Moorgate Mercantile Co. Ltd v Twitchings* [1976] 1 QB 225 (CA), 241 (Denning MR).

[215] A Bradley, K Ewing and C Knight, *Constitutional & Administrative Law*, 17th edn (Harlow, Pearson Education, 2018) 667.

[216] [2002] UKHL 8, [2002] 4 All ER 58.

[217] ibid [35].

[218] For instance *Fisher v Brooker* [2009] UKHL 41, [2009] WLR 1764 [63] (Lord Neuberger). For a strong exploration of this issue see: E Cooke, *The Modern Law of Estoppel* (Oxford, Oxford University Press, 2000) ch 6.

[219] *Reprotech* (n 216) [34].

[220] *Minister of Agriculture and Fisheries and Food v Matthews* [1950] 1 KB 148, 153 (Cassels J); *Vestry of the parish of St. Mary, Islington v Hornsey Urban District Council* [1900] 1 Ch 695, (CA) 704–705; Craig, *Administrative Law* (2016) 705.

[221] *Reprotech* (n 216) [35].

had earlier been communicated, as HMRC in such an instance is simply carrying out the statutory function of collecting taxes.[222]

IV. Non-court Remedies

If there were a triangle representing legal disputes, it would only be those at the apex of the wedge which actually make it to litigation. Many more disputes are settled at a much earlier stage. Where a dispute arises in relation to reliance on HMRC advice, taxpayers should first seek to resolve the issue with HMRC directly.[223] HMRC will have another look at the decision and if the taxpayer is still unhappy with the outcome, then a different official independent of the original decision-maker will review the complaint and give a final response.[224] This 'second look' is known as internal review and has proved to be not unfavourable for taxpayers, with 49 per cent of reviews in 2013/14, for instance, resulting in HMRC's decision being cancelled or varied.[225]

If a taxpayer is still unhappy, she may approach the Adjudicator and if still unhappy can be referred by her local MP to the Ombudsman. The Adjudicator and Ombudsman may recommend a range of remedies.[226] The Adjudicator may recommend ex gratia payments, recompense and other payments to complainants such as covering expenses incurred in pursuing complaints and compensation for loss of time in pursuing complaints. HMRC generally agrees to implement recommendations, other than in exceptional circumstances or where the recommendation would require HMRC to depart its published standards, guidance and codes of practice.[227] The Ombudsman has broader jurisdiction and may recommend a wide range of remedies, from the issuance of an apology[228] to financial compensation,[229]

[222] See *GUS Merchandise Corporation Ltd v Normal Motor Factors Ltd* [1978] VATTR 20; *Animal Virus Institute v The Commissioners* [1988] VATTR 56 (cited in Cooke, *Estoppel* (n 218) 137, fn 137).

[223] HMRC, 'Complain about HMRC. To see who deals with the different disputes, see: HMRC, Code of governance for resolving tax disputes' (October 2017).

[224] This is a statutory process, though the particularities may depend on the type of tax. See for Taxes Management Act 1970, ss 49A–49I; Oil Taxation Act 1975, Sch 2, paras 14A–14I; Inheritance Act 1984, ss 223A–223I. See further P Hamilton, *Hamilton on Tax Appeals* (West Sussex, Bloomsbury Professional, 2016) ch 9.

[225] M Boddington, 'Taxpayers should take up internal reviews' *Accountingweb* (19 May 2016). The article cites statistics in 'HMRC's Reviews and Appeals – 2013–14'.

[226] See ch 5 in text at n 119.

[227] The Adjudicator's Office, HMRC and VOA, 'Service Level Agreement for the provision of complaints adjudication services for HM Revenue & Customs and Valuation Office Agency by the Adjudicator's Office' (July 2018) paras 5.19–5.20.

[228] Parliamentary Commissioner for Administration, 'Third report of the parliamentary commissioner for administration' (HC 1973–74, 281) 12; Parliamentary Commissioner for Administration, 'Annual report for 1988' (HC 1988/89, 301) 16; Parliamentary and Health Service Ombudsman, 'Annual Report 2010–11' (HC 2010–11, 1404) 17.

[229] Parliamentary Commissioner for Administration, 'Second report of the Parliamentary Commissioner for Administration' (HC 1973–74, 106) 7.

which seek to restore the complainant to the position she would have been in had the maladministration not occurred.[230] Though as noted already[231] neither body is vested with formal powers to bind HMRC to its recommendations, a review of case studies from the Adjudicator and Ombudsman reveals that they can be effective in holding HMRC to its advice.[232] This is despite the fact that neither body is in theory supposed to investigate complaints where a legal remedy, such as a claim based on legitimate expectations, is available.[233] Moreover, the case of *R (Bradley) v Secretary of State for Work and Pensions*[234] adds some legal force to recommendations from the Ombudsman and Adjudicator.[235] HMRC should only reject the findings of either body if there are 'cogent reasons'[236] for doing so and the courts may quash the rejection if it is deemed to be irrational.[237]

A. The Adjudicator

The Adjudicator is more constrained in the remedies that can be issued than the Ombudsman and regularly repeats that the Office has 'no jurisdiction to ask HMRC to act outside of their guidance or instructions'.[238] But this does not prevent the Adjudicator from holding HMRC to its advice, or at least compensating taxpayers, even where the advice is incorrect. This is because HMRC may have a practice or policy of following incorrect advice. For instance, HMRC guidance provides that persons may be entitled to compensation for reasonable costs directly caused by their mistakes or delays.[239] Thus in a case study from the Annual Report 2012, a company complained that HMRC's National Advice Service had given misleading advice.[240] Initially HMRC did not accept it had made any errors for which redress should be considered. The Adjudicator asked for a further independent review to be undertaken. In addition, she asked one of her investigators to obtain and listen to recordings of the two telephone calls made to the NAS. Having reviewed

230 Parliamentary and Health Service Ombudsman, 'Equitable Life: a decade of regulatory failure' (HC 2007–08, 815-I) 377.

231 See ch 5 in text at nn 137, 152 and 119.

232 On the utility of the Ombudsman see also Weeks, *Soft Law* (2016) ch 12, who arrives at a similar conclusion.

233 See Parliamentary Commissioner Act 1967, s 5(2), though there is an exception where the Commissioner believes it to not be reasonable to expect the citizen to pursue proceedings in a court or tribunal. Adjudicator, HMRC and VOA, 'Service Level Agreement' (n 227) para 5.12 provides that the Adjudicator cannot look at issues that the courts could have considered or could consider.

234 [2008] EWCA Civ 36, [2009] QB 114.

235 See ch 5 in text at n 152.

236 *Bradley* (n 234) [51], [72] (Sir John Chadwick).

237 ibid [95] (Sir John Chadwick).

238 See, for instance, Adjudicator's Office, 'Annual Report 2012: A year of challenges' (July 2012) 13. See Adjudicator, HMRC and VOA, 'Service Level Agreement' (n 227) paras 5.1, 5.2 and 5.20 on the scope of the Adjudicator's remit to that end.

239 See HMRC, 'Complain about HMRC'.

240 Adjudicator's Office, 'Annual Report 2012' (n 238) 17.

this evidence, the Adjudicator found that a mistake had been made by HMRC and recommended that the body pay the costs arising from the misleading advice. HMRC agreed and, as an aside, also issued an apology for its poor complaints handling. Moreover, HMRC does have a policy of following its incorrect advice (as has already been set out) provided that the taxpayer can satisfy HMRC's strict tests, which notably includes demonstrating financial detriment. Where HMRC provided an assurance to taxpayers who traded in a partnership that their supply of tuition services was VAT exempt and later tried to go back on the advice (on the basis that in fact a third party provided the tuition on behalf of the partners), the Adjudicator upheld the complaint on the basis that the taxpayers would suffer detriment if held to the correct legal position.[241]

A case study from the Annual Report 2010 serves to bear out, meanwhile, that the Adjudicator is capable of holding HMRC to its general advice, regardless of whether the taxpayer has sought to rely on it (much as the doctrine of legitimate expectations also ensures consistency of administrative action). HMRC gave up tax otherwise payable in respect of Mr F, whose difficulties began when he retired and took a part-time job in 2003.[242] His PAYE personal allowances were duplicated for both sources of income. In November 2006, Mr F received tax calculations for 2004–05 and 2005–06, showing significant amounts of tax owing. Mr F then instructed an accountant who wrote to HMRC, but HMRC took a long time to give a detailed reply. The Adjudicator recommended that HMRC should not pursue the underpayments of tax as it was not reasonable to assume that Mr F should have been able to work out that he had not been paying enough tax, particularly as he had not received any tax codes for those years. This money was payable as a matter of law, but the Adjudicator was relying upon HMRC guidance (ESC A19).

These examples serve to demonstrate that the Adjudicator is a useful option for taxpayers. However, its utility from the perspective of holding HMRC to its advice should not be overstated. First, its remit is restricted and in the examples above the Adjudicator should not in fact have considered the issues given that a remedy in the courts on the basis of the doctrine of legitimate expectations would have been available. More problematically, the remedies that are available are 'soft' rather than 'hard' in the sense that should HMRC disagree with the Adjudicator's recommendation then it would be necessary to go to court to seek its enforcement.

B. Ombudsman

The reports of the Ombudsman are also replete with examples of the body holding HMRC to its advice. The 'Annual report for 1990' provides two such examples.[243]

[241] See for instance Adjudicator's Office, 'Annual Report 2006' (2006) 34–35.

[242] Adjudicator's Office, 'Annual Report 2010 continuous improvement driving performance learning lessons' (September 2010) 19.

[243] Parliamentary commissioner for administration, 'Annual report for 1990' (HC 1990–91, 299) 14.

HMRC's practice on reimbursing taxpayers for expenses arising by reason of official error on the part of the department is set out in general HMRC advice.[244] In one case, the Ombudsman found that a solicitor's costs fell squarely within the terms of the concession and the department agreed to reimburse the expense. In another case, the Ombudsman found that a taxpayer fell within the terms of a concession relating to sick pay (the now obsolete ESC A26),[245] but the department had overlooked to apply it in the case at hand. It was agreed that the complainant should be endowed with an ex gratia payment totalling £96.

The Inland Revenue's refusal to apply another concession, namely ESC A19, which forgives tax where there are delays on HMRC's part, to cases which fell within its terms came in for much criticism in the 'Annual report for 1991'.[246] The Ombudsman's opposing opinion that the taxpayers concerned did actually fall properly within the terms of ESC A19 was sufficient to provoke the Inland Revenue to give the taxpayers the benefit of the concession.[247] In one case, the Revenue had initially refused to apply the concession because a separate governmental department, the Department of Social Security (DSS),[248] caused the delay. The DSS had acquiesced in its duty to pass information concerning the state pension to the Inland Revenue. After the Ombudsman's intervention, the Inland Revenue agreed to compensate the taxpayer to the tune of £598.14. In a similar case, the taxpayer had been aware that the DSS had this arrangement with the Inland Revenue and accordingly relied upon this mechanism, rather than informing the Inland Revenue himself of his state pension. The Ombudsman recommended that the taxpayer obtain the benefit of the concession for the delay caused, again by the DSS's tardiness in passing on information. He received an exceptional ex gratia payment of £975.

Given that the remit of the Ombudsman's jurisdiction is to investigate complaints of *maladministration causing injustice*, the Ombudsman may recommend that an individual be compensated to produce an effect equivalent to an incorrect, more favourable tax assessment to which the taxpayer thought she was entitled.[249] To this end, where HMRC provides advice to a taxpayer which is incorrect as a matter of law, the Ombudsman may recommend that the taxpayer be compensated to in effect put that taxpayer in the position as if the incorrect position continued to apply. In one case, for instance, a taxpayer was compensated for failure on the part of a Customs and Excise officer to advise him of a

[244] Initially, it was set out in Statement of Practice A31, which was replaced by Code of Practice 1 on 17 February 1993.

[245] Rendered obsolete in 1999, see: Inland Revenue 'IR1' (August 1999).

[246] Parliamentary Commissioner for Administration, 'Annual report for 1991' (HC 1991–92, 347).

[247] ibid 13–14.

[248] Now has been subsumed within the Department for Work and Pensions.

[249] See: Parliamentary Commissioner for Administration, 'Annual report for 1986' (HC 1986/87, 248) 11 noted in HWR Wade and C Forsyth, *Administrative Law*, 11th edn (Oxford, Oxford University Press, 2014) 285.

more 'tax efficient' way of structuring the refurbishment of his house.[250] VAT relief was available for DIY house-builders who had built a new dwelling, but was not available for reconstructions. The complainant had incorporated an old building in a new structure (which would not qualify for the relief) but the Customs and Excise office gave the impression that it might be available and failed to intervene when it became apparent that the complainant was under a false impression. The Department compensated the taxpayer to the tune of £961.67 (representing the VAT paid on the building materials) thereby effectively arriving at the result the taxpayer had hoped, notwithstanding the fact that the taxpayer clearly did not come within the scope of the law properly applied.

The efficacy of the Ombudsman in holding HMRC to its advice, whilst helpful, also suffers similar shortcomings to that of the Adjudicator. Its remedies are 'soft' as evidenced by *Bradley* in that the claimant in that case had to take the relevant body to court in order for the body to be bound by the decision of the Ombudsman. Secondly, its remit is limited to issues of maladministration which cannot be resolved in the court, a limitation which is built into its jurisdiction in order, at least in principle, to separate issues of law from administration.[251]

V. Conclusion

For HMRC advice to guide taxpayers as to the legal consequences of their actions, it is necessary that there be some mechanism(s) to ensure that HMRC does not resile from previous commitments. In the case of individual advice (outside the context of binding rulings) or general advice, the taxpayer will have available various remedies. However, as this chapter has sought to demonstrate, there are serious shortcomings in respect of these in terms of providing protection for taxpayers.

Public law provides the most robust protection for taxpayers in the form of the doctrine of legitimate expectations. However, this is hampered by problems where the advice is incorrect, HMRC's desire to maintain control, issues around clarity, the ubiquity of qualifications in the advice and restrictions on access to justice. The extent to which the ECHR and EU law can supplement the common law doctrine of legitimate expectations is limited at best. That is not to say that the doctrine of legitimate expectations fails to find an appropriate balance between individual interests and the interests of the general public. It is, rather, that it is inapt for the purpose of providing reliability for taxpayers in respect of HMRC advice. Private law, meanwhile, is underdeveloped in this area. Finally, the assistance that the Adjudicator and Ombudsman may provide should neither be

[250] Parliamentary Commissioner for Administration, 'Fifth report for session 1983–84' (HC 1983–84, 322) 26–27.

[251] R Kirkham, 'Parliamentary Ombudsman: Withstanding the Test of Time' (HC 2006–07, 421) 5.

understated, in that evidence can be produced to demonstrate that both bodies can be effective in holding HMRC to its advice, nor overstated, in that their remit and the enforceability of their recommendations are limited.

The fact that there are such shortcomings in the protections available to taxpayers is a matter of concern not just from the perspective of the rule of law, but also operationally for HMRC. The production of advice is warranted on the basis that it facilitates collection of tax and hence HMRC performing its primary statutory duty. The judgment in *Gaines-Cooper*, however, suggests that taxpayers should not rely on general advice, but rather should approach HMRC directly whenever an issue of difficulty arises. This may require significant correspondence in order to ensure that there is absolute agreement of the scope and application of the advice provided. This in turn will have the effect of increasing the costs of collection otherwise reduced by the provision of general advice in the first place![252]

[252] Williams, 'The Multiple Doctrines of Legitimate Expectations' (n 33) 651–652.

7

Reforms

First you have to decide what the law is, then you have to decide how it should be changed, and then you have to persuade Parliamentary counsel to find the words to express this clearly and precisely enough for the parties and judges who will have to apply it in future.*

I. Introduction

Given the problems that have been assessed in the previous chapters in terms of the correctness, clarity, accessibility, scrutiny and reliability of HMRC advice, the question which must follow is, what can be done? The purpose of this chapter is to propose a package of solutions to ameliorate the issues in the UK in relation to HMRC advice. It begins by critiquing the possibility of introducing a broad binding rulings system. The chapter then moves to collating the recommendations that emanate from findings in earlier chapters.

II. Binding Rulings

The section will propose that a broad binding rulings regime should be introduced in the UK, encompassing both rulings for individuals and for a general class of taxpayers. The section first provides some background to the proposals. It then considers the operation of a rulings regime for individual taxpayers before considering in detail how a regime for binding general advice would operate in the UK. The section will then consider the permissibility of binding rulings from the perspective of Parliamentary sovereignty. The final matter to consider in this section is the viability of the proposal in terms of ensuring that Parliament, the Government and HMRC buy in to the proposal.

* Lady Hale, 'Legislation or judicial law reform: where should judges fear to tread?' (Society of Legal Scholars Conference 2016, Oxford, 7 September 2016) 14.

A. Background

i. Private Rulings

Binding rulings for individuals are generally known as 'private rulings'.[1] The UK already operates a scheme for binding rulings for individual entities and persons, but they are only available in a very narrow set of circumstances.[2] At one time, in fact, there was serious consideration of the introduction of a more general regime for private rulings. The Inland Revenue in 1994 launched a consultation about the prospect of introducing a regime for post-transaction rulings – in other words, rulings on the tax effect of a transaction after the transaction has been undertaken, but before the relevant return has been submitted.[3] Though at the time the consultation was launched, the Financial Secretary to the Treasury (then Stephen Dorrell MP) in a speech at the annual dinner of the Association of Her Majesty's Inspectors of Taxes and Senior Revenue Officials talked up the merit of *advance* (ie pre-transaction) rulings, rather than post-transaction rulings:

> Rulings are a logical part of customer service. It is helpful when the Revenue can provide guidance for taxpayers about prospective transactions where the application of the law is uncertain. Advance rulings would benefit industry and the ordinary taxpayer. They would provide a clearer, more certain system, consistent with the principles of self-assessment.[4]

In any event, the Inland Revenue duly ran a pilot scheme for non-statutory, and hence informal, post-transaction rulings,[5] which of course still operates today.[6] The following year the Inland Revenue launched a further consultation, but this time on the prospect of introducing pre-transaction rulings.[7] The Government, however, decided not to proceed with the introduction of a formal scheme for pre-transaction rulings.[8] Despite general support from practitioners,[9] there were concerns about the impact of any formal scheme on the (then) arrangements for giving informal advice on the application of the law; the additional amount of information required to obtain a ruling; and the charging of a fee for the ruling sufficient to recover the Revenue's costs in providing the ruling.

[1] See OECD, 'Tax Administration 2017: Comparative Information on OECD and Other Advanced and Emerging Economies' (September 2017) 94.

[2] See ch 2 in text at n 19.

[3] [1994] 20 *Simon's Tax Intelligence*.

[4] ibid.

[5] [1994] 47 *Simon's Tax Intelligence*.

[6] See ch 2 in text at n 14.

[7] Inland Revenue, 'Pre-Transaction Rulings: A Consultative Document' (November 1995), reported in [1995] 46 *Simon's Tax Intelligence*.

[8] [1996] 40 *Simon's Tax Intelligence*.

[9] See the Law Society's response to the consultation in [1996] 24 *Simon's Tax Intelligence*; The Institute of Chartered Accountants of Scotland submission in [1996] 15 *Simon's Tax Intelligence*; and the Chartered Institute of Taxation's submission in [1995] 12 *Simon's Tax Intelligence*.

This development is disappointing when viewed in light of the rule of law rationale for HMRC advice. Whilst there can undoubtedly be other benefits to binding rulings, such as reducing the overall cost of disputes and obtaining pertinent information about taxpayer activities,[10] it is obvious that binding rulings would further the rule of law by generating more reliable guidance as to the consequences of taxpayers' actions.

The justification for binding private rulings has greater force, from the perspective of the thin account of the rule of law, in the case of pre-transaction as opposed to post-transaction rulings. Human dignity, the value underpinning the thin account, is respected where we are given assurances as to the consequences of transactions we are contemplating. It is less engaged[11] after the transaction has been undertaken, where the consequences that a taxpayer would wish to know are those that relate to submitting a tax return on the basis of that transaction (or, in the case of a PAYE taxpayer, whether she is tax compliant). As the taxpayer has already acted, she would be seeking with post-transaction 'insurance' against the future actions of HMRC. As Sandler argues, this 'insurance' can already be provided by the tax system through disclosure on a tax return.[12] Further, informal rulings can also provide this insurance, as can HMRC's general advice. The problem from the perspective of human dignity is that problems persist in relation to this advice and in particular that HMRC in practice may go back on previous assurances.[13] To this end, the concerns that are addressed by a post-transaction ruling scheme are better addressed not by taxpayers obtaining binding retrospective assurances, but by, first, a taxpayer engaging with HMRC, assuming that reforms can be made to shore up the inadequacies prevalent in the current regime for HMRC advice, and, second, by HMRC not acting retrospectively.[14] That is before one even considers the myriad practical issues that would arise were a general binding post-transaction regime to be introduced, such as taxpayers seeking assurances on every aspect of a proposed return. For these reasons, binding post-transaction rulings will not be considered in this book as a means of advancing the rule of law. But the prospect of binding pre-transaction rulings does call for greater consideration given its impact on the human dignity aspect of the rule of law.

ii. Public Rulings

A public ruling is binding advice that is produced not for an individual taxpayer, but for a group of taxpayers. It is a published statement on the way the law applies

[10] A Sawyer, 'Binding Rulings in New Zealand – An Assessment of the First Ten Years' (2006) 12 *Canterbury Law Review* 273, 276; D Oliver 'Advance Rulings' [1996] 6 *British Tax Review* 578, 579.

[11] But still engaged! See ch 6 in text at n 53.

[12] D Sandler, *A Request for Rulings* (London, Institute of Taxation, 1994) 36–37.

[13] See ch 4 in text at n 139.

[14] On which, see the recommendation in text at n 270 that HMRC changes its practice on retrospective changes to advice.

in defined circumstances that are common to a general class of taxpayers.[15] There are very few instances where this presently exists in the UK tax code. An example is VAT Notices. These notices will have the force of law where the relevant legislation makes provision for HMRC to make determinations with binding effect. Take for instance VAT Notice 731, which relates to 'Cash Accounting',[16] the process by which a business accounts for VAT on sales on the basis of payments received, rather than on tax invoices issued. Regulation 57 of The Value Added Tax Regulations 1995 provides that a taxable person can use cash accounting provided that the business satisfies 'such conditions as are described in a notice published by the Commissioners'. There are no formal conditions as to how HMRC goes about producing these notices. There may be consultation, as occurred in the case of VAT Notice 700/22: 'Making Tax Digital for VAT' for instance,[17] but consultation is not mandated.

This book shall propose that a regime, based on the Australian model, for the production of public rulings is desirable given the ability of such a scheme to advance the rule of law. The development of the Australian system of public rulings is owed in particular to two significant events. The first was the introduction of the Freedom of Information Act in 1982. Until that point, the Commissioner had used an internal system for disseminating information on the application of tax law to staff[18] since at least the 1920s.[19] The system in place then for producing advice for the public, however, could best be described as 'sporadic'.[20] The Freedom of Information Act forced the publication of this internal advice.[21] The next significant event was the introduction of self-assessment in the latter half of the 1980s.[22] The shift in responsibilities to taxpayers was said to merit the introduction of a formal rulings regime, which would provide greater 'certainty' for taxpayers as to how they should arrange their affairs.[23]

Public rulings are binding on the Australian Tax Office (ATO).[24] A taxpayer can rely on a public ruling if her circumstances fall within its terms. If the advice

[15] See OECD, 'Tax Administration 2017' (2017) 94.

[16] HMRC, 'Cash Accounting Scheme' (VAT Notice 731) (August 2018).

[17] HMRC Consultation outcome. 'Draft legislation: The Value Added Tax (Amendment) Regulations 2018' (March 2018).

[18] Auditor General, 'The Australian Taxation Office's Administration of Taxation Rulings' (2001) 175.

[19] L Edmonds, Working for all Australians 1910–2010: A brief history of the Australian Taxation Office (Canberra, Australian Tax Office, 2010) 33.

[20] G Cooper, 'Improving the operation of the Income Tax Rulings system' Discussion Paper: Report for the Australian Society of CPAs (1998) 9.

[21] Joint Committee of Public Accounts, 'An Assessment of Tax – A Report on an Inquiry into the Australian Taxation Office' (July 1993) para 2.50; Commissioner of Taxation, 'Sixty-Second Annual Report' (Commonwealth Government Printer 1983) 7.

[22] Commonwealth of Australia, 'Discussion Paper: Review of Aspects of Income Tax Self Assessment' (March 2004) (ROSA Discussion Paper) 3.

[23] Edmonds, *Working for all Australians* (2010) 223. The case of *David Jones Finance v Commissioner of Taxation* (1991) 21 ATR 1506 was apparently the catalyst; see Joint Committee of Public Account and Audit, 'Tax Administration' (June 2008) 122.

[24] See Taxation Administration Act 1953 (TAA 1953), Sch 1, subs 357–60.

turns out to be incorrect and the taxpayer mistakenly submits an incorrect tax return as a result, she will be protected from paying tax that would otherwise be payable under the law, in addition to protection from interest and penalties.[25] Conversely, a ruling does not bind the taxpayer, who is free to apply the law if it provides a more favourable result for her than the ruling, though if a court finds later that the ruling is correct she may be subject to a penalty.[26] The Commissioner has wide discretion to issue rulings on provisions relating to inter alia income tax, fringe benefits tax, indirect tax, excise duty and the administration or collection of those taxes levies and duties.[27] It is notable that the scope of issues for which rulings may be provided has expanded over time.[28] When initially introduced, rulings were reserved *only* for interpretations, guidelines, precedents, practices or procedures which established a new interpretation of administration of the tax laws that affected a group of taxpayers.[29]

Public rulings are grouped into different series, such as the Taxation Rulings series, Product Grants and Benefits Rulings series and Excise Rulings series.[30] There are also specific public rulings, known as product[31] and class rulings,[32] available for tax schemes. One entity or taxpayer asks for advice on the tax consequences of a transaction or arrangement which affects multiple taxpayers, such as in the case of a financial product or where an employer seeks advice on the tax consequences of retention bonuses. These are administratively efficient as the ATO can provide a single ruling rather than multiple substantively identical rulings. However, the process for the production of these is significantly different from that of public rulings generally and more akin to the process for producing private rulings. Whereas public rulings are generated generally at the discretion of the ATO, product and class rulings are produced following specific requests from taxpayers.[33]

Whilst many jurisdictions operate public rulings regimes,[34] the system in Australia merits detailed consideration for three reasons. The first is that there is symmetry between the two jurisdictions, not just by reason of common law, but

[25] See ATO, 'TR 2006/10: Public rulings' (February 2018).

[26] See TAA 1953, Sch 1, subs 184-15(1) and 284-15(3)(d).

[27] TAA 1953, Sch 1, subs 357-5.

[28] ATO, 'TR 2006/10: Public rulings' (2018) para 13; Explanatory Memorandum to the Tax Laws Amendment (Improvements to Self Assessment) Bill (No 2) 2005 para 3.22. See also: J Ralph, R Allert and B Joss, 'Review of Business Taxation: A tax system redesigned. More certain, equitable and durable' (Australian Government Publication Services 1999) (Ralph report) 37, 137–38.

[29] See ATO, 'TR 92/1' (July 1992) para 9.

[30] ATO (n 25) para 22.

[31] ATO, 'PR 2007/71' (September 2018). Product rulings were introduced in 1998. See: Commonwealth of Australia, 'ROSA Discussion Paper' (2004) 13.

[32] ATO, 'CR 2001/1' (September 2013). Class rulings were introduced in 2001. See JCPAA, *Tax Administration* (2008) 94.

[33] See ATO, 'When to consider applying for a class ruling' (March 2017) and ATO, 'Applying for a product ruling' (August 2017).

[34] See for instance OECD, 'Tax Administration 2015 Comparative Information on OECD and Other Advanced and Emerging Economies' (August 2015) 289.

also in respect of the legal framework for the tax authorities as well as, critically, rationales for the provision of advice. The allocation of responsibility in terms of tax administration is almost identical to the UK framework. The ATO is the chief revenue-collecting body in Australia, which is led by the Commissioner of Taxation and three Second Commissioners of Taxation.[35] The Commissioners are accountable to ministers and Parliament.[36] The primary role of the ATO is to effectively manage and shape the tax and superannuation (or pensions) systems.[37] This includes collecting revenue, administering the goods and services tax (GST)[38] on behalf of the Australian states and territories, and administering the major aspects of Australia's superannuation system. The ATO's authority for this general administration is to be found in the relevant primary legislation. Generally, the Acts, or parts thereof,[39] will contain a provision which states that 'the Commissioner shall have the general administration of this Act' or 'the Commissioner has the general administration of this Act'.[40] In interpreting the scope of the ATO's power of general administration, the courts have acknowledged that the Commissioner must be empowered to undertake any necessary actions incidental to the effectuation of this provision.[41]

Importantly for present purposes, the principle underpinning the general powers of administration has long been recognised as allowing the ATO to engage with the public in order to help individuals, entities and undertakings to understand their obligations and rights under the law.[42] Commissioner Patrick McGovern in 1958 put it thusly:

> It has been remarked that there is no justification for a programme to improve the relations between taxpayers and the Tax Administration. Taxes, like death, are certain it is said – there is no escaping them. The Administration is clothed with adequate power to enforce payment. So why bother about what the taxpayers think of the Administration?
>
> Both experience and common sense provide an emphatic denial to the validity of these views in present day conditions.
>
> … There is in these days a desire to understand and be understood.
>
> It would be futile to expend effort on improving public relations unless the basic conditions for the success of the effort were present. Fortunately, this is the case. Equitable tax administration has existed in the Commonwealth for nearly fifty years. This enables a positive approach to be made to improve relations between the Administration and

[35] TAA 1953, s 5.

[36] Commissioner of Taxation, 'Annual Report 2017–18' (October 2018) 152.

[37] ibid 2.

[38] GST is a broad-based tax on most goods, services and other items sold or consumed in Australia.

[39] See for example Superannuation Industry (Supervision) Act 1993, s 6.

[40] For instance Income Tax Assessment Act 1936, s 8; Superannuation Guarantee (Administration) Act 1992, s 43; Excise Act 1901, s 7.

[41] See Commonwealth of Australia, 'An "Extra-Statutory Concession" Power for the Commissioner of Taxation?', Discussion Paper (12 May 2009) para 14.

[42] ibid para 19.

> the public. There are two branches of this positive approach – first – the promotion of an understanding of taxation law itself and second – the furthering of confidence in the organisation entrusted with the administration of the law.[43]

What is notable about this approach is its symmetry to that of HMRC in the UK in relation to the importance of engaging with the public and proactively providing advice.[44] The successful adaptation of any programme for reform relies upon the fundamentals being present in the first place. The congruity of approaches to the effectuation of the primary duty accordingly augurs well for the positive implementation of reforms based upon the Australian model for the provision of binding general advice.

Secondly, the Australian model would satisfy to a greater extent one of the normative benchmarks, namely scrutiny. The Australian public rulings system incorporates an expert oversight body, in the form of the Public Advice and Guidance Panel, into the regime. This is comprised of several of the most senior ATO personnel as well as external representatives who are respected tax practitioners and academics.[45] The Public Advice and Guidance Panel came into being in 2016 and took over the role previously played by what were known as 'public rulings panels'.[46] The primary role of the panel is to discuss the technical and practical merits of the draft ruling presented to it and to advise on the proposed interpretation of the law.[47] The presence of expert external oversight distinguishes the Australian regime from the public rulings systems in similar jurisdictions such as New Zealand.[48]

Thirdly, the presence of this expert scrutiny, as will be seen, has a positive effect also on the correctness, clarity and accessibility of tax authority advice, with consequent positive knock-on effects on reliability.

It should be noted that a greater amount of attention shall be granted to the consideration of public rulings rather than rulings for individuals. This is for two reasons. Public rulings involve a greater departure from the norm than rulings for individuals, which already operates in the UK albeit on a limited scale.[49] Secondly, proposals for private rulings have already been subject to serious detailed consideration by others.[50]

[43] See Edmonds (n 19) 97; Commissioner of Taxation, 'Annual Report 1957–58', 29.

[44] See ch 3 in text at n 74.

[45] ATO, 'PS LA 2008/3: Provision of advice and guidance by the ATO' (February 2014) para 33.

[46] ATO, 'Australian Taxation Office Submission to the Standing Committee on Tax and Revenue' (November 2016) para 100.

[47] ATO, 'How we develop public advice and guidance' (February 2018).

[48] See generally, New Zealand: Tax Administration Act 1994, Pt 5A in particular ss 91D–91DE.

[49] See ch 2 in text at n 19.

[50] See for instance B Alarie, K Datt, A Sawyer and G Weeks 'Advance Tax Rulings in Perspective: A Theoretical and Comparative Analysis' (2014) 20 *New Zealand Journal of Taxation Law and Policy* 362; Sandler, *Rulings* (1994); J Prebble, 'Advance Rulings on Tax Liability' (Wellington, Victoria University Press/Institute of Policy Studies, 1986).

B. Proposal for Private Rulings

Many commentators over the years have proposed the introduction of a more general formalised rulings system in the UK[51] and this book too considers binding pre-transaction rulings to be an appropriate tool to advance the rule of law, having regard to the normative framework adopted. The word 'transaction' here is used loosely so as to encompass not just contractual transactions concerning the transfer of consideration in return for an asset, but also situations where taxpayers decide to arrange their affairs in a manner which results in legal changes which are pertinent to tax.[52] To that end, 'transaction' should be taken to include not just, for instance, the purchase or sale of an asset, but also an arrangement such as a change in residence.

The goal here is not to set out in detail how such a regime would operate, but to highlight how the benchmarks from the normative framework would apply to a formal pre-transaction rulings regime. In particular, such a regime would improve accessibility and reliability.

i. Correctness and Clarity

The benchmarks of correctness and clarity can be dealt with together on the basis that a rulings regime per se does not automatically bring about improvements in these areas. Although with a binding regime an individual taxpayer might be nonplussed about the correctness of the HMRC advice, it is unhelpful in terms of the rule of law.

Correctness and clarity of HMRC advice are essentially issues that HMRC controls, but the introduction of a formal pre-transaction rulings regime would call for a means of allowing experts to review rulings, such as through the establishment of a central rulings body[53] or of a framework to accommodate expert review. For instance, in Australia, binding rulings are prepared by ATO staff in the relevant major business line,[54] together sometimes with technical specialists from the Tax Counsel Network,[55] the ATO's most senior tax technical specialists.[56] Moreover, scrutiny can be provided by other taxpayers or members of representative groups,

[51] See for instance A Taylor, 'Proposing a tax rulings system' (2017) 4605 *Taxation* 8; W Chan, 'Binding Rulings' (1997) 18 *Fiscal Studies* 189; Sandler (n 12); E Troup, 'Unacceptable Discretion: Countering Tax Avoidance and Preserving the Rights of the Individual' (1992) 13 *Fiscal Studies* 128, 138.

[52] See for instance Australia: Income Tax Assessment Act 1997, subs 995-1(1).

[53] Sandler (n 12) 43; C Waerzeggers and C Hillier, 'Introducing an Advance Tax Ruling (ATR) regime' (2016) 2 *Tax Law IMF Technical Note* 6.

[54] For the Business Lines, see the left-hand column in ATO, 'ATO organisational structure' (January 2019).

[55] Inspector-General of Taxation, 'Review of aspects of the Australian Taxation Office's administration of private binding rulings' (May 2010) 87.

[56] ibid 91.

which can be instrumental in achieving correctness and clarity *if* individual rulings are published (as will be suggested).

There might be a temptation to argue that formal rulings give rise to the possibility that HMRC could adopt an approach which is either overly favourable to the Exchequer, or conversely, where a rogue officer is involved, overly favourable to taxpayers. In terms of the former, HMRC is not incentivised to interpret legislation in a manner overly favourable to the Exchequer. HMRC's primary objective is to 'Collect revenues *due* and bear down on avoidance and evasion'.[57] One of the tools used to estimate the performance in respect of this objective is the tax gap that calculates the difference between the amount of tax that should, in theory, be collected by HMRC against what is actually collected.[58] Thus, the operations of HMRC are driven by the objective of collecting only the tax that is *due*. To interpret the law to maximise revenue per se would result in an increase in the size of the amount of tax which ought to be collected by HMRC and hence would make the tax gap look larger than it is, in turn indicating underperformance. The incentive is more likely to be that HMRC would not wish to provide a ruling in a case of genuine doubt, owing to the duty to collect taxes.[59] Responding to that problem requires a broader shift in mindset – becoming more comfortable with the idea that certainty for taxpayers as a whole can trump the importance of collecting every penny that is due.[60] In terms of the latter, Nick Petroulias was a former Assistant Tax Commissioner who used his position in the tax office to secure private tax rulings for companies in which he had a financial interest.[61] But that is a straightforward case of fraud. Though formal rulings could be said to present another opportunity for fraud, the fault for engaging in such an illegal practice lies with the individuals concerned, not at the feet of the rulings system. There are in any event other opportunities for fraudsters working in HMRC to engage in nefarious activities.[62]

ii. Accessibility

In terms of entitlement to apply for pre-transaction rulings, jurisdictions ought to strive to give the greatest provision possible in line with the principle of the rule of law, but resource constraints will require compromises to be made. This will especially be the case in respect of the timeliness of rulings. The focus must be on whether deviations from the principle that all should be treated equally are justified.

[57] HMRC, 'HM Revenue and Customs single departmental plan' (June 2019) (emphasis added).

[58] HMRC, 'Measuring tax gaps 2019 edition – tax gap estimates for 2017–18' (June 2019) 3.

[59] T Pagone, 'Tax Uncertainty' (2009) 33 *Melbourne University Law Review* 886, 905.

[60] On which, see in text at n 250.

[61] For more, see: *Petroulias v R* [2014] NSWCCA 108, [58]–[80].

[62] See for instance R Covill, 'Former HMRC worker sentenced for tax credits fraud' *The Business Desk* (December 2018).

In terms of practical restrictions on accessibility, it is possible to establish the system so as to entitle all UK taxpayers to pre-transaction rulings.[63] Given that a rulings regime requires input in terms of resources, it is permissible for tax authorities to charge for the service.[64] The amount that should be charged will be a reflection of the balance between the extent to which the ruling is viewed as beneficial to the taxpayer specifically and the ruling is beneficial for society generally.[65] That a taxpayer may bear some of the burden is appropriate too not just in terms of benefit, but also to ensure that the services of tax authorities are not simply used in substitution for private professional services. A fee, meanwhile, would have the effect of deterring unmeritorious requests. The amount that should be charged would have to depend on the nature of the ruling requested – for instance, a complex transaction ruling will be resource-intensive – and the taxpayer, as it would be necessary to try to avoid taxpayers being financially unable to ask for a ruling.

Given the cost involved in providing a ruling, there may be a temptation to make rulings binding on the taxpayer as well as on HMRC, or to apply penalties for failing to follow a ruling.[66] A balance accordingly needs to be struck between, on the one hand, encouraging compliance with rulings and, on the other, the rights of taxpayers. However, given the importance that is stressed upon producing correct tax outcomes, penalties are undesirable, as they would have the effect of giving rulings a superior place to that of the underlying law. As Cooper has noted, 'in a Westminster-style democracy, taxpayers should be penalised for infractions of legislation, not the [the tax authority's] view of it'.[67] This could be achieved by a clarification, either by HMRC or by legislative amendment, that the failure to take reasonable care, which attracts penalties in the UK,[68] is not engaged, absent other aggravating factors, simply where a taxpayer refuses to follow an HMRC ruling.

As for the scope of what may be requested by way of ruling, it is possible to provide that a taxpayer could be entitled to ask for a ruling on any provision of the UK tax code.[69] Of course, it is already HMRC and Treasury policy to bear down on tax avoidance and evasion[70] and it would be unlikely that it would be possible to convince the relevant stakeholders that rulings should be provided even in tax avoidance situations, such as in relation to the General Anti-Abuse Rule (GAAR).[71] Whilst this could be said to stand in tension with the rule of law,

[63] In Australia, for instance, every taxpayer is entitled to apply for a private ruling on how a relevant provision applies: TAA 1953, Sch 1, subs 359-10(1) and 'Explanatory Memorandum to the Tax Laws Amendment (Improvements to Self Assessment) (No 2) Bill 2005', para 3.67.

[64] On which see Sandler (n 12) 65; OECD (n 1) 95.

[65] Society will benefit from the rule of law aspect of rulings, but it should be remembered that tax authorities are funded by the government which relies upon the general body of taxpayers.

[66] Penalties can apply in Australia in respect of public rulings. See TAA 1953, Sch 1, subs 284-75(1) which allows the levying of penalties where a taxpayer's position is not 'reasonably arguable'.

[67] Cooper, 'Income Tax Rulings system' (1998) 51.

[68] See for instance Finance Act 2007, Sch 24, paras 1 and 3.

[69] See in the case of Australia, TAA 1953, Sch 1, subs 359-5(2).

[70] HMRC, 'Single departmental plan' (2019).

[71] For the relevant provisions on the General Anti-Abuse Rule, see generally Finance Act 2013, Pt 5.

it is to be remembered that deviations from the normative framework advanced here can be accommodated.[72] More generally, HMRC should retain a discretion to refuse to issue rulings where it would not be conducive to the performance of HMRC's duties. For instance, where the applications are frivolous; or where complying with the request would conflict with another duty, such as the duty of confidentiality or moreover the duty to collect taxes which would augur against providing a ruling in a case of genuine uncertainty; or where the ruling would be unreasonably costly or where the matters to which they refer are those that are discretionary decisions vested in HMRC, such as resource allocations which come within HMRC's general managerial discretion or whether to mitigate penalties,[73] which is a specific discretion.[74] In Australia, this is achieved by a provision which states that the Tax Office can refuse a request where the ruling would prejudice or unduly restrict the administration of a taxation law.[75] More practically, HMRC should not be required to issue a ruling where one has already been provided, or where the taxpayer provides insufficient information or is not timely with the provision of information, or where the transaction has already been completed. These practical issues could be set out as individual conditions for the provision of a ruling.[76] Whenever a ruling is refused, the taxpayer should be given reasons – a specification that could be set out in statute,[77] though could be argued to be a norm of good administration in any event.[78]

Where a taxpayer applies for a ruling, it should be provided promptly, though resource constraints may have an impact upon how promptly this may take place. In Australia, taxpayers can expect rulings to be provided within 60 days,[79] which seems a sensible starting point as it is broadly in line with international comparisons.[80] This could not be a strict limit as there would have to be some accommodation for the fact that certain transactions will be far more complex and time-consuming than others.

Beyond practical restrictions, there is a need to consider how binding pre-transaction rulings can alleviate the problems caused by lack of publication, retrospectivity and mingling. In terms of publicising rulings, it follows that in order so that all taxpayers for whom the advice may be relevant could have access to the

[72] See ch 4 in text at n 109.

[73] See for instance Taxes Management Act 1970, s 102; Value added Tax Act 1994, s 70.

[74] On specific discretion, see ch 3 in text at n 55.

[75] See TAA 1953, Sch 1, subs 359-35(1)(a); ATO, 'TR 2006/11' (16 August 2017) para 39.

[76] See, for instance, TAA 1953, Sch 1, subs 359-35(2)(a), which provides that a ruling will not be given where 'the matter sought to be ruled on is already being, or has been, considered by the Commissioner for you'.

[77] See TAA 1953, Sch 1, subs 359-35(4).

[78] See, for instance, M Elliott, 'Has the Common Law Duty to Give Reasons Come of Age Yet?' [2011] 1 *Public Law* 56.

[79] See TAA 1953, Sch 1, subs 359-50.

[80] OECD, 'Tax Administration 2015' (2015) 289 and 332–33.

advice, all binding pre-transaction rulings should be published but with confidential information redacted.[81] As rulings should be stable over time, retrospectivity then should be guarded against. However, a change to a ruling may be necessitated where it is realised that it is incorrect or where a court decision supersedes it.[82] Where this occurs, rulings should be changed prospectively, whilst allowing the ruling to have effect for the remainder of the tax year to which the ruling relates.[83] Finally, the problems caused by mingling for the taxpayer stem from the fact that a taxpayer may be put in an unwittingly precarious position, but this is neutralised in the case of binding rulings. The publication of rulings meanwhile produces the possibility that there can be greater oversight so as to scrutinise potential inconsistency with the underlying law.

iii. Scrutiny

As with correctness or clarity, the introduction of a binding pre-transactions rulings scheme would not automatically bring about improvements of scrutiny and, to that end, the hope that there would be any increased supervision should be downplayed. As for internal arrangements, a framework for involving experts in the process of providing rulings (highlighted already) would be beneficial, and this could be overseen at a macro level by the HMRC Tax Assurance Commissioner, who reviews the most sensitive tax settlements.[84]

Meanwhile, the publication of redacted rulings will ensure that there will be public scrutiny of rulings – whether that is the general body of taxpayers, their advisers, professional groups or non-governmental organisations. The insertion of feedback links[85] on the site where the rulings are published would provide those interested with the means of communicating to HMRC where improvements or changes could be made. Further, the Adjudicator's Office ('Adjudicator') and Parliamentary and Health Service Ombudsman ('Ombudsman') would become involved also, with the added oversight these bodies provide,[86] as taxpayers would bring disputes to these bodies in relation to HMRC's decisions on rulings. Finally, greater scrutiny could be achieved as part of a broader change in the role currently adopted by the bodies that are formally charged with scrutinising HMRC advice, in particular with the tribunals and courts becoming more proactive and the

[81] This occurs, for instance, in Australia and Canada. See ATO, 'Publishing of private rulings' (May 2018); Canada Revenue Agency, 'Information circular: IC70-6R9' (April 2019) para 51.

[82] See, for instance, in New Zealand: Tax Administration Act 1994, s 91EI.

[83] New Zealand: Tax Administration Act 1994, s 91EI(3).

[84] See, for instance, HMRC, 'How we resolve tax disputes: The Tax Assurance Commissioner's Annual Report 2015–16' (July 2016) 4–6.

[85] As has been recommended by the Office of Tax Simplification in the context of HMRC guidance. See Office of Tax Simplification, 'Guidance for taxpayers: a vision for the future' (October 2018) 6 and 30. Disclosure: the author met with the Office of Tax Simplification to discuss HMRC advice when the team was preparing the report.

[86] See ch 5 in text at n 129.

Comptroller and Auditor General (CAG) along with the National Audit Office (NAO) taking on more responsibility for HMRC advice.[87]

iv. Reliability

The greatest contribution that a formal pre-transaction rulings regime can make is in respect of reliability in that rulings become binding on HMRC. This eliminates the issues caused by the second limb of the legitimate expectations test as there is no possibility to consider whether there is good reason to depart from a binding ruling. That is at least the case where a taxpayer has applied for a ruling. In such an instance, legislation should provide that the ruling is binding.[88] Where the taxpayer seeks to rely on a published, redacted ruling of another taxpayer, she should seek her own ruling from HMRC. Meanwhile where there is inconsistency between rulings, the later ruling should take precedence.[89]

If a taxpayer disagrees with a ruling provided to her, there should be a mechanism to allow her to challenge it.[90] Where the decision of HMRC is to refuse to provide a ruling, then the ordinary principles of judicial review ought to apply as the refusal is a discretionary decision of HMRC.[91] Where a taxpayer seeks to challenge the ruling provided, then the challenge should lie not in review, but in appeal. The first argument in support of this proposal is the likelihood that the adjudicators would, in review, defer in some respect to the view of the statutorily empowered, institutionally competent HMRC.[92] But this relinquishes power in favour of HMRC, allowing the body to control the decision which will be arrived at. A more preferable state of affairs would be for the tribunals and then courts to have control over the dispute. Both appeal and review ought to take place in the first instance in the Tax Chamber of the First-tier Tribunal (FTT). However, this would require a change of approach, as the FTT is generally not competent to decide issues of judicial review,[93] as will be elaborated below.[94]

Of course, the fact that rulings would be binding does not alter the fact that there can still be disputes as to whether the taxpayer falls properly within the scope

[87] See in text at n 277.

[88] See, for instance, New Zealand: Tax Administration Act 1994, s 91EA.

[89] See, for instance, TAA 1953, Sch 1, subs 357–75.

[90] See TAA 1953, ss 14ZYB and 14ZZ for guidance.

[91] Of course, if the refusal is simply because HMRC has misunderstood whether the relevant conditions for the provision of a ruling have been satisfied, it might be said that the refusal is not discretionary. But in such a case, the ordinary principles of judicial review would suggest that HMRC has acted unlawfully because it has failed to properly take into account relevant considerations. On the obligation to take into account considerations expressed in statute, see: *Secretary of State for Education and Science v Tameside MBC* [1977] AC 1014 (HL), 1065 (Lord Diplock).

[92] On which, see T Endicott, *Administrative Law*, 4th edn (Oxford, Oxford University Press, 2018) 238–41.

[93] See, for instance, *Metropolitan International Schools Ltd v HMRC* [2019] EWCA Civ 156, [2019] STC 632 [20]–[22].

[94] See in text at n 295.

of a ruling, just as disputes arise in respect of the doctrine of legitimate expectations as to whether a legitimate expectation arises in favour of the taxpayer. These disputes should, however, be reduced by virtue of the fact that there can be no ambiguity as to whether an assurance has actually be given[95] – as a ruling is either given or it is not – and the taxpayer and HMRC should be closer to one mind on the scope of the ruling than arises in the case of general assurances, given that both parties will need to be more specific in their communications.[96] Further, the potential benefits to clarity brought about by binding individual rulings should also have a beneficial impact on the potential reliability, just as lack of clarity negatively impacts reliability.[97]

C. Proposal for Public Rulings

The introduction of public rulings in the UK, based loosely on the Australian regime, presents an opportunity to make significant improvements to the provision of advice by HMRC. To flesh out such a proposal, it is necessary first to examine the Australian regime and how it performs in respect of correctness, clarity, accessibility, scrutiny and reliability. Thereafter this section will consider the mechanics of a public rulings regime in the UK, looking initially at the steps that are involved in public rulings, before considering what matters would be appropriate for public rulings, the relevant stakeholders that would need to be involved and the legislative amendments that are necessary to accommodate public rulings.

i. Public Rulings in Australia

a. Correctness and Clarity

Although the Australian system took off with some turbulence,[98] subsequent commentary has attested to the increased quality of rulings in terms of correctness and clarity. As might be expected of a system which stresses the importance of incorporating the scrutiny of experts and the public, the rulings regime has been found to have enhanced the technical quality of publications which go through it. Indeed, the two elements are interwoven. The increased quality of rulings is related to the increased use of consultation and public engagement.[99]

In his report on the rulings system almost a decade after its introduction, the Auditor General concluded that the 'processes for the production of public

[95] For a case where this dispute arose, see *Hanover Company Services Ltd v HMRC* [2010] UKFTT 256 (TC).

[96] See, for instance, *R (Biffa Waste Services Ltd) v Revenue and Customs* [2016] EWHC 1444 (Admin), [2017] Env LR 10.

[97] See ch 6 in text at n 87.

[98] JCPA, 'Assessment of Tax' (1993) xxiii para 21.

[99] ibid para 6.21.

rulings of high technical quality operate effectively overall'.[100] This conclusion was supported by evidence from the private sector that the quality of public rulings had increased since the regime's inception by reason of the variety of measures taken by the ATO, such as the introduction of rulings panels and the priority rulings system.[101] The ATO likewise submitted that the introduction of rulings panels to review public rulings was a 'significant factor in the ATO improving the quality of its public rulings'.[102]

The report of the Joint Committee of Public Accounts and Audit (JCPAA) on 'Tax Administration' in 2008 reached a similar conclusion.[103] The Institute of Chartered Accountants in Australia advised the Committee that the Public Rulings Panel had improved the standard of public rulings:

> [T]he establishment of a Public Rulings Panel and an International Public Rulings Panel,[104] which include external tax experts, to supplement a public consultation process, in which professional bodies participate, has gone some way to ensure the quality of public rulings and, more particularly, public confidence in these rulings.[105]

On the indirect tax front, meanwhile, private practitioners have commended the ATO on the quality of GST rulings:

> I should state at the outset that the overall standard of public GST rulings is high, and that nothing I say below should be taken to diminish that conclusion. While I do not always agree with the conclusions expressed in public GST rulings, nor the reasons advanced in support of those conclusions, the rulings demonstrate a high level of technical expertise and clarity.[106]

The history of public rulings suggests that consultation with public rulings panels has resulted often in a change of direction of the public ruling, sometimes very significantly, from the initial ATO position, as noted by the Auditor General.[107] Although there are no publicly available data on the performance of the rulings panels[108] or the new entity known as the Public Advice and Guidance Panel (as the advice is confidential), their impact can be surmised from the history of individual rulings. If an initial view published by the ATO in the form of

[100] Auditor General, 'Administration of Taxation Rulings' (2001) 16.
[101] ibid 85.
[102] ibid.
[103] JCPAA, 'Tax Administration' (2008) 99.
[104] This panel was later subsumed by the Public Rulings Panel.
[105] JCPAA (n 23) 99.
[106] K O'Rourke, 'The GST Rulings System – Is it Failing?' (2002) 11 *Revenue Law Journal* 79, 86. See also Cooper (n 20) 53.
[107] Auditor General (n 18) 83.
[108] ibid 85. Granted, this report was in 2001, but the author has not found yet any specific data on the performance of the Public Rulings Panels or Public Advice and Guidance Panel. In its follow-up audit, the Auditor General considered that the ATO had 'fully implemented' the Auditor General's recommendation in the 2001 report to introduce performance indicators for the public rulings system (Auditor General, 'Administration of Taxation Rulings: Follow-up Audit' (August 2004) para 4.22). But none of the indicators related to the performance specifically of the Panels in augmenting the quality of public rulings.

non-binding guidance, such as an 'Interpretative Decision', is contrasted with a subsequently published draft ruling on the same issue, it can reasonably be inferred that at least on some of the occasions the Panel has forced the ATO to reconsider its view.

In other instances where there is a perceived inconsistency with the underlying law, the public rulings regime forces the ATO to defend its interpretations. The ATO now often publishes contrary views in its rulings.[109] The evolution of 'Tax Ruling 98/15: Income tax: taxation consequences of trading in a previously leased asset for a replacement leased asset'[110] illustrates the utility of the consultative framework in forcing the ATO to deal with contrary interpretations. The initial draft ruling, *TR 95/D28*,[111] did not mention the High Court decision of *AL Hamblin Equipment*[112] on the treatment of trade-ins. The ATO advised that it did not consider the *Hamblin* case to be relevant. However, in response to submissions on the draft ruling, the ATO published its reasons for believing the case to be irrelevant. These were contained in the final ruling when it was published three years later.

Of course, the interposition of the rulings process does not absolutely prevent rulings from being inconsistent with the underlying law,[113] nor from being ambiguous (which in turn frustrates the utility of the ruling).[114] But it is more likely to produce better quality advice than would arise in its absence.

It should be noted that it has been claimed that there may be a 'revenue bias'[115] in the production of public rulings – a cause that, if made out, would undermine the ability of the regime to ensure that rulings are consistent with the law. The basic argument to this effect is that the ATO seeks to produce rulings which err on the side of caution in the interpretative process.[116] But that is not bias, but rather conservatism driven by the primary duty to collect tax.[117] In any event, both the Auditor General's 2001 report[118] and the ROSA discussion paper[119] held that it was

[109] These are often found in the compendium to public rulings. See, for instance, ATO, 'TR 2010/6EC: Ruling Compendium'.

[110] ATO, 'TR 98/15: Income tax: taxation consequences of trading in a previously leased asset for a replacement leased asset' (September 1998).

[111] ATO, 'TR 95/D28: Income tax: leasing – trade-ins and balloon payments' (November 1995).

[112] *AL Hamblin Equipment Pty Ltd; AL Hamblin Constructions Pty Ltd v Federal Commissioner of Taxation* (1974) 131 CLR 570.

[113] Eg see: *Commissioner of Taxation v Indooroopilly Children Services (Qld) Pty Ltd* [2007] FCAFC 16 [3]–[6] Allsop J, with which Stone J concurred [1]; [43]–[47] Edmonds J.

[114] D Scolaro, 'Tax Rulings: Opinion or Law? The Need for an Independent "Rule-Maker"' (2006) 16 *Revenue Law Journal* 109, 124–46; J Prebble, 'Avoidance and Other Consequences of Publishing Commissioner's Interpretation Guidelines' (2004) 19 *Australian Tax Forum* 245, 250–64.

[115] Scolaro (ibid); D Bentley, 'A Proposal for Reform of the Australian Ruling system' (1997) 26 *Australian Tax Review* 57; Cooper (n 20) 36; T Rumble, 'Ralph Review Submission No 30' (December 1998) 41.

[116] Scolaro, 'Tax Rulings' (2006) 121; Bentley (ibid) 63; M Allars, *Introduction to Australian Administrative Law* (Sydney, Butterworths, 1990) ch 6.

[117] Pagone, 'Tax Uncertainty' (2009) 905.

[118] Auditor General (n 18) 95.

[119] Commonwealth of Australia (n 22) 24.

difficult to determine whether there was any validity to the accusation of bias. The best available evidence which can illuminate whether there is a pro-revenue bias in interpretations arises in the context of private rulings. Importantly, such rulings do not go through the formal consultative process in place for public rulings. As a result, if there is pro-revenue bias to be found anywhere, it will at the very least be where there is little oversight. The Inspector-General of Taxation (IGT), an independent statutory agency created to review systemic tax administration issues,[120] prepared a report in 2008 on potential revenue bias in private binding rulings.[121] There were no examples of undue revenue bias submitted to the review.[122] The IGT considered whether Tax Office processes and records of internal thinking that produced a private binding ruling indicated any evidence of an intention to impose more revenue than was open on a purposive interpretation of the law, as the ATO understands it. The sample did not exhibit evidence of such intentions.[123] The review concluded that there was no evidence of undue revenue bias:

> Based on a survey of representative large corporate PBR applicants' views, submissions to the review, the proportion of favourable PBRs given, the pattern of external review of the Tax Office's PBR objection decisions, and review of a random sample of Tax Office files undertaken by the staff of the Inspector-General, this review has found no evidence of undue revenue bias.[124]

b. Accessibility

There are four strands to accessibility to be considered. In terms firstly of practical restrictions, public rulings are all available online on the ATO's legal database and are printed in the *Gazette* (a printed publication of the Australian Government). Additionally, public rulings may be produced on any matter related to the application of a provision,[125] including, therefore, not just interpretation of a provision, but also how the ATO administers a provision or exercises discretion.[126] Public rulings can also be produced on the application of the Australian General Anti-Avoidance Rule.[127] However, unsurprisingly, given the binding and general nature of public rulings, that there have been complaints about their timeliness.[128]

Meanwhile in terms of publication, several aspects of the Australian system act to safeguard against unpublished advice. Although the decision to produce a

[120] Inspector-General of Taxation Act 2003, s 3.
[121] Inspector-General of Taxation, 'Review of the potential revenue bias in private binding rulings involving large complex matters' (February 2008).
[122] ibid para 2.3.
[123] ibid para 2.4.
[124] ibid para 2.5.
[125] TAA 1953, Sch 1, subs 358-5.
[126] ATO (n 25) paras 66A–B.
[127] See, for instance, ATO, 'TD 2010/10' (March 2010). For the Australian GAAR, see generally Income Tax Assessment Act 1936, Pt IVA.
[128] See, for instance, Commonwealth of Australia (n 22) 23.

ruling is a matter of discretion for the Commissioner, the engagement of taxpayers through consultative forums and in particular through the work of the National Tax Liaison Group reduces the prospect of this occurring. When the IGT reviewed the self-assessment system in 2012,[129] it was concluded that collaboration with tax professionals has led to a better assessment of what the priority areas of uncertainty were, as well as improving the ATO's understanding and its capacity to address them effectively.[130] This appears to likewise be the understanding amongst senior ATO staff:

> [T]he ATO's law experts and leaders need to have ongoing engagement with the tax profession about contentious and uncertain issues. During the last year or so, this has started to happen more and more, but I think a wider range of law experts (and not just the senior officers) need to be engaging this way. This type of ongoing open and frank discussions with the accounting and law firms should help to provide a better understanding of contentious issues and areas of uncertainty in the laws, as well as developing a more constructive relationship between the ATO and the profession. It would also enable a greater understanding of each other's views and perspectives.[131]

As regards retrospective changes to advice, the ATO seeks only to change interpretations prospectively.[132] This is equivocally the case in respect of rulings. A public ruling binds the Commissioner from the time it is published or at a separate earlier or later time as specified in the ruling.[133] Where a public ruling is withdrawn, it is published in the *Gazette* or, if set out in the ruling, ceases from the date set out therein.[134] Importantly, previous versions of rulings can be found via a weblink at the bottom of the page where the relevant ruling is found online. In spite of this prospective-only rule, a perception of ATO 'U-turns', namely retrospective changes to guidance, has proliferated amongst taxpayers.[135] To this end, the IGT investigated the issue in 2010 and issued a report on U-turns.[136] The IGT concluded that, in certain circumstances, taxpayers' perception of changes in ATO views or practices were justified, but crucially not in respect of one piece of binding advice clearly changing a previous piece.[137] The crux of the matter was disagreement over whether a previous view or practice existed at all and, if it did exist, whether the

[129] Inspector-General of Taxation, 'Review into improving the self assessment system' (August 2012).

[130] ibid para 2.141.

[131] ibid, citing K Fitzpatrick, 'A Long Innings – Valedictory Address by Kevin Fitzpatrick' (2012) 46 *Taxation in Australia* 394.

[132] See above: ATO, 'PS LA 2011/27 Matters the Commissioner considers when determining whether the Australian Taxation Office view of the law should only be applied prospectively' (October 2015).

[133] TAA 1953, Sch 1, subs 358-10(1).

[134] ATO, PS LA 2008/3 (2014) paras 40–41.

[135] See, for example, 'Minutes of the National Tax Liaison Group meeting' (4 June 1998), Item 5; Press Release, Corporate Tax Association, 'Greater Accountability Needed for ATO' (April 1998) as noted in Cooper (n 20) 28. See also: *MacQuarie Bank v FCT* [2013] FCAFC 119.

[136] Inspector-General of Taxation, 'Review into delayed or changed Australian Taxation Office views on significant issues' (March 2010).

[137] ibid iii.

subsequent view constituted a change.[138] In respect of these concerns, the IGT recommended that the solution lay in increased transparency and due process.[139] Early, collaborative engagement through the consultative framework, in particular through the use of the National Tax Liaison Group, with the taxpaying community was crucial to assuaging concerns of change.[140] Other internal changes, such as counteracting taxpayer misconceptions early[141] and making sure that a new interpretation does not conflict with a previous approach,[142] were similarly recommended.

In respect of mingling binding and non-binding advice, the issue was seemingly prominent when public rulings were first introduced.[143] As one critic noted at the time, 'the vast majority of verbiage that appears in tax rulings and determinations does not form part of the public ruling'.[144] However, it is inherent in the nature of the production of publicly binding advice that there be some background explanation to the binding interpretation. As the Auditor General has noted:

> [I]f a taxation ruling were to provide only the material that is legally binding on the Commissioner and did not provide an explanation for its interpretation of the law, taxation rulings would be less meaningful to taxpayers than they are now.[145]

The pragmatic solution proposed, and thereafter adopted accordingly, was that rulings should state in the preamble which parts of the ruling are binding.[146]

Although on the whole the Australian regime has, accordingly, evolved over the years to include various facets that enhance accessibility for taxpayers, one minor problem with the system is the failure of the rulings to make mention of the relevant legal provisions to which they relate. This hinders the taxpayers' access to the applicable law.

A criticism that can also be levelled against the rulings system relates to the link with the penalties regime – something which policymakers might think desirable given the costs that are incurred in producing rulings (even if the presence of penalties does not impact accessibility per se). As a taxpayer may be punished for failing to follow a public ruling, the regime is clothed with punitive force.[147] This is something that has been stitched into the regime since its inception.[148] Penalties

[138] ibid.
[139] ibid.
[140] ibid 42–43.
[141] ibid 44.
[142] ibid 27–28.
[143] S Bernhardt, 'The Bellinz Case and the Rulings System' (1998) 27 *Australian Tax Review* 117, 119; Cooper (n 20) 25. See also: *Crestani v FCT* (1998) 98 ATC 2219 (AAT).
[144] Bernhardt (ibid) 119.
[145] Auditor General (n 18) 91.
[146] ibid 94.
[147] Cooper (n 20) 34.
[148] Commonwealth of Australia, 'A Full Self Assessment of Taxation – A Consultative Document' (Canberra, 1990) paras 1.6–1.7 and 6.23. For a critique, see Cooper (n 20) 18–19; JCPA (n 21) paras 6.72 and 6.80 recommended severing the link with penalties.

will be avoided where a taxpayer adopts a 'reasonably arguable' position.[149] A matter is reasonably arguable if it would be concluded in the circumstances, *having regard to relevant authorities*, that what is argued for is about as likely (or more likely) to be correct as incorrect (emphasis added).[150] Crucially, a 'relevant authority' for the purposes of the penalty regime may be a public ruling.[151] The fact that there is a public ruling that contradicts the taxpayers approach does not necessarily mean that alternative treatments to that suggested by the public ruling cannot be reasonably arguable.[152] However, it is a difficult threshold to overcome.[153] The fact that there are alternative arguments alone does not mean that the taxpayer's interpretation is reasonably arguable. Rather, there must be 'sound reasons' for adopting the alternative position.[154] Furthermore, a ruling will generally incorporate any potential alternative interpretations, which likewise will not necessarily equate to having a reasonably arguable position.[155] The disincentives against challenging an ATO public ruling amongst other issues have led commentators, including the JCPA, to conclude that rulings are de facto law.[156] When faced with the possibility that failing to follow the public ruling may result in an additional penalty, the taxpayer will be more inclined to follow the ruling rather than challenge the ATO's view. This has the effect of potentially placing rulings in a superior position to the underlying law, thereby undermining the ideal of providing rulings which are consistent with the law. The link with penalties accordingly is undesirable.[157]

c. Scrutiny

Public rulings other than product and class rulings may, and until recently generally did, go through a comprehensive development process before being released in final form. This included public consultation, including publication of drafts, and importantly for our purposes consultation with an independent, expert body. The standard process used to be as follows:

- *Stage 1* – An issue is identified that may need to be resolved by a public ruling. The ATO considers whether to issue a public ruling in response to an identified risk (as set out above). The process involves consultation with taxpayers and

[149] See: TAA 1953, Sch 1, subs 284-75(2). Also arises under subs 284-75(2) – penalty relating to statements; para 284-160(1)(b) – base penalty amount for Part IVA schemes; para 284-160(2)(b) and subs 284 160(3) table items 1 and 2 – base penalty amount for transfer pricing schemes; and subparas 290-65(1)(b)(i) and 290-65(1)(b)(ii), and subs 290-65(2) – meaning of tax exploitation scheme.

[150] TAA 1953, Sch 1, subs 284-15(1). See also: *Walstern Pty Ltd v Commissioner of Taxation* [2003] FCA 1428.

[151] TAA 1953, Sch 1, subs 284-15(3).

[152] ATO, 'MT 2008/2: Shortfall penalties: administrative penalty for taking a position that is not reasonably arguable' (April 2015) para 46.

[153] Cooper (n 20) 19.

[154] ATO, 'MT 2008/2' (2015) para 47.

[155] ibid para 48.

[156] For instance JCPA (n 21) xx, para 9; Scolaro (n 114) 109–10.

[157] Cooper (n 20) 51.

professional groups to ensure that the selected issues are indeed of concern to taxpayers.

- *Stage 2* – The topic is added to the public rulings programme. If the ATO decides on the basis of the consultation to proceed with the ruling, the topic is added to the public rulings programme. This is accessible to taxpayers on the ATO website.
- *Stage 3* – A draft public ruling is prepared. This is done in most cases, and taxpayers and professional groups are invited for consultation again.
- *Stage 4* – The draft public ruling is internally approved. The ruling goes through a comprehensive technical quality review, which includes the public rulings panel, the Deputy Chief Tax Counsel or Chief Tax Counsel. This is an important step in the process, as will be further detailed below.
- *Stage 5* – The draft public ruling is released for comment. The draft public ruling is published on ato.gov.au, with notification also posted on the government's website. The draft ruling includes contact details of an ATO officer who will receive feedback and discuss details. The standard feedback period for draft public rulings is six weeks.
- *Stage 6* – The final public ruling is prepared. There is a further consideration of comments on the draft public ruling and amendments are accordingly made where appropriate. Again, taxpayers and professional groups are consulted throughout the preparation of the final public ruling.
- *Stage 7* – The final public ruling is internally approved. The process for approving the final public ruling is identical to that for the draft public ruling. In other words, the final ruling goes through technical scrutiny from a panel of independent experts. A compendium of comments on the draft ruling is prepared, containing a summary of comments received and the ATO response or action taken.
- *Stage 8* – The final public ruling is published. The final public ruling and the compendium of comments are made available on the ATO's website. Details of the final public ruling are also published in the *Gazette* and tabled in Parliament. ATO officers are available to discuss details.
- *Stage 9* – Post-publication matters. Within seven days of the final public ruling being issued a compendium of comments is sent to all who submitted comments. Further comments can be submitted through a feedback mechanism on the ATO Legal Database. The ATO also conduct formal post-implementation reviews for significant public rulings to assess their effectiveness. Public rulings are also reviewed regularly and updated as necessary to maintain the currency, accuracy and consistency of the precedential ATO view.[158]

[158] This information was taken from an ATO publication: ATO, 'ATO advice and guidance' (July 2015) which is no longer available on the internet. All that remains now is ATO, 'How we develop public advice and guidance' (2018).

The previous ATO guidance which set out these steps was changed sometime in 2016, but is relevant in so far as previous reports prepared, for instance, by the IGT, JCPAA and Auditor General on the correctness, clarity and accessibility of public rulings were prepared on the basis of that process. Accordingly, scrutiny of the process for producing public rulings in the past operated at two important levels beyond the ATO itself. The first was through rulings panels at both stages 4 and 7 in the above consultative framework. The second was through public consultation. Today, the Public Advice and Guidance Panel is still involved and public rulings are issued initially as drafts for public consultation,[159] but it is not clear if all steps outlined above are still included. It is likely that there is less involvement from than Panel than was provided by the rulings panels in the past. The recent shift in leadership of the ATO has resulted in a change of ethos within the body. The focus is now placed on the provision of timely advice and sees the use of the Panel reduced[160] given the impact which it can have upon the expediency of the provision of rulings.[161]

When the rulings scheme was introduced in 1992, it did not contain a mechanism for robust scrutiny of the rulings produced by the ATO. The introduction of rulings panels is owed to a report from the JCPA in 1993 which reviewed the new system[162] and recommended that greater attention be given to contrary views.[163] The Public Advice and Guidance Panel today is responsible accordingly for discussing the technical and practical merits of draft rulings presented to them and for advising on the proposed interpretation of the law.[164] The Panel's role is not just limited to considering public rulings, but general advice also. It is far from a bureaucratic box-ticking exercise, with some discussions requiring several meetings of the Panel.[165]

The Panel is made up of senior ATO officers, respected tax specialists, academics and a representative from the states and territories when goods and services tax (GST) rulings are discussed. A Deputy Chief Tax Counsel or Special Tax Adviser chairs the Panel, with up to three members from outside the ATO on a topic-by-topic basis. As well as giving advice about interpretative matters and technical accuracy, the Panel advises the ATO on a range of related issues associated with the preparation of public rulings, including whether a ruling is the best way to clarify the law, or whether an alternative should be used (such as legislative amendment or litigation); whether the structure and wording of the proposed ruling can be improved to make it easier to understand; whether there are realistic examples

[159] ATO (n 47).
[160] ATO, 'Future public advice and guidance' (July 2015); Agenda Item 2.3 in National Tax Liaison Group, 'Minutes: 10 September 2015 meeting' (September 2015).
[161] Auditor General (n 18) 85.
[162] ibid 83.
[163] JCPA (n 21) para 6.26.
[164] See generally ATO (n 47).
[165] Auditor General (n 18) 83.

which can be included to make the ruling more useful; the most appropriate date of effect for the proposed ruling; and whether there are other related topics that may also be appropriate for rulings. The Panel may support, challenge or disagree with aspects of the proposed position and make recommendations on the interpretation to be taken. The Panel does not, however, decide on the ATO position, nor are the Panel's recommendations publicly available. The authoring team will decide on the approach to be taken. In practice, however, there is a strong emphasis on obtaining consensus among external members concerning the direction taken in the public ruling.[166]

Thereafter, the relevance and performance of the public rulings programme is monitored by the National Tax Liaison Group,[167] a stewardship committee which consists of representatives of the major tax, law and accounting professional associations and senior members of the ATO and Treasury.[168] Topics on the programme arise from or reflect suggestions made either internally through ATO issue escalation processes, or from external sources such as tax professional and industry representative bodies.[169] A recent innovation in relation to monitoring the performance of the public rulings programme is the use of private bodies, entities and persons to update old rulings.[170]

As well as these formal supervisory bodies, public consultation acts as an informal means of scrutinising the rulings. There is particular emphasis placed on early and frequent public consultation.[171] To this end, public comment is sought at stages 1–3, 5–6 and 9 of the consultation framework set out above. Further, transparency is ensured by the wide circulation of the rulings through publication on the ATO website and the *Gazette*. These steps underline the importance of transparency[172] and public engagement,[173] allowing the taxpaying community to scrutinise the work of the ATO in respect of public rulings.

On the whole, the processes for scrutinising public rulings have been perceived to be successful in ensuring that a variety of views on the correct operation of the relevant laws are considered, thereby ensuring robust legal analysis of the rulings concerned.[174] The Auditor General, in his 2001 report, was highly complimentary:

> In the audit we found that the drafting and approval processes for public rulings were exhaustive. The drafting and approval processes involved wide consultations with affected taxpayers and/or their representatives and in some cases examination by the relevant Public Rulings Panel (whose membership consists of very senior technical

[166] ibid.
[167] ATO (n 45) para 32.
[168] See: ATO, 'National Tax Liaison Group' (July 2019).
[169] ATO (n 45) para 32.
[170] Commissioner of Taxation, 'Annual report 2014–15' (October 2015) 97.
[171] ATO (n 47). See also JCPA (n 21) para 6.21.
[172] Auditor General (n 18) 54–55.
[173] ibid 55.
[174] See in text at n 99.

> officers in the ATO and eminent external tax professionals). Overall, ANAO concludes that the ATO has undertaken significant measures to ensure that the process of preparing and issuing public rulings provides for extensive technical review and community consultation …[175]
>
> Overall the ATO has a well-developed public rulings system, which draws on the expertise of ATO staff with detailed knowledge of taxation law, industry and community group experts, academics and the general public.[176]

Approximately 40 per cent of private sector tax professionals surveyed for the 2001 report rated consultation as highly effective, with a similar number concluding that consultation as moderately effective.[177] Ann O'Connell, a member of the Public Advice and Guidance Panel, is similarly complimentary of the level of deliberation which takes place during meetings of the Panel: 'Discussion is robust and the focus is on getting the correct interpretation, not necessarily the one that is most advantageous to the revenue'.[178] Former judge of the Supreme Court of Victoria Tony Pagone remarked in relation to public rulings that: 'The Commissioner has adopted an impressive array of measures to ensure taxpayer representation in his decision-making or decision forming internal bodies and processes'.[179] Former Commissioner Michael D'Ascenzo, who was highly influential in the evolution of the rulings regime, similarly compliments the process:

> The existence of this Panel, which includes external experts, to advise the Commissioner on this important aspect of tax administration provides extra legitimacy to the quality and integrity of public rulings.[180]

d. Reliability

Public rulings issued since 1992 are binding on the ATO. This augmentation of the reliability of rulings over other ordinary forms of general advice is underlined by the case of *Bellinz Pty Ltd & Ors v Commissioner of Taxation*.[181] Therein the appellant taxpayers claimed inter alia that the ATO was bound by advice it had issued prior to 1992, in other words prior to the introduction of formally binding rulings. Merkel J in the Federal Court noted first that these pre-1992 publications were informative but could not supplant the terms of the law.[182] Secondly, any assessment of whether the ATO would be held to the terms of such a ruling would be

[175] Auditor General (n 18) 206.
[176] ibid 20.
[177] ibid 81. There were 209 private sector parties submitted responses to the survey; see ibid 248.
[178] A O'Connell, 'The ATO and the Giving of Advice' (Cambridge, UK, Centre for Tax Law Workshop, 12 July 2011) 18.
[179] T Pagone, 'Tax Uncertainty' (Annual Tax Lecture, Melbourne Law School, 20 August 2009) 26.
[180] M D'Ascenzo, 'Modernising the Australian Taxation Office: Vision, people, systems and values' (2015) 13 *eJournal of Tax Research* 361.
[181] [1998] FCA 615, (1998) 39 ATR 198.
[182] See: ATO, Taxation Ruling 1 (1983).

dictated by fairness, thereby drawing upon the early UK cases on the law of legitimate expectations.[183] Fairness to the taxpayers in turn would need to be balanced with the Commissioner's duty to collect taxes:

> But where the question arises as to the inclusion of an amount in assessable income or the allowance of an amount as a deduction, where no question of discretion arises and where the Commissioner is charged to administer the law (cf s 8 of the Act), and one might say bound so to do in accordance with the language used in the statute as passed by Parliament, it is difficult to see how the Commissioner can properly be said to have acted unfairly, even if there is an element of discrimination, where he has acted in accordance with the law itself.[184]

The appellants' claim accordingly failed. Notably, this balancing exercise is analogous to that which is undertaken in the UK in the case of a legitimate expectation claim.[185] Had the appellants' circumstances fallen within the provisions of a ruling produced after 1992 on the other hand, however, the judge stressed that the ATO would have to be held to its published position, regardless of the correct legal position:

> The Commissioner is bound in respect of an existing ruling, not withdrawn for relevant purposes, to assess tax in accordance with the ruling even where the tax law, in accordance with the relevant statute, might have otherwise resulted in more tax being payable.[186]

The case therefore underlines the distinction between rulings and other ATO publications, highlighting the binding nature of the former and hence reliability from the perspective of the taxpayer.

Although the binding nature of rulings is an admirable feature of the Australian system, it comes fused with an inevitable reluctance to produce rulings in cases of genuine doubt.[187] This in-built conservativism is reinforced by the ATO's concern for horizontal equity and the duty to collect tax due from the perspective of the community:

> Errors made by the Commissioner, in the taxpayer's favour, in legally binding material impact on the general community. It is the community that forgoes the revenue lost because of the error. In addition, those taxpayers, who are able to rely on that erroneous view of the law, may be able to obtain a benefit that is unavailable to other taxpayers. It is these unfavourable outcomes that the Commissioner is avoiding by not being bound by all general publications.[188]

[183] *Inland Revenue Commissioners v National Federation of Self-Employed and Small Businesses Ltd* [1982] AC 617 (HL); *In re Preston* [1985] 2 WLR 836, [1985] STC 282 (HL); *R v Inland Revenue Commissioners, ex parte Unilever plc* [1996] STC 681 (CA).

[184] *Bellinz* (n 181) 210.

[185] See ch 6 in text at n 22.

[186] *Bellinz* (n 181) 211; ATO (n 45) para 24.

[187] Pagone (n 59) 905; JCPA (n 21) para 6.26.

[188] ATO (n 45) para 69.

However, in spite of the fact that the decision to promulgate a public ruling lies exclusively with the ATO,[189] an innovation in the process has been to involve stakeholders as a means of assessing areas in which the ATO ought to issue a ruling. The decision as to when a public ruling should be promulgated, other than in the case of a product or class ruling being requested by an individual or entity, is a matter of discretion for the ATO, of course. There is no rule or provision specifying when a ruling should be issued. But decisions to issue a public ruling are made by the ATO as part of its risk management strategy, in consultation with stakeholders:

> [P]ublic rulings arise out of our risk mitigation strategies. Risk processes are governed at an ATO level by the Enterprise Risk Management Framework (ERMF). All BSLs [Business and Service Lines] have risk management processes in place consistent with the ERMF (see for example LB&I [the Large Business and International BSL], Indirect Tax, and S&ME [the Small and Medium Enterprises BSL] risk intranet pages). It is generally through these processes that public rulings are internally sourced, including risks escalating out of private rulings work.[190]
>
> Identification and prioritisation of potential topics for rulings and determinations is largely a demand-driven consultative and collaborative process involving representatives from the tax profession, such as the technical sub-committees of the National Tax Liaison Group (NTLG) and the NTLG Public rulings Steering Committee. Discussion with these groups already includes consideration of the appropriate vehicle for ATO advice or guidance on any given topic …[191]

This involvement of stakeholders tempers the ATO's conservativism by placing the body under pressure to produce rulings in areas of high priority.

A further by-product of this reluctance is the use of caveats and qualifications so as to prevent rulings consuming more factual scenarios than the ATO is willing to accept in its advice.[192] Since *Bellinz*, however, qualifying words such as 'likely' and 'generally' have been avoided as far as possible.[193]

Despite the continued calls for, and legislative amendments to produce,[194] increased use of the rulings system for a broader range of topics,[195] the ATO has been accused of not producing sufficiently broad rulings. In the 2009 review of the ATO's administration of public binding advice, the IGT noted that in spite of the widening of the broadening of the scope for ATO rulings, the tax office advice had nevertheless become 'more limited, cautious and conditional'.[196] However, this

[189] See TAA 1953, Sch 1, subs 358-5.

[190] IGT, Review into improving the self assessment system (2012) para 2.140.

[191] ibid para 2.137.

[192] Cooper (n 20) 30.

[193] O'Connell, 'The ATO' (2011) 16.

[194] Tax Laws Amendment (Improvements to Self Assessment) Bill (No 2) 2005, para 1.12.

[195] Commonwealth of Australia, 'Outcome of the Review of Aspects of Income Tax Self Assessment', Media Release No 106 of 2004 (December 2004); Commonwealth of Australian, 'Review of Aspects of Income Tax Self Assessment' (August 2004) 10–12; Ralph Report (1999) 37, 137–40; Commonwealth of Australia, 'Tax reform: not a new tax, a new tax system' (1998) 27, 147; Cooper (n 20) 51.

[196] Inspector-General of Taxation, 'Review of the Tax Office's administration of public binding advice' (April 2009) 9.

conclusion is disputed by the ATO[197] and, in fact, the issuance of binding rulings has been consistently on the increase since the introduction of the regime.[198]

The lesson to be drawn from this is that in order for the system of binding rulings to have proper efficacy, it is necessary for the tax office to feel comfortable to be bound by particular pieces of advice. Reliability cannot be enhanced by the framework for the provision of binding rulings alone, but rather requires the tax office to buy in to the objectives underlying the framework.

ii. Public Rulings in the UK

a. The Framework: From Identification to Post-publication Challenges

Although the process for producing public rulings in Australia may have changed recently, it is nevertheless recommended for now that the process for public rulings in the UK should consist of the following 10 stages (though not for product or class rulings, which should be processed in the same way as binding pre-transaction rulings):

- Stage 1 – An issue for ruling is identified. In consultation with taxpayers, representative groups and the Working Together Group (discussed further below),[199] and through internal communications, an issue is identified that should be resolved by a public ruling. The identification process should interact advantageously with the private rulings regime from the perspective of HMRC as the body may be able to identify from the requests which areas are in greater need of a public ruling than others.
- Stage 2 – The topic is added to the public rulings programme. If HMRC then decides on the basis of the consultation to proceed with the ruling, the topic will be added to the public rulings programme. This will be accessible to taxpayers through the HMRC website.
- Stage 3 – A draft ruling will be prepared internally. Taxpayers and professional bodies representing taxpayers may be invited for consultation. An official within the relevant team in HMRC will be assigned expressly with responsibility for the particular ruling.
- Stage 4 – The draft public ruling is internally approved. It must go through a comprehensive technical quality review which includes the Public Advice and Guidance Panel. Although in the Australian model it is not compulsory for each public ruling to be analysed by the Panel, this book takes the stricter approach of utilising the Panel for all public rulings. The Office of Tax Simplification (OTS) also recommends that the UK introduces an Advice and Guidance

[197] ibid 55.
[198] IGT (n 129) paras 2.87–2.91.
[199] See in text at n 216.

Panel, but in respect of general HMRC advice.[200] Whilst it might be desirable for such a Panel to assist in relation generally to interpretive matters, it is recommended instead here that the Panel only be utilised in relation to public rulings. This is because rulings should be considered a far greater priority for scrutiny given that they will be binding. The primary role of the Panel will be to discuss the technical and practical merits of the draft ruling presented to it and to advise on the proposed interpretation of the law. It should also advise HMRC on the following matters related to the preparation of public rulings:

- whether a ruling is the best way to clarify the law, or whether an alternative should be used (such as legislative amendment, guidance or litigation);
- whether the structure and wording of the proposed ruling can be improved to make it easier to understand;
- whether there are realistic examples which can be included to make the ruling more useful;
- the most appropriate date of effect for the proposed ruling;
- whether there are other related topics that may also be appropriate for rulings.

The recommendations of the Public Advice and Guidance Panel should not be made publicly available. Although there is a strong public interest in the process being as transparent as possible, in this instance there is the countervailing consideration of protecting the Panel members' independence. As will be detailed below, some of the members for the Panel are to be drawn from the pool of professional practitioners. If their advice were to be public, there is a risk that members would not be able to be completely frank given potential conflicts with clients' interests. It is vital that the advisors are in a position to give an impartial, independent view on the matters before them.

- Stage 5 – The draft public ruling is then released for public comment. It will be published on hmrc.gov.uk, with notification also posted on the Government's general website, gov.uk. The draft ruling should include contact details of the relevant HMRC officer, who will receive feedback and discuss details. The standard feedback period should be at least eight weeks for draft public rulings. This is in line generally with HMRC's commitment to subject secondary legislation, which imposes significant new obligations and responsibilities, and Finance Bills to eight weeks' consultation.[201] HMRC may decide, as a matter of discretion, if there should be a longer consultation period in any given case.
- Stage 6 – The final public ruling is prepared. The comments received on the draft ruling are to be considered by the HMRC officer in charge of the relevant public ruling. Amendments are made where appropriate to the final ruling,

[200] OTS, *Guidance for taxpayers* (2018) 6 and 17.
[201] HM Treasury and HMRC, 'Tax Consultation Framework' (March 2011) 4.

whilst taxpayers and professional groups are consulted throughout the preparation of the final public ruling.

- Stage 7 – The final public ruling is internally approved. The process for approving the final public ruling will be identical to that for the draft public ruling. In other words, the final ruling will go through technical scrutiny from the Panel members. A compendium of comments on the draft ruling shall be prepared, containing a summary of comments received and the HMRC response or action taken.
- Stage 8 – The final public ruling is published. This, and the compendium of comments, will be published on HMRC's website, whilst a notice should be published on the gov.uk website.[202] The relevant HMRC officer should again be available to discuss details. The ruling will include also contrary views to those expressed in the ruling, an important feature from an accessibility standpoint. HMRC should, where permissible, elaborate upon why the contrary views are not accurate. Such a regime forces HMRC to squarely confront the aspects of the advice which might be at odds with the underlying law, in turn acting as a subtle means of protecting the primacy of law. In this respect, although the advice from the Public Advice and Guidance Panel will be confidential, HMRC should distinguish its own view in the ruling from the advice of the Panel. In terms of combatting retrospection, the ruling should set out the date from which it applies. Where there are any changes to the ruling, it should expressly be noted only to take effect prospectively, whilst a link should remain at the bottom of the webpage on which the ruling is located to all permutations (and dates of effect) of the ruling. As for 'mingling', which likewise undermines accessibility, the paragraph at the beginning of the ruling should set out explicitly what elements of the ruling are binding. Importantly, the ruling should stress that it is only binding on HMRC, but that a taxpayer may choose to rely instead upon the law. Finally, the ruling should contain a link to the relevant underlying law.
- Stage 9 – Post-publication matters. A compendium of comments will be sent to all who submitted comments within seven days of the final public ruling being issued. Further comments can thereafter be submitted through a feedback mechanism on the HMRC website. HMRC should also conduct formal post-implementation reviews for significant public rulings to assess their effectiveness. Public rulings should also be reviewed regularly and updated as necessary to maintain their currency, accuracy and consistency. This process should involve the Public Advice and Guidance Panel, the Working Together

[202] It must be accepted that this is obviously not helpful from the perspective of digital exclusion (see Office of National Statistics, 'Exploring the UK's digital divide' (March 2019)), though the issue might be said to be tempered by the fact that HMRC helpline officials would search for relevant public rulings for those digitally excluded.

Group and taxpayers. Where significant changes need to be made, the previous eight stages of this framework should be revisited. Whether this is necessitated should be decided by HMRC, with the option to consult the Public Advice and Guidance Panel, the Working Together Group, taxpayers and representative groups.

- Step 10 – Challenging the ruling. In the Australian model, there is a disincentive for the taxpayer to challenge the ATO's ruling by reason of the link with penalties. There is no need to import that link to the UK. To this end, taxpayers should not be subject to an additional penalty for failing to follow an HMRC public ruling per se. In terms of challenging a public ruling, it should be possible for a taxpayer who has been assessed by HMRC to challenge it directly in the tribunals and then the courts. Bearing in mind that the public ruling is only binding upon HMRC, the tribunals and courts can host adversarial proceedings in which the taxpayer will defend her view of the law and how it applies in the particular case, whilst HMRC can defend why its view should govern the scenario. The same should arise also where there is no disagreement between the parties about the interpretation set out in the ruling, but only over whether it applies in the circumstances. This type of dispute is identical in nature to precisely the types of disputes that the tribunals and courts hear in tax cases. In order to streamline disputes about rulings with ordinary tax disputes, it would be necessary to amend the governing legislation.[203] At this juncture, however, the possibility that epistemic deference would arise and influence the tribunal or court's view as to the correct interpretation of the law must be accepted. The problem would be that the tribunal or court would in practice place significant weight upon the interpretation set out in the ruling, rather than approaching the issue completely *de novo*. It cannot be denied that this risk could materialise in practice, and faith must simply be placed in the integrity of the independent tribunals and courts to arrive at an independent view on such matters.[204] At any rate, it should also be stressed that this can occur in practice as it stands with HMRC advice today and at least with a public rulings regime, there would be greater transparency and also the possibility to participate in the drafting of the public ruling.

A potential problem of duality can arise whereby two streams of appeal could occur at once. The first would concern a substantive dispute in relation to the underlying law; the second would concern the public ruling. Let's say, for instance, that HMRC has issued a public ruling on residency which is at odds with the underlying law. At the same time, the taxpayer argues that her affairs come within

[203] Appeals to the tribunals against any particular decision of HMRC in respect of tax are governed the legislation relating to that particular tax or decision. Thus, appeals in respect of VAT are governed by the Value Added Tax Act 1994, Pt V. Each piece of legislation which allows for appeals must be amended accordingly.

[204] On epistemic deference, see ch 3 in text at n 33.

the terms of the public ruling on residency. Two issues accordingly have to be resolved: on the facts, what is the taxpayer's residency status as a matter of law? And, do the taxpayer's affairs fall within the scope of the ruling? The fact that there could be parallel disputes such as this arising within the same tribunal is not problematic and is in fact much more preferable to the situation which currently exists where a taxpayer could argue that their affairs fall squarely within the law, but in the alternative that they have a legitimate expectation, arising out of reliance upon HMRC advice, not to be taxed. This can result in dual proceedings in separate courts where the determination of one issue can render the determination of another redundant.[205] Having the one tribunal hear arguments on two separate points – one going to substance and the other going to reliance upon the ruling – allows the tribunal to consider whether findings of fact are necessary for determining both points, or whether a finding on one point will vitiate the need to make a finding on the other and vice versa.

The tribunal can also apply its expertise in deciding which issues ought to be resolved first. This would have the effect of avoiding the unfortunate situation which arose in the case of *R (Davies) v HMRC; R (Gaines-Cooper) v HMRC.*[206] In the Supreme Court, two sets of judicial review proceedings were heard together. The procedural history of the two was quite distinct, however. The first appellants had stayed the substantive hearing until after the judicial review whilst the second appellant had pursued the substantive appeal through the First-tier Tribunal (at the time the relevant body was known as the Special Commissioners) and thereafter instituted proceedings. Given that a successful judicial review would render the investment of time and resources by HMRC in challenging the case redundant, Lord Wilson labelled it 'unfortunate' that the course taken in the case of the first appellants was not taken in the case of the second.[207]

b. What Matters should be Considered for Public Rulings?

The process for producing a public ruling will evidently be time-consuming and resource-intensive. But HMRC produces vast quantities of general advice, whilst also developing internally many interpretative and policy positions. It is obvious that it is not feasible for all these pieces of advice to be processed through this public rulings framework. Whilst ultimately the decision whether to promulgate a public ruling will and should reside with HMRC, a helpful benchmark rule could be formulated to assist HMRC. Given the principle underpinning this book is that advice is desirable because it provides guidance to taxpayers as to the legal consequences of their actions, the rule could be as follows: *advice which has a significant*

[205] At the moment, there is a means of allowing the Upper Tribunal to hear both disputes. See in text at n 305.

[206] [2011] UKSC 47, [2012] 1 All ER 1048 (*Gaines-Cooper*).

[207] ibid [6].

impact on the rights or obligations of taxpayers, by reason of creating, substantially amending or removing them, ought to become a public ruling. In practice, HMRC does already decide to consult on changes to rules which have a significant impact on taxpayers.[208]

Of course, not all forms of advice might be considered appropriate for entrenchment in a ruling.[209] Most obviously appropriate for public rulings are those forms of advice which require a greater degree of legal analysis. Thus, substantive and explanatory advice would be unlikely to benefit greatly from the rulings regime, as with advisory advice which applies to a class of taxpayers, unless the law in question is complex or difficult to administer. Interpretative advice would be more likely to benefit than the three above categories. It might be queried whether concessionary advice or administrative advice in respect of specific statutory discretion[210] could be appropriately processed through the rulings regime. In both, there is a potential conflict with legislative intent: in the former, HMRC should not seek to produce rulings inconsistent with the underlying law and, in the latter, the legislative intention is that the decision on how to proceed should be taken by HMRC rather than some other body. Neither, in fact, would result in a conflict with legislative intent. In the case of the latter, it should be recalled that the decision is ultimately left with HMRC as to the scope and substance of the public ruling. The intermediate steps merely seek to provide a framework within which issues can be alleviated, but do not prevent HMRC from exercising control over the final ruling. HMRC would need to ensure, however, that there is some flexibility left in the way the ruling will be administered so as not to conflict with the rule against fettering discretion.[211]

The issue is more complicated in respect of concessionary advice. Whilst HMRC should generally not seek to depart from the law as prescribed by Parliament, concessionary advice can be justified by recourse to legitimate interpretation or to HMRC's managerial discretion.[212] Concessionary advice can accordingly be put through the public rulings process, which, it should be noted, provides safeguards to ensure that there is not an inconsistency with the underlying law, something which does not exist at present for concessionary advice.

Ultimately, however, it must be accepted that although in principle all forms of general advice could be processed through the public rulings regime, HMRC will be unlikely to seek to relinquish the de facto discretion that it has acquired in respect of broadly worded anti-avoidance provisions,[213] or codify the exercise

[208] Take the example of changes to IR35 for instance which concerns intermediaries. See: HMRC, 'Intermediaries Legislation (IR35): discussion document' (July 2015).

[209] On the different categories, types and forms of advice, see generally ch 2.

[210] On specific discretion, see ch 3 in text at n 55.

[211] For instance, *R (Sandiford) v Secretary of State for Foreign and Commonwealth Affairs* [2014] UKSC 44, [2014] 1 WLR 2697 [54]. See ch 3 in text at n 24.

[212] See S Daly, 'The Life and Times of ESCs: A defence?' in D de Cogan and P Harris (eds), *Studies in the History of Tax Law: Volume 8* (Oxford, Hart Publishing, 2017) 177–83.

[213] See ch 3 in text at nn 28 and 37.

of specific statutory discretions it has, such as to issue an Accelerated Payment Notice[214] or to invoke the GAAR.[215] It is further unlikely on account of HMRC's primary objective being to bear down on tax avoidance and evasion.[216]

c. Details of the Relevant Participators in the Process

There will be three participators in the public rulings scheme other than HMRC. These will be the Working Together Group, the Public Advice and Guidance Panel, and taxpayers generally combined with representative bodies.

Working Together

A notable difference between the proposal here and the Australian regime is the displacement of the National Tax Liaison Group in favour of what is known as the Working Together Group. The reason for this is that the Working Together Group already exists and more or less mirrors the activities of the National Tax Liaison Group. In Australia, the National Tax Liaison Group is a steering committee comprised of members from the major tax, law and accounting professional associations and senior members of the ATO and Treasury. The Working Together initiative, on the other hand, is a partnership between HMRC and a wide range of representative agent bodies.[217] HMRC works with 19 bodies as part of this initiative, including prominent institutions such as the Institute of Chartered Accountants of England and Wales and the Chartered Institute of Taxation. The purpose of the National Tax Liaison Group is to identify significant issues and drive improvements in relation to the tax system. The Working Together initiative similarly seeks to look for ways to improve HMRC's operations for the benefit of tax agents, their clients and HMRC. Although the remits are slightly different, the remit of the Working Together Group would allow it to consider public rulings as these relate to HMRC operations. The National Tax Liaison Group meets quarterly, whilst the Working Together meetings take place digitally in 'Talking Points': weekly online interactive presentations usually 45 minutes in duration that focus on topics agents have highlighted as being of interest, or on emerging issues that HMRC identify as impacting on agents.

In turn, a subset of the Working Together Group is the Issues Overview Group, a joint forum of HMRC and professional bodies that progresses important operational issues or problems raised on the online Agent Forum, or otherwise identified by HMRC or professional bodies representing tax agents and advisers.[218] The purpose of the Issues Overview Group is to focus inter alia on the delivery of the Working Together initiative; ensure that the systemic issues raised

[214] See Finance Act 2014, s 219.
[215] See Finance Act 2013, Sch 1, para 3.
[216] HMRC (n 57).
[217] See generally HMRC, 'Working Together'.
[218] HMRC, 'Issues Overview Group'.

via the Working Together network are investigated effectively; identify areas or unresolved main priority issues and escalate them; and review suggestions raised via the professional bodies and agent members of the Working Together network regional groups.

The combination of the two groups generates a particularly broad representation of the interests of taxpayers, both by engaging with the separate regions of the country and by incorporating agents from 19 professional bodies. It is worth highlighting also that the 19 professional bodies engaged in this initiative have hundreds of thousands of members and as such their submissions to HMRC generally, whether in the context of Working Together or not, focus on a wide range of issues, from reforms which affect wealthy non-domiciled individuals[219] to those affecting ordinary workers[220] and small and medium-sized enterprises.[221]

In light of the above, there is clearly scope to incorporate engagement with public rulings within the remit of the existing UK groups. The role of the Working Together Group in conjunction with the Issues Overview Group in respect of rulings thus will be to identify significant issues of concern that should be considered for resolution by public ruling. The groups should also consider the operation of the existing rulings and establish whether any amendments should be made.

Public Advice and Guidance Panel

The establishment of a bespoke body in the form of the Public Advice and Guidance Panel is necessitated. Members of the Panel should be drawn from the pool of senior HMRC officers, respected tax specialists and academics. Of the latter two categories, there is an abundance of personnel in the UK who dedicate a significant amount of time and resources to communicating with HMRC in respect of tax policy. The willingness of tax practitioners to contribute was highlighted already in respect of the Working Together initiative. Meanwhile, the UK, like Australia, is endowed with considerable academic expertise in the field of taxation with personnel dedicated to making improvements in the field of taxation. HMRC should produce a consultation document calling for all interested personnel to submit to HMRC their expression of interest in the project, with a brief description of their qualifications and areas of expertise. A formal list thereafter can be drawn up by HMRC. There should be regular calls for expression of interest so as to keep the list up to date.

[219] See, for instance, R Mace, 'Reforms to the taxation of non-domiciles: further consultation – CIOT comments' (October 2016) available at: www.tax.org.uk/policy-technical/submissions/reforms-taxation-non-domiciles-further-consultation-ciot-comments.

[220] See, for instance, Ruth Mace, 'Off-payroll working in the public sector: reform of the intermediaries legislation – CIOT comments' (August 2016) available at: www.tax.org.uk/policy-technical/submissions/payroll-working-public-sector-reform-intermediaries-legislation-ciot.

[221] See, for instance, Ruth Mace, 'Soft Drinks Industry Levy – CIOT comments' (October 2016) 4–5, available at: www.tax.org.uk/policy-technical/submissions/soft-drinks-industry-levy-ciot-comments.

The make-up of the Public Advice and Guidance Panel in any case will be decided on a topic-by-topic basis by HMRC, but it should be balanced in order to ensure that a broad range of perspectives are taken into account. The need for diversity of decision-makers when resolving legal questions has been supported by those in the highest judicial offices in the UK.[222] Indeed, this was the original plan for the GAAR Panel in the UK also. There will be at least three members on the Public Advice and Guidance Panel for each ruling, but more may be added if considered necessary in the circumstances by the chair, who in turn will be a senior officer from HMRC's legal department.[223] It is the chair who will have ultimate control of the composition of the panel in any given instance.

The reason that the chair should be an HMRC officer is a reflection of the role of the Panel, namely to advise HMRC on its public ruling. From a practical perspective the HMRC officer will be more knowledgeable of institutional needs and even the language that should be used to communicate the message from the panel most clearly. The matter was also considered in Australia, and reform by way of having a representative external to HMRC chair the Panel was rejected not just by the ATO, but also the panel members. In addition to practical concerns, it was considered to be inappropriate as the role of the Panel is to advise[224] (whereas the decision on the ruling ultimately resides with the tax authority). There is some force to this argument. The provision of advice to taxpayers is legitimised in the hands of HMRC by reason of its endowment with responsibility by Parliament for the collection and management of taxes. It is appropriate to this end that the management of the Public Advice and Guidance Panel and the advice that it produces should reside with HMRC.

The cultural make-up of the Panel is also of particular concern. There must be buy-in to the process. The role of the Panel is to provide balanced, impartial, robust advice; it is to get the correct interpretation, not be driven by what would be most advantageous for either taxpayers or the Exchequer.[225] To this end, the independence of the members is critical, as is the need to draw upon the views not just of HMRC officers, but also tax experts and academics on any given ruling. There should be a strong emphasis on obtaining consensus among external members concerning the direction taken in the public ruling, but if disagreement persists, this should form part of the advice that the Panel issues to HMRC.

Taxpayers and Representative Groups

The third category of participant other than HMRC in the process is the general body of taxpayers and the representative groups, including professional bodies, to

[222] See, for instance, T Etherton, 'Liberty, the Archetype and Diversity: A Philosophy of Judging' [2010] *Public Law* 727; B Hale, 'Equality and the Judiciary: Why Should We Want More Women Judges?' [2001] *Public Law* 489.

[223] Note that the GAAR panel composition is also decided by HMRC; see: Finance Act 2013, Sch 43, para 1(1).

[224] Auditor General, *Follow-up Audit* (2004) para 2.20.

[225] O'Connell (n 178) 18.

whom there will be consultation on what matters might require a ruling and on the rulings themselves. The representative groups act in this capacity on behalf of taxpayers generally, although HMRC consultations do seek the views additionally of individual taxpayers.[226] It has already been evidenced that HMRC are committed to consulting widely and seeking the input of taxpayers,[227] and as such the inclusion of consultation with taxpayers builds upon a pre-existing initiative.

One criticism which can be raised in relation to this structure, however, is that the process can get hijacked by dominant lobbying groups who may exert considerable pressure in order to extract favourable treatment for the parties they represent.[228] The problem with this argument is that the possibility arises regardless of whether there is an open forum for participation. Dominant groups over the years have been able to extract concessionary treatment, for instance in respect of miners' coal.[229] This was in spite of the fact that there was no formal system for participation. The opening of the forum for consultation is a pragmatic improvement upon the previous structure. Less powerful classes of taxpayers are given the opportunity to engage. As Paul Craig has written: 'The introduction of a more structured system of participatory rights at least gives the less advantaged groups a chance to air their views'.[230]

d. Legislative Amendment

As with the Australian model, it will be necessary to make a legislative amendment so as to bind HMRC to its public rulings. This is necessary by reason of the fact that without such a law, there would be not be sufficient means of enforcing a ruling against HMRC. Additionally, it is necessary to amend legislation dealing with appeals, so as to allow taxpayers to challenge whether a ruling properly governs their dispute with HMRC.[231] There is a question, however, as to whether anything else is in need of legislative introduction. The possibilities would be to enshrine the aforementioned stages in legislation or the formation and composition of the relevant groups. These do not necessitate legislative changes, however, and could readily be accommodated within HMRC's managerial discretion by reason of the fact that they pertain to HMRC's management of taxes and would be driven by a desire to improve overall the collection of taxes. It is preferable for the time being to allow the system to develop in a more organic fashion, as occurred

[226] Anybody can generally provide a submission to an HMRC consultation document. See, for instance, HM Treasury and HMRC, 'Tax deductibility of corporate interest expense: consultation on detailed policy design and implementation' (May 2016) 7.

[227] See ch 5 in text at n 283.

[228] See, for instance, R Baldwin, *Rules and Government* (Oxford, Clarendon Press, 1995) 74–80.

[229] Inland Revenue, 'A List of Extra Statutory Wartime Concessions given in the Administration of Inland Revenue Duties' (October 1944) Cmd 6559. See ch 4 in text at n 14.

[230] P Craig, *EU Administrative Law*, 3rd edn (Oxford, Oxford University Press, 2018) 319.

[231] See n 203.

in Australia. The proper functioning in practice of the system may require subsequent unforeseen changes and it would be advisable to retain flexibility.

D. Parliamentary Sovereignty and Binding Rulings

The idea that the UK could introduce a broad system for binding rulings comes into tension with Parliamentary sovereignty. Parliament has legislative supremacy and, more importantly in the tax context, Article 4 of the Bill of Rights Act 1688/9 provides that taxes may only be levied with the consent of Parliament. The complication brought about by a system of rulings is that there is a new source of 'law' that builds up from rulings.

But where the ruling is consistent with the underlying law, it merely fills in the detail and does not amount to the introduction of a law at odds with Parliament's intent. The real issue is where the ruling is not consistent with the underlying law. Five points are made in response. First, there already exist avenues by which HMRC can be compelled to act in a manner which is at odds with the underlying tax law. There are formal binding rulings in the UK, but it is merely that the category of taxpayers to whom they are available is very narrow. The doctrine of legitimate expectations too can force HMRC to follow incorrect advice, whilst recommendations from the Adjudicator and Ombudsman can persuade HMRC not to follow the correct application of the law.[232] Secondly, the tension with Parliamentary sovereignty arises regardless of whether there operates a formal system of binding rulings, if it is recalled that administrative advice itself has de facto binding features.[233] Having a formal system for binding administrative advice merely prevents HMRC from reneging on a position it subsequently realises to be incorrect. Thirdly, an argument can be made that Parliamentary sovereignty already accommodates the idea of binding rulings on the basis of the principle of good administration: that Parliament intends that public authorities act according to the principle of good administration. Allowing HMRC to renege on a previous assurance could be characterised as a misuse of powers itself as it is contrary to the ideal of good administration.[234] Fourthly, Parliamentary sovereignty, whilst undoubtedly important, is just one principle. The rule of law is another important constitutional principle.[235] Given the narrowness of the proposition here – that there could be an extension to a scheme of binding rulings which already

[232] See ch 6 in particular in text at nn 66, 238 and 243.

[233] See ch 3 in text at n 28. See also G Weeks, 'The Public Law of Restitution' (2014) 38 *Melbourne University Law Review* 198, 203.

[234] See, for instance, P Craig, *Administrative Law*, 8th edn (London, Sweet and Maxwell, 2016) 703; *Laker Airways Ltd v Department of Trade* [1977] QB 643, 707 (CA) (Lord Denning); S Daly, 'Recent developments in tax law: vires revisited' [2016] 2 *Public Law* 190, 192 and 197.

[235] See, for instance, *R (Jackson) v Attorney General* [2005] UKHL 56, [2006] 1 AC 262 [107] (Lord Hope).

has been sanctioned by Parliament – a balancing of the two principles[236] ought to come down in favour of permitting a greater range of assurances to taxpayers as to the legal consequences of their actions. Finally, binding rulings would need to be introduced by way of primary legislation. That is the only way of ensuring that HMRC would be bound without condition to the representation. The doctrine of legitimate expectations does not suffice because the second limb of the doctrine asks HMRC whether reneging on an expectation is unlawful.[237] Making the rulings binding removes this second limb. As the binding mechanism would be introduced by primary legislation, Parliament would have assented to the lawfulness of executive action at odds with other primary legislation.

E. Buy-in from Parliament, the Government and HMRC

Aside from the demonstrable benefits which the regime would bring in terms of correctness, clarity, accessibility, scrutiny and reliability, the successful adoption of the programme proposed herein hinges upon Parliament, the Government and HMRC buying in to its objectives.

In terms of Parliament, the requisite legislation must be passed. From the perspective of the House of Commons, any move that could compromise, or could be perceived to compromise, its primacy in respect of tax policy-making would be unacceptable.[238] However, this would not be the effect of introducing a rulings regime. The present model does not seek to substitute itself for the use of law. Advice in the form of rulings is intended to supplement the underlying law, thereby giving greater effect to the rule of law. The need for rulings merely reflects the fact that 'legislators cannot cover every eventuality that daily life throws up.'[239]

The concern in relation to the Government would be that the new regime would provide an opportunity to abdicate responsibility to produce reasonably clear laws, by purposefully drafting laws more broadly, knowing that the rulings regime would fill the gaps.[240] As forcefully put by Gammie, '[T]he substitution of rulings or revenue guidance for clear and simple legislation is no more than an abrogation by Parliament of its democratic duty.'[241] In response, it is first worth noting that

[236] If a balancing is necessary. It may well be the case that Parliamentary sovereignty encompasses the rule of law. See, for instance, A Venn Dicey, *Introduction to the law of the constitution* (Indianapolis, Liberty Classics, 1982) 273.

[237] See ch 6 in text at n 22.

[238] Treasury Select Committee, 'Letter from the Chairman to the Exchequer Secretary regarding tax policy' (3 November 2010).

[239] Foreword to Sandler (n 12) viii.

[240] Of course, a positive case could be made for drafting legislation more broadly. See, for instance, J Freedman, 'Improving (not perfecting) tax legislation: rules and principles revisited' [2010] *British Tax Review* 717; J Black, 'Forms and paradoxes of principles-based regulation' (2008) 3 *Capital Markets Law Journal* 425.

[241] Foreword to Sandler (n 12) viii.

this concern arises regardless of whether the framework proposed herein would be adopted. It has already been noted that there is at times a practice of drafting broad laws which can be narrowed through HMRC guidance.[242] The potential for this to arise might be said to be increased in the case of a rulings regime and this moral-hazard-type risk must be accepted. A rulings regime would, however, bring greater transparency to the system, thereby allowing concerned taxpayers to take up the issue through traditional democratic channels. Additionally, the new system allows for greater participation by concerned taxpayers and experts. If there is abdication of responsibilities through drafting widely, the merit of the proposed regime is that it imposes democratic features. Further, insofar as HMRC's views may be taken into account during the lawmaking process, the body should urge legislators to articulate intent clearly through legislation.

The successful implementation of the regime also relies upon a significant amount of goodwill on the part of HMRC. In the case of public rulings, the body will have control over the Public Advice and Guidance Panel by virtue of having an officer as chair. The decisions as to which pieces of advice should become rulings and which parts of the rulings should be binding rest with HMRC. It is within the power of HMRC to decide that a longer or shorter period for consultation is required, which persons should be invited to the Panel for any given topic and what, ultimately, the ruling will look like. Meanwhile HMRC will have the power to refuse to provide private rulings. However, a rulings regime which forces HMRC to be bound to its rulings comes inevitably fused with conservativism as to the breadth of reliance the body is comfortable to allow. This produces an obvious tension. In response, three points should be made. First, it would be materially in HMRC's interests to fully engage with the proposed rulings regime as a system of binding rulings would reduce operational costs for HMRC. As stressed by Moses LJ in the Court of Appeal hearing of *Gaines-Cooper*[243] in the context of general advice and cited with approval in the Supreme Court by Lord Wilson:[244] 'The importance of the extent to which thousands of taxpayers may rely upon guidance, of great significance as to how they will manage their lives, cannot be doubted'.[245]

Public rulings, meanwhile, should obviate the need for taxpayers to individually consult HMRC, thereby reducing costs.[246] Thus, whilst it is certainly true as Greg Weeks has suggested that poorly drafted guidance places risk on the taxpayer,[247] it also places a financial burden on the public authority concerned in

[242] See ch 3 in text at n 135.

[243] *R (Davies) v HMRC; R (Gaines-Cooper) v HMRC* [2010] EWCA Civ 83, (2010) STC 860 (*Gaines-Cooper* (CA)).

[244] *Gaines-Cooper* (n 206) [25].

[245] *Gaines-Cooper* (CA) (n 243) [12].

[246] On this, see: R Williams, 'The Multiple Doctrines of Legitimate Expectations' (2016) 132 *LQR* 639, 651–652.

[247] G Weeks, Soft Law and Public Authorities: Remedies and Reform (Oxford, Hart Publishing, 2016) 118.

respect of resolving disputes. Given budgetary constraints and the need generally to allocate resources in an efficient manner, avoiding this eventually is undoubtedly in HMRC's interests.

Secondly, HMRC is already de facto committed consulting outside parties on its advice[248] and being bound to the advice it produces,[249] these two components being fundamental to the proposal. That HMRC will be unlikely to provide rulings in respect of tax avoidance should be accepted, though it should not be assumed that taxpayers would only seek to use a rulings regime to abuse the law.

Thirdly, HMRC could consider becoming more relaxed about the possibility of making mistakes on the law, which might result in less tax being collected than is due. This change of mindset would not come into conflict with the primary duty to collect tax.[250] Given the benefits that this would bring to taxpayers – providing them with greater certainty as to the consequences of their actions – it is desirable also from the perspective of the rule of law and human dignity.[251]

III. Proposals in Respect of Individual and General Advice

The rulings regime proposal can bring significant improvements to HMRC advice. Private rulings will assist principally in respect of accessibility and reliability, but their impact will necessarily be limited in respect of correctness, clarity and scrutiny. Further, private rulings will only apply pre-transaction and not post-transaction. Public rulings, meanwhile, will bring about improvements in relation to all of these benchmarks, but the more rigorous process for producing a public ruling (other than a product or class ruling) can only apply to a modest amount of the general advice promulgated every year by HMRC. Moreover, there are many items of HMRC advice which might not be considered by HMRC to be appropriate for public ruling.

There is a need to consider also as part of a package of reforms proposals that deal with individual and general advice that will not come in the form of binding private or public rulings. These proposals emanate from findings in earlier chapters.

A. Correctness and Clarity

The correctness and clarity of HMRC advice are essentially internal issues that HMRC ought to strive to enhance and a proper internal framework for the

[248] See ch 5 in text at n 283.
[249] See ch 6 in text at n 1.
[250] See ch 6 in text at n 45.
[251] See ch 6 in text at n 53.

promulgation of general advice, which presently does not exist,[252] can assist (as discussed further below).[253] Further, greater levels of external scrutiny (as will be proposed) will be instrumental to achieving greater levels of correctness, clarity and accessibility. But there are some suggestions which can be made in respect of practices when promulgating advice. To focus the minds of HMRC staff, the following questions (which in turn should be enshrined in HMRC's internal framework) should be considered when promulgating advice:

- Is the advice consistent with the law?
- Is the advice sufficiently clear so that it allows the particular taxpayer to better understand their rights and obligations under the law?
- Does the advice contain unnecessary qualifying language?

When considering whether the advice is sufficiently clear to the particular taxpayer to whom it is directed, it seems prudent to take on board the recommendation of the OTS on the categorisation of taxpayers.[254] There should be three levels, according to the OTS. On the first level is simple guidance, for the majority of individual taxpayers. On the second level is more advanced guidance, primarily aimed at more sophisticated taxpayers and others in business. And on the third level is HMRC's technical manuals, primarily for tax advisers.

Shifting away from using qualifying language may be difficult, but could come about through a broader change in mindset about taxpayers obtaining benefits which might be legally undue. As stressed already, it is lawful, and in certain circumstances normatively desirable, for HMRC to stick to incorrect advice or to provide advice which results in taxpayers obtaining benefits which they are not strictly due.

Finally, the provision of binding private rulings can benefit the production of advice as redacted rulings can be used as examples in general advice thereby providing more detailed guidance for taxpayers. The 1955 Royal Commission on the Taxation of Income and Profits also suggested something along these lines: '[T]he kind of publication we have in mind is one which would describe preferably with illustrative examples, the effect that a particular branch of the tax code is understood to have'.[255]

B. Accessibility

In respect of restrictions on accessibility, the focus of HMRC ought to be on the justifications for any limitations. Resource constraints provide an obvious

[252] See ch 2 in text at n 157.
[253] See in text at n 274.
[254] See OTS (n 85) 5.
[255] Royal Commission on the taxation of profits and income, 'Final Report' (Cmd 9474, 1955) para 983 noted in Sandler (n 12) 31.

limitation; whilst, meanwhile, it is unlikely that HMRC is going to change its position on the provision of advice concerning tax avoidance.[256] Critical issues in respect of non-publication, retrospection and mingling can benefit from practical suggestions. These suggestions should operate in addition to the improvements to accessibility brought about by greater internal and external scrutiny of advice. One particular area of concern in relation to non-publication of general advice is in relation to HMRC Manuals. Redactions in HMRC Manuals, for instance, are commonplace.[257] The relevant information is removed and in its place is the line: 'This content has been withheld because of exemptions in the Freedom of Information Act 2000'. It is not clear on what ground the information in the HMRC Manuals is exempted under the Freedom of Information Act 2000 (FOIA 2000).[258]

In light of HMRC's vague guidance on the scope of its duty of confidentiality, and its contradictory approach to the legality of disclosures of taxpayer information, an argument can be made that some of the information redacted in HMRC Manuals under the guise of protections under FOIA 2000 might not be exempt under the Act. It is recalled that in *Privacy International*, the Court held that HMRC had misconceived its duty of confidentiality and hence that a blanket refusal to the request of the claimant in the case was unlawful.[259] Conversely in *R (Ingenious Media and McKenna) v HMRC*,[260] however, HMRC contended that it had a relatively broad power to disclose information.[261] The inconsistency in HMRC's approach to the boundaries of its duty of confidentiality opens up the possibility that it has an equally inconsistent approach to the scope of the exemptions in relation to FOIA 2000. This is because there is a close relationship between the information protected by both. For instance, both sets of rules cover information provided in confidence[262] and cover information which contains personal information.[263] Moreover, section 23 of the Commissioners for Revenue and Customs Act 2005 makes it explicitly clear that information which cannot be disclosed as a result of HMRC's duty of confidentiality is also exempt under the FOIA 2000 if its release would identify, either expressly or by implication, the taxpayer concerned. Furthermore, there is evidence, too, of information in HMRC Manuals being redacted under the guise of being exempted by the FOIA 2000 which is not in fact exempted. A section of HMRC's Statutory Payments Manual was previously redacted owing to a purported exemption under the FOIA 2000.

[256] See ch 4 in text at n 108.

[257] See, for instance, HMRC, 'AGL6200: Aggregates Levy Guidance' (August 2016); HMRC, 'AWRS60300: Alcohol Wholesaler Registration Scheme' (July 2016).

[258] See generally, Freedom of Information Act 2000 (FOIA 2000), Pt II.

[259] *Privacy International v HMRC* [2014] EWHC 1475 (Admin), [2015] STC 948. See ch 4 in text at n 77.

[260] [2013] EWHC 3258, [2014] STC 673; upheld: EWCA Civ 173, [2015] STC 1357; overturned: [2016] UKSC 54, [2016] 1 WLR 4164.

[261] *Privacy International* (n 259) [60].

[262] FOIA 2000, s 41; Commissioners for Revenue and Customs Act 2005 (CRCA 2005), s 18.

[263] FOIA 2000, s 40; CRCA 2005, s 22.

A subsequent Freedom of Information request, however, revealed that the information had been redacted in error.[264]

There is precedence for the relevant body, namely the Information Commissioner's Office, to investigate whether undisclosed HMRC advice is actually exempted under FOIA 2000.[265] On 18 September 2006 there was a complaint to the Commissioner about the way a taxpayer's request for information under FOIA 2000 had been handled.[266] The complainant specifically asked the Commissioner to investigate the refusal by HMRC to disclose the information that the body held which supported its interpretation of section 95(2) of the Taxes Management Act 1970 that a repayment (whether actually made or not) represents a negative amount of tax payable. The complainant had requested a copy of the relevant section of the HMRC Manual or other guidance notes that were used to determine the penalty that HMRC sought to impose. The Commissioner in turn contacted HMRC on 29 January 2007 to ask for a copy of the information being withheld and any further representations HMRC wished to make. HMRC responded on 7 February 2007 enclosing a copy of the withheld information, which consisted of legal advice, an email chain and worked examples to explain the advice given. HMRC clarified the purpose of the advice received and referred the Commissioner to its previous responses to the complainant for its arguments in maintaining the exemption. The Commissioner was satisfied thereafter that the information was properly exempted under FOIA 2000. Although the information which was exempted did not in the end come from an HMRC Manual, the process highlights the ability of the Information Commissioner to assess whether HMRC is properly applying FOIA 2000.

To this end, it is recommended that there should be a review of the instances in the Manuals where information is redacted purportedly on the basis of FOIA 2000 exemptions, something which was previously recommended by the Low Incomes Tax Reform Group.[267] As it would be overly burdensome for the Information Commissioner's Office to investigate all of these instances individually, it is instead recommended that HMRC departments should conduct reviews into the Manuals they produce, in liaison with HMRC's Freedom of Information Team. Such a review was already undertaken in relation to the Statutory Payments Manual by the Statutory Payments Technical Team and the Freedom of Information Team following the aforementioned Freedom of Information request which identified the erroneous redaction of information.[268] The Information Commissioner's Office should thereafter investigate a random sample of the redacted information remaining in HMRC Manuals to check whether the information should indeed

[264] 'Request for redacted information from SSP manual', available at: www.whatdotheyknow.com/request/request_for_redacted_information.

[265] FOIA 2000, ss 47–49.

[266] Information Commissioner's Office, 'Decision Notice FS50133903' (March 2007).

[267] Low Incomes Tax Reform Group, 'Is HMRC transparent?' (February 2011).

[268] See n 264.

still be redacted.[269] If dissatisfied, the Information Commissioner's Office should then conduct a more comprehensive review.

As for the other accessibility issues of retrospection and mingling, more minor remedial action is recommended. In respect of HMRC's approach to retrospection, HMRC's current position is that it will generally retrospectively change its advice where it turns out to be incorrect.[270] It is suggested that HMRC take a less stringent approach than that which it currently adopts as part of a broader change in mindset. Furthermore, as a means of properly equipping it with the information to make an informed decision as to the comparative unfairness or otherwise of a retrospective change of policy, HMRC should consult affected parties, as occurred in the case of the change of policy in relation to the tax treatment of unremitted foreign income or gains used as collateral for a loan enjoyed in the UK.[271]

In terms of mingling, the processing of concessions through the rulings regime will have a beneficial impact generally on this problem. The mingling of concessionary elements within other pieces of general advice is particularly problematic in terms of accessibility.[272] A further step in this direction would be for HMRC, in its continuing analysis of Extra-Statutory Concessions (ESCs) in the aftermath of *Wilkinson*, to move pieces of advice which are found to contain concessionary elements into the actual list of published ESCs. Additionally, if HMRC are not willing to adopt a change of mindset, the published list of ESCs should also highlight in its introduction that HMRC will generally not consider itself to be bound by concessions which are incorrect in law. Although a minor shift, it would at least render taxpayers informed as to the risk that they take by relying upon concessions.

C. Scrutiny

There are serious shortcomings in respect of the scrutiny that is currently afforded to HMRC advice. Scrutiny, properly conducted, can be instrumental in bringing about improvements to HMRC advice, as can be gleaned from the examination of the relationships of the Adjudicator and Ombudsman with HMRC, in addition to the benefits brought about by consultation.[273] The first area in need of rectification is internal scrutiny.[274] As part of an internal framework, there ought to be checks to ensure that general advice is properly categorised, so as to alleviate the

[269] This is a similar process to that conducted for the 'Park' report: National Audit Office, 'Settling large tax disputes' (June 2012).

[270] HMRC, 'When you can rely on information or advice provided by HM Revenue and Customs' (March 2009). See ch 6 in text at n 3.

[271] See HMRC News, 'Remittance Basis' (August 2014); HMRC, 'Revenue and Customs Brief 16 (2015): remittance basis treatment of foreign income and gains used for loan collateral' (October 2015).

[272] See ch 4 in text at n 154.

[273] See ch 5 in text at n 129.

[274] See ch 2 in text at n 157.

problem of taxpayers being placed in an unknowingly precarious position by relying on concessionary advice. Further, it appears that there is no existing process to ensure that advice is passed by legal experts in HMRC, which in turn will lead to errors of law being made and muddled, unclear advice. This affects the correctness, clarity and reliability of advice, given that these factors diminish the likelihood of a successful legitimate expectations claim. To this end, it is recommended that HMRC review its internal processes for the production of general advice and consider whether a coherent and consistent approach can be adopted which would allow for internal legal review. The framework should seek to ensure that drafts are properly scrutinised and responsibility for each piece of advice clearly allocated. Though taxpayers also receive individual advice, the framework for the promulgation of general advice is of critical concern given that advice given to taxpayers individually should be derived from HMRC policies and interpretations which will often be found in general advice.

In terms of scrutiny from external parties, several proposals are made. The first is that taxpayers and representative groups should be given greater opportunity to provide assistance through the provision of feedback links incorporated into HMRC's online general advice.[275] These can be found already in some HMRC publications,[276] but there seems no reason why more feedback links could not be inserted.

Secondly, critically, there is a need for a formal scrutinising mechanism whereby one body or party is responsible for properly overseeing HMRC advice. The expertise of the CAG and the NAO might lie generally in the auditing of accounts, but there is good reason to think that the role could be expanded.[277] The CAG and NAO would be capable of taking responsibility for overseeing, at a high level, HMRC advice. The CAG is generally a highly experienced qualified accountant and would be capable of asking questions of HMRC about a selected sample of HMRC advice, focusing in on issues of correctness, clarity and accessibility. Freedman, however, has noted that the shortcomings in terms of tax expertise of the offices of the CAG and NAO were highlighted by the fact that retired tax judge Sir Andrew Park had to be drafted in to conduct the report into the 'Settlements' scandal.[278] But that episode can be distinguished from the expansion of the role envisaged here. The CAG and NAO would not be required to approach the advice *de novo* and come

[275] See OTS (n 85) 6 and 30.

[276] See, for instance, HMRC, 'BIM Feedback' (May 2019).

[277] This suggestion came up in a conversation with Nigel Mellor. It was a free-flowing conversation and it is not that Nigel Mellor proposed or supports this idea, but rather that it would be inaccurate to say that the author came up with the idea all by himself. Others have also suggested that HMRC could be represented in Parliament by a minister: see J Freedman, 'Five Recommendations for Restoring Trust in HMRC' (2017) 1342 *Tax Journal* 6, 7. That, however, is a broader suggestion dealing with accountability, whereas this book is focused purely on how HMRC advice can be bettered. In respect of the latter, it is difficult to see how a non-expert minister could provide any great assist.

[278] J Freedman, 'Managing Tax Complexity: The Institutional Framework for Tax Policy-Making and Oversight' in C Evans, R Krever and P Mellor, *Series on International Taxation*, Vol 53: *Tax Simplification* (Alphen aan den Rijn, Kluwer Law International, 2013) 277.

to a determination about the correct answer, as occurred with the settlements, but would simply be asking questions of HMRC about the advice it has produced. The CAG should work closely with the Tax Assurance Commissioner in relation to private rulings and check to ensure that the system is operating appropriately.

Thirdly, as Weeks has argued, soft law breaches require soft law remedies.[279] The findings in this book chime with those of Weeks in that the Adjudicator and Ombudsman can be effective at scrutinising HMRC advice. To this end, the current settlement should be permitted to continue, in addition to scrutiny of HMRC being expressly acknowledged to be a function of these bodies.

Finally, the tribunals and courts should take a more positive role in checking general HMRC advice. The cases of *Malone v UK*,[280] *Silver v United Kingdom*,[281] and *R (Purdy) v Director of Public Prosecutions* ('*Purdy*')[282] and *R (Nicklinson) v Ministry of Justice* ('*Nicklinson*')[283] in particular, highlight the role that can be played by judges in ensuring that HMRC's advice satisfies the normative requirements of correctness, clarity and accessibility.[284] The interventions from the tribunals and courts should be explicit, rather than simply critical of HMRC, as occurred with *Vestey*[285] and *Wilkinson*.[286,287] When intervention should occur is a matter of discretion generally for the tribunals and courts, outside the specific circumstances in which the failure to promulgate sufficiently clear and accessible advice amounts to an infringement of human rights as in *Purdy* and *Nicklinson* or otherwise mandated by law.[288] The tribunals and courts can, however, be guided as to when they should direct HMRC on its advice. In such relevant cases, the following considerations should be taken into account:

- Whether HMRC's advice is inconsistent with the law.
- Whether the production of HMRC advice, or amendment of existing advice, would better inform taxpayers as to their rights and obligations under the law.
- Whether HMRC's advice undermines the ability of taxpayers to rely upon it by virtue of having unnecessary caveats, qualifications and provisos.
- Whether HMRC's advice has retrospective elements. If this is the case, tribunals and courts should enquire as to whether this results in comparative unfairness, detriment due to earlier reliance or other injustice. If the retrospection is lawful because of an error in the advice, then the tribunals and courts should direct HMRC to amend its advice accordingly.

[279] G Weeks, 'The Use and Enforcement of Soft Law by Australian Public Authorities' (2014) 42 *Federal Law Review* 181, 216.

[280] (1985) 7 EHRR 14.

[281] (1983) 5 EHRR 347.

[282] [2009] UKHL 45, [2010] 1 AC 345.

[283] [2014] UKSC 38; [2014] 3 WLR 200.

[284] See generally ch 3 in text at n 103.

[285] *Vestey v IRC* [1980] AC 1148 (HL); *Vestey v IRC (No 2)* [1979] Ch 198 (Ch) 202; *Vestey v IRC (No 1)* [1979] Ch 177 (Ch).

[286] *R (Wilkinson) v IRC* [2005] UKHL 30, [2006] STC 270.

[287] See ch 5 in text at n 241.

[288] See ch 3 in text at n 148.

D. Reliability

There are five primary limitations to the doctrine of legitimate expectations when applied to HMRC advice, which have the effect of diminishing the reliability of HMRC advice.[289] The first and third are correctness and clarity respectively, which reduce reliability – but if the number of mistakes was to be reduced, and clarity enhanced, by virtue of the added scrutiny suggested here then these problems could be reduced. More particularly, in respect of the problem caused by HMRC seeking to reserve control to prevent taxpayers obtaining benefits not strictly due, it is open to HMRC to change its policy. It may be lawful for HMRC to frustrate a legitimate expectation which is predicated on a legal error, but HMRC could take an approach which is less strict having regard to the importance of taxpayers on the whole being able to plan their lives in reliance on the advice.[290] A consequence of HMRC's current approach is that taxpayers may never be certain when they can rely upon HMRC advice, as the treatment promised in the advice might subsequently turn out to be incorrect, prompting HMRC to resile from the promised position. A broader change in mindset could also have the consequence of reducing the amount of qualifying language, the routine presence of which is the fourth factor limiting the utility of the doctrine of legitimate expectations in this context.

The fifth limitation, namely accessibility, could be cut down by broadening the avenues for relief available to taxpayers. Whilst it is open to taxpayers to bring complaints to the Adjudicator and Ombudsman, it is recommended that taxpayers should be made more explicitly aware of the possibility of having the complaint resolved by these bodies. The relevant HMRC advice, such as the Administrative Law Manual, which advises taxpayers on the consequences of advice being incorrect,[291] and HMRC's general guidance on when taxpayers can rely upon information provided by HMRC,[292] should be amended accordingly.[293] Meanwhile, section 84 of the Criminal Justice and Courts Act 2015 produces an unnecessary barrier on access to justice and ought to be repealed,[294] though this is highly unlikely to occur.

Further, serious consideration should be given to allowing the First-tier Tribunal to consider legitimate expectations. The FTT is, for the most part, prevented from hearing public law claims.[295] For the ordinary taxpayer, the difference in costs

[289] See ch 6 in text at n 39.
[290] See ch 6 in text at n 45.
[291] HMRC, 'Admin Law Manual: ADML1300' (July 2016).
[292] HMRC, *When you can rely* (2009).
[293] The House of Lords Economic Affairs Committee has also recommended that greater taxpayer access to the Adjudicator should be considered. In response, the Government agreed and committed to considering whether there was a need to publicise the role earlier in the complaints process: HM Government, 'The Powers of HMRC: Treating Taxpayers Fairly (House of Lords Paper 242): Government Response' (January 2019) 13.
[294] See ch 6 in text at n 179.
[295] *Metropolitan International Schools* (n 93) [20]–[22].

between litigating in the tribunal and litigating in court is significant.[296] It is in fact a perennial problem. In the 1930s, William Robson espoused the benefits of the tribunals over the courts in the following terms:

> It is, indeed, the very backwardness of the court process which enables the departments of state to use the right of access to the courts as a weapon of the most tyrannous character. Compare, for instance, the cheap, informal and entirely admirable system of Income Tax Appeals before the Special Commissioners of Income Tax, an example of a true administrative tribunal, which the Committee admits 'gives general satisfaction by its impartiality,' with the oppressive costliness and lengthiness of the system of appeals from the Special Commissioners on questions of law to the High Court, the Court of Appeal, and the House of Lords. Only the wealthiest persons or corporations can afford to continue a dispute with the Inland Revenue once the threat of litigation has been made.[297]

This restriction of the FTT's jurisdiction is unjustified. The FTT already has the requisite competence and expertise to consider public law issues and the broadening of its jurisdiction would have cost benefits in reducing duplication.[298] For instance, the Tribunal is already entitled to consider issues concerning the major grounds of judicial review, namely illegality,[299] irrationality,[300] procedural impropriety,[301] proportionality[302] and legitimate expectations.[303] Although there is no universally accepted means of categorising the various grounds of review,[304] no reasonable public lawyer would dispute that these are established grounds of review, and this goes to the point that Parliament has already entrusted the body with the power to consider the full range of public law issues. Extending the jurisdiction would also be prudent as it would allow a single tribunal to consider both substantive disputes and public law claims, the resolution of either of which might render the other redundant, or in any event might produce findings which would be of assistance in resolving the other dispute.[305] At the moment, there is a means of allowing the Upper Tribunal (UT) to consider both sets of disputes at the same time, but it requires the consent of the Presidents of the FTT and UT

[296] See ch 6 in text at n 170.

[297] W Robson, 'The Report of the Committee on Ministers' Powers' [1932] *The Political Quarterly* 346, 361–62.

[298] For the author's fuller argument on expanding the jurisdiction of the FTT, see S Daly, 'Public Law in the Tax Tribunals and the Case for Reform' [2018] 1 *British Tax Review* 94.

[299] See, for instance, *Pegasus Birds Ltd v CC&E* [1999] STC 95 (QBD) 101.

[300] See *Kohanzad v CC&E* (*Kohanzad*) [1994] STC 967 (QBD), 969 (Schiemann J) on how to interpret the Value Added Tax Regulations 1995 (SI 1995/2518), reg 29(2).

[301] See, for instance, *Aqua Products Ltd v HMRC* [2013] UKFTT 340 (TC) [18]–[59], which considered the compliance of the tax rules in the case with Art 6 of the European Convention on Human Rights.

[302] See, for instance, *Trinity Mirror plc v HMRC* [2014] UKFTT 355 (TC).

[303] *Aleena Electronics Ltd v HMRC* [2011] UKFTT 608 (TC) [38]–[44] considering compliance with Art 1 of Protocol 1 of the ECHR.

[304] M Elliott and R Thomas, *Public Law*, 3rd edn (Oxford, Oxford University Press, 2017) 497.

[305] See Daly, 'Public Law in the Tax Tribunals' [2018] 103–07.

and both parties to the dispute,[306] though HMRC's consent may not always be forthcoming.[307]

The preferred approach to expanding the FTT's jurisdiction would be through legislative change,[308] but this is unlikely to be forthcoming for the foreseeable future. In response to a recent recommendation from the House of Lords Economic Affairs Committee, the Government rejected giving the FTT the power to conduct judicial reviews:

> Any change to the Judicial Review process would need to be led by the Ministry of Justice in consultation with the judiciary. This would fundamentally alter the nature and purpose of the First-tier Tribunal which is to make findings of fact in a relatively quick and inexpensive way.[309]

But in any event, an expanded jurisdiction for the FTT can be achieved through judicial innovation. In *Oxfam v HMRC* ('*Oxfam*'),[310] Sales J (as he then was) considered that the jurisdiction of the FTT to hear public law claims was broader than previously understood.[311] Such an interpretation was defensible on the basis that the FTT is particularly well positioned to make judgements about the fair treatment of taxpayers by HMRC and it avoids the cost, delay and potential injustice and confusion associated with proliferation of proceedings.[312] It is plausible that Parliament would have had the avoidance of these issues in mind when drafting the provision.[313] In *Noor v HMRC* ('*Noor*'),[314] the UT, which featured the (then) President of the Tax and Chancery Chamber of the UT, Mr Justice Warren, and the President of the FTT Tax Chamber, Judge Bishopp, rejected Sales J's analysis. If Parliament had intended to allow the FTT to consider public law issues in such a manner, the UT contended, it would have expressly done so and subjected the jurisdiction to do so to specific conditions, as it did in the case of the UT.[315] The judgment in *Noor* has in practice been accepted as the leading authority.[316]

Nevertheless the reasoning of Sales J aligns generally with that of the Supreme Court in the subsequent case of *R (Cart) v Upper Tribunal*.[317] The Supreme Court took a broad reading of Tribunals, Courts and Enforcement Act 2007 (TCEA 2007) in order to develop a means of judicially reviewing decisions of the UT. Although

[306] Tribunal Procedure (First-tier Tribunal) (Tax Chamber) Rules 2009 (SI 2009/273) r 28.
[307] See, for instance, *Reed Plc v HMRC* [2010] UKUT B24 (TCC) [12].
[308] See Daly (n 298) 109–11.
[309] HMRC, 'The Powers of HMRC' (2019) 9.
[310] *Oxfam v HMRC* [2009] EWHC 3078 (Ch), [2010] STC 686 [73].
[311] ibid [61]–[79].
[312] ibid [70].
[313] ibid.
[314] [2013] UKUT 71 (TCC), [2013] STC 998.
[315] ibid [29], [76]–[78].
[316] See *Reed Employment plc and others v HMRC* [2014] UKUT 160 (TCC), [2014] STC 1982, 2068; *British Disabled Flying Association v HMRC* [2013] UKUT 162 (TCC), [2013] STC 1677, 1689.
[317] [2011] UKSC 28, [2011] STC 1659.

the statute states that the UT is a superior court of record,[318] the Supreme Court held that this did not preclude judicial review of the UT's decisions. In terms of the mechanics of such judicial review, the Supreme Court used the language of TCEA 2007 to develop a novel approach that the courts ought to take.[319] The Supreme Court justified the invention inter alia by reference to the need to spare judicial resources.[320] To this end, the judgment supports Sales J's assessment in *Oxfam*,[321] specifically, that having two sets of proceedings dealing with effectively the same issue is a poor use of judicial resources and hence contrary to the intention of Parliament.[322] The Supreme Court judgment in *Cart* was not, however, mentioned in *Noor*.

One could respond that the jurisdiction to hear judicial review cases has been rendered purposefully narrow by Parliament. Judge Mosedale in *LH Bishop v HMRC*[323] put the argument in the following terms: Parliament cannot have intended for challenges to, effectively, the fairness of a provision to be brought in an unrestricted manner.[324] By limiting such claims to judicial review, and therein having a permission filter to weed out unmeritorious claims, it could be said that there is merit in preventing the tribunal from hearing public law issues without limit.[325] But this, similarly to the approach of the UT in *Noor*, is to imply that Parliament, without using express words, intends to restrict access to justice. This goes directly contrary to the principle of legality, which provides that restrictions on fundamental rights must be expressed in clear terms rather than implied as a matter of interpretation.[326] The argument is further bolstered by the case of *R (Unison) v Lord Chancellor*,[327] wherein the Supreme Court held that tribunal fees, introduced by secondary legislation,[328] were unlawful by reason of their impact on access to justice.[329]

It is envisaged that this change, whereby the FTT could deal with all issues concerning a dispute in relation to HMRC advice, not just legitimate expectation claims but also indirectly scrutinising HMRC advice, could integrate well with

[318] TCEA 2007, s 3(5).

[319] On which see *Cart* (n 317) [128]–[134] (Lord Dyson).

[320] ibid [47] (Lady Hale) [89] (Lord Phillips), [100] (Lord Brown), [104] (Lord Clarke), [124]–[126] (Lord Dyson).

[321] *Oxfam* (n 310) [5].

[322] It is notable likewise that TCEA 2007 was intended to produce a coherent structure for the delivery of administrative justice. Lord Chancellor's Department, 'Tribunals for Users: One System, One Service – Report of the Review of Tribunals by Sir Andrew Leggatt, Terms of Reference' (March 2001).

[323] [2013] UKFTT 522 (TC).

[324] ibid [143]–[146].

[325] ibid.

[326] *R v Secretary of State for Defence ex p Smith* [1996] QB 517 (CA) at 554E–G (Bingham LJ); *R v Lord Chancellor ex p Witham* [1998] QB 575 (DC) at 581E–F (Laws LJ); *R v Secretary of State for the Home Department ex p Pierson* [1998] AC 539 (HL) at 575 (Lord Browne-Wilkinson).

[327] *R (Unison) v Lord Chancellor* [2017] UKSC 51, [2018] 1 CMLR 35.

[328] The relevant primary legislation – the Tribunals, Courts and Enforcement Act 2007 – allowed the Lord Chancellor to introduce tribunal fees (s 42).

[329] *Unison* (n 327) [90]–[98] (Lord Reed).

the process recommended for appeals in relation to public rulings.[330] The most complicated issue which could arise would be a three-tiered dispute before the FTT revolving around a substantive dispute on the correct application of law, the application of a ruling, and a legitimate expectation in respect of some assurance. For instance, a dispute might arise in relation to a taxpayer's residence. The taxpayer might contend that on the basis of the application of the substantive law she is not resident in the UK. She might also contend that she can rely upon a ruling to this effect. She might finally contend that she had a legitimate expectation that she was not resident, on the basis of HMRC advice on residence. All of these arguments might then be placed before the FTT in the same hearing. Although this might seem complicated at first glance, it is less so on closer inspection. The resolution of any one of these issues in favour of the taxpayer will resolve the immediate dispute. Having the FTT, being equipped with all the relevant facts, decide the case is again preferable to dual proceedings arising before the Tribunal and the High Court. The Tribunal can decide which argument has greatest merit, can resolve what findings of fact are necessary for the expedient resolution of the case, and can choose to stay issues which would be irrelevant upon resolution of other issues.

IV. Conclusion

This chapter has set out a range of proposals which can be adopted in the UK in order to advance the rule of law in respect of HMRC advice. Most notably, the book recommends the establishment of a broad binding rulings regime incorporating both private and public rulings. Binding pre-transaction rulings ought to be available, and though product and class rulings are technically public rulings, these should be provided in the same manner as private rulings whereby taxpayers, rather than HMRC, initiate their production. In respect of private rulings, there would need to be legislation setting out that rulings can be applied for and that the ruling will be binding, but also entitling HMRC to refuse to issue rulings, for instance where it would jeopardise the exercise of a statutory discretion. Legislation would also need to be amended in order to allow the FTT to have jurisdiction to hear disputes in relation to private rulings. Further, there would need to be established an internal framework for the promulgation of private rulings, which could allocate responsibility and incorporate legal expertise.

In terms of the mechanics of operating a public rulings scheme, there ought to be a nine-stage process involved in the promulgation of rulings in addition to a tenth stage allowing for challenges to rulings to be brought. Public rulings should be promulgated in respect of general advice which *has a significant impact on the rights or obligations of taxpayers, by reason of creating, substantially amending or*

[330] See in text at n 204.

removing them. Legislative amendment is necessary so as to allow public rulings to be binding and to allow the tribunals and courts to consider appeals. As for the relevant actors, the Working Together Group should be consulted so as to assist HMRC in determining which items of general advice ought to become public rulings. Beyond these practical changes to accommodate the introduction of a broad-binding rulings regime it is worth highlighting that whilst the conflict with Parliamentary sovereignty is more illusory than real, there would need to be buy-in from Parliament, the Government and HMRC to ensure the effective operation of the regime.

Private rulings primarily assist in relation to accessibility and reliability, but only apply to pre-transaction problems. Meanwhile, not all issues can, or might be considered appropriate to, go through the public rulings process. To that end, there is a need to consider reforms beyond the introduction of a broad rulings regime. A change of mindset within HMRC, whereby the body is more comfortable with relinquishing control over the advice and the possibility of taxpayers receiving benefits perceived to be undue, would be beneficial in terms of advancing the rule of law. This could lead to a reduction in the use qualifying language in advice, prospective-only changes in advice and allowing incorrect advice to have effect. A change of mindset should be more palatable for HMRC if accompanied by the reforms suggested which seek to ensure that better processes are involved in the production and scrutiny of advice.

In terms of the normative benchmarks for testing whether the rule of law is being advanced, the ideals of correctness and clarity could be achieved to a greater extent if HMRC directed itself specifically to these when drafting advice. Redacted rulings could also be used as part of general advice in the form of examples to assist taxpayers.

On accessibility, the Information Commissioner should investigate the FOI protected information contained in HMRC Manuals to ensure that these are protected by the FOIA. Parties affected by retrospective changes, if HMRC is not going to change its general approach, ought to be consulted so that HMRC is equipped with the information relevant to taking such a decision. The list of published ESCs, meanwhile, ought to be updated to include all items of general advice which contain concessions relevant to the general body of taxpayers. The list should also highlight the precarious position that taxpayers are placed in by relying on concessions.

Scrutiny will be assisted by the development of an internal framework, incorporating oversight from HMRC lawyers. Meanwhile external feedback should be augmented by the provision of feedback links in general advice for taxpayers and representative groups. Greater responsibility could be taken by the CAG and NAO, whilst other parties, particularly the tribunals and courts, ought to take the opportunity to be more involved in scrutinising HMRC advice.

In terms of reliability, alleviating the problems of correctness, clarity and accessibility, will necessarily have a beneficial effect. A change of mindset would be particularly beneficial as this would lead to HMRC being clearer in its positions, through using less qualifying language, in addition to accepting that it is lawful and desirable not to frustrate legitimate expectations. Further, the restriction on the jurisdiction of the FTT is unjust and ought to be removed, preferably through legislation but, if not, through judicial innovation. If possible, section 84 of the Criminal Justice and Courts Act 2015 additionally ought to be repealed.

Finally, even if all the proposals recommended in this chapter are accepted, that should not be the end of the story. There is a need for the system to grow organically and to be amended if necessary to adapt to as yet unforeseen exigencies. The regime for binding private and public rulings will need to be monitored, particularly in the early years and thereafter at regular intervals, in order to safeguard its proper development. The evolution of the rulings system in Australia into its current highly respectable state is due in no small part to the constant scrutiny that it has been placed under by the Treasury, the IGT and the JCPAA. The other proposals in respect of HMRC advice will equally be in need of supervision to ensure that they are both put into effect and are effective. To this end, the final recommendation is that the CAG and NAO should prepare reports at regular intervals, more frequently in the early years, on the performance of both the rulings regime and HMRC advice generally in respect of correctness, clarity, accessibility, scrutiny and reliability.

8

Conclusion

> [The resignation of David Heaton from the GAAR Panel] was not just bad luck or an indication that the wrong person was chosen. It is the result of a failure to create a robust institution with a clear function. That in itself is the result of rushing developments, partial consultation with busy people and lack of an underlying route map about where we are going with our tax institutions.*

The Aaronson Report recommended that the General Anti-Abuse Rule (GAAR) Advisory Panel, a body to be established to update HMRC's GAAR guidance[1] and provide opinions on cases where HMRC considers the GAAR may apply,[2] should be made up of members of HMRC and a majority of independent tax experts, including an independent chair.[3] The reason for such a balanced composition was not fleshed out in the Report, but given the findings in this book it is obvious such a constitution would better ensure robustness, deliberation and balance, taking into account the considerations from both an external and internal perspective. This, unfortunately, was overlooked in subsequent developments. A 'significant majority' of respondents to the Government's consultation objected to HMRC's membership in the Panel.[4] The formality and powers of the panel in turn grew, further deviating from the original intent, with the advisory opinion of the GAAR Panel becoming a mandatory consideration for the tribunals and courts.[5] The 'odd constitutional role' now adopted by the Panel rendered the membership of HMRC officials untenable. With membership a contested feature, eyes turned to the appropriateness of the other members.[6]

* J Freedman, 'Creating new UK institutions for tax governance and policy making: progress or confusion?' [2013] *British Tax Review* 373, 380.

[1] G Aaronson, 'GAAR Study: A study to consider whether a general anti-avoidance rule should be introduced into the UK tax system' (November 2011) (Aaronson Report) 8, 26, 29–30, 34.

[2] ibid 8, 26, 33–34, 52, 58 and 72–73.

[3] ibid 26, 42, 33, 42, 52–53, 58 and 73.

[4] HMRC, 'Summary of Responses: A General Anti-Abuse Rule' (December 2012) 20, cited in J Freedman, 'Creating new UK institutions for tax governance and policy making: progress or confusion?' [2013] *British Tax Review* 373, 378.

[5] Finance Act 2013, s 211(2), cited in Freedman, 'Creating new institutions' (ibid) 378. The original vision was that the courts would be entitled to take into account the GAAR Panel's opinion. See: Aaronson Report 2011) 42, 50.

[6] Freedman, 'Creating new institutions' [2013] 378.

On 27 June 2013, David Heaton presented some tips on minimising tax liability at a conference entitled '101 Ideas for Personal Tax Planning'.[7] These would serve as a means of keeping money 'out of the Chancellor's grubby mitts'.[8] The following month, he was appointed to the GAAR Panel.[9] On 16 September, a BBC Panorama documentary, 'Tax, Lies and Videotape', featuring footage of David Heaton speaking at this conference, was scheduled to be aired. A few days prior, he took the opportunity to resign from the Panel.[10] Had the original purpose of the Panel been more clearly expressed and better understood, and had the subsequent departure from the original vision not taken place, it is most likely that the resignation of a tax-planning expert from an expert panel tasked with advising on the acceptability of tax-planning practices would not have been inevitable.[11]

The episode serves as a cautionary tale, which this book bears in mind. It is necessary to clearly set out the underlying reasons for, and the precise details of, the necessary components of any reforms. In this book, the provision of legal advice by a public authority, specifically the UK's tax authority, was comprehensively examined (though the lessons could be valuable in the context of other public authorities who provide advice to the public). As a matter of principle, HMRC advice is desirable by reason of the rule of law: the advice gives taxpayers guidance as to the tax consequences of their actions, thereby respecting the capacity of individuals to make choices affecting their lives. But in order for the advice to perform this function it is necessary that it be correct, clear and accessible. So as to achieve these ends, the advice ought to be scrutinised, whilst taxpayers should be able to rely on the advice, thereby requiring there to be some remedy to prevent HMRC from reneging on its promised position. These indicia, derived from the rule of law, form the normative framework against which the provision of advice by HMRC should be tested.

The testing of HMRC advice against this normative framework in chapters four to six demonstrates that there are shortcomings in the present UK system. These chapters did not seek to comprehensively set out all of the shortcomings, but rather to highlight particular areas of concern. Others may find different problems in the present system – but one of the book's critical contributions lies in the framework for assessing any such problems and accordingly examining potential reforms. These chapters highlighted the areas where reform ought to be forthcoming and in chapter seven the book set out a future vision for HMRC advice revolving principally around the introduction of a comprehensive binding rulings regime.

[7] M McLaughlin, 'Conference Report: 101 Ideas for Personal Tax Planning' (August 2013), available at www.bloomsburyprofessionalonline.com/applib/newsitem/404/conference-report-101-ideas-for-personal-tax-planning.

[8] G Parker and V Houlder, 'Revenue adviser caught listing ways to avoid "chancellor's grubby mitts"' *Financial Times* (13 September 2013).

[9] R Lovell, 'Revenue reveals new GAAR panel' *Accountingweb* (22 July 2013).

[10] C Carter, 'Government tax adviser quits after talk on how to keep money out of George Osborne's 'grubby mitts'' *The Telegraph* (13 September 2013).

[11] See Freedman (n 4) 379–80.

Ultimately, the book takes as its starting point the status quo – that tax law will continue to be promulgated in such a way that HMRC advice necessarily helps taxpayers and tax officials to understand their rights and obligations. HMRC advice should not be used so as to allow legislators to obviate their duty to draft reasonably clear laws. HMRC advice should be a supplement to, not substitute for, tax law. The rule of law and indeed democratic principles mandate that this be the case.

BIBLIOGRAPHY

Books and Articles

Aaronson G, Cordara R, Cullinane J, Johnson P and Smith D (eds), *Plucking the Goose: A century of taxation from the Great War to the Digital Age* (Croydon, Tolley, 2016)

Allars M, *Introduction to Australian Administrative Law* (Sydney, Butterworths, 1990)

Allen CK, *Law and Orders*, 3rd edn (London, Stevens and Sons, 1965)

Asimow M, 'Nonlegislative rulemaking and regulatory reform' [1985] *Duke Law Journal* 381

Baldwin R, *Rules and Government* (Oxford, Clarendon Press, 1995)

Baldwin R and Hawkins K, 'Discretionary Justice, Davis Reconsidered' [1984] *Public Law* 570

Baldwin R and Houghton J, 'Circular Arguments: The Status and Legitimacy of Administrative Rules' [1986] *Public Law* 239

Baldwin R, Scott C and Hood C, *A Reader on Regulation* (Oxford, Oxford University Press, 1998)

Beighton L, 'The Finance Bill process: scope for reform?' [1995] 1 *British Tax Review* 33

Bentley D, 'A Proposal for Reform of the Australian Ruling system' (1997) 26 *Australian Tax Review* 57

Bernhardt S, 'The Bellinz Case and the Rulings System' (1998) 27 *Australian Tax Review* 117

Black J, 'Which Arrow: Rule Type and Regulatory Policy' [1997] *Public Law* 94

—— *Rules and Regulators* (Oxford, Oxford University Press, 1997)

—— 'Talking about Regulation' in Michael Harris and Martin Partington, *Administrative Justice in the 21st Century* (Oxford, Hart Publishing, 1999)

—— 'Law and Regulation: The Case of Finance' in C Parker, C Scott, N Lacey and J Braithwaite (eds), *Regulating Law* (Oxford, Oxford University Press, 2004)

—— 'Forms and paradoxes of principles-based regulation' (2008) 3 *Capital Markets Law Journal* 425

Black J, Hopper M and Band C, 'Making a Success of Principles Based Regulation' (2007) 1 *Law and Financial Markets Review* 191

Bingham T, 'The Rule of Law' [2007] *Cambridge Law Journal* 67

—— *The Rule of Law* (London, Penguin Press, 2011)

Booth J, *Stand and Deliver! The Inland Revenue and Non-statutory Taxation* (Winchester, Waterside Press, 1998)

Bowler-Smith M and Ostik H, 'Towards a classification of the Central London congestion charge as a tax' [2011] *British Tax Review* 487

Braithwaite J, 'Making tax law more certain: A theory' (2003) 31 *Australian Business Law Review* 72

Braithwaite J, Makkai T and Braithwaite V, *Regulating Aged Care: Ritualism and the New Pyramid* (Cheltenham, Edward Elgar, 2007)

Bradley A, Ewing K and Knight C, *Constitutional & Administrative Law*, 17th edn (Harlow, Pearson Education, 2018)

Cannon P, 'New SDLT general anti-avoidance rule' (2007) 874 *Tax Journal* 6

Chamberlain E, 'Treasury Sixth Report on Inland Revenue' [1999] *British Tax Review* 445

—— 'Home loans: an update on common Inheritance Tax mitigation schemes' (2013) *Step Journal* 26

Chamberlain E and Whitehouse C, 'HMRC debacle? The efficacy of home loan schemes is in question.' (2011) 167 Taxation 15, 16

Chan W, 'Binding Rulings' (1997) 18 *Fiscal Studies* 189

Chinkin CM, 'The Challenge of Soft Law: Development and Change in International Law' (1989) 38 *International and Comparative Law Quarterly* 850

Cockburn R, *Small Business Tax Planning: All you need to know from start-up to retirement* (Petersfield, Harriman House Publishing, 2011)

de Cogan D, 'UK Uncut Legal Action v HMRC: legal inaction and a return to Fleet Street' [2013] 4 *British Tax Review* 552

—— 'A Changing Role for the Administrative Law of Taxation' (2015) 24 *Social & Legal Studies* 251

—— '*CIR v National Federation of Self-Employed and Small Businesses* (1981): All Grievances Converging on Tax Law' in D de Cogan and J Snape, *Landmark Cases in Revenue Law* (Oxford, Hart Publishing, 2019)

de Cogan D, P Tuck and Snape J, 'A Tale of the Merger between the Inland Revenue and HM Customs & Excise' in P Harris and D De Cogan (eds), *Studies in the History of Tax Law: Volume 9* (Oxford, Hart Publishing, 2019)

Collins J, 'Analysis – The tax assurance commissioner's first annual report' (2013) 1181 *Tax Journal* 22

Cooke E, *The Modern Law of Estoppel* (Oxford, Oxford University Press, 2000)

Cooper G, 'Improving the operation of the Income Tax Rulings system' Discussion Paper: Report for the Australian Society of CPAs (1998)

Cory R, 'The Human Rights Act 1998 and the Treasury consents regime' [2005] *British Tax Review* 412

Craig P, 'Representations by Public Bodies' (1977) 93 *LQR* 398

—— 'Formal and substantive conceptions of the rule of law: an analytical framework' [1997] *Public Law* 467

—— *Administrative Law*, 8th edn (London, Sweet and Maxwell, 2016)

—— *EU Administrative Law*, 3rd edn (Oxford, Oxford University Press, 2018)

D'Ascenzo M, 'Modernising the Australian Taxation Office: Vision, people, systems and values' (2015) 13 *eJournal of Tax Research* 361

Daintith T and Page A, *The Executive in the Constitution: Structure, Autonomy, and Internal Control* (Oxford, Oxford University Press, 1999)

Daly P, *A Theory of Deference in Administrative Law: Basis, Application and Scope* (Cambridge, Cambridge University Press, 2012)

—— 'Administrative Law: A Values-Based Approach' in J Bell, M Elliott, J Varuhas and P Murray (eds), *Public Law Adjudication in Common Law Systems: Process and Substance* (Oxford, Hart Publishing, 2015)

Daly S, 'Recent developments in tax law: vires revisited' [2016] 2 *Public Law* 190

—— 'Fairness in tax law and revenue guidance: *R (Hely-Hutchinson) v HMRC*' [2016] 1 *British Tax Review* 18

—— 'Oversight of HMRC soft law: lessons from the Ombudsman' (2016) 38 *Journal of Social Welfare and Family Law* 343

—— 'The Life and Times of ESCs: A defence?' in D de Cogan and P Harris (eds), *Studies in the History of Tax Law: Volume 8* (Oxford, Hart Publishing, 2017)

—— 'Tax Exceptionalism: A UK Perspective' (2017) 3 *Journal of Tax Administration* 95

—— 'Legitimate expectations and HMRC advice' (2018) 77 *Cambridge Law Journal* 265

—— 'Public Law in the Tax Tribunals and the Case for Reform' [2018] 1 *British Tax Review* 94

—— 'Drawing the boundaries of HMRC's discretion' in R de la Feria and G Loutzenhiser (eds), *Essays in Honour of Judith Freedman* (forthcoming Oxford, Hart Publishing, 2020)

Daly S and Tomlinson J, 'Administrative Inconsistency in the Courts' (2018) 23 *Judicial Review* 190

Davis KC, 'Judicial Control of Administrative Action' (1966) 66 *Columbia Law Review* 635

—— *Discretionary Justice: A Preliminary Inquiry*, 2nd edn (Baton Rouge, Louisiana State University Press, 1971)

Dicey AV, *Introduction to the law of the constitution* (Indianapolis, Liberty Classics, 1982)

Diller M, Kortebusch P, Schneider G and Sureth-Sloane C, 'Boon or Bane? Advance Tax Rulings as a Measure to Mitigate Tax Uncertainty and Foster Investment' (2017) 26 *European Accounting Review* 441

Drewry G (ed), *The New Select Committees*, 2nd edn (Oxford, Oxford University Press, 1989)

—— 'Public Law' (1995) 73 *Public Administration* 41

Dworkin R, *Taking Rights Seriously* (London, Gerald Duckworth & Co, 1977)
Elliott M, 'The Demise of Parliamentary Sovereignty? The Implications for Justifying Judicial Review' (1999) 115 *LQR* 119
—— 'Asymmetric Devolution and Ombudsman Reform in England' [2006] *Public Law* 84
—— 'Has the Common Law Duty to Give Reasons Come of Age Yet?' [2011] 1 *Public Law* 56
Elliott M, Bell J, Varuhas J and Murray P (eds), *Public Law Adjudication in Common Law Systems: Process and Substance* (Oxford, Hart Publishing, 2015)
Elliott M and Thomas R, *Public Law*, 3rd edn (Oxford, Oxford University Press, 2017)
Endicott T, *Vagueness in Law* (Oxford, Oxford University Press, 2000)
—— *Administrative Law*, 4th edn (Oxford, Oxford University Press, 2018)
Etherton T, 'Liberty, the Archetype and Diversity: A Philosophy of Judging' [2010] *Public Law* 727
Evans C, Freedman J and Krever R (eds), *The Delicate Balance: Tax, Discretion and the Rule of Law* (Amsterdam, International Bureau of Fiscal Documentation, 2011)
Evans C, Krever R and Mellor P (eds), *Tax Simplification* (Alphen aan den Rijn, Kluwer Law International, 2015)
Fairpo A, 'Tax Research – Online Resources' (2008) 923 *Tax Journal* 17
Fernandes D and Sadiq K, 'A principled framework for assessing general anti-avoidance regimes' [2016] *British Tax Review* 172
Finnemore M and Toope S, 'Alternatives to "Legalization": Richer Views of Law and Politics' (2001) 55 *International Organization* 743
Finnis J, *Natural Law and Natural Rights*, 2nd edn (Oxford, Oxford University Press, 2011)
Fitzpatrick K, 'A Long Innings – Valedictory Address by Kevin Fitzpatrick' (2012) 46 *Taxation in Australia* 394
Flinders M, *Delegated Governance and the British State* (Oxford, Oxford University Press, 2008)
Forsyth C, 'The Provenance and Protection of Legitimate Expectations' (1988) 47 *Cambridge Law Journal* 238
—— 'Wednesbury Protection of Substantive Legitimate Expectations' [1997] *Public Law* 375
—— (ed), *Judicial Review & the Constitution* (Oxford, Hart Publishing, 2000)
Forsyth C and Hare I (eds), *The Golden Metwand and the Crooked Cord* (Oxford, Oxford University Press, 1998)
Forsyth C and Wade W, *Administrative Law*, 11th edn (Oxford, Oxford University Press, 2014)
Frankfurter F, Forward to 'Discussion of Current Developments in Administrative Law' (1938) 47 *Yale Law Journal* 515
Freedman J (ed), *Beyond Boundaries: Developing Approaches to Tax Avoidance and Tax Risk Management* (Oxford, OUCBT, 2008)
—— 'Improving (not perfecting) tax legislation: rules and principles revisited' [2010] *British Tax Review* 717
—— 'Creating new UK institutions for tax governance and policy making: progress or confusion?' [2013] 4 *British Tax Review* 373
—— 'Managing Tax Complexity: The Institutional Framework for Tax Policy-Making and Oversight' in Evans C, Krever R and Mellor P, *Series on International Taxation, Vol 53: Tax Simplification* (Alphen aan den Rijn, Kluwer Law International, 2013)
—— 'UK institutions for tax governance: reviewing tax settlements' [2016] *British Tax Review* 7
—— 'Five Recommendations for Restoring Trust in HMRC' (2017) 1342 *Tax Journal* 6
Freedman J, Loomer G and Vella V, 'Corporate tax risk and tax avoidance: new approaches' [2009] *British Tax Review* 74
Freedman J and Vella J, 'HMRC's Management of the UK Tax System: The Boundaries of Legitimate Discretion' in Evans C, Freedman J and Krever R, *The Delicate Balance: Tax, Discretion and the Rule of Law* (Amsterdam, IBFD, 2011)
—— 'Revenue Guidance: The Limits of Discretion and Legitimate Expectations' (2012) 128 *LQR* 192
Fuller L, *The Morality of Law*, revised edn (New Haven, Yale University Press, 1969)
Galligan D, 'The nature and function of policies within discretionary power' [1976] *Public Law* 332

—— *Discretionary Powers*: A Legal Study of official *Discretion* (Oxford, Clarendon Press, 1986)
—— *Due Process and Fair Procedures* (Oxford, Oxford University Press, 1994)
Gammie M, '"Revenue Practice": A Suitable Case For Treatment' [1979] *British Tax Review* 304
—— 'Extra-Statutory Concessions' [1980] *British Tax Review* 308
—— 'Shooting the messenger: the proposed enabler penalty' [2017] *British Tax Review* 142
Ganz G, 'Allocation of Decision-Making Functions' [1972] *LP* 215, 215
—— *Quasi-legislation: recent developments in secondary legislation* (London, Sweet and Maxwell, 1987)
Giddings P, 'Select Committees and Parliamentary Scrutiny: Plus Ca Change' (1994) 47 *Parliamentary Affairs* 669
Givati Y, 'Resolving Legal Uncertainty: The Fulfilled Promise of Advance Tax Rulings' (2009) 29 *Virginia Tax Review* 137
Goodall A, 'Taxpayer Confidentiality: Hartnett sets out HMRC view for MPs' (2011) 1098 *Tax Journal* 2
Goslinga S, Van Der Hel-Van Dijk L, Mascini P and van Steenbergen A (eds), *Tax and Trust* (The Hague, Eleven International Publishing, 2018)
Greenberg D, 'Dangerous Trends in Modern Legislation' [2015] 1 *Public Law* 96
Gregory R and Giddings G, *Practice and Prospects of the ombudsmen in the United Kingdom* (Lampeter, Edwin Mellon Press, 1995)
Griffiths S, '"No discretion should be unconstrained": considering the "care and management" of taxes and the settlement of tax disputes in New Zealand and the UK' [2012] 2 *British Tax Review* 167
Hale B, 'Equality and the Judiciary: Why Should We Want More Women Judges?' [2001] *Public Law* 489
Hamilton P, *Hamilton on Tax Appeals* (London, Bloomsbury, 2016)
Harlow C and Rawlings R, *Law and Administration* (Cambridge, Cambridge University Press, 2009)
Harris T, McLaughlin M, Wunschmann-Lyall I and Erwood C, *Core Tax Annual: Inheritance Tax 2011/12* (West Sussex, Bloomsbury Professional, 2011)
Harrison C and Stainer D, 'Back to basics: When can you rely on HMRC statements?' (2014) 1235 *Tax Journal* 12
Hart HLA, 'Positivism and the Separation of Law and Morals' (1958) 71 *Harvard Law Review* 593
Hartnett D, 'CGT Treatment of Employee Share Options – Letter to the Editor' (2009) 1000 *Tax Journal* 4
Hawkins K (ed), *Uses of Discretion* (Oxford, Oxford University Press, 1992)
Hayek FA, *The Road to Serfdom* (Abindgon, Routledge, 1944)
Hill P, 'Binding GST Rulings – A Proposed Framework' (2003) 18 *Australian Tax Forum* 177
Hinds W, 'Estopping the taxman' [1991] *British Tax Review* 191
Hoffmann L, 'Tax Avoidance' [2005] *British Tax Review* 197
James M, *Taxation of Small Businesses 2016–2017*, 9th edn (London, Spiramus Press, 2016)
James S and Wallschutzky I, 'The Design of an Appropriate System of Tax Rulings' (1995) 5 *Revenue Law Journal* 175
Johnston A, *Inland Revenue* (London, George Allen & Unwin, 1965)
Jones JA, 'Tax Appeals: The Case for Reform' [1994] *British Tax Review* 3
—— 'Tax law: rules or principles?' [1996] 6 *British Tax Review* 580
—— 'The reform of the tax tribunals: a story of uncompleted business' [2006] *British Tax Review* 282
—— 'The equity of the executive: A commentary' in Turner P (ed), *Equity and Administration* (Cambridge, Cambridge University Press, 2016)
Jowell J, 'The Legal Control of Administrative Discretion' [1973] *Public Law* 179
—— *Law and Bureaucracy: Administrative Discretion and the Limits of Legal Action* (New York, Dunellen, 1975)
Jowell J and Oliver D (eds), *The Changing Constitution*, 5th edn (Oxford, Oxford University Press, 2004)
Kay J and King M, *The British Tax System*, 5th edn (Oxford, Oxford University Press, 1990)

Keane A and McKeown P, *The Modern Law of Evidence*, 10th edn (Oxford, Oxford University Press, 2014)
Kirkham R, 'The Constitutional Role of the Ombudsman' (2006) 10 *The International Ombudsman Yearbook* 120
Klabbers J, 'Informal instruments before the European Court of Justice' (1994) 31 *Common Market Law Review* 997
—— 'The Redundancy of Soft law' (1996) 65 *Nordic Journal of International Law* 167
—— 'The Undesirability of Soft Law' (1998) 67 *Nordic Journal of International Law* 381
Kramer M, *Objectivity and the Rule of Law* (Oxford, Oxford University Press, 2007)
Laugharne P, 'The Treasury and Civil Service Select Committee during the Thatcher Administration' (2007) 26 *Parliamentary History* 225
Law J (ed), *Oxford Dictionary of Law*, 9th edn (Oxford, Oxford University Press, 2015)
Lawson N, *The View from No 11* (London, Bantam Press, 1992)
Laws J, 'Law and democracy' [1995] *Public Law* 72
Lee N, *Revenue Law: Principles and Practice*, 30th edn (West Sussex, Bloomsbury Professional, 2012)
—— "Editorial" (2013) *Private Client Business* 143
Lewis C, 'Judicial review: time limits and retrospectivity' [1987] *Public Law* 21
Leyland P and Anthony G, *Textbook on Administrative Law*, 8th edn (Oxford, Oxford University Press, 2016)
Lino D, 'The Rule of Law and the Rule of Empire: A.V. Dicey in Imperial Context' (2018) 81 *MLR* 739
Loutzenhiser G, *Tiley's Revenue Law*, 9th edn (Oxford, Hart Publishing, 2016)
Maugham J, 'What can you legitimately expect?' (2013) 1114 *Tax Journal* 13
Mba O, 'Transparency and accountability of tax administration in the UK: the nature and scope of taxpayer confidentiality' [2012] *British Tax Review* 187
McCarthy HL, 'Statutory appeal or judicial review?' (2014) 1234 *Tax Journal* 15
McCarthy HL and Black S, 'UBS and DB Group Services: a departure from the conventional approach?' [2016] *British Tax Review* 257
McFall J, 'The Treasury Select Committee: its reach and its role in the financial crisis' (2009) 29 *Economic Affairs* 53
McHarg A, 'Administrative Discretion, Administrative Rule-making, and Judicial Review' (2017) 70 *Current Legal Problems* 267
McKay W, Hutton M and Sandall A (eds), *Erskine May's Treatise on the Law, Privileges, Proceedings and Usage of Parliament*, 23rd edn (Oxford, Butterworths, 2004)
McLaren J, 'The Distinction Between Tax Avoidance and Tax Evasion Has Become Blurred in Australia: Why Has it Happened?' (2008) 3 *Journal of the Australasian Tax Teachers Association* 141
McLaughlin M, Wünschmann-Lyall I and Erwood C, *Core Tax Annuals: Inheritance Tax 2015/16* (West Sussex, Bloomsbury Professional, 2015)
Meade J, *The Structure and Reform of Direct Taxation* (London, George Allen & Unwin 1978)
Megarry RE, 'Administrative Quasi-Legislation' (1994) 60 *LQR* 125
Micheau C, 'Tax selectivity in European law of state aid: legal assessment and alternative approaches' (2015) 40 *European Law Review* 323
Mirrlees J, *Tax by Design: the Mirrlees Review* (Oxford, Oxford University Press, 2011)
Morris PE, 'The Revenue Adjudicator – the first two years' [1996] *Public Law* 309
Moules R, *Actions against Public Officials: Legitimate Expectations, Misstatements and Misconduct* (London, Sweet and Maxwell, 2009)
Nason S, *Reconstructing Judicial Review* (Oxford, Hart Publishing, 2016)
Nias P and Belgrano B, 'Analysis: HMRC's refreshed LSS: no "soft" option' (2012) *Tax Journal* 15
Nolan M, 'The Unsatisfactory State of Current Tax Law' [1981] 3 *Statute Law Review* 148
O'Rourke K, 'The GST Rulings System – Is it Failing?' (2002) 11 *Revenue Law Journal* 79
Oliver DBO, 'Advance Rulings' [1996] 6 *British Tax Review* 578
Oliver D, 'Ombudsmen in search of a role' (1978) 41 *MLR* 446
—— 'Is the ultra vires rule the basis of judicial review?' [1987] *Public Law* 543

Osofsky L, 'The Case Against Strategic Tax Law Uncertainty' (2011) 64 *Tax Law Review* 489
Owens D, 'A Simple Theory of Promising' (2006) 115 *Philosophical Review* 51
Pagone T, 'Tax Uncertainty' (2009) 33 *Melbourne University Law Review* 886
Parker C, Scott C, Lacey N and Braithwaite J (eds), *Regulating Law* (Oxford, Oxford University Press, 2004)
Perry A, 'The Flexibility Rule in Administrative Law' (2017) 76 *Cambridge Law Journal* 375
Poirier J, 'The functions of intergovernmental agreements: post-devolution concordats in a comparative perspective' [2001] *Public Law* 134
Prebble J, *Advance Rulings on Tax Liability* (Wellington, Victoria University Press/Institute of Policy Studies 1986)
—— 'Should tax legislation be written from a principles and purpose point of view or a precise and detailed point of view?' [1998] *British Tax Review* 112
—— 'Avoidance and Other Consequences of Publishing Commissioner's Interpretation Guidelines' (2004) 19 *Australian Tax Forum* 245
Prebble J and Prebble R, 'Does the Use of General Anti-Avoidance Rules to Combat Tax Avoidance Breach Principles of the Rule of Law?' (2010) 55 *St Louis University Law Journal* 21
Prosser T, 'Towards a Critical Public Law' (1982) 9 *Journal of Law and Society* 1
—— *The Economic Constitution* (Oxford, Oxford University Press, 2014)
Raz J, 'The Rule of Law and its Virtue' (1977) 93 *LQR* 195
—— *The authority of law: Essays on law and morality* (Oxford, Clarendon Press, 1979)
Robson W, 'The Report of the Committee on Ministers' Powers' [1932] *The Political Quarterly* 346
—— *Justice and Administrative Law*, 2nd edn (London, Stevens and Sons 1947)
Rowland A, 'Is the Revenue being Fair? Revenue Statements and Judicial Review' [1995] *British Tax Review* 115
Sabine B, *A History of Income Tax*, 1st edn (London, George Allen & Unwin, 1966)
Sales P and Steyn K, 'Legitimate expectations in English public law: an analysis' [2004] *Public Law* 564
Salter D, '*Zim Properties Ltd v Proctor* (1985): Compromise of Action, Compensation and CGT' in D de Cogan and J Snape, *Landmark cases in Revenue Law* (Oxford, Hart Publishing, 2019)
Sandler D, *A Request for Rulings* (London, Institute of Taxation, 1994)
Sanitt G, 'Ingenious Media and HMRC's duty of confidentiality' (2015) 1256 *Tax Journal* 8
Sawyer A, 'Binding Tax Rulings: The New Zealand Experience' (1997) 26 *Australian Tax Review* 11
—— 'What are the Lessons for Australia from New Zealand's First Comprehensive Remedial Review of its Binding Rulings Regime?' (2000) 29 *Australian Tax Review* 133
—— 'Binding rulings in New Zealand. An assessment of the first ten years' (2006) 12 *Canterbury Law Review* 273
Sawyer A, Alarie B, Datt K and Weeks G, 'Advance Tax Rulings in Perspective: A Theoretical and Comparative Analysis' (2014) 20 *New Zealand Journal of Taxation Law and Policy* 362
Schoenbrod D, *Power without Responsibility – How congress abuses the people through delegation* (New Haven, Yale University Press, 1993)
Schofield P, Pease-Watkin C and Blamires C (eds), *The Collected Works of Jeremy Bentham: Rights, Representation, and Reform: Nonsense upon Stilts and Other Writings on the French Revolution* (Oxford, Oxford University Press, 2002)
Scotchmer S and Slemrod J, 'Randomness in Tax Enforcement' (1989) 38 *Journal of Public Economics* 17
Schwartz B and Wade HWR, *Legal Control of Government: Administrative Law in Britain and the United States* (Oxford, Oxford University Press, 1972)
Schwarz J, 'Rights and powers: protecting the legitimate interests of taxpayers' [2009] *British Tax Review* 306
Schwebel S (ed), *The effectiveness of International Decisions* (Sijthoff, Leiden, 1971)
Scolaro D, 'Tax Rulings: Opinion or Law? The Need for an Independent 'Rule-Maker'' (2006) 16 *Revenue Law Journal* 109
Senden L, *Soft Law in European Community Law* (Oxford, Hart Publishing, 2004)
Seneviratne M, *Ombudsmen: Public Services and Administrative Justice* (Oxford, Butterworths, 2002)

Shaw M, *International Law*, 8th edn (Cambridge, Cambridge University Press, 2017)
de Smith SA, 'Sub-delegation and circulars' (1949) 12 *MLR* 37
de Smith SA, Woolf H and Jowell J, *Judicial Review of Administrative Action*, 5th edn (London, Sweet and Maxwell, 1995)
Sherry M, 'Muddled thinking on Mansworth v Jelley' (2003) 3891 *Taxation* 363
Simpson E, 'The Ramsay Principle: A Curious Incident of Judicial Reticence' [2004] *British Tax Review* 358
Smith A, *The Wealth of Nations* (Oxford, 1776)
Smith K and Doran R, 'GSTS Pathology LLP: When do legitimate expectations end?' (2013) 1177 *Tax Journal* 16
Snape J, *The Political Economy of Corporation Tax: Theory, Values and Law Reform* (Oxford, Hart Publishing, 2011)
Stacey F, *Ombudsmen Compared* (Oxford, Clarendon Press, 1978)
Stebbings C, 'The equity of the executive: Fairness in tax law in nineteenth-century England' in Turner P (ed), *Equity and Administration* (Cambridge, Cambridge University Press, 2016)
Stewart R, 'The Reformation of American Administrative Law' (1975) 88 *Harvard Law review* 1667
Steyn L, 'Democracy through law' [2002] *European Human Rights Law Review* 723
Sugarman N, 'Federal Tax Rulings Procedure' (1954) 10 *Tax Law Review* 1
Sunstein C, *Legal Reasoning and Political Conflict*, 2nd edn (Oxford, Oxford University Press, 2018)
Tallon D, 'Comparative Law: Expanding Horizons' (1969) 10 *Journal of the Society of Public Teachers of Law* 265
Tallon D, Young I, Elliott P and Dave D, *Inland Revenue Practices and Concessions: 1984/85 Bound Volume* (London, Oyez Longman, 1984)
Tasioulas J, 'The Rule of Law' in Tasioulas J (ed), *The Cambridge Companion to the Philosophy of Law* (Cambridge, Cambridge University Press, forthcoming)
Taylor A, 'Proposing a tax rulings system' (2017) 4605 *Taxation* 8
Tomkins A and Turpin C, *British government and the constitution: text and materials*, 7th edn (Cambridge, Cambridge University Press, 2011)
Torgler B, 'Tax morale, rule governed behaviour and trust' (2003) 14 *Constitutional Political Economy* 119
—— *Tax Compliance and Tax Morale: A Theoretical and Empirical Analysis* (Cheltenham, Edward Elgar Publishing, 2007)
Tridimas T, 'Indeterminacy and legal uncertainty in EU law' in Mendes J (ed), *EU Executive Discretion and the Limits of the Law* (Oxford, Oxford University Press, 2019)
Troup E, 'Unacceptable Discretion: Countering Tax Avoidance and Preserving the Rights of the Individual' (1992) 13 *Fiscal Studies* 128
Truman M, 'Tax prat of the year' (2013) 171 *Taxation* 8
—— 'Angelic tax' (2012) 170 *Taxation* 31
Turner P (ed), *Equity and Administration* (Cambridge, Cambridge University Press, 2016)
Waldron J, 'Vagueness in Law and Language: Some Philosophical Issues' (1994) 82 *California Law Review* 509
Wallis D, 'The Tax Complexity Crisis' (2006) 35 *Australian Tax Review* 274
Waerzeggers C and Hillier C, 'Introducing an Advance Tax Ruling (ATR) regime' (2016) 2 Tax Law IMF Technical Note
Warren N, 'Enough is enough' (2016) 4540 *Taxation* 9
Weeks G, 'The Public Law of Restitution' (2014) 38 *Melbourne University Law Review* 198
—— 'The Use and Enforcement of Soft Law by Australian Public Authorities' (2014) 42 *Federal Law Review* 181
—— *Soft Law and Public Authorities: Remedies and Reform* (Oxford, Hart Publishing, 2016)
Wellens K and Borchardt G, 'Soft law in European Community law' (1989) 14 *European Law Review* 267
Wheare KC, *Maladministration and its Remedies* (London, Stevens and Sons, 1973)

de Widt and Oats L, 'Risk Assessment in a Co-operative Compliance Context: A Dutch-UK Comparison' [2017] *British Tax Review* 230
Wilks E, *Death Magic* (New York, Berkley Sensation, 2011)
Williams D, 'Extra-Statutory Concessions' [1979] *British Tax Review* 137
Williams D, Morse G and Eden S, *Davies: Principles of Tax Law*, 8th edn (London, Sweet and Maxwell, 2016)
Williams R, 'The Multiple Doctrines of Legitimate Expectations' (2016) 132 *LQR* 639
Whyatt J, *The Citizen and the Administration: The Redress of Grievances. A Report by JUSTICE* (London, Stevens and Sons, 1961)

Australian Governmental Documents

Auditor General

'Administration of Taxation Rulings Follow-up Audit, Audit Report no. 7 2004–05' (August 2004)
The Australian Taxation Office's Administration of Taxation Rulings' (2001)

Commissioner of Taxation

'Annual report 2014–15' (October 2015)
'Sixty-Second Annual Report, Commonwealth Government Printer' (1983)

Commonwealth of Australia

'A Full Self Assessment of Taxation – A Consultative Document' (Canberra, 1990)
'Administrative Accountability in Business Areas Subject to Complex and Specific Regulation' (November 2008)
'An "Extra-Statutory Concession" Power for the Commissioner of Taxation?: Discussion Paper' (12 May 2009)
'Australia's future tax system: Report to the Treasurer' (December 2009)
'Discussion Paper: Review of Aspects of Income Tax Self Assessment' (March 2004)
'Outcome of the Review of Aspects of Income Tax Self Assessment, Media Release No 106 of 2004' (December 2004)
'Review of Aspects of Income Tax Self Assessment' (August 2004)
'Tax reform: not a new tax, a new tax system' (Commonwealth of Australia 1998)

Inspector-General

'Review into delayed or changed Australian Taxation Office views on significant issues' (March 2010)
'Review into improving the self assessment system' (August 2012)
'Review into the ATO administration of class rulings' (September 2011)
'Review of the potential revenue bias in private binding rulings involving large complex matters' (2008)
'Review of the Tax Office's administration of public binding advice' (April 2009)

Joint Committee of Public Accounts

Report No 326, 'An Assessment of Tax – A Report on an Inquiry into the Australian Taxation Office' (1993)

Joint Committee of Public Accounts and Audit

Report No 410, 'Tax Administration' (June 2008)
Report No 432, 'APS – Fit for Service' (2012)

Parliamentary Debates

Commonwealth Parliamentary Debates (Senate), 15 June 1989, 4129 (Senator Collins)
Peter Baldwin, Second Reading Speech Taxation Laws Amendment (Self-Assessment) Bill 1992 House of Representatives Hansard Reports 26 May 1992

Parliamentary Papers

Ralph J, Allert R and Joss B, 'Review of Business Taxation: A tax system redesigned. More certain, equitable and durable' (Australian Government Publication Services, 1999)
Review of Business Taxation, 'A Strong Foundation: Discussion Paper' (1998)
Argument S, 'Papers on Parliament No 15, Parliamentary Scrutiny of Quasi-legislation' (1992)

Senate Standing Committee on Legal and Constitutional Affairs

Parliamentary Paper No 217/1987, 'Income Taxation Rulings' (1987)

Newspaper Articles

Carter C, 'Government tax adviser quits after talk on how to keep money out of George Osborne's "grubby mitts"' *The Telegraph* (13 September 2013)
Covill R, 'Former HMRC worker sentenced for tax credits fraud' *The Business Desk* (20 December 2018)
Fearnside A and Willis K, 'HMRC guidance: difficulties with out-of-date, inaccurate and hard to find guidance' *Tax Adviser* (1 May 2018)
Houlder V, 'Revenue whistleblower fearful for future' *The Financial Times* (31 March 2012)
Houlder V and Parker G, 'Backlash builds against Google tax deal' *The Financial Times* (25 January 2016)
Kynasto D, 'Tory conviction politician who broke ranks early as a leading "wet" under Thatcher' *The Financial Times* (24 September 2007)

Leigh D, Ball J, Garside J and Pegg D, 'HSBC files show how Swiss bank helped clients dodge taxes and hide millions' *The Guardian* (8 February 2015)
Mather J, 'Chris Jordan v Ali Noroozi in "personality clash" over ATO scrutiny' *The Australian Financial Review* (17 March 2017)
Mostrous A, Schlesinger F and Watson R, 'Screen play: how movie millions are moved offshore' *The Times* (21 June 2012)
Pannick D, 'Why judicial review needs protection from our politicians' *The Times* (20 February 2014)
Public Leaders Network, 'Public accounts committee 'theatrical exercise in public humiliation'' *The Guardian* (9 March 2012)
Rozenberg J, 'Mea culpa, Lord Bingham' *The Guardian* (7 September 2013)
Young H, 'Democracy is in crisis if we have to rely on the Lords' *The Guardian* (18 December 2001)

OECD Documents

'Tax Administration 2015 Comparative Information on OECD and Other Advanced and Emerging Economies' (August 2015)
'Tax Administration 2017: Comparative Information on OECD and Other Advanced and Emerging Economies' (September 2017)
'Tax Administration in OECD and Selected Non-OECD Countries: Comparative Information Series' (2010) (March 2011)

UK Governmental Sources

Customs and Excise

'Business Brief 8/95' (May 1995)

HM Treasury

'Appropriation Accounts' (HC 1981–82, 76-IX)
'Financing Britain's Future – Review of the Revenue Departments' Cm 6163 (2004)

HM Treasury and HMRC Documents

'Tax Consultation Framework' (March 2011)
'Tax deductibility of corporate interest expense: consultation on detailed policy design and implementation' (May 2016)
'Tax policy making: a new approach' (June 2010)
'The new approach to tax policy making: a response to the consultation' (December 2010)
'The Patent Box' (June 2011)
'The Patent Box: December 2011 response to consultation' (December 2011)

Inland Revenue Documents

Board of Inland Revenue, 'Extra-statutory concessions in operation at 8 August 1980' (IR1 (1980))
—— 'Extra-statutory concessions in operation at 8 August 1980' (IR1 (1980))
—— 'Extra-statutory concessions in operation at 31 December 1993' (IR1 (1994))
—— 'Extra-Statutory Concessions Supplement' (IR1 (Supp) (1987))
—— 'Inland Revenue extra-statutory concessions as at June 1985' (IR1 (1985))
—— 'The Path to Tax Simplification and The Path to Tax Simplification: A Background Paper' (HMSO, 1995)
Inland Revenue, 'A List of Extra Statutory Wartime Concessions given in the Administration of Inland Revenue Duties (October 1944)' Cmd 6559
—— 'IR1' (August 1999)
—— 'IR1' (August 2002)
—— 'IR1' (Supp) (1991)
—— 'IR1' (2004)
—— 'Pre-Transaction Rulings: A Consultative Document' (November 1995)
—— 'Press Release', 25 September 1987, [1987] *Simon's Tax Intelligence* 724
—— 'Tax Bulletin: Issue 18' (August 1995)
—— 'Tax Bulletin: Issue 50' (December 2000)
—— 'Tax Bulletin Issue 32' (1997)
—— 'Tax Bulletin: Issue 55' (October 2001)
—— 'Tax Bulletin: Special Edition' (May 2001)
—— 'Technical Note' (January 2003)

Office of National Statistics

'Exploring the UK's digital divide' (March 2019)

Office of Tax Simplification

'Guidance for taxpayers: a vision for the future' (October 2018)
'Review of tax reliefs Final report' (March 2011)

Other UK Government Documents

Aaronson G, 'GAAR Study: A study to consider whether a general anti-avoidance rule should be introduced into the UK tax system' (November 2011)
Cabinet Office, 'Categories of public bodies: a guide for departments' (December 2012)
—— 'Giving evidence to Select Committees: Guidance for Civil Servants' (October 2014)
—— 'Guide to Making Legislation' (July 2017)
Colcutt P and Hourihan M, 'Review of the Public Sector Ombudsmen in England' (Cabinet Office 2000)
Department for Business Innovation and Skills, 'Bevin Boys'
Lord Chancellor's Department, 'Tribunals for Users: One System, One Service – Report of the Review of Tribunals by Sir Andrew Leggatt, Terms of Reference' (March 2001)

Home Office, 'Revised Code of Practice for the Detention, Treatment and Questioning of Persons by Police Officers' (May 2015)
HM Government, 'The Powers of HMRC: Treating Taxpayers Fairly (House of Lords Paper 242): Government Response' (January 2019)
Ministry of Justice, 'Pre-Action Protocol for Judicial Review'
—— 'Judicial Review: proposals for reform' (December 2012)
—— 'Judicial Review: Proposals for further reform' (September 2013)
The Director of Public Prosecutions, 'Policy for Prosecutors in Respect of Cases of Encouraging or Assisting Suicide' (February 2010)

UK Non-departmental Public Body Documents

Adjudicator's Office

'Annual Report 2003' (March 2003)
'Annual Report 2006' (2006)
'Annual Report 2007' (September 2007)
'Annual Report 2009' (September 2009)
'Annual Report 2010: continuous improvement driving performance learning lessons' (September 2010)
'Annual Report 2011: A year of record breaking performance' (July 2011)
'Annual Report 2012: A year of challenges' (July 2012)
'Annual Report 2013: The Adjudicator calls for greater organisational learning' (June 2013)
'Annual Report 2014: Learning is paramount!' (July 2014)
'Annual Report 2015' (September 2015)
'Annual Report 2015–16' (September 2016)
'The Role of the Adjudicator' (August 2017)
'Annual Report 2018' (July 2018)
Adjudicator's Office, HMRC and VOA, 'Service Level Agreement for the provision of complaints adjudication services for HM Revenue & Customs and Valuation Office Agency by the Adjudicator's Office' (July 2018)

Information Commissioner's Office

'Decision Notice FS50133903' (March 2007)

UK Parliamentary Sources

Committee on Ministers' Powers Report

Cmd 4060 (1932)

Comptroller and Auditor General

'Appropriation accounts on the sums granted by Parliament for classes XIII–XIV for the year ended 31st March 1981' (HC 1981–82, 76-IX)
'Appropriation accounts of the sums granted by Parliament for civil services, classes I–V, for the year ended 31st March 1968' (HC 1968–69, 53-LI)
'Appropriation accounts of the sums granted by Parliament for revenue departments for the year ended 31st March 1953' (HC 1953–54, 12-XXIV)
'General report of the comptroller and auditor general' (HC 1997–98, 251-XIX)
'General report' (HC 1997–98, 251-XIX)
'Revenue departments appropriation accounts 1946–47' (HC 1946–47, 24)

Constitution Committee

'Sixth Report: The accountability of civil servants' (HL 2012–13, 61)

Hansard

Criminal Justice and Courts Bill Deb, col 106 (13 March 2014)
Finance Bill Deb HC cols 754–55 (17 June 2008)
HC Deb Vol 744 col 1006 (11 April 1967)
HC Deb Vol 592, cols 851–55 (11 February 2015)
HC Deb Vol 63 col 1171 (11 July 1984)
HC Deb Vol 915, col 187 (12 July 1976)
HC Deb Vol 75, col 151 (12 March 1985)
HC Deb Vol 79, cols 188–89 (16 May 1985)
HC Deb Vol 582, col 697 (17 June 2014)
HC Deb Vol 734, col 51 (18 October 1966)
HC Deb Vol 445, col 924 (2 May 2006)
HC Deb Vol 445, col 925 (2 May 2006)
HC Deb Vol 462, col 248 (26 June 2007)
HC Deb Vol 462, col 254 (26 June 2007)
HC Deb Vol 462, cols 250–51 (26 June 2007)
HC Deb Vol 166, cols 329–30 (31 March 1862)
HC Deb Vol 922, cols 66–67W (6 December 1976)
HL Deb Vol 669, col GC275 (22 February 2005)
HL Deb Vol 754, col 1557 (30 June 2014)

House of Commons Briefing Papers

Maer L and Everett M, 'The Parliamentary Ombudsman: role and proposals for reform' (Briefing Paper: Number CBP7496, March 2016)
Seely A, 'Tax avoidance and tax evasion' (House of Commons Briefing Paper 7948, May 2019)
—— 'The Budget and the annual Finance Bill' (House of Commons Briefing Paper 813, July 2019)

House of Lords Select Committee on Economic Affairs

'The Finance Bill 2008: Volume 1 Report' (HL 2007–08, 117-I)
'Tackling Corporate Tax Avoidance in a Global Economy: is a New Approach Needed?' (HL 2013–14, 48)

Joint Committee on Tax Law Rewrite Bills

'Income Tax (Trading and Other Income) Bill: Evidence' (2004–05, HL 37, HC 285)

National Audit Office

'An Introduction to the National Audit Office'
'HM Revenue & Customs 2005–06 Accounts: The Comptroller and Auditor General's Standard Report' (7 July 2006)
'HM Revenue & Customs 2006–07 Accounts: The Comptroller and Auditor General's Standard Report' (6 July 2007)
'Increasing the effectiveness oftax collection: a stocktake of progress since 2010' (February 2015) (HC 2014–15, 1029-I)
'Settling large tax disputes' (June 2012)
'The quality of service for personal taxpayers' (HC 2016–17, 17)

Parliamentary and Health Service Ombudsman

'Annual Report 2005–06' (HC 2005–06, 348)
'Annual Report 2006–07' (HC 2006–07, 838)
'Annual Report 2007–08' (HC 2007–08, 1404)
'Annual Report 2008–09' (HC 2008–09, 786)
'Annual Report 2009–10' (HC 2009–10, 274)
'Annual Report 2010–11' (HC 2010–11, 1404)
'Annual Report 2011–12' (HC 2011–12, 251)
'Consultation on direct access to the Parliamentary Ombudsman' (2011)
'Equitable Life: a decade of regulatory failure' (HC 2007–08, 815-I)
'Principles of Good Administration' (February 2009)
'Tax Credits: Getting it Wrong?' (HC 2006–07, 1010)
Kirkham R, 'Parliamentary Ombudsman: Withstanding the Test of Time' (HC 2006–07, 421)

Parliamentary Commissioner for Administration

'Annual report for 1970' (HC 1970–71, 261)
'Annual report for 1976' (HC 1976–77, 116)
'Annual Report 1977' (HC 1977–78, 157)
'Annual Report for 1978' (HC 1978–79, 205)
'Annual report for 1979' (HC 1979–80, 402)
'Annual report for 1980' (HC 1980–81, 148)
'Annual report for 1982' (HC 1982–83, 257)

'Annual Report for 1983' (HC 1983–84, 322)
'Annual report for 1984' (HC 1984–85, 262)
'Annual report for 1986' (HC 1986–87, 248)
'Annual report for 1987' (1987–88 HC 363)
'Annual report for 1988' (HC 1988–89, 301)
'Annual report for 1990' (HC 1990–91, 299)
'Annual report for 1991' (HC 1991–92, 347)
'Annual Report for 1993' (HC 1993–94, 290)
'Annual report for 1994' (HC 1994–95, 307)
'Annual report for 1995' (HC 1995–96, 296)
'Annual report for 1996' (HC 1996–97, 386)
'Fifth report for session 1983–84' (HC 1983–84, 322)
'Fifth report of the parliamentary commissioner for administration [cases investigated 1st February to 30th April, 1976]' (HC 1975–76, 496)
'Report for 1983' (HC 1983–84, 322)
'Second report of the Parliamentary Commissioner for Administration' (HC 1973–74, 106)
'Selected cases 1981 – volume 2' (HC 1980–81, 250)
'Third report of the parliamentary commissioner for administration' (HC 1973–74, 281)

Parliamentary Ombudsman

'Annual report 1999–00' (HC 1999–00, 593)

Public Accounts Committee

'First, second and third reports from the Committee of Public Accounts together with the proceedings of the committee, minutes of evidence, appendices and index' (HC 1967–68 (156-I, 233-I, 314)-V)
'Further written evidence from Osita Mba in the matter of the Public Interest Disclosure Act 1998, HM Revenue & Customs procedures for settling tax disputes' (HC 2010–12, 1531)
'HM Revenue & Customs 2010–11 Accounts: tax disputes' (HC 2010–12, 1531)
'HM Revenue & Custos performance in 2014–15: Sixth Report of Session 2015–16' (HC 2015–16, 393)
'Holding Government to Account: 150 years of the Committee of Public Accounts' (House of Commons 2007)
'Public Accounts – Minutes of Evidence' (HC 2013–14, 112)
'Second report from the committee of public accounts' (HC 1897–98, 261-VIII)
'Second report: Inland Revenue Department' (HC 1990–91, 71)
'Special report and first, second and third reports from the Committee of Public Accounts together with the proceedings of the committee, minutes of evidence, appendices and index' (HC 1953–54 (67-1, 101-1, 183-1, 231-1)-IV)
'Third, fourth and fifth reports from the Committee of Public Accounts together with the proceedings of the committee, minutes of evidence, appendices and index' (HC 1966–67 (369-I, 529-I, 647-I-VII)
'Twenty second report' (HC 1981–82, 339)

Public Administration Committee

'Smaller Government: Shrinking the Quango State' (HC 2010–11, 537)

Public Administration Select Committee

Annual Report of Parliamentary Ombudsman, Fourth Report (HC 1999–2000, 106)

Royal Commission Reports

'Final Report of the Royal Commission on the Taxation of Income and Profit' (1955 Cmd 9474)

Select Committee on Procedure

'First Report' (HC 1977–78, 588-I)

Select Committee on the Parliamentary Commissioner for Administration

'First Report from the Select Committee on the Parliamentary Commissioner for Administration' (Cmnd 4729, 1971))
'First report from the Select Committee on the Parliamentary Commissioner for Administration' (HC 1974–75, 454)
'First report from the Select Committee on the parliamentary commissioner for administration together with the proceedings of the committee relating to the report and minutes of evidence' (HC 1970–71, 240-XLII)

Treasury and Civil Service Select Committee

'Budgetary reform in the UK' (HC 1981–82, 137)
'Budgetary Reform in the UK' (HC 1981–82; 137-vi)
'Civil service pay' (HC 1982–83, 19-I)
'Civil service recruitment, training & career management & public service manpower' (HC 1986–87, 358-I)
'Efficiency of the Civil Service' (HC 1979–80, 333-II, IV, V and VII)
'Eighth report: Progress in the next steps initiative' (HC 1989–90, 481)
'Fifth report' (HC 1986–87, 84)
'Fifth report: Developments in the Next Steps Programme' (HC 1988–89, 348)
'Fifth report: The new system of departmental reports' (HC 1990–91, 290)
'Fifth report: The 1981 budget and the government's expenditure plans 1981–82 to 1983–84' (HC 1980–81, 232)
'First report: Cross border shopping' (HC 1994–95, 35)
'First report: The 1990 autumn statement' (HC 1990–91, 41)
'First report: The future of the Civil Service Department' (HC 1980–81, 54)
'First special report' (HC 1982–83, 46)
'Financial Services Regulation: Minutes of evidence' (HC 1994–95, 187-I)
'Fourth report' (HC 1979–80, 712)
'Fourth report' (HC 1986–87, 45)

'Fourth report: Civil Service manpower reductions' (HC 1979–80, 712)
'Fourth report: International monetary arrangements: international lending by banks' (HC 1982–83, 21)
'Fourth report: Simplified estimates and resource accounting together with the proceedings of the committee, minutes of evidence and appendices' (HC 1994–95, 212)
'Fourth report: The 1984 budget' (HC 1983–84, 341)
'Fourth report: The 1988 budget' (HC 1987–88, 400)
'Inland revenue: tax office delays' (HC 1985–86, 165-I)
'International credit and capital markets' (1985–86 HC 464-I)
'Manpower losses in the revenue departments' (1988–89, 155-I)
'Memoranda on long-term trends in resources and public expenditure' (HC 1984–85, 141)
'Memorandum on efficiency and effectiveness in the civil service' (HC 1982–83, 118)
'Official economic statistics' (HC 1988–89, 181-I)
'Official economic statistics' (HC 1988–89, 181-II)
'Official economic statistics' (HC 1989–90, 671)
'Second report: The budget and the government's expenditure plans 1980–81 to 1983–84' (HC 1979–80, 584)
'Second report: The government's public expenditure plans 1988–89 to 1990–91' (HC 1987–88, 292)
'Second report: The structure and form of financial documents presented to Parliament' (HC 1984–85, 110)
'Second report: The work of the valuation office' (HC 1989–90, 223)
'Seventh report: Civil service manpower reductions' (HC 1980–81, 423)
'Sixth report' (HC 1986–87, 293)
'Sixth Report: Estimates 1984–85' (HC 1983–84, 516)
'Seventh report: Public expenditure and estimates' (HC 1987–88, 506)
'Sixth Report: Estimates 1984–85' (HC 1983–84, 487-I)
'Sixth Report: Estimates 1984–85' (HC 1983–84, 516)
'Sixth report: Public expenditure' (HC 1989–90, 466)
'Sixth report: The government's expenditure plans 1985–86 to 1987–88' (HC 1984–85, 213)
'Sixth report: The presentation of information on public expenditure' (HC 1988–89, 217)
'Sixth report: The role of the Civil Service (Interim report)' (HC 1992–93, 390)
'Supply estimates' (HC 1985–86, 38-i)
'Supply estimates 1985–86' (HC 1984–85, 369-I)
'Supply estimates 1987–88' (HC 1986–87, 332-I)
'Supply estimates 1987–88' (HC 1986–87, 332-I)
'The 1981 budget and the government's expenditure plans 1981–82 to 1983–84' (HC 1980–81, 232-I)
'The city research project: Minutes of evidence' (HC 1994–95, 533)
'The financial and economic consequences of UK membership of the European communities' (HC 1984–85, 57-II)
'Third report' (HC 1986–87, 153)
'Third report: Efficiency and Effectiveness of the Civil Service' (HC 1981–82, 236)
'Third report: International debt strategy' (HC 1989–90, 138)
'Third report the European Commission's proposals on the approximation of indirect taxation' (HC 1987–88, 248)
'Third special report: The Structure of Personal Income Taxation and Income Support' (HC 1982–83, 386)

Treasury and Civil Service Committee Sub-committee

'Acceptance of outside appointments by Crown servants' (HC 1983–84, 302)
'Efficiency and effectiveness in the Civil Service' (HC 1980–81, 360-II)
'Efficiency and effectiveness in the Civil Service' (HC 1980–81, 360-III)

'Tax changes in the March 1980 Budget' (HC 1979–80, 554-I, II and III)
'The civil service management reform: the next steps' (HC 1987–88, 494-I)
'The financial and economic consequences of UK membership of the European communities' (HC 1984–85, 57-I)
'The role of the Civil Service' (HC 1993–94, 27-I)
'The role of the Civil Service' (HC 1993–94, 27-VIII)
'The role of the Civil Service: minutes of evidence' (HC 1992–93, 390-VII)
'The role of the Civil Service: minutes of evidence' (HC 1992–93, 390-VIII)
'The structure of personal income taxation and income support' (HC 1981–82, 331)
'The structure of personal income taxation and income support' (HC 1982–83, 20-I)
'The structure of personal income taxation and income support' (HC 1982–83, 20-II)

Treasury Committee

'Principles of Tax Policy' (HC 2010–11, 753)

Treasury Select Committee

'16th Report: Administration and effectiveness of HM Revenue and Customs' (HC 2010–12, 731)
'29th Report – Closing the Tax Gap: HMRC's record at ensuring tax compliance' (HC 2010–12, 1371)
'6th Report: The administration of tax credits' (HC 2010–12, 811)
'7th Report: The Administrative Costs of Tax Compliance' (HC 2003–04, 269)
'Administration and effectiveness of HMRC – uncorrected evidence – 24 October 2012' (HC 2012–13, 673)
'Administration and effectiveness of HMRC – uncorrected evidence – 31 October 2012' (HC 2012–13, 673-II)
'Appointment of Edward Troup as Executive Chair of HMRC' (HC 2016–17, 498)
'Appointment of Jon Thompson as Chief Executive of HMRC' (HC 2016–17, 232)
'Child Trust Funds follow up' (HC 2007–08, 537-I)
'Closing the Tax Gap: HMRC's Record at Ensuring Tax Compliance' (HC 2010–12, 1371)
'First report: the cross border market in excise products' (HC 1995–96, 24)
'Fourth Report: The Handling of the Joint Inland Revenue/Customs and Excise Steps PFI Project' (HC 2002–03, 184)
'HM Revenue and Customs and HSBC' (HC 2014–15, 1071)
'HMRC's operation of the PAYE system' (HC 2010–12, 479-I)
'Inland Revenue: Self Assessment Systems' (HC 2001–02, 681)
'Making Tax Digital' (HC 2016–17, 927)
'Minutes of Evidence for 14 March 2007' (HC 2006–07, 382-I)
'Minutes of Evidence for 17 November 2004' (HC 2003–04, 1281-I)
'Minutes of Evidence for 21st July 2004' (HC 2003–04, 835-I)
'Minutes of Evidence for 22 November 2006' (HC 2006–07, 51-I)
'Minutes of Evidence for 24 January 2007' (HC 2006–07, 192-I)
'Minutes of Evidence for 25 June 2008' (HC 2007–08, 852-I)
'Minutes of Evidence for 26 and 12 October 2005' (HC 2005–06, 524-I, II)
'Minutes of Evidence for 29 October 2008' (HC 2007–08, 1097-III)
'Minutes of Evidence for 30 June 2004' (HC 2003–04, 908-I)
'Minutes of Evidence for 30 November 2005' (HC 2005–06, 738-I)
'Minutes of Evidence for Wednesday 1 November 2000' (HC 1999–00, 953)
'Minutes of Evidence for Wednesday 14 November 2001' (HC 2001–02, 371-I)

'Minutes of Evidence for Wednesday 19th June 2002' (HC 2001–02, 975)
'Minutes of Evidence for Wednesday 26th June 2002' (HC 2001–02, 1011)
'Minutes of Evidence for Wednesday 1 November 2000' (HC 1999–00, 953)
'Minutes of Evidence for Wednesday 4 June 2003' (HC 2002–03, 746-I)
'Minutes of Evidence for Wednesday 6th March 2002' (HC 2001–02, 681-I)
'Ninth Report: The Merger of Customs & Excise and the Inland Revenue' (HC 2003–04, 556)
'Second Report' (HC 1999–00, 53)
'Second special report' (HC 1995–96, 24)
'Sixth Report' (HC 1998–99, 199)
'Sixth Report' (HC 2000–01, 237)
'Disputing Tax' (HC 2017–19, 1914)
'Tenth Report: Inland Revenue Matters' (HC 2002–03, 834)
'Third report: the 1995 budget' (HC 1995–96, 79)
'Third Report: the 1996 Budget' (HC 1996–97, 129)

Other Sources

Australia

Black J, 'Managing Discretion', paper presented at Australian Law Reform Commission Conference, Penalties: Policies, Principles and Practice in Government Regulation, Sydney, June 2001
Commonwealth of Australia, Business Consultation website
Cooper C, 'Improving the operation of the Income Tax Rulings system' Discussion Paper: Report for the Australian Society of CPAs (1998)
Corporate Tax Association, 'Press Release: Greater Accountability Needed for ATO' (28 April 1998)
Explanatory Memorandum to the Tax Laws Amendment (Improvements to Self Assessment) (No 2) Bill 2005
National Tax Liaison Group, 'Minutes of the National Tax Liaison Group meeting' (4 June 1998)
National Tax Liaison Group, 'Minutes: 10 September 2015 meeting' (September 2015)
O'Connell A, 'The ATO and the Giving of Advice', Centre for Tax Law Workshop, Cambridge UK, 12 July 2011
Pagone T, 'Tax Uncertainy', Annual Tax Lecture, Melbourne Law School, 20 August 2009
Quigley B, 'The Commissioner's powers of general administration: How far can he go?', 24th National Convention, Sydney, 12 March 2009
Taxation Institute of Australia, 'Submission on the Rulings System published as "Public rulings and Determinations"' (1995) 3 *Taxation in Australia (Red Edition)* 157

UK

[1993] 13 *Business Law Review* 98
[1987] *Simon's Tax Intelligence* 724
[1994] 20 *Simon's Tax Intelligence*
[1995] 46 *Simon's Tax Intelligence*
[1994] 47 *Simon's Tax Intelligence*
[1995] 12 *Simon's Tax Intelligence*
[1996] 15 *Simon's Tax Intelligence*
[1996] 24 *Simon's Tax Intelligence*
[1996] 40 *Simon's Tax Intelligence*

Boddington M, 'Taxpayers should take up internal reviews' *Accountingweb* (19 May 2016)
Bowler T, 'HMRC's Discretion: The Application of the Ultra Vires Rule and the Legitimate Expectation Doctrine' (Institute for Fiscal Studies, 2014)
—— 'Countering tax avoidance in the UK: which way forward?' (Institute for Fiscal Studies' 2009)
BT, 'Smarter Working in public services: The HMRC experience so far' (September 2018)
Cabinet Office, 'Prime Minister David Cameron's speech to the World Economic Forum in Davos' (January 2013)
Canada Revenue Agency, 'Information circular: IC70-6R9' (April 2019)
Cave R, 'Limited audience for HMRC letters' (22 April 2016)
Chartered Institute of Taxation, 'Tackling complexity in the tax system' (2000)
—— 'Taxed by Law; Untaxed by Concession' (2005)
—— 'Draft TAAR – Chartered Institute of Taxation Comments' (9 February 2007)
—— 'Targeted Anti-Avoidance Rule (TAAR) for Capital Losses Comments of the Chartered Institute of Taxation' (1 June 2007)
Chartered Institute of Taxation and Association of Taxation Technicians, 'Professional Conduct in relation to Taxation' (November 2016)
Devereux M, Freedman J and Vella J, 'Tax Avoidance' (OUCBT, 2012)
Edmonds L, 'Working for all Australians 1910–2010: A brief history of the Australian Taxation Office' (Canberra, Australian Tax Office, 2010)
'Explanatory Notes to the Income Tax HC Bill' (2006–07)
Fuller C, 'GAAR panel member steps down after Panorama sting' (September 2013)
Greenberg D, 'Dangerous Trends in Modern Legislation … and How to Reverse Them' (Centre for Policy Studies. 2016)
Hale (Lady), 'Legislation or judicial law reform: where should judges fear to tread?', Society of Legal Scholars Conference 2016, Oxford, 7 September 2016
Homer L, 'HMRC priorities 2013' (June 2013)
—— 'Letter to Andrew Tyrie, Chair of the Treasury Select Committee' (3 July 2014)
Institute for Fiscal Studies, 'Making Tax Law: IFS Tax Law Review Committee Discussion Paper No 3' (March 2003)
—— 'The Case for the Abolition of Stamp Duty' (November 2016)
Institute of Chartered Accountants in England and Wales, 'Legitimate Expectation and Reliance on HMRC Guidance' (Technical Release 06/13)
Judge (Lord), 'Ceding Power to the Executive; the Resurrection of Henry VIII', King's College London, April 2016
Judiciary for England and Wales, 'The Administrative Court Judicial Review Guide 2018' (July 2018)
Keats A, 'When to claim costs at a tax tribunal', *AccountingWeb* (8 February 2019)
Lovell R, 'Revenue reveals new GAAR panel' (July 2013)
Low Incomes Tax Reform Group, 'Is HMRC transparent?' (February 2011)
McLaughlin M, 'Conference Report: 101 Ideas for Personal Tax Planning' (August 2013)
Mace R, 'Off-payroll working in the public sector: reform of the intermediaries legislation – CIOT comments' (August 2016)
—— 'Reforms to the taxation of non-domiciles: further consultation – CIOT comments' (October 2016)
—— 'Soft Drinks Industry Levy – CIOT comments' (October 2016)
Mullan R, 'I have a tax dream' (2015) *Tax Adviser*
National Audit Office and Tax Administration Research Centre, 'The effect of HMRC Taxpayer Assistance on compliance: An experimental investigation' (December 2017)
Owen R, 'Building our Future: transforming how HMRC serves the UK' (July 2014)
Pinsent Masons, 'Tax expert: rush to enact 2015 Finance Bill leaves no time for proper parliamentary scrutiny' (March 2015)
Restore UK, 'The Restore UK Project: a summary'
Ross Martin Tax Consultancy, 'Mansworth v Jelly loss claims' (13 June 2014)

Rutter J, 'The Strange Case of Non-Ministerial Departments' (Institute for Government, October 2013)
Senior President of Tribunals, 'Costs in Tribunals: Report by the Senior President of Tribunals' (December 2011)
Southern D, 'Changes to the taxation of compensation (ESC D33)' (March 2015)
The General Council of the Bar, 'Taxation and Retirement Benefits Guidance', 6th edn (2012)
The Tax Faculty of the Institute of Chartered Accountants in England and Wales, 'Avoidance through the creation and use of capital losses' (8 February 2007) Taxrep 07/07
Turnbull-Hall C and Thomas R, 'Tax Legislation as a Measure of Complexity' (Office of Tax Simplification, 2012)
Tyrie A, 'Letter to David Gauke: Tax Policy' (3 November 2010)
Wales CJ and Wales CP, 'Structures, processes and governance in tax policy-making: an initial report' (OUCBT. 2012)
Warren N, 'Liable Not Liable: The concession not mentioned in HMRC's registration manual' *Accountingweb* (21 August 2018)

Websites

webarchive.nationalarchives.gov.uk
www.accountingweb.co.uk
www.ato.gov.au
www.bloomsburyprofessionalonline.com
www.hmrc.gov.uk
www.intelligencesquared.com
www.tax.org.uk
www.whatdotheyknow.com

INDEX